WOMEN, MADNESS AND THE LAW: A FEMINIST READER

London • Sydney • Portland, Oregon

WOMEN, MADNESS AND THE LAW: A FEMINIST READER

Edited by
Wendy Chan, Dorothy E Chunn and Robert Menzies

glasshouse press

London • Sydney • Portland, Oregon

First published in Great Britain 2005 by
The GlassHouse Press, The Glass House,
Wharton Street, London WC1X 9PX, United Kingdom
Telephone: + 44 (0)20 7278 8000   Facsimile: + 44 (0)20 7278 8080
Email: info@cavendishpublishing.com
Website: www.cavendishpublishing.com

Published in the United States by Cavendish Publishing
c/o International Specialized Book Services,
5824 NE Hassalo Street, Portland,
Oregon 97213-3644, USA

Published in Australia by The GlassHouse Press,
45 Beach Street, Coogee, NSW 2034, Australia
Telephone: + 61 (2)9664 0909   Facsimile: +61 (2)9664 5420
Email: info@cavendishpublishing.com.au
Website: www.cavendishpublishing.com.au

British Library Cataloguing in Publication Data
Chan, Wendy, 1966–
Women, madness and the law
1 Mentally ill women – Legal status, laws, etc
2 People with mental disabilities and crime
3 Mentally ill offenders 4 Sex discrimination in criminal justice administration
I Title II Chunn, Dorothy E III Menzies, Robert
346'.0138'082

Library of Congress Cataloguing in Publication Data
Data available

ISBN 1-90438-509-5
ISBN 978-1-904-38509-7

1 3 5 7 9 10 8 6 4 2

Printed and bound by Antony Rowe Ltd, Eastbourne

Acknowledgments

As ever in a group venture of this kind, there are many to acknowledge and finite space (and capacity of memory) with which to do so. Our advance apologies, therefore, to all those whom, through oversight, or just plain insensitivity, we succeed in overlooking here. With that caveat in place – and most mindful of (and grateful to) everyone credited in individual chapters – we wish to single out the following for special thanks.

Beverley Brown, Commissioning Editor, and Cara Annett have been steadfast believers in this project from conception to completion (and an immense pleasure to work with). Without their abiding commitment to feminist scholarship, and to this book, the collection would never have emerged from the shadows of proposal purgatory. Sanjeevi Perera, Project Manager for Cavendish, has overseen the editing and production process with acumen and finesse; and Marketing Director Ruth Phillips has expertly steered the book into the public realm.

For, in their various ways, keeping us honest and alert (and, we hope, humble), we are much beholden to our many colleagues, friends, partners and collaborators in all things academe, and otherwise. The long list includes, but is scarcely exclusive to, Robert Adamoski, Susan B Boyd, Susan C Boyd, Joan Brockman, Shelley Gavigan, Richard Fredericks, Margaret Jackson, Dany Lacombe, John Lowman, John McLaren, Ted Palys and Claire Young.

We also extend our appreciation to Simon Fraser University for supplying the needed resources, stimulation and surroundings, and the opportunity to shepherd this project through to completion in the midst of a demanding academic year.

Chapters 1, 3, 6 and 8 are selective, updated and/or revised versions of papers originally appearing as, respectively: Ussher, JM, 'Women's madness: a material-discursive-intra psychic approach', in Fee, D (ed), *Psychology and the Postmodern: Mental Illness as Discourse and Experience*, 2000, London: Sage, pp 207–30; Labrum, B, 'Looking beyond the asylum: gender and the process of committal in Auckland, 1870–1910' (1992) 26 The New Zealand Journal of History 125; Caplan, PJ, 'Sex bias in psychiatric diagnosis and the courts' (2004) The Journal of Trauma Practice 1; and Chan, W, *Women, Murder and Justice*, 2001, Basingstoke: Palgrave, Chapters 2 and 4. Figure 5.2 originally appeared in Ballou, M, Matsumoto, A and Wagner, M, 'Toward a feminist ecological theory of human nature: theory building in response to real-world dynamics', in Ballou, M and Brown, LS (eds), *Rethinking Mental Health and Disorder: Feminist Perspectives*, 2002, New York: Guilford. Thanks to the publishers and editors concerned for granting permission to adapt these materials. Every effort has been made to trace all the copyright holders but if any have been inadvertently overlooked, the publishers will be pleased to make the necessary arrangements at the earliest opportunity.

Penultimately, we owe an incalculable debt to the 15 authors who share their accumulated knowledge, wisdom and counsel in the pages that follow. The process of editing and learning from their words has been a memorable, and invaluable, experience for us all.

And last but far from least, welcome to the planet, Alexander and Benjamin (and do get accustomed to that order of introduction, Benjamin). You will both be amazed.

About the Editors and Contributors

Bonnie Burstow, PhD, is a critically informed counterhegemonic academic, a feminist therapist, and an active member of a number of social justice movements including the women's movement(s), antipsychiatry and penal abolition. She has been a core member of such antipsychiatry organisations as Phoenix Rising, Ontario Coalition to Stop Electroshock, Resistance Against Psychiatry and, currently, Coalition Against Psychiatric Assault. She is a prolific author whose works include *Radical Feminist Therapy: Working in the Context of Violence* (1992) and *Shrink Resistant: The Struggle Against Psychiatry in Canada* (co-edited with Don Weitz, 1988). She currently teaches full time in the Department of Adult Education and Counselling Psychology at Ontario Institute for Studies in Education (University of Toronto).

Paula J Caplan, PhD, is a clinical and research psychologist who has worked for 25 years in the legal system and an Adjunct Professor at Washington College of Law, American University and at Brown University. A former Professor at the Ontario Institute for Studies in Education, where she headed the Community Psychology and School Psychology Programs and the Centre for Women's Studies, she is author of 12 books, including *They Say You're Crazy: How the World's Most Powerful Psychiatrists Decide Who's Normal* (1996), and she is co-editor of the recent *Bias in Psychiatric Diagnosis* (2004). She is a frequent expert witness in civil and criminal cases ranging from family law to murder cases, and she also advises attorneys on interpretation of mental health experts' reports and on cross-examination of clinical experts and also of social science researchers.

Wendy Chan is Associate Professor in the School of Criminology at Simon Fraser University. Her research interests are in the areas of feminist and critical criminology, racism, immigration and crime control, welfare and social exclusion. Her recent publications include *Women, Murder and Justice* (2001), and *Crimes of Colour: Racialization and the Criminal Justice System in Canada* (co-edited with Kiran Mirchandani, 2001). Some of her ongoing research projects involve examining immigrant perceptions of deportation practices, studying the impact of welfare surveillance on people of colour, exploring the role of the media in shaping issues of 'illegal' immigration, analysing deportation appeal cases from the Immigration and Refugee Board, and investigating the impact of safe housing for low income women in Vancouver's downtown eastside.

Dorothy E Chunn teaches in the School of Criminology and is co-director of the Feminist Institute for Studies on Law and Society at Simon Fraser University. Her current research projects focus on: the historical regulation of sex in the Canadian welfare state; feminism, law, and social change in Canada since the 1960s; and poor women's experiences of health and housing. Among her other recent edited books are *Law as a Gendering Practice* (with Dany Lacombe, 2000); *Contesting Canadian Citizenship: Historical Readings* (with Robert Adamoski and Robert Menzies, 2002); and *Regulating Lives: Historical Essays on the State, Society, the Individual and the Law* (with John McLaren and Robert Menzies, 2002).

Eileen Fegan is a Lecturer in Law at the Queen's University of Belfast, where she specialises in gender and law, and in women's human rights. She has also held lecturing posts in Lancaster University, New College, Oxford and Cardiff Law School. She has published widely on feminist legal theory and is currently researching the relationship between gender, law and culture.

Kathleen Kendall teaches sociology in the School of Medicine at Southampton University. Her research interests generally lie in the intersection between crime and mental health. Her recent published work has focused upon critical examinations of correctional cognitive behaviouralism (in Carlen, P (ed), *Women and Punishment: The Struggle for Justice*, 2002; Bloom, B, *Gendered Justice: Addressing Female Offenders* (with Shoshana Pollack), 2003; Lindsay, W, Taylor, JL and Sturmey, P (eds), *Offenders with Developmental Disabilities*, 2004; and Mair, G (ed), *What Matters in Probation*, 2004). Her ongoing research includes a qualitative study on depression with colleagues from Southampton University; an examination of human experimentation in Canadian prisons with Dorothy Proctor; and a study of female criminal lunatics at Rockwood Asylum, Canada.

Bronwyn Labrum teaches in the History Department at the University of Waikato, New Zealand. She is the author of *Women's History: A Short Guide to Researching and Writing Women's History in New Zealand* (1993), co-editor of *Fragments: New Zealand Social and Cultural History* (2000), and has contributed numerous articles on women's and welfare history. Her current project is a book which is provisionally entitled *Family Needs and Family Desires: Families and State Welfare in New Zealand, 1920–1970*.

Pierre Landreville is Professor and Director at the School of Criminology, Université de Montréal. He specialises in questions related to penology, the functioning of the criminal justice system, and more generally the sociology of social control.

Hannah Lerman, PhD, is a psychologist currently in practice in Las Vegas, Nevada. She is the author of two books about women's mental health issues, editor of a third and is also the compiler of an annotated bibliography about sexual abuse by therapists and other professionals.

Ann Lloyd is a writer and freelance journalist. Her first book, *Doubly Deviant, Doubly Damned* (1995), about society's attitudes towards women who are violent, was published by Penguin. Her second, about personal faith journeys, is to be published later this year by Darton Longman and Todd. She specialises in women's issues, 'spiritual/belief' matters, psychology and health.

Robert Menzies teaches criminology at Simon Fraser University. He has written extensively on medico-legal regulation, psychiatric and public health history, and the sociology of academic criminology. Three recent edited books are *Contesting Canadian Citizenship: Historical Readings* (with Robert Adamoski and Dorothy E Chunn, 2002), *Regulating Lives: Historical Essays on the State, Society, the Individual and the Law* (with John McLaren and Dorothy Chunn, UBC Press, 2002), and *Toxic Criminology: Environment, Law and the State in Canada* (with Susan C Boyd and Dorothy E Chunn, 2002). In September 2005, he will be commencing a two-year term as JS Woodsworth Resident Scholar in the Humanities at SFU.

Daphné Morin is Research Associate at the Collectif de recherche sur l'itinérance, la pauvreté et l'exclusion sociale (CRI). A graduate of the Université du Québec à Montréal (sociology), she specialises in the study of marginality and social control. She has done extensive research on the criminalisation of mental illness and homelessness.

Shirley Roy is Professor of Sociology at the Université du Québec à Montréal and Director of the CRI research team on homelessness and extreme poverty. She teaches methodology, marginality and social exclusion. Her areas of expertise are related to homelessness, social exclusion and the use of social control systems in relation to various situations (mental illness, poverty, drug abuse). These projects have been informed by a gendered perspective and qualitative approaches to research.

Marielle Rozier is Research Associate at the Collectif de recherche sur l'itinérance, la pauvreté et l'exclusion sociale (CRI). Her research interests are focused on homelessness and extreme poverty. In these areas, she is currently engaged in research on issues of intervention (for example, practices, models, harm reduction, community intervention) and social representations (for example, money, health, illness, HIV). These projects have been informed by a gendered perspective and qualitative approaches to research.

Joe Sim is Professor of Criminology in the School of Social Science at Liverpool John Moores University. His major publications include *Medical Power in Prisons* (1990), *British Prisons* (with Mike Fitzgerald, 1982), *Prisons Under Protest* (with Phil Scraton and Paula Skidmore, 1991) and *Western European Penal Systems* (co-edited with Vincenzo Ruggiero and Mick Ryan, 1995). He is currently writing a book on penal developments in England and Wales since 1974 to be published by Sage under the title of *The Carceral State: Prisons and Punishment in a Hard Land*.

Julie Stubbs is an Associate Professor and Deputy Director of the Institute of Criminology, Faculty of Law, University of Sydney. Her research interests relate primarily to violence against women and include domestic violence, battered women syndrome, defences to homicide, a critical assessment of restorative justice, feminist law reform initiatives, sexual assault and race and gender issues in criminology. Her publications include *Negotiating Child Contact and Residence Against a Background of Domestic Violence* (with Kaye and Tolmie, 2003), *Women, Male Violence and the Law* (1994) and *Gender, Race and International Relations: Violence Against Filipino Women in Australia* (with Cunneen, 1997).

Julia Tolmie is a senior lecturer in criminal law at Auckland University, New Zealand. Prior to that she was a lecturer/senior lecturer at the Law Faculty at Sydney University for 10 years. She has an LLB (Hons) from Auckland University and an LLM from Harvard University. An area of deep and enduring interest for her throughout her years as an academic has been the issue of extending the defences for murder to battered women who have killed their perpetrators.

Jane M Ussher is Professor of Women's Health Psychology at the University of Western Sydney. She is author of a number of books, including *Women's Madness: Misogyny or Mental Illness?* (1991), *Fantasies of Femininity: Reframing the Boundaries of Sex* (1997), and *Managing the Monstrous Feminine* (forthcoming). Her research focuses on women's sexual and reproductive health, with particular emphasis on premenstrual experiences.

Contents

Introduction

Robert Menzies
Dorothy E Chunn
Wendy Chan

For most women (the middle-class-oriented), psychotherapeutic encounter is just one more instance of an unequal relationship, just one more opportunity to be rewarded for expressing distress and to be 'helped' by being (expertly) dominated.

Phyllis Chesler, *Women and Madness* (1972, p 108)

In many criminological studies female offenders are not mentioned at all: either their very existence is ignored or they are held to be too insignificant to be worthy of consideration. The deviant, the criminal or the actor is always male; it is always *his* rationality, *his* motivation, *his* alienation, or *his* victim. And this is more than a convenient choice of words; the selection of the male pronoun may be said to be inclusive of the female but in reality it is not; it merely excludes women and makes them invisible.

Carol Smart, *Women, Crime and Criminology* (1976, p 177)

Prefacing the collection

The idea for the book gradually emerged out of our common research and teaching encounters with the subjects of women, gender, madness,[1] forensic psychiatry and psychology, criminality and legal regulation. Much of our respective work has focused on the psycho-legal control of women in its endless incarnations and points of application. It has brought us into contact with the remarkable profusion of feminist writing that is now available on the experiences of psychiatrised women, and on psycho-legal ideas, systems and practices that state and society have established to contend with women's 'disorders' of the mind, and their relation to crime, punishment and the gendered social order. Through our engagement with this legion of work, it occurred to us that an integrated collection of essays, featuring the contributions of leading international theorists, researchers and activists, would help to fill a gaping hole in the existing scholarship. It was evident that a feminist-informed mapping of women's relation to madness and law – one which could locate the many ways in which gender configures the development, regulation and control of women's mental health – was both needed and timely. Whereas a number of exceptionally important and illuminating texts and readers are now available on the general subject of women's madness, and while a virtual infinity of clinical and socio-legal publications on forensic psychiatry and psychology populate library shelves around the world, this collection represents the very first attempt to canvass selectively, on an international basis, the available wealth of writing that exists on the inter-connected topics of women, madness and the law.

---

1 While we favour the expression 'madness' as best capturing the cultural, discursive properties of psy power, and as being most in line with the thinking of feminists, antipsychiatrists and psychiatric survivor activists, the book's authors engage with a variety of related constructs including mental 'disorder', 'disability' and 'illness'.

The 13 chapters that comprise this book, therefore, are chosen to reflect the wide range of issues, themes and interests that penetrate the diverse feminist study of women's relation to mental health and legal cultures, institutions, agencies and practitioners around the world. The contributors comprise 18 academics, researchers, activists and journalists, working in six countries (Australia, Canada, England, New Zealand, Northern Ireland and the United States), who between them have generated, over many years, an impressive body of writing in the disciplines of women's studies, law, history, sociology, psychology and criminology. The collection combines original essays with selected contributions where authors have re-tailored previously published material to incorporate current literature and integrate it with the book's main themes. In so doing, we have tried to strike a balance between established scholarship and cutting-edge treatment of contemporary issues and problems.

The issues and perspectives rippling through this collection reflect our desire to highlight and explain how the structures, languages and practices of legal and psychiatric institutions sculpt our understandings of women's mentalities. These studies of women's conflicts with law, psychology and medicine all point to the many factors that influence public and professional understandings of women labelled as mentally disordered. They consider in their various ways how such views both represent and perpetuate myths and stereotypes about the nature of women's madness, and about women's social roles throughout the realm of the social, and within psychiatry and law.

This is nothing if not a multi-vocal effort. The essays purposively scan a dizzying range of subject fields. For their part, the authors bring a diversity of values, theoretical perspectives and prescriptions for praxis to bear upon their respective topics – and on feminism, madness, psychiatry, psychology and the law more generally. At the same time, a common commitment to critical feminist scholarship galvanizes the contributions, offering a unifying set of themes, purposes and directions to which all 18 authors adhere. In various ways, feminist ideas and ideals inform, and are readily evident in, every one of these 13 essays.

The book begins with two chapters (Ussher and Kendall) that explore how women's madness, and the relations between gender, law and madness, have taken form through prevailing cultural practices, academic and medico-legal theories, and the apparatuses and activities of social control institutions. Next are two studies (Labrum, and Menzies and Chunn) on, respectively, the treatment of New Zealand women asylum inmates around the turn of the 20th century, and the forensic regulation of a Canadian 'murderess' in the mid-1900s that locate our understanding of women's madness historically. These essays are followed by writings on five major themes exploring the connections between gender, mental disorder, the 'psy' sciences and the law: (1) professional psychiatric diagnoses and understandings of women's mental disorders (Lerman and Caplan); (2) psychiatrised women's experiences with homelessness, poverty and marginalisation in the trans-institutional urban 'community' (Morin, Roy, Rozier and Landreville); (3) expert constructions of violent women subjects (Chan); (4) the pathologisation of women litigants, defendants and victim/survivors through invoking 'post-abortion syndrome' and 'battered woman syndrome' (Fegan, Stubbs and Tolmie); and (5) the confinement and treatment of woman inmates in carceral and forensic settings (Sim and Lloyd). We conclude the book on a challenging but affirmative note, with Burstow's review of women's empowering strategies to resist legal and psychiatric regulation, and her consideration of past, present and potential future contributions of the women's movement to antipsychiatry praxis.

A number of themes bridge these essays. First, in one way or another, the authors all consider how the professional appropriation of and attention given to women's experiences of madness, both in law and the 'psy' sciences, have operated to suppress women's capacity to speak for themselves and take a greater role in determining and shaping their lives. However, at the same time, these studies are overflowing with expressions of women's agency. In the least-expected spaces, and under the most mind-deadening of conditions, we find so-called 'insane' and criminally deviant women creatively resisting the psycho-legal powers that surround them, transgressing norms of good, sane womanhood, and struggling to transform their lives.

Secondly, we stress that the forces impinging on women and men are not entirely discrete. Our choice to focus this book on psychiatrised women and law should not be read to downplay the potent psycho-legal forces that govern men's lives too – along with those whose identities traverse conventional sex/gender lines of division. Indeed, women, men and transgendered alike are recurrently caught up in identical or confluent cultural and institutional currents of control. As these essays will attest, women's encounters with psy regulation do not unfold in isolation, and are seldom constituted by gender alone. Instead, the forensic experiences of women are inherently, and intersectionally, bound together with relations of class, race, ethnicity, sexuality, generation and (dis)ability. For this same reason, we refrain from hypostatising or dichotomising gender, just as we approach other central ideas in this book – law, madness, medicine, power, and so on – as sinuous, contested and ever-changing categories that come to being through the contingent operations of power, discourse, and social practice.

Thirdly, the institutions of psychiatry and psychology themselves are likewise heterogeneous. Far from being a single-chord diatribe against the abuses of an inevitably and transhistorically oppressive institution, this collection engages the psy sciences within their wider social context, recognising the plurality of their forms and practices, and tempering critique and condemnation with a search for better ways to contend with madness in women and society.

Fourthly, and following from these last points, none of us subscribes to a single, unreflexive or iconoclastic conception of feminism. For us, feminism is both an epistemological and a material medium for addressing women's relations to law, madness, and the gendered social order more generally. It is a gender-conscious way of seeing and acting upon the world. It affords a window into, and myriad prescriptions for, transforming the oppressions and deprivations of women of all classes, colours, sexualities and mentalities, and all other disenfranchised and subaltern groups. A feminist theory and politic is, therefore, always necessarily about the human rights and empowerment of oppressed people everywhere, whatever their gender. In the world, and in this book, feminism assumes many guises, enters into complex relations with patriarchal and other forms of power, and is inextricably bound up with myriad other progressive, transformative systems of thought and practice. Thus, it is not by accident that the collection begins with Jane

Ussher's stimulating call for a dialectical approach to women's madness that would theoretically conjoin the material, discursive and intrapsychic realms. Nor is it by chance that we conclude with Bonnie Burstow's advocacy of a multiple-front praxis through which feminists, activists and their allies might unite in the interests of women and men, psychiatrised people and others who face discrimination and oppression in the name of law, medicine, psychology and other modernist formations.

Conventional and critical forensic moments

For the better part of a millennium now, madness and law have been performing an intricate and arcane *pas de deux* in the public institutions and civic cultures of 'western' nation states. From the earliest, embryonic efforts to inscribe an elemental notion of responsibility and competency in legal doctrine, to the Byzantine operations of the modern psy-law complex, successive generations have grappled with questions about the relevance of mind-state to problems of crime, punishment and social order. Since the mid 19th century, the 'developed' English-speaking jurisdictions that geographically frame this book have witnessed a truly staggering profusion of statutory and common law, institutional structures, diagnostic schemes, professional organisations, and scientific theories, languages and practices aimed at distinguishing the mad from the bad from the putatively normal. In this age of what Castel, Castel and Lovell (1982) have termed the 'psychiatric society', the forensic occupations have proliferated globally and are involved in a galaxy of functions related to the adjudication of psychiatric status and the treatment of pathology in both criminal and civil legal contexts.

Today, virtually every sector of society finds itself engaged in one aspect or another, and in radically divergent ways, with the enigma of the 'mentally disordered offender'. The 'criminally insane' being has become a true cipher of contemporary ideology and discourse – a metaphoric, liminal character (Harris, 1999; Horwitz, 2002; Mechanic, 1999) who incites a welter of fears and apprehensions throughout the political, institutional and cultural order. He or (variably) she also assumes many different forms and shades of meaning. As many commentators have observed through the years, the images and imaginings of the 'madly bad' subject are wildly polymorphous, and they shift dramatically from one social location to the next.

To philosophers, questions of mental capacity and criminal responsibility elicit primal questions about what it means to be competently human, to exercise rational choice in a world that is filled with untold compulsions and necessities. For legal scholars and practitioners, the main quandary is where to situate partially or fully unfit, or irresponsible, or dangerously pathological persons within the realm of legal subjecthood. Mountains of legislative decrees, case holdings, legal opinions and articles have piled up with a view to codifying the law's response to 'insanity' in a manner that would predictably balance free will and determinism, individual freedoms and public securities, mercy and punishment. Civil libertarians, ethicists, antipsychiatrists, and critical and feminist activists, for their part, concern themselves with the human attributes and citizenship rights of psychiatrised people who come into conflict with the state's social control apparatus. They denounce the arrogance that inevitably informs efforts to adjudicate the mental state of others. They underscore our proven inability to distinguish reliably between madness and sanity, and our long-established penchant for depriving cognitively and emotionally troubled people of basic liberties in the name of science, therapy and due process. Forensic psychiatrists, psychologists and other clinical professionals, in contrast, approach 'criminally insane' or otherwise defective or deficient wrongdoers as scientific or technical problems in need of evaluation, classification and rehabilitation. Their solution to the problem of madness in law is an inherently modernist one that promises ever-improving services to courts and prisons, and ever-increasing protection to the 'mentally ill' and the public, through the progressive advance of medical and academic knowledge, method, and instrumentation.

With perhaps even greater consequence, the community outside the walls of courts, prisons and hospitals is a central player, too, in the fashioning of narratives about law and madness. The contemporary social order is awash with fear-inspiring depictions of the criminally insane as violently and permanently crazed anti-citizens who are impervious to normal legal regulation, and who must therefore be constrained or contained by means of exceptional, supra-legal measures. However wrongheaded and prejudicial, such visions of dangerous criminal 'lunatics' running loose through the population erupt from a litany of cultural, media and scholarly sources. They pervade the public realm, and they reverberate back upon the state's medical-legal edifices, shaping official responses to psychiatrised people – especially those whose lives become entangled in law – in myriad ways (for example, Kutchins and Kirk, 1997; Petrunik, 2003; Wahl, 1995).

At the level of everyday policy and practice, however, it is the clinical professions – and particularly forensic psychiatry and psychology – that have come to exercise the most potent and lasting influence over the fates of mentally 'disordered' persons who collide with law as defendants, litigants, witnesses and victim/survivors. The impact of medical and psychological models is everywhere evident in legal settings. Forensic clinicians are key players in decisions about what constitutes mental dysfunction or 'disease', in rulings about who requires or merits diversion from judicial to therapeutic spaces (and under what conditions), in the delivery of court verdicts and dispositions, in the tailoring of treatment regimes in clinics, prisons and hospitals, and in the determination of length and location of confinement and the circumstances of an individual's release back to the community. Correspondingly, the mammoth scholarly, research and policy literature on forensic matters is overwhelmingly aligned with a clinical, positivist paradigm. With rare exceptions, on an international scale we find that the publications of government agencies and professional associations, and the leading academic texts, journals, and educational programs consistently privilege the interests and voices of forensic clinicians over those of more sceptical perspectives – and to the virtual exclusion of psychiatric survivors, consumers and their advocates.

By the same token, the discourse on mental disorder and law is far from univocal. Enriched by the vibrant antipsychiatry, critical psychiatry and C/S/X[2]

---

2 Consumer/survivor/ex-patient.

movements of which it is a part (see below), a counterhegemonic perspective on forensic psychiatry and psychology has emerged on several fronts over the past three or four decades. Critical writers and researchers have charted the involvements of the psycho-legal professions in the state's less benign regulatory practices. They have revealed how the participation of clinical practitioners in criminal, mental health, family, and other areas of law has operated to erode legal entitlements and imperil human rights. They have challenged psychiatric and psychological claims to benevolence by documenting the inherently hierarchical character of 'therapeutic' relations in coercive legal settings. They have exposed the daily lived reality that mental health remedies are often more corrosive to liberty and life than the overtly punitive judicial outcomes they reputedly replace. Moreover, they have shown how policies, decisions and encounters that unfold at the junction points between psy sciences and law are inescapably informed by the vertical social arrangements of class, race, ethnicity, sexuality, generation, (dis)ability, and other axes of power and subordination; and as the contributors to this book will rehearse in evocative detail, these forensic experiences are also intensely gendered in character, form and consequence (Allen, 1987; Chunn and Menzies, 1990; Kendall, 2000; Menzies, Chunn and Webster, 1992).

The feminist engagement with psychiatry

Out of the second-wave feminist movements of the 1960s and 1970s, an influential body of writing began to circulate on the gendered properties of madness, and on the impact of psychiatric theories, discourses, structures and practices on the lives of psychiatrised and ostensibly normal women alike. Much of this work flowed from the cumulative experiences of countless women, extending over many generations, with a malestream medical profession that harboured scarcely coded gynaephobic ideas about the cognitive, affective and moral deficits of female bodies and mentalities – and the supposedly 'natural', biogenetic vulnerabilities of women to conditions of defect and unreason. From the asylum building and 'moral management' movements of the 1800s, through the successive 20th century waves of eugenics, mental hygiene, psychoanalytic theory, somatic 'treatment' and community mental health, women found themselves either relegated to the margins of psychiatric interest, or singled out for grievous, and sometimes lethal, forms of intervention in the name of mental therapy.

At the same time, women found soon enough that the antipsychiatry movement of that same era was hardly speaking to their own experiences with the androcentric organisations and agents of mental health and illness (Smith and David, 1975; Ussher, 1991). European activists who applied Marxian analyses of class and labour relations under capitalism (Ingleby, 1980; Navarro, 1976; Scheper-Hughes and Lovell, 1987) were given to ignore or downplay the maddening forces of familial, patriarchal and reproductive relations in the private sphere. At the same time, however galvanizing his *Madness and Civilization* (1965) might have been during those formative years, Foucault's magisterial treatment of (un)reason, knowledge, power, truth and order in the age of Enlightenment was far from being a feminist-informed tract. British antipsychiatrists (Cooper, 1967; Laing, 1969, 1985; Miller and Rose, 1986), inspired by the insights of continental existentialists and phenomenologists, addressed the contradictions of reality and meaning that constituted madness in a crazy-making world (Pearson, 1975; Sedgwick, 1982). However, their consideration of women's and men's experiences seldom entered the realm of structured gender conflicts (moreover, their invocation of the 'schizophrenigenic mother' and the 'big nurse' bordered precariously on the blaming of women for their own intrapsychic problems).

In the United States, the writings of Goffman (1961), Scheff (1966, 1975), and assorted other (male) scholars of constructionist and neo-Chicagoan leanings (Pearson, 1975; Ussher, 1991, Chapter 6; Vice, 1992) afforded an unprecedented window into the totalitarian features of mental asylums, as a way of conceiving mental 'illness' as a manufactured cultural product, and as a set of sanctions to be unleashed against those outsiders who violate deeply entrenched 'residual rules' of mind and manner. However, their work largely proceeded as if gender (and race, and ethnicity, and social class, and sexuality, and generation) did not exist. As for the most renowned among that first generation of antipsychiatrists, women soon learned that Thomas Szasz's (1961, 1963) excoriation of psychiatry as a pseudo-scientific witchhunt, and of mental illness as a fiction, was fatally undermined by his crude promotion of a libertarian politic and rationalist system of contractual social relations which ignored the structured inequality, and the crushing conditions of poverty and abuse that so many women, 'mad' and otherwise, were facing daily (Goldstein, 1980; Vatz and Weinberg, 1983).

Responding to these many exclusions and distortions at the hands of both institutional psychiatry and its legions of adversaries, women authors and activists began to tell their own stories of psychiatry, mentality, gender and power. The 1972 publication of Chesler's *Women and Madness* was a watershed moment for this new feminist paradigm. In her book, Chesler conducted the reader through a sweeping odyssey of oppression, maltreatment and neglect. Chesler's analysis illustrated how, through the centuries, the very idea of madness had been culturally rooted in prevailing images of normative femininity. Mustering a dazzling array of historical and contemporary sources, she linked the 'madwoman' and her treatment in society and psychiatry to a wider misogynistic impulse that associated womanhood with irrationality, inferiority, sexuality, biological imperative, pathology, deceit, dependency and danger. She showed how generations of cultural conceptions and academic theories of 'mental illness' either arrogantly effaced women's subjectivities and needs, or relied on bizarre and hurtful stereotypes which, in turn, were invoked to justify all manner of atrocities against women in the name of 'treatment'. Moreover, Chesler's chronicling of women's long experience with organised psychiatry exposed the deeply masculinist roots of a profession that, in ideology and function, both reflected and gave content to the patriarchal structures and relations that enveloped it.

In the more than three decades since the release of *Women and Madness*, a truly remarkable, internationally-based body of English-language feminist scholarship on women, mind-state and psychiatry has entered the public and academic realms. It is clearly impossible, in this brief introduction, to begin to take stock of that literature in all its complexity and effect. Instead, we simply note, in passing, four of the main currents and themes that run through the collected work.

First, feminists and other scholars have ushered forth a groundswell of research on the historical roots of women's pathologisation. Reacting to the gender-neutral content of writings on the genealogy of psychiatry prior to the 1980s, Showalter's *The Female Malady* (1987) recounted how the Victorian age came to constitute the madwoman as a central figure of 19th century discourse about danger, order and purity. The feminisation of madness became equated with the ascendancy of the public asylum system, which was increasingly dominated by a powerful male medical superintendency. In the ensuing two decades, feminists working in British, continental European, North American and Antipodean locales have reconstructed many aspects of women's historical encounters with madness control systems. They have charted, among other subjects: the shifting ideas about gender, lunacy, morality and defect that propelled psychiatric practices through those early years; the complex transactions that prevailed between medical and legal doctrine and officialdom in the making of women mental patients; the contradictory roles played by families in the commitment of mothers, wives, sisters and daughters; the gendered categories (hysteria, puerperal insanity) and interventions (reproductive surgery) that specifically targeted women; and the gendered worlds that evolved inside the asylum through women's relations with their male physicians, their 'keepers' and nurses, and each other (de la Cour and Reaume, 1998; Davies, 1987; Dwyer, 1987; Finnane, 1985; Geller and Harris, 1994; Kelm, 1992; Labrum, 1992; Matthews, 1984; Mitchinson, 1991; Prestwich, 1994; Reaume, 2000; Ripa, 1990; Theriot, 1993; Tomes, 1990).

Secondly, a number of feminist and feminist-informed theoretical treatments of women and madness have materialised over the past two decades throughout the English-language jurisdictions that concern this book (Astbury, 1996; Ballou and Brown, 2002; Burman, 1990, 1996; Russell, 1995; Ussher, 1991, 1997b; Wenegrat, 1995; Willie, Perri Reiker, Kramer and Brown, 1995). From varied analytic standpoints, these authors have been exhuming and contesting androcentric, rationalist ideas about the gendered meanings and properties of mental 'illness' that have held sway over many centuries. In their rethinking of 'western' philosophical systems and social theorists from Aristotle, Descartes and Marx to Freud, Lacan and Foucault, they have shown how the enduring 'woman problem' has variously eluded, confounded or corrupted malestream ontologies, phenomenologies and practices of all stripes. When it comes to the psy sciences, these authors demonstrate that the belief systems and professional activities permeating women's forensic encounters are welded to the hegemonic, patriarchal status of modern medicine and psychology. Such institutional and cultural regimes of 'truth', 'reason', 'knowledge' and 'power', they assert, are remorselessly viricentred in their nature and effects. They are also deeply engrained into prevailing scientific rationalities, medical fields of discourse and theatres of operation. And when transposed into law, they ignite powerful forces, to the general detriment of women patients, defendants and prisoners.

Third, we are now able to mine a rich vein of literature on the syndromisation of women through the marketing of the American Psychiatric Association's controversial DSM-IV-TR[3] (see Caplan, 1995; Kirk and Kutchins, 1992; Kutchins and Kirk, 1997), along with sundry other schemes, constructs, taxonomies and instruments designed to categorise chaotic and 'diseased' states of mind. Several of the contributors to this book (Caplan, 1995; Fegan, 1999; Kendall, 1991; Lerman, 1996; Stubbs and Tolmie, 1999) have written extensively about the impact on women's identity, agency and fortunes of such already-entrenched or proposed diagnoses as premenstrual dysphoric disorder (PMDD), battered women's syndrome (BWS), post-abortion syndrome (PAS) and self-defeating personality disorder (SDPD). Other illuminating exposés of the psychological categorisation process, and its implications for the objectification of women, include Becker's (1997) deconstruction of borderline personality disorder (BPD), and Raitt and Zeedyk's (2000) critique of the implicit psycho-legal agenda informing other labels trained upon women, among them rape trauma syndrome (RTS) and false memory syndrome (FMS). The appropriation by the men's and fathers' rights movements of such disputed categories as Munchausen's syndrome by proxy (MSBP) and parental alienation syndrome (PAS) has been the subject of devastating critique (Allison and Roberts, 1998; Bruch, 2001). For their part, Chan and Rigakos (2002) have considered how the burgeoning risk assessment industry, in proposing to rank the population according to actuarial levels of threat and endangerment, harbours ominous implications for women's status in legal, mental health and other contexts. These various feminist contributions, and others, are unified in their assertion that imputing psychiatric classifications is an intensely gendered affair that is about women's moral transgressions, and their violations of normative femininity, as much as it is their implied mental aberrations.

Fourthly, emerging from a dynamic mad movement and its constituency of mental health consumers, survivors and ex-patients – and deeply informed by feminist sensibilities – an evocative body of first-person writing now exists on the thoughts, words and deeds of psychiatrised women, and their encounters with (usually male) medical authority in both institutional and community contexts (Capponi, 2003; Chamberlin, 1979; Everett, 1994; Millett, 1990; Shimrat, 1997). Complementing this important literature are other works chronicling the involvement of the psy professions in the abusive treatment and control of women (Breggin, 1993; Collins, 1988; Hudson, 1987; Lloyd, 1995; Penfold, 1998); explorations of feminist-informed therapies and other involvements as catalysts for the healing and empowerment of women clientele (Burman, 1990; Burstow, 1992; Harden and Hill, 1997; Penfold and Walker, 1984; Ussher and Nicolson, 1992); and depictions and considerations of the past, present and future prospects of feminist, survivor-centred and antipsychiatry advocacy (Brandon, 1991; Burstow and Weitz, 1988; Dain, 1994). These widely dispersed treatments of women's lived relations with medical powers find common expression in their centring of women as agentic beings in their own life narratives, in their privileging of experiential over scientific knowledge, and in their self-conscious embracing of an avowedly feminist, activist, human-rights oriented politic.

---

3   Diagnostic and Statistical Manual, 4th edn, text-revised (2000).

Women, madness and the law[4]

As with the psychiatric orthodoxy more generally, the traditional clinical literature on women, criminality, mental 'illness' and the law has been, in the main, distressingly devoid of feminist influence. Indeed, much forensic writing, teaching and research have transpired as though women were no more than statistical instances of the binary 'sex variable' but here, too, recent years have witnessed an encouraging turn of fortune and perspective. In many respects, Carol Smart's *Women, Crime and Criminology* (1976) was as paradigmatic on this subject as was Chesler's book on madness four years earlier. Through the intervening years, feminists, and others inspired in various ways by a feminist politic, have been exploring the many troubling points of engagement between women and a hybrid psycho-legal control system. Many of the contributors to this book have been involved in both prompting and promoting this seismic shift in thought and knowledge about women, madness and crime.

They are in good company. Writings have now appeared on an absorbing complex of related topics, including public images of 'criminally insane' women (Knelman, 1998; Myers and Wight, 1996; Shipley and Arrigo, 2004; Skrapec, 1994); the cultural, expert and legal apprehension of women's criminal responsibility (Ward, 1997; White-Mair, 2000); the contradictions of gender-specific offences like infanticide (Backhouse, 1984; Kramar, 2000; Laster, 1989; Ward, 1999); the psycho-judgments conferred upon women by the criminal and civil courts (Allen, 1987; Chan, 2001; Edwards, 1984; Mosoff, 1997; Neave, 1995) along with other criminal justice contexts (Eaton, 1986); the regulation and 'therapy' meted out to captive women (Carlen, 1983, 1985; Comack, 1996; Dobash, Dobash and Gutteridge, 1986; Hannah-Moffat, 2001; Hannah-Moffat and Shaw, 2000; Hudson, 1987; Rafter, 1990); and the impact of mentality and competency on the capital punishment of women (Rapaport, 2000; White-Mair, 2001).

These collected writings, as with the current volume, together chart the many topographies, ideologies, languages, activities and influences of medicine, psychology and law. In various ways, they show how 'psy' power and legal power are mutually enhancing, with particularly crucial consequences for women and other subaltern groups. By conferring a legitimising set of scientific discourses and practices upon judicial decisions and penal sanctions, the forensic professional serves as a medium for the confluence of medicine and justice into an amalgam of control regimes that is far more potent than either system in isolation. The scientific veneer of impartiality and precision becomes a catalyst and justification for the invoking of carceral outcomes. Far from being 'diverted' out of law's reach, women deemed 'mentally disordered' find themselves channelled into polycentred realms of regulation where their characters and mentalities are as much on trial as their criminal deeds.

Overarching much of the prevailing work on women, crime and madness has been the recurrent finding that criminal justice agents and criminologists are

---

4 Portions of this section are adapted from pp 36–38 of Chunn and Menzies, 1990.

predisposed to explaining female offenders in germs of bio- and psycho-genetic motivations which are premised on assumptions about inherent sex differences (Gavigan, 1987; Heidensohn, 1996; Morris and Gelsthorpe, 1981; Smart, 1976). As Allen (1987) has argued, for example, mental health assessors routinely assign pathological labels to women accused of serious violence offences. These images gain currency, in large part, because the victims of violent women are usually children, partners and other relatives, yet even women charged, sentenced and imprisoned for non-violent crimes are systematically deemed abnormal, despite the frequent absence of an identifiable mental 'illness', and are subjected to regimes of treatment and resocialisation (Carlen, 1983, 1985; Comack, 1996; Dobash, Dobash and Gutteridge, 1986; Hannah-Moffat, 2001; Hannah-Moffat and Shaw, 2000; Kendall, 2000; Sim, 1990).

Although feminists agree that psy authorities and criminal justice agents more frequently depict women offenders through the lens of pathology in comparison to their male equivalents, they have tended to split over whether this discrepancy translates into less severe dispositions for women. Allen's important work comparing female and male violent offenders in the UK (1987) – a Foucauldian analysis of medico-legal discourses embedded in forensic judgments – concluded that forensic decisions are consistently biased in favour of female offenders, particularly in relation to serious violent crime. According to Allen, the 'chivalry' phenomenon occurs because the gender-neutral provisions of the criminal law get undercut by the gender-specific assumptions about women and men to which psy professionals adhere. Psycho-legal decision-makers therefore routinely dissolve or expunge the legal guilt of violent women by transforming them into pitiful victims who lack moral guilt, while they simultaneously impose doubly inculpating judgments on their male counterparts. Consequently, men with ascribed mental pathologies still end up in prison, where similarly psychiatrised women are more likely to return home to the scene and victim(s) of their offence.

Allen's book, while pivotal, is also controversial. Her conclusions were based almost entirely on cases involving serious violence, which are highly atypical of the crimes committed by the vast majority of women, psychiatrised and other, who enter into conflict with the law (Chunn and Menzies, 1990; Dell and Gibbens, 1971; Menzies, 1989). Moreover, Allen ultimately adopts the same dichotomous approach to theorising about women, crime and madness which she repudiates in the conventional, malestream literature (1987, pp 9–13). While Chesler (1972) and many other feminist writers on madness have exposed the many oppressions of women by an androcentric psychiatric enterprise, Allen maintains that forensic ideologies and practices consistently privilege psychiatrised women while they discriminate against men.

In contrast, the majority of feminist research on women and crime establishes that legal decision-making reflects the ideologies and practices which are dominant within a given form of political and social organisation (Carlen and Worrall, 1987; Chunn and Lacombe, 2000; Comack, 1999; Daly, 1987; Smart, 1989). We cannot begin to unravel the relation between psychiatrised women and crime – or any other legal problematic – by invoking transhistorical, unitary categories, whether these be related to gender, class, race, ethnicity, sexuality, generation, (dis)ability, or any other axis of social relation. Analyses of 'therapeutic' and legal practices must be historically specific and account for similarities between, as well as differences among, all offender categories of social position and experience.

Inside the ordering practices of the 21st century (neo-)liberal democratic state, what contributes most to maintaining the capitalist, patriarchal, racialised status quo is not only the overt oppression of specifically targeted outsiders, but also the direct influence of ideologies and discourses on decision-makers, including those who enact and administer the law and its ancillary institutions like forensic psychiatry and psychology. Of particular significance are the class, gender, racial and sexual norms encapsulated in familial ideology (Barrett, 1988; Barrett and McIntosh, 1982; Collier, 1995; Gavigan, 1997). The research on women, crime and madness – including the contributions to this reader – reveals most clearly that, historically, both legal and extra-legal criminal justice agents have judged their 'clients' in relation to the (usually) implicit standards of normative thinking, morality and conduct that are associated with the nuclear, eurocentric bourgeois family model based on a heterosexual marriage relationship and the sexual division of labour. Accordingly, criminalised women, and men, who contravene the dictates of familial ideology find themselves subject to intensified regimens of regulation and treatment that frequently transcend unitary categories of gender, class, race, ethnicity, sexuality, and so on (Chunn and Menzies, 1990, p 38; Daly, 1987; Eaton, 1986; Edwards, 1984; Kendall, 2000).

At the same time, this 'constructed normality' (and innocence, and competency, and responsibility, and inoffensiveness) which familial, legal and psychiatric ideologies represent is unremittingly white, patriarchal, heterosexist, and middle class. Criminal 'offenders' who receive the harshest psycho-legal judgments and treatments are the double, triple and multiple failures – the women and men who have failed to negotiate the class, gender, racial, ethnic, sexual and other 'deals' which are characteristic of 'normal' people (Carlen, 1985; Chan and Mirchandani, 2002). They eschew, ignore, or otherwise transgress the discipline, deferred gratification and hard work that are the assumed requisites for a rational, competent, risk-free relation to the private and public spaces they inhabit. They have not assumed their rightful roles as wives/mothers/daughters, or as husbands/fathers/sons, in a nuclear family unit. They are socially inept, verbally inarticulate, morally labile, mentally aberrant and often dangerous misfits living on the marginal edge of their constructed categories, and the world around them (see, for example, Morin, Roy, Rozier and Landreville, Chapter 7 of this book).[5]

In the everyday ordering of women forensic subjects, psycho-legal authority articulates with gender, class, race, ethnicity, sexuality and other hierarchical categories of life according to complex and mutually elaborative patterns, and through the multiple discourses that infuse legal spaces and the ancillary systems

---

5   In contemporary neo-liberal states, familial ideology intersects with the ideology of (formal) equality that governs family-related law and policy. A focus on equality as sameness has supported the increasing recognition of relationships that are *analogous* to traditional marriage and the nuclear family (ie, same-sex and opposite-sex common-law relationships). Thus, family-related law and policy are no longer explicitly premised on a 'homemaker/breadwinner' model (ie, difference), but the influence of familial ideology remains strong.

that surround them. Accordingly, it would be simplistic, and usually wrong, to interpret the feminist research on women, madness and law – including the contents of this book – as suggesting that psy and legal agents are knowingly complicit in a conspiratorial coercive enterprise aimed at openly oppressing women, or men. To the contrary, the unexamined assumptions about normality underlying psycho-legal discourses and practices are rarely, if ever, explicitly stated. Forensic authority is, rather, deeply rooted in the power of therapeutic discourse and the hegemonic realms of psychiatry, psychology, law, criminal justice, and penality. It is through their role as mediators between the mechanisms and languages of scientific and legal order – and in their ability to deflect political, structural and cultural explanations in favour of theories grounded in personal pathologies – that forensic clinicians come to exercise and justify state control over marginal citizens of both genders. It is here that they most clearly contribute to the maintenance of gender, class, race and other inequalities.

Outlining the book

This final section of the introduction is a brief overture to the contents of this edited collection. The conceptual framework of the book's wider themes and problematics, as outlined above, provides the scaffolding for the 13 essays. We underscore how the authors have connected their respective theoretical and substantive studies to the wider questions that we pose about the impact of psycho-legal thinking, ideology, language and practice – and of wider regulatory systems and discourses – on the lives of psychiatrised, criminalised and other women, in both historical and contemporary contexts.

Jane M Ussher launches the collection by carving out a philosophical terrain that, we feel, is sufficiently reflexive, dynamic, multi-factorial and fluid to subsume the breadth of feminist work that follows in this book. Ussher begins with a devastating critique of the positivist-realist tradition that has dominated cultural and clinical thinking about women and 'insanity' since the time of the Enlightenment – with its reductionist, empiricist, individualising vision of the internally, often biologically perverse and pathological 'madwoman'. Correspondingly, she maintains (in accord with the discussion earlier on in this Introduction) that the successor epistemologies of social constructionism and interpretivism, founded in culturalism, relativism and a wholesale repudiation of materiality, have failed to yield an emancipatory politic or praxis for women. In their place, Ussher advances a critical-realist epistemology and a material-discursive-intrapsychic (MDI) approach to comprehending and intervening into women's madness. From such a dialectical, multi-factorial space, Ussher argues, these various 'aspects of experience can all be examined without privileging one level of analysis above the other, within an epistemological and methodological framework that does not make *a priori* assumptions about causality and objectivity, or about what type of methods can or should be used'. Through example, Ussher considers how this model might be invoked for theoretical and clinical purposes, such that the material conditions of women's lives, the normalising discursive fields they inhabit, and the intrapsychic pains they live through can be simultaneously addressed and overcome through feminist praxis.

Chapter 2, by Kathleen Kendall, complements Ussher's analysis by opening a theoretical window into the psycho-legal construction of 'criminal lunatic' women. Kendall reaffirms Ussher's call for a feminist understanding and practice that would simultaneously engage the discursive and material realms. For Kendall, the public fixation on Aileen Wuornos as 'America's first female serial killer' epitomises the ambivalence, turbulence and fear that haunt our assorted efforts – in culture, law and science – to explain and domesticate madly bad women. According to Kendall, women such as Wuornos 'endanger the social order not only through their actions but because they threaten to expose the fissures and failures within the myriad of methods designed to understand and manage society's miscreants'. As Kendall keenly observes, this making of criminally insane women occurs through a multi-sited and conflicting torrent of dominant and subordinate discourses. At the same time, these cultural practices are immanently tied to 'political rationalities and relations of power' that enact themselves through structure and language; they have real-world, lived consequences when targeted on the minds and bodies of ostensibly afflicted, defective and dangerous 'female offenders'. For Kendall, a feminist praxis that would subvert and transcend these rationalities must, first and foremost, be 'self-reflexive', acknowledging our own complex relations to dominant thought-forms about women, madness and crime. It must also take seriously these women's lives, words and subjectivities. 'If we wish to propose a more astute and possibly emancipatory framework,' Kendall concludes, 'we must not assume that we can simply speak on their behalf.'

The next two chapters combine to establish some basic historical parameters for the anthology. In Chapter 3, 'The Boundaries of Femininity', Bronwyn Labrum revisits her landmark research on the committal of women to the Auckland Lunatic Asylum, New Zealand, between 1870 and 1910. Informed by her patient-centred analysis of historical case file records, Labrum excavates the ideologies and practices of gender, family, class, race, nationhood and indigeneity that together propelled 'lunatic' women and men into the colonial asylum. She observes that economic circumstances, domestic crises, female 'trangressions' and normative prescriptions for 'quiescent, decorous and neat' femininity were all deeply implicated in cultural and medico-legal responses to madwomen during this era. At the same time, Labrum's data confirm that gender alone cannot account for these women's experiences in a context where so many intrusive material, political and cultural forces were impinging on their lives. Following a parallel trajectory, Chapter 4, by Robert Menzies and Dorothy E Chunn, retraces the steps of one woman forensic patient who entered the forensic machinery of the west coast Canadian province of British Columbia during the middle years of the 20th century. In reconstructing the case of 'Charlotte Ross', a diagnosed schizophrenic woman found unfit to stand trial for murdering her husband, they reveal how the forces of psychiatry and criminal law combine to shape the diagnostic and institutional careers of female carceral subjects. Working from the massive clinical records compiled by hospital authorities through her many years of institutionalisation, Menzies and Chunn reveal the psycho-legal theorising that informed authoritative depictions of Charlotte's violent crime, her moral condition, and her state of mind. They argue that, despite her vigorous, longstanding and often inspired efforts to prove her mental competency and gain her day in court, Charlotte's protests and transgressions were no match for the medical powers that radiated beyond the asylum and inscribed themselves profoundly into legal process.

Chapters 5 and 6 consider and critique the professional classification of women's mental states. In 'Women's Misery: Continuing Pigeonholes into the 21st Century', Hannah Lerman addresses the role played by the DSM-IV-TR ('the bible of the mental health field') in representing and entrenching wider masculinist ideologies and discourses about the essential pathology and frailty of women. As a practising feminist clinician, Lerman maintains that the DSM, with its pantheon of diagnostic categories, represents a pseudo-scientific expression of the pandemic 'definition of women by men' that pervades modern life. Beyond mere deconstruction, however, Lerman advocates continuing pressurisation of psychiatry, and reflective feminist engagement with 'the seats of power of our various professions', including the embracing of gender-sensitive and woman-empowering alternatives to the DSM. In Chapter 6, Paula J Caplan begins and concludes her essay with the critical point that sexism is so ideologically engrained in the cultural consciousness of modern society that it frequently goes undetected and, therefore, rendering sexism transparent must be a central imperative of feminist praxis in psychology and law, as elsewhere. To this end, Caplan enlists her own professional experience, along with a varied collection of case law, clinical research and feminist writing, to enumerate myriad 'manifestation[s] of sexism' in relation to psychology, criminality and the law. The positioning and pathologising of women in courts and prisons, family law cases and therapeutic settings, as Caplan compellingly observes, collectively reflect 'a troubling combination of intermittent invisibility and hypervisibility for women'.

From here, the essays turn to the policies and patterns of response to criminalised, psychiatrised and 'violent' women. Chapter 7, by Daphné Morin, Shirley Roy, Marielle Rozier and Pierre Landreville, navigates the daunting world of homeless women – many of them with longstanding mental health and criminal histories – who inhabit the streets and other public spaces of the contemporary urban landscape. In their case file study of 25 Montreal 'multi-problem' women during the late 1990s, Morin and her colleagues show how these women's chronic marginality, poverty and homelessness, and the conflicts and disruptions that typify their daily lives, combine to situate them at the boundary between judicial and psychiatric spheres of reference. Moreover, as 'hard-core', 'unclassifiable' cases, these women expose the many shortcomings, collaborative tensions and conflicting values of a polycentred care and control network that is ill-equipped to contend with women, and men, who transgress prevailing structural and conceptual frontiers. In the post-decarceration world of the city streets, 'community mental health' has mutated into a patchwork of revolving doors, widening nets, locked van therapy, and 'spirals of exclusion'. By means of three poignant case studies extracted from their files, the authors chart the hybrid responses of 'mobilization, abdication and vacillation' that these women variously trigger, while at the same time demonstrating why '[r]ecourse to the criminal justice system and incarceration measures' remains such an expedient and common 'management strategy' for everyone involved.

In Chapter 8, Wendy Chan enters the realm of the criminal courts to study the psychiatrization of 'intimate homicide' defendants. Chan conducts an intensive file analysis of Crown records for 25 accused persons (nine women and 16 men) diagnosed as mentally ill in five regions of England and Wales between 1985 and 1991 (most of whom entered pleas of diminished responsibility under s 2 of the Mental Health Act 1957). Chan's unpacking of the psychiatric and legal discourses endemic in these cases shows how gender-based apprehensions of subjectivity, agency and accountability are constitutive of experts' opinions about the criminal (ir)responsibility of male and female homicide offenders. What comprises 'abnormality of mind', for the purposes of legal judgment and disposition, hinges on gender-contingent ideas about mentalities and capabilities. 'Female defendants,' Chan asserts, 'do not act, but only respond to the events that occur in their lives', while in stark contrast, 'Male defendants' pathological personalities do not diminish their choice-making activity; they simply place limits on how well they can make these choices'. Psycho-legal narratives of pathology, responsibility and homicide are therefore governed by an androcentric state of mind – and outlook on mind-state – through which women violent offenders are cast as passive, non-agentic, in need of leniency, and at worst semi-culpable, victims of circumstance and affliction. As Chan concludes, 'What is missing from this portrait of female defendants', and what feminist scholars and practitioners must help inscribe into psycho-legal discourse and process, 'is a more multi-dimensional understanding and explanation of women's mental condition'.

The syndromisation of women – in public culture, psy science and the courts – is the subject of Chapters 9 and 10. In her provocative chapter 'Reclaiming Women's Agency', Eileen Fegan assembles the testimonies of 15 Canadian women, recounting their diverse experiences with abortion, to de- and re-construct the anti-choice, psychologizing discourses that contrive to forge causal links between the abortion experience and mental health trauma for women. Through these interviews, and through her deconstructions of wider psycho-legal languages and practices, Fegan exposes the political origins and disempowering effects on women of 'post abortion trauma syndrome' (PAS). Like related gender-specific constructs, Fegan argues, PAS is embedded in a matrix of public, religious, medical and legal myths about women's biological fragility and mental incompetency, and is buttressed by objectifying claims about women's lack of agency over their own reproductive lives. In this way, PAS reflects and entrenches anti-choice ideologies constructing abortion as 'anomalous and exceptional', and as dangerous to women's minds and bodies. For Fegan, feminists must contest the psycho-legal propaganda circulating around PAS, by affording women (especially those with abortion experience) better recognition 'of the effects of PAS propaganda upon their own suffering', and by connecting such understandings to 'the material obstacles they must overcome to access [abortion] in a gender unequal society'.

In Chapter 10, Julie Stubbs and Julia Tolmie deploy feminist legal scholarship, and their incisive critique of judicial reasoning in recent Australian criminal law, in an effort to 'shift the analysis of battered women's homicide cases from a singular focus on the failings of BWS to a broader consideration of the criminal justice process'. They observe how, its initial embrace by many feminists notwithstanding, the BWS construct has come to dovetail with and reinscribe the abiding 'psychological individualism' of criminal law. Psychiatric discourse, prevailing narratives of normative femininity, notions of 'learned helplessness', the racialisation of indigenous women and the 'privatisation of justice' through plea bargaining and sentencing practices combine to divorce women's 'domestic' killings of men from their circumstances of structured disadvantage and frequent long-term physical abuse. In the process, the complexities of women's experiences and rationalities, and women's contextually reasonable, agentic efforts to defend themselves, get translated into law as the expressions of gender- and racially-tainted inadequacies, dependencies, and afflictions. As Stubbs and Tolmie argue – whatever the limitations and contradictions of any feminist engagement with law – those involved in the defence of women homicide offenders need to consider and promote 'social framework evidence' as 'a strategy that is preferable to BWS evidence and has the explicit purpose of moving beyond narrow, individualistic conceptions of women's offending'.

In Chapters 11 and 12, Joe Sim and Ann Lloyd address the imprisonment and treatment of criminalised and 'criminally insane' women, respectively, in the UK. Sim's unnerving essay 'At the Centre of the New Professional Gaze: Women, Medicine and Confinement' picks up the 21st century threads of his 1990 *Medical Power in Prisons* by: (1) depicting how recent trends in 'health promotion' for imprisoned women reinscribe their status as 'less eligible subjects' in a remorselessly gender-contoured and increasingly racialised carceral realm that inexorably widens its terrain and consolidates its grip over captive women and men; (2) charting the manoeuvres of a new generation of experts in the criminality of women, whose 'cleansing psychological and psychic interventions are designed to create the born-again, nurturing, female subject'; (3) linking medico-penal power over and against women to the 'authoritarian modernisation of the criminal justice system' sponsored by Tony Blair's New Labour, and the gender scripts and familial/community ideologies that fuel its policies toward 'deviant' and 'deficient' women 'in need'; and (4) arguing, unsettlingly, that the 'new' regimes of therapy, care, health promotion and risk management are inherently latticed to, and inevitably serve, 'the coruscating discourses of paramilitary discipline and neo-liberal, financial managerialism that dominate contemporary penal arrangements'. In a similar vein, in Chapter 12, Ann Lloyd revisits her work with the women forensic inmates of the Ashworth special (now 'security') hospital in England, whose voices figured prominently in Lloyd's 1995 book *Doubly Deviant, Doubly Damned*. Ten years on, Lloyd returns to Ashworth and conducts a series of provocative interviews with women 'patient-prisoners', clinicians and reformers. Complementing these narratives with her critical review of selected government reports and clinical studies, Lloyd unleashes a forceful condemnation of a psycho-legal institutional machinery that – its pretensions to modernisation, due process and reform aside – continues to neglect and abuse the marginalised 'criminally insane' women under its purview. Lloyd delivers passionate advocacy for a system that would acknowledge 'the fundamental importance of gender and social inequalities', informed by a wider recognition that the resolution of these women's psycho-legal problems ultimately resides 'not in a secure hospital or in a medium secure unit set up, not in the government organised system of care, but in the society of which they are a part'.

Lastly, in Chapter 13 Bonnie Burstow shares her critical reflections on the prospects and possibilities for a feminist-informed praxis advancing the human rights of women and psychiatrised people, and against the oppressions of a malestream psychiatric profession. As both a feminist and an antipsychiatry activist, Burstow poses challenging questions for those involved in the two movements, and for those who seek to establish a united front in the interests of genuine transformation. In her recounting of recent history, Burstow notes both the promises and limitations of women's struggles against mentalist ideology, involuntary commitment, electroshock, the psycho-pharmaceutical industry, the psychiatric abuse of women 'patients', and other issues at the forefront of antipsychiatry praxis over the past generation. While mindful of the factors that have impeded progress – and of the need for renewed self-reflection and critical engagement – Burstow is also encouraged about the opportunities for a galvanizing social justice movement that would simultaneously proceed along multiple fronts. One answer among many, argues Burstow, is to acknowledge the common needs, identities, social positions and potential contributions of women and men, feminists and their allies, activists and scholars, psychiatric survivors and those involved in assorted other local and global struggles against oppression and subordination. For Burstow, the transcendent ideals of feminism, and the activist agendas of antipsychiatry, are both best realised through co-ordinated praxis that aligns itself with such related contemporary social justice movements as 'disabilities rights, antiglobalisation, antipoverty, anti-racism, and penal abolition'. In that sense, a feminist antipsychiatry praxis, too, is ultimately 'aimed at a fundamental transformation of the world'.

Burstow's final thoughts, we believe, afford us a clear and hopeful, if monumentally challenging, passageway through this diverse collection of feminist essays, and through the field more generally. If we are to genuinely change as well as interpret the world of psychiatrised, criminalised and other 'deviant' women, we need to consider how our understandings might translate into involved social praxis on behalf of all those who run afoul of cultural conventions and control institutions in our hyper-modern, ultra-regulated 21st century civilization. Certainly the book will have special application, on an international level, to women and men working in the disciplines of women's studies, criminology, sociology, law, psychiatry and psychology, but our hope is that the writing, and the subject matter, might resonate more widely still. If we have done our job, the essays will register not only with scholars, students, practitioners and activists with interest in forensic matters, but with anyone involved in the study of and resistance against cultural prejudices, human rights abuses and the marginalisation of disempowered people, regardless of their gender – and whatever the socio-legal, ideological, institutional and human circumstance.

Chapter 1
Unravelling Women's Madness: Beyond Positivism and Constructivism and Towards a Material-Discursive-Intrapsychic Approach[1]

Jane M Ussher

1.1 Introduction

Women's madness is a subject that has fascinated artists, poets, playwrights and novelists for centuries. Representations of woman as mad, ranging from the dangerous harridan in the attic, to the melancholic maiden languishing helplessly on her bed, all stand as reminders of the potential danger or vulnerability lurking beneath the mask of beauty that otherwise signifies 'woman'. However, making madness synonymous with femininity isn't merely a matter of misogynistic fantasy or fear. Mental health statistics which record the number of individuals diagnosed or treated for the myriad disorders of the mind which are deemed worthy of statutory regulation attest to the preponderance of women deemed mad.[2] Prior to puberty, boys may be represented in significantly greater numbers (by a factor of approximately 4:1) in the whole gamut of psychological or behavioural problems experienced by children. However, after puberty the situation is reversed, so estimates of the ratio of women to men suffering from disorders such as depression or anxiety range from 6:1 to 5:3. Community surveys, hospital admissions and statistics on outpatient treatment (both medical and psychological) all concur: women report more mental health problems than men, and are more likely to be diagnosed and treated for madness (Bebbington, 1996; Busfield, 1996; Stoppard, 2000; World Health Organisation, 2003).

For decades, researchers have searched for the factors underlying this gender difference, claiming that if we can explain it, we will have the key to understanding mental health problems *per se* (for example, Bebbington, 1996). Numerous competing biological, psychological and social aetiological theories have been put forward as a result. The professions of psychiatry, clinical psychology, psychotherapy and social work dispense expert knowledge and care in the attempt to ameliorate or prevent such problems. Lay texts proliferate offering myriad self-help suggestions or 'alternative' treatments. Women's madness has clearly moved from mythology to mass industry. No longer a mystery, we are assured that it can be categorised, contained and cured.

---

1 A previous version of this chapter was published as 'Women's madness: a material-discursive-intra psychic approach', in Fee, D (ed), *Psychology and the Postmodern: Mental Illness as Discourse and Experience*, 2000, London: Sage, pp 207–30. The current chapter is revised and updated.

2 I will use the term 'madness' to refer to the discursively constructed category which effectively defines individuals so categorised as Other, as fearful or fragile, and 'mental health problems/symptoms' to refer to the symptoms women report.

However, these institutionalised investigations and interventions have not gone unquestioned. A range of critics, including antipsychiatrists, post-modernists and feminists from a number of different ideological camps have subjected expert analyses of women's madness to critical deconstruction. Much of what has for decades (perhaps centuries) been taken for granted has been dissected and discarded as biased, misconceived, or misogynistic in the extreme. Reading many of these critiques, one could be forgiven for concluding that a revolution is underway; that everything which has gone before has been overturned and that the very categorisation of women as 'mad' has been rejected. But this is not the case. In mainstream research and clinical practice very little has changed. Madness as an illness remains unchallenged. Science categorises symptoms into syndromes that are operationally defined and analysed in objective research. Individual women are offered reductionist explanations, and invariably a bio-medical cure, for symptomatology they experience. Psychological interventions may not blame the body, but they still focus, in the main, on the individual woman (or on her mind). The gap between critical analysis and the institutionalised regulation or treatment of madness seems impossible to bridge.

The question is, why is this the case? And what can be done to effect change? In this chapter I will address these two questions head on, reviewing both mainstream positivist and critical interpretivist approaches to the phenomenon of women's madness, as well as the relationship between the two. I will argue that the positivistic and realist epistemological perspectives which underlie mainstream psychological and medical research and clinical intervention should be replaced not by an interpretivist approach, but by a material-discursive-intrapsychic perspective, grounded within a critical realist epistemological paradigm. Such a perspective, I argue, recognises the materiality of mental health problems as they are experienced by women, their intrapsychic pain and defences, and the discursive construction of madness and femininity, without privileging one level of analysis above the other.

1.2 A reflexive pause

Before I embark upon this analysis I would like to clarify my own interest in this debate and outline the reasons why I have arrived at this particular position at this point in time. My interest in women's madness was first inspired by my own mother's mental health problems and her subsequent treatment at the hands of myriad professionals when I was an adolescent, as I have described elsewhere (Ussher, 1991, 2000). This meant that I discovered the stigma of 'madness' very early in life. It was a subject that could not be spoken of, and which clearly inspired fear and dread in all those associated with it. I learned to live with my mother's mental health problems without ever naming as madness the problems she experienced, either to her or to anyone else. Naming them now is only possible because of the 25-year distance which has now elapsed (and also because she is now no longer deemed 'mad'). In contrast, my training as a psychologist equips me not only to name, but to research, diagnose and treat other women who suffer similarly. I have spent many years doing so, yet there was a time, for a number of years, when I stopped; I could no longer reconcile my academic and professional training with my knowledge of feminist and social constructionist thinking on the subject of women's madness. I felt that I could only take part in critical analysis or deconstructive debate.

However, I no longer believe that this is enough, for myself at least. Critical thinking is essential; deconstruction of madness as a concept must be done, yet we cannot ignore the pain and suffering experienced by the women (and men) who are deemed mad; we cannot dismiss mental health problems as linguistic constructions or mere justifications for regulatory control; we need to offer something more concrete than critique for women who come forward for help. At the same time, we need to address head on the fact that post-modern and feminist thinking has not had the impact it should have done on mainstream research and clinical practice in this sphere – the fact that it is invariably dismissed or ignored. And rather than wringing our hands at the injustice of this situation, we need to offer a way forward. This is what I want to try to do here.

At the time of writing, I am personally engaged in research, clinical practice and critical thinking on the subject of women's madness. I no longer feel that there is an irreconcilable tension between these three levels of analysis or exploration. The research and clinical practice I am engaged in is not on the margins (at least as I see it), but situated in the mainstream of psychology. My aim is to have an impact not only on critical thinking, but on the way mainstream research constructs and treats women deemed 'mad'. For example, women suffering from premenstrual syndrome (PMS), who are regarded by the mainstream medical profession to have a bio-medical disorder, have been found to be attributing relationship conflict to PMS, and are thus inappropriately internalising, and being blamed for, relational issues (Ussher, 2003b). The way I have achieved this integration between my clinical and academic thought and practice is not through compromise or sleight of hand, but through an epistemological shift. Thus, the focus of this chapter will be largely on epistemology, rather than on the arguments that unravel the relationship between gender and madness, outlined elsewhere (Ussher, 1991). Mainstream bio-medical and psycho-social theories and interventions for women's madness may appear to have little in common, or even to stand in opposition to each other. What is often overlooked is the fact that researchers in both fields share the same epistemological assumptions[3] and, as a consequence, adopt the same methodology and methods in investigating women's madness. It is because researchers and clinicians have adopted the realist/positivistic epistemology that has dominated science since the 17th century, that little attention has hitherto been paid to what has become a taken-for-granted fact. Yet arguably it is the particular nature of the positivist/realist standpoint that has resulted in the refusal to engage with constructivist and feminist debates, and thus the resulting reductionism and negation of historical and cultural factors in this field, as I will outline below. However, this critique of positivism does not lead to my making a plea for interpretivist or constructivist models – the

---

3   In a critical analysis of the epistemological assumptions of science and social science, Sandra Harding (1987) has defined epistemology as a theory of knowledge which sets out who may legitimately be deemed a 'knower', what requirements information or beliefs must meet in order to be legitimated as 'knowledge', and what kinds of 'facts' may be known. Epistemology therefore determines both methodology – the 'theory and analysis of how research does or should proceed' (Harding, 1987, p 3) – and research methods – the techniques deemed legitimate or appropriate for gathering evidence or information.

conclusion drawn by many post-modern researchers (see Fee, 2000) – but rather to the adoption of a critical-realist epistemological standpoint, and more specifically, a material-discursive-intrapsychic model for understanding and responding to women's madness.

1.3 Explaining women's madness: a critique of mainstream accounts

As the term 'positivism' has often been used in a loose and general manner, it may be helpful to outline a definition at this point. Keat (1979) identified two major elements within the positivist position. The first element is methodological naturalism, the demand for homogeneous methods and approaches in both the social and natural sciences, with the latter providing the model for the former. Secondly, science is conceived within the following criteria: it is asserted that knowledge is only possible as the result of observation, and the only things that can be observed are those which are accessible to the senses; causality is understood in terms of antecedent conditions and general laws governing phenomena; facts and theories are clearly separated from values, with only the former being the legitimate focus of scientific interest. The fundamental premise of a realist perspective is that objects have real existence independent of any perceiver, or of any cultural knowledge or practice. The implications of the dominance of both positivist and realist epistemological standpoints in mainstream analyses of women's madness, in terms of theory, research and clinical practice, will be outlined below.

1.3.1 Methodological naturalism in the analysis of women's madness

The influence of methodological naturalism is clearly evident in mainstream analyses of women's madness. In both bio-medical and psycho-social research, the models of research that are adopted clearly mimic those extant in the natural sciences. This has resulted in the emphasis on the homogeneous use of hypothetico-deductive methodologies, and on standardised, validated measures of both dependent and independent variables (mental health problems and their causes), with an emphasis on objectivity, reliability and replicability, in research.

The limitations of hypothetico-deductive methodologies have been well rehearsed elsewhere (for example, Harre and Secord, 1972; Henriques, Hollway, Urwin, Venn and Walkerdine, 1984; Hollway, 1989; Ingleby, 1982; Ussher, 1996). They include: the artificiality of controlled studies; the limited number of variables that can be studied at any one time; the limitations of quantitative analysis; the assumption that the individual can and should be studied separately from cultural and historical factors; the assumption that the individual should be the sole focus of attention at all; the notion that objectivity is possible in either theory, analysis or the conduct of research; and the limitations of predictive models of cause and effect. Each of these critiques will be explored in more detail below.

1.3.2 Categorisation and consensus definitions of mental illness: knowledge through observation

Following a thesis of methodological naturalism, the desire for valid and reliable comparison across epidemiological and treatment studies, and the need to facilitate research into aetiological mechanisms, have precipitated the desire to establish consensus definitions of mental health problems: the diagnostic categories reified in the Diagnostic and Statistical Manual of the American Psychiatric Association (DSM) being the archetypal case. The desire for uniform definitions of mental health problems may appear on the surface to be a necessary first step for both research and clinical intervention. However, the very notion of categorisation of madness into psychiatric syndromes has been criticised from many different venues.

First, the focus on diagnostic categories reifies the notion of madness as a series of discrete clinical entities that occur in a consistent and homogeneous way, that have an identifiable aetiology, and that are perceived to have *caused* the symptoms women report. This reification of madness acts to deny the social and discursive context of women's lives, as well as the gendered nature of science, which defines how women's bodies and lives are studied (Keller, 1985). In contrast, as many critics have argued (Fee, 2000; Littlewood and Lipsedge, 1982; Ussher, 1991), madness can be conceptualised as a social category created by a process of expert definition. In this view, madness is a socially constructed label, based on value-laden definitions of normality. Parallel arguments have been made about many other 'disorders', both physical and psychological (Foucault, 1965; Sedgwick, 1982), leading to a deconstruction of expert diagnosis, and to a questioning of the existence of many 'syndromes'.

Secondly, if a phenomenon cannot objectively be observed and measured using reliable, standardised techniques, then it cannot be 'known' within a positivist paradigm. As a consequence, the analysis of women's madness and its possible aetiology has come to be driven by methodology rather than theory. For example, the role of unconscious factors cannot be easily assessed within a hypothetico-deductive frame, and so such factors are not included in the majority of mainstream analyses (for example, see Bebbington, 1996). Equally, as historical, political and wider societal factors are not easily operationalised and assessed, they are only addressed within social constructionist or feminist critiques (Chesler 1972; Fee, 2000; Showalter, 1987; Ussher, 1991). According to a positivist paradigm, madness is construed as an individual problem – a disorder affecting an individual woman, on whom bio-medical or psycho-social factors impact and produce symptomatology.

The woman who presents with problems is implicitly positioned as passive and devoid of social context in positivist/realist analyses of madness, since agency is not easy (if at all possible) to observe. Therefore, it is inevitable that it is her body, or her symptoms, that are the entire focus of attention, yet women are not passive objects in relation to the interpretation of physical or psychological symptoms, or in relation to the discursive construction of madness. Recognition of, or self-referral for treatment for mental health problems is a process of active negotiation of symptomatology, current life events and lifestyle, and hegemonic cultural, medical or psychological discourses about madness. Many women make sense of their experiences through positioning themselves as suffering from depression, anxiety or problems such as PMS – a process that has been described as subjectification (Ussher, 2003a). Others may experience symptoms but not make ascriptions of any of these problems. To position these women as 'false negatives', as they are in the case of PMS research (Hamilton and Gallant, 1990), is to misinterpret the active negotiation and resistance of dominant discourse associated with madness in which many women engage. It is to reinforce the notion of women as passive dupes, rather than active agents who continuously make sense of and interpret the social sphere, and their own psychological or bodily experiences (see Ussher, 2002). As psychological symptoms are not visibly apparent, they have to be observed through the interface of subjective accounts. As the latter may easily fall outside the required standards of objectivity and replicability, in empirical research they are often assessed through the use of standardised instruments. This is why there has been an inordinate amount of attention given over to developing reliable and valid standardised questionnaire measures for assessing the incidence of specific mental health problems, such as depression, anxiety or PMS. In mainstream research in this area there is almost total reliance on quantitative methods of data collection and statistical analysis of results. Thus, the complexity and contradictions evident within women's subjective accounts are negated, and a potentially rich source of data is left uncollected and unexamined.

Equally, within a positivist/realist frame, women are made to fit the researcher's model of each of these syndromes, in contrast to grounded methods of data collection and analysis, where the constraints of *a priori* assumptions are not imposed upon participants' accounts, which are collected in a more open, qualitative manner (Henwood and Pigeon, 1994). The use of questionnaires also assumes that 'symptoms' can be categorised and classified in a dichotomous manner as existing or not, with the only added complexity being the notion of a *degree* of symptomatology. That a woman might reply that she sometimes has a symptom and sometimes does not; that it depends on what is happening in her life, whether she has recently eaten, what she is thinking, or how recently she has had sex, amongst other factors, is not acknowledged at all; neither is her assessment of the meaning of her symptoms.

1.3.3 Focusing within the person: biology or cognitions

Within a positivist/realist paradigm, the body is implicitly considered to be more fundamental or 'real' than psycho-social variables, resulting in the emphasis within mainstream medical research on measurable aspects of biology. This historical attribution of women's 'abnormality', discontent, anger, or illness to the body, or to the vagaries of reproduction, has led to the disparity between the number of bio-medical and psycho-social aetiological theories and therapies for women's mental health problems (Ussher, 1989). The focus on the physical body is a direct result of the assumption that bio-medical factors can be observed and measured in the most 'objective' manner, removing the potentially confounding interface of the woman's subjective interpretation, or reports of a symptom. In what is a totally reductionist viewpoint, biology is conceptualised in terms of physical processes – the action of hormones, neurotransmitters, or ovarian functions, considered separately from any meaning, or from social-cultural contexts.

However, there have been many critiques of the notion that the body, or biology, as an objective entity can be understood separately from socio-historical knowledge, experience or subjectivity (see Foucault, 1979; Henriques *et al*, 1984). Individuals do not experience symptoms in a socio-cultural vacuum. The bodily functions we understand as a sign of 'illness' vary across culture and across time (Littlewood and Lipsedge, 1982; Payer, 1988; Sedgwick, 1982). Women's recognition or interpretation of physical and psychological changes cannot be understood outside of the social and historical context in which they live. Our interpretation of changes will be influenced by the *meaning* ascribed to these changes in a particular cultural context. For example, in a cultural context where change across the menstrual cycle is pathologised and positioned as a hormonal disorder, and where women are expected to be calm, in control and able to cope at all times, it is not surprising to find women taking up the diagnostic category of PMS (see Ussher, 2003a). In contrast, in cultural contexts where there are different regimes of truth associated with menstrual cycle change, and where PMS does not circulate as a diagnostic category, women are less likely to report premenstrual 'symptoms', or to attribute changes across the menstrual cycle to PMS (see Chandra and Chaturvedi, 1989; Dan and Monagle, 1994). Equally, definitions of sexuality as a sign of madness differ greatly between the 19th century and today. In the 19th century it was arguably the sexual woman who was at risk of being defined as mad; today it is the *a*sexual woman (Ussher, 1997a). These differences impact upon women's interpretation of the sexual body, and of 'sexual disorder'.

Expert knowledge and understanding of the influence of the body are also socially and historically situated. For example, it was in the context of the 'discovery' of sex hormones in 1905 (Oudshoorn, 1990) that hormonal theories of women's madness (see below), and arguably the very existence of syndromes such as PMS or PND (post-natal depression) as illnesses, evolved. Rather than accepting the body as something which exists above and beyond the measurement tools and definitions of science, it can be argued that the aspects of biology and the body we are allowed to 'know' are those which meet the criteria of the measurement tools currently in use. The development of new technology for calibrating the body will undoubtedly lead to a new set of meta-theories for women's madness. In psychological models of madness, the emphasis on cognitions (see below) is arguably equally reductionist; the focus here may be on biology, but it is still an essentialist view of madness, looking within the woman for the problem, and following a simple model of cause and effect.

1.3.4   *The adoption of unilinear models of cause and effect*

Within the existing research on women's madness, each of the variables which appear in the bio-medical, psycho-social or multifactorial models are clearly operationally defined, reinforcing the assumption that they are discrete antecedent entities which exert independent causal influence in the aetiology of specific syndromes. Within this framework, both mental health problems and the resulting symptoms are positioned as independent variables in research, invariably conceptualised in a dichotomous way as existing or not existing (Ussher, 2003a;

Walker, 1995). The need to test the influence of these antecedent variables within a hypothetico-deductive model has led to the almost universal adoption of unilinear models in both bio-medical and psycho-social research, where the reporting of symptoms is correlated with a single predictive factor.

Given the predominance of these unilinear models of aetiology, it is not surprising to find that unidimensional approaches also dominate research on the effectiveness of both bio-medical and psycho-social treatment. One worrying consequence of adopting a unilinear approach to treatment is that causal assumptions are often made on the basis of treatment effectiveness. For example, in a study which reported the positive benefits of fluoxetine for treating premenstrual complaints, Menkes, Taghavi, Mason and Howard (1993, p 101) concluded that 'these findings thus support the proposed role of serotonergic hypoactivity in the aetiology of PMS'. Similarly, in a study of oestradiol patches, Watson, Studd, Savvas and Garnett (1989, p 731) argue that their positive result 'supports the earlier observation of a link between premenstrual syndrome and ovarian function'. However, the finding that a particular treatment reduces premenstrual symptoms does not necessarily have implications for aetiology. Aspirin is an effective cure for headache, and inhalation of CO_2 an effective treatment for panic attacks, yet we would not propose that either aspirin or CO_2 are implicated in the aetiology of either disorder.

The very premise of a causal relationship is also flawed, as the discovery of a *correlation* between reported symptoms, and a particular bio-medical or psycho-social substrate does not mean that the substrate *caused* the symptoms. Each may be related to a third variable, or not related at all. Indeed, as Bebbington (1996) pointed out, correlations between scores of neuroticism on personality questionnaires and measures of depression may reflect the fact that similar questions are used on both, rather than any association between neuroticism and depression. It is probable that there is a complex and fluid interaction between a number of different factors, which cannot be encapsulated within a narrow positivist frame. Thus, the search for general laws underlying gender differences in mental health problems is potentially blinding us to the complexity of the phenomenon, and to the complexity of women's experience.

1.3.5 Multifactorial models: moving away from linear models of madness?

A number of suggestions have been offered in an attempt to resolve the contradictions and inconsistencies in mainstream research and theory. Many researchers still continue to search for the holy grail – the single underlying cause or treatment for mental health problems. Others (for example, Bancroft, 1993) have focussed on the disciplinary divide between medical and psychological approaches, and as a result have suggested the adoption of multifactorial models, where biological and psycho-social vulnerability can be addressed within a framework that acknowledges the interaction between the two. Alternatively, there have been suggestions of an interaction between cognitive and social vulnerability, with certain women being more prone to depression or anxiety as a result of the interaction of environmental factors such as loss or stress, and cognitive factors such as the overvaluation of one goal at the expense of others.

While these multifactorial models have provided a lead in moving away from narrow unidimensional thinking about women's madness, they offer only a partial answer and arguably operate almost solely at the level of theory, having had little influence on research practice, which continues to be conducted in a unidimensional vein. For example, Paul Bebbington, in acknowledging the aetiological complexity of women's depressions, concludes:

> clinical experience suggests that depression arises because of a complex cascade, whereby for instance external circumstances interact with cognitive sets and induce physiological responses that in turn change the way circumstances are appraised. This may then change cognitions and physiological status, leading to a further spiral ... If this is actually how depression develops, *it becomes extremely hard to research*, and progress has to fall back on the integration of piecemeal approaches (Bebbington, 1996, p 299, emphasis added)

Depression is only 'extremely hard to research' within the constraints of methodological naturalism, outlined above. It is only researchers who adopt this epistemological stance (myself included, until recently) who feel constrained to remain within their own professional boundaries and to pay no more than lip service to the notion of a multifactorial model at the conceptual level. There are a number of reasons why this is so: the practical difficulties of crossing professional boundaries, which include professional rivalries, differences in epistemological or methodological training, and the pressure to locate research funding in one institution as a result of research assessment exercises cannot be overlooked. At the same time, within a positivist paradigm, to measure the influence of myriad multi-layered factors simultaneously could be seen as a sign of poor research design. It contravenes the notion of clear predictability, and introduces the likelihood of type one errors – where significant relationships between symptomatology and putative predictive variables are found by chance, due to the large number of variables being examined. The use of causal or structural equation modelling has been used to overcome this problem in other areas of psychology, but not, to date, in examining women's madness. In addition, these multifactorial models are still framed within a positivist/realist epistemology, and so all of the criticisms which I have outlined thus far still apply.

1.3.6   Objectivity: the separation of facts from values

Underpinning the whole of the positivist/realist endeavour is the commitment to scientific objectivity. The goals of the scientific enterprise are to remove the possibility of bias, and to examine research questions or test hypotheses in a precise, value-free manner that can be replicated by other researchers in order to ascertain the reliability and validity of results. This emphasis on objectivity and neutrality leads to the elevation of the views of the scientific expert over the views of untrained observers – in this case, women diagnosed as mad. Thus, any information on symptomatology is collected in a systematic and objective manner, with any inconsistencies which are found used as confirmatory evidence for the unreliability of women's subjective accounts.

The fact that women reporting mental health problems are considered to be biased or subjective, yet researchers are not, illustrates the absence of reflexivity in positivist/realist research, and the refusal to acknowledge the influence of values, politics, and the constraints of disciplinary boundaries on the way research is conducted or interpreted. However, as it has been argued elsewhere (Billig, 1991; Harding, 1987; Hollway, 1989), the ideological stance of researchers inevitably affects the research questions they ask, the epistemologies and methodologies they adopt, and their interpretations of the data they collect. Research or theory that is explicitly conducted within a feminist framework (Chesler, 1972; Ussher, 1991), challenging the dominance of bio-medical models of women's madness, and arguing instead for attention to the social-political context in which diagnoses are made, is often dismissed or ignored by positivist/realist researchers. It is not seen to meet the criteria for 'good science', because it is deemed biased or political (see Koeske, 1983 for an example of this in relation to PMS research). However, it is equally political and ideological to conduct research within a narrow positivist model that ignores the subjective meaning of madness and of symptomatology for women; to negate the role of discursive constructions of madness in the social construction of gender; and to conceptualise mental health problems within a narrow realist frame. It is political and ideological to elevate the researcher or the clinician to a position of power which implies that he or she is the only one qualified to 'know' (Foucault, 1989). It is political and ideological to reify the notion of madness as an illness (see Chesler, 1972; Ingleby, 1983). The emphasis on objectivity does not strengthen positivist/realist research; it undermines it.

1.3.7 Moving beyond positivism/realism

Many of the above critiques of the concept of madness, and of research into gender differences in mental health problems, have been made previously. Unfortunately, as was noted above, thus far they appear to have had little influence on mainstream research and clinical intervention. This is not because mainstream researchers are unaware of many of these critiques, as they are certainly implicitly acknowledged in many recent reviews. However, whilst researchers or reviewers are happy to acknowledge the importance of social or psychological aetiological factors (for example, Bancroft, 1993; Bebbington, 1996; Busfield, 1996), they are less comfortable with including any mention of the historical or cultural construction of madness, or of gender. Equally, they rarely question the right of experts to intervene. Their reluctance reflects the continuing conceptualisation of women's madness within a positivist/realist frame.

It is arguably exactly because many of the critics of mainstream theories and therapies have *rejected* positivism/realism and embraced a social constructionist or interpretivist epistemology that they have had such little impact on mainstream research and clinical practice. Social constructionism is seen as incompatible with positivist/realist research and theory, largely because it contravenes many of the assumptions of this particular model of science. A further reason for the lack of impact of these critiques is the fact that, as Mary Parlee (1991, p 29) has commented about feminist research, 'very few feminist researchers have over the last few decades gone to the scientific heart of the matter by outlining or carrying out *doable* alternatives in research'. This, in my view, is the challenge to critical theorists, of whatever persuasion.

1.4 Social constructionist and interpretivist critiques

1.4.1 Social constructionism and feminism

Positivist/realist approaches have been challenged in many areas of health and illness (Foucault, 1965; Ingleby, 1983; Nicolson, 1986; Stainton-Rogers, 1996; Ussher, 1997b; Yardley, 1997); the above critiques are not unique to women's madness. Alternative models of conceptualising, researching, and, if necessary, treating symptomatology have been developed from within a broadly social constructionist perspective (see Fee, 2000). Social constructionist approaches take a critical stance towards taken-for-granted knowledge; they acknowledge cultural and historical specificity; they agree that knowledge is sustained by social practices, and that knowledge and social action go together (Burr, 1995). Social constructionists challenge the realist assumptions of traditional bio-medical and psychological research, arguing instead that subjectivity, behaviour, and the very definition and meaning of 'health' and 'illness' are constructed within social practices and rules, language, relationships, and roles; they are always shaped by culture and history. Science is part of this constructive process and, as a consequence, research or clinical intervention can never be seen as objective or neutral; it is a social practice that partly shapes and constructs knowledge. This does not mean that scientific research is pointless, but merely that reflexivity in theory and practice is an essential part of the scientific enterprise.

Social constructionism has also been used as the epistemological basis of much research and clinical practice (McNamee and Gergen, 1992; Shotter and Gergen, 1989), where the gaze of the researcher is on the 'social' rather than on the individual, and where methodological naturalism is explicitly rejected. For example, there has recently been a move towards the use of discursive theories and methods which focus specifically on the role of language and its relation to cultural practices. These discourse analytic approaches draw upon principles from ethnomethodology (Garfinkel, 1967), post-structuralism (Henriques *et al*, 1984) and conversation analysis and linguistics, in viewing discourse as constructive of reality and action-oriented (Potter and Wetherell, 1986). The term 'discourse' refers to a set of shared cultural beliefs and practices, which are utilised in everyday life in order to construct meaning and interpretation about the world (Parker, 1992). It is also argued that discourses are constitutive of subjectivity, and that the meanings of objects and events are inseparable from the way in which they are constituted within particular discourses (Foucault, 1979; Potter and Wetherell, 1986). Constructionist models stand in direct contrast to traditional psycho-social research that conceptualises factors such as cognitions as fixed entities that can be reliably measured. Here, the very notion of *a* cognitive style is dismissed, as interpretation and meaning are continuously negotiated within discourse. From a methodological point of view, this leads to the use of qualitative methods, and again to reflexivity in research practice (for examples, see Ussher, 1999a; Wilkinson and Kitzinger, 1995).

Many of the now numerous feminist critiques of women's madness, and of the treatment of women within the mental health professions, could also be placed under a broad social constructionist umbrella. Feminist critics have argued that: misogynistic assumptions about gender roles and normal femininity are used to diagnose and treat women who deviate as mad; assumptions about the proper position of women within the institution of heterosexuality are used to prescribe notions of normality; the age-old practice of locating distress or deviancy in the womb (or in reproductive hormones) reinforces notions of woman as more animalistic or biologically driven than man, as well as dismissing all legitimate anger or discontent as the result of 'raging hormones'; and social and political inequalities which understandably produce symptoms of distress are ignored (see Chesler, 1972; Penfold and Walker, 1984; Stoppard, 2000; Ussher, 1991, 2005). This has led to critical feminist analyses of mental health research and treatment, to a deconstruction of the very concept of women's madness, and, more recently, to the development of women's centred research and therapy.

1.4.2 The limitations of social constructionist and interpretivist analyses

Despite the welcome addition of these recent critiques in the field of mental health, there are many issues that potentially remain unaccounted for within a social constructionist epistemological frame.

One of the main problems is that in adopting a social constructionist perspective, or in arguing that 'madness' exists entirely at a discursive level, we are implicitly denying the influence of biology or genetics, or we may appear to relegate the body to a passive subsidiary role, which has meaning or interpretation imposed upon it (Turner, 1984; Yardley, 1996). Whilst the emphasis on social and discursive phenomena is understandable as a reaction against biological reductionism, positioning the body as irrelevant in the aetiology, interpretation, or meaning of madness or psychological symptomatology is clearly inappropriate. Other material aspects of women's lives may also be negated in a discursive analysis: the influence of age, social class, power, economic factors, ethnicity, sexual identity, personal relationships and social support, or a prior history of sexual abuse, amongst other factors.

Equally, within a social constructionist or discursive approach, the 'reality' of mental health problems may appear to be denied; madness can appear to be conceptualised as merely a social label or category. One of the conundrums facing feminist critics is the contradiction between the social or cultural construction of madness that pathologises and dismisses women, and the increasing number of women who seek treatment for mental health problems, as they perceive them to have a significant influence on their lives. As Parlee (1989, p 20) notes, 'what is strategically difficult for feminists, is that many women now derive genuine benefits in their personal lives from an ideology that functions to explain and obscure social contradictions in their lives and those of other women'. Ironically, many women adopt a biological discourse in explaining their psychological symptoms; the body is blamed for what is clearly positioned as 'illness'. Social constructionist analyses may seem to have little to say to these women; they stand in opposition to what women 'know', and may be further rejected for appearing to suggest that madness is a myth. This is a problem facing all those who would put forward a radical critique of mental illness: how to reconcile a deconstructive critique at a macro-level with the needs of individuals at a micro-level (Ussher, 2005).

In addition, it is not clear how a social constructionist critique which 'normalises' madness, and denies its status as pathology, would impact upon clinical intervention. Whilst social constructionist and feminist therapy *has* been developed in a number of areas, it is notably absent at the level of official discourse – in training on mainstream clinical courses, as well as in articles in refereed academic journals. If we are to deconstruct the very notion of madness, how can we offer women treatment for this problem without being accused of reifying its existence? If we are focusing on the social or discursive construction of madness, is the woman an appropriate focus of attention? Does this not reify the notion of madness as an individual illness, to be solved by the woman herself? If we are rejecting realism, does that mean we are embracing relativism, with all the problems that entails?

1.5 Moving forward: a material-discursive-intrapsychic analysis of women's madness within a critical realist epistemological framework

In order to understand women's mental health problems, we need an epistemological shift away from a positivist/realist position, since so many aspects of the phenomenon of 'madness' are excluded from the gaze of the researcher by the narrow definition of 'science' that this approach implies. However, moving to a hard line social constructionist position leaves us with questions unanswered, for the reasons outlined above. What I would suggest is a move toward a critical-realist epistemological standpoint, where material, discursive and intrapsychic aspects of experience can all be examined without privileging one level of analysis above the other, within an epistemological and methodological framework that does not make *a priori* assumptions about causality and objectivity, or about what type of methods can or should be used.

Critical realism affirms the independent existence of reality (for example, biological or economic factors), but recognises that our experience of it is always mediated by culture, language and politics (Bhaskar, 1989). Critical realism is described as a 'third way', which overcomes the limitations of both positivism and interpretivism (Wainwright and Forbes, 2000). It rejects the anti-empiricism and apparent relativism of social constructionist and post-structuralist theory, as it does the positivist position that 'reality' can be observed or measured through scientific methods that are objective or value free (Williams, 2003). A variety of *sceptical* methodological approaches, both qualitative and quantitative, are suggested, with the particular choices dependent upon the 'nature of the object of study and what one wants to learn about it' (Sayer, 2000, p 19). There is also acceptance of the legitimacy of lay knowledge and subjective experience, often marginalised or ignored in mainstream psychological research (Ussher, 1996). Critical realism explicitly rejects the 'predictive pretensions' of natural science because, in examining human behaviour and the social sphere, we are dealing with open systems and therefore can only explain and describe, not predict (Williams, 2003). Critical realism leads naturally to a material-discursive-intrapsychic approach, which can reconcile both the bio-medical and psycho-social aspects of experience, as well as acknowledge the cultural and historical context in which individual women and men are positioned, and in which meaning about experience is created.

'Material-discursive' approaches have recently been developed in a number of areas of psychology, such as sexuality, reproduction, and mental or physical health (see Ussher, 1997a, 1997b; Yardley, 1997). Their emergence in the discipline results from both a frustration with traditional psychology which has tended to adopt a solely materialist standpoint, thus serving to negate discursive aspects of experience, and a dissatisfaction with the negation of the material aspects of life in many discursive accounts. This integrationist material-discursive approach is to be welcomed, yet, arguably, it does not always go far enough, as the intrapsychic is often still left out, for the reason that it is seen as individualistic or reductionist, or not easily accessible to empirical investigation. Equally, when intrapsychic factors are considered (for example, in psychoanalytic or cognitive theorising), they are invariably conceptualised separately from either material or discursive factors.[4] It is time that all three levels together are incorporated into academic theory and practice, in order to provide a multi-dimensional analysis of women's lives, of madness as a discursive category, and of the mental health symptoms many women experience. So what is meant by a material-discursive-intrapsychic approach?

1.5.1   The level of materiality

To talk of materiality is to talk of factors which exist at a corporeal, societal or institutional level: factors which are traditionally at the centre of bio-medical or sociological accounts. These would include biological factors which are associated with psychological symptomatology; material factors which institutionalise the diagnosis and treatment of mental health problems as madness; and gender inequalities and inequalities in heterosexual relationships which legitimate masculine power and control. The latter would encapsulate: economic factors which make women dependent on men; presence or absence of accommodation which allows women in destructive relationships to leave; and support for women of a legal, emotional and structural kind, which allows protection from further harassment or abuse. It would include issues of social class which lead to expectations of 'normal' behaviour for women and men, and which are implicated in educational or employment opportunities available to both, as well as in the way individuals are treated by external institutions such as social services or the mental

---

4   There are exceptions. For example, the feminist psychoanalyst Karen Horney (1931) developed theories of sexuality and gender relationships which encapsulated material, discursive and intra-psychic levels of experience.

health professions. The fact of whether children are present in the relationship (or are in custody battles withheld), and the material consequences of being married (or not) are also part of this level of analysis. Equally, previous history of abuse or bereavement is partly a material event, as is family history – the number of siblings, parental relationships and factors such as parental divorce or separation from parents in childhood. There are also many material consequences of experiencing or being treated for mental health problems, in terms of physical or psychological vulnerability, as well as powerlessness at an economic or societal level. The social isolation which can be a consequence of mental health problems, or which can act to exacerbate its effects, is partly a material issue. Sex, ethnicity and sexuality are also associated with materiality – with the reproductive body, with gendered or sexual behaviour, and with physical appearance. Within a feminist perspective it is recognised that material factors frequently militate against women: women are often economically, physically and socially disadvantaged in relation to men.

1.5.2 The level of the discursive

To focus on the 'discursive' is to look to social and linguistic domains – talk, visual representation, ideology, culture, and power. What is arguably of most relevance in analyses of women's madness is the discursive construction of madness, of medical or psychological expertise (Foucault, 1965), as well as the analysis of the relationship between representations of 'woman' and 'man' and the social roles adopted by individual women and men. As the discursive construction of 'madness' as an illness, as an individual problem, and as justification for expert intervention has already been explored (see above), here I will focus only on the discursive construction of gender. Within a discursive account, rather than femininity being seen as pre-given or innate, it is seen as something which is performed or acquired. In the process of becoming 'woman', it is argued that women follow the various scripts of femininity that are taught to them through the family, through school, and through the myriad representations of 'normal' gender roles in popular and high culture, as well as in science and the law (Ussher, 1997a). They have to choose between the contradictory representations of femininity which are available at any point in time, in order to find a fit between what they wish to be, and what is currently allowed (Ussher, 1997a). The fact that many women take up the archetypal position of 'woman' – always positioned as secondary to 'man' – is attributed to the dominance of patriarchy, and the fact that gender is constructed within a 'heterosexual matrix' (Butler, 1990).

Within a heterosexual matrix, the traditional script of femininity tells us that women live their lives through a man. To have a man, and keep him, is the goal of every girl's life. Girls are weaned on fairy stories that reinforce the importance of this tale (and remind them of the terrible fate of women who fail): Cinderella and her ugly sisters; Snow White and her wicked step-mother. In adulthood, women are reminded of it through romantic fiction, women's magazines, television soap operas or Hollywood films: the good wife and the femme fatale, who in film noir always meets an unseemly end. In the 21st century, 'getting' still means monogamy, and usually marriage or motherhood; this is the script for the 'respectable' woman.

Not getting means being positioned as sad or bad: the spinster on the shelf, or the shameful whore. And the sexual woman, the whore, is always deemed to deserve all the condemnation that she gets (see Ussher, 1997a).

In the traditional discursive construction of heterosexuality, 'man' is positioned as powerful, and 'woman' as passive and beholden to man. The institutionalised couple they together form is positioned as immune from scrutiny or intervention from outside. At the same time, 'man' is idealised as the answer to a woman's dreams: the fairy tale prince who will sweep her off her feet; 'Mr Right' who will bring happiness, contentment and fulfilment of her heart's desires – the 'happy ever after' ending we are promised at the end of romantic fiction and fairy tales. However, it is also acknowledged that this relationship can result in violence, oppression and neglect. The traditional discursive representation of heterosexuality provides an explanation for this experience that ensures that many women stay: the myth of 'Beauty and the Beast'. We are taught that a good woman can always tame or transform the monstrous brute or beast; through her ministrations or example the frog will turn into the prince, the violent man into the charming thoughtful lover. The woman who *can't* enact this transformation is positioned as to blame; she must try harder, be more self-sacrificing, or attempt with greater vigour to be the 'perfect woman'. Even if she fails, though, and the beast is never transformed, we are reminded by the fairy stories and by romantic fiction that underneath it all the brute is a vulnerable and needy man, and that he is the most sexy or desirable partner a woman could find (Mr Darcy, Rhett Butler ...). And if all else fails, women still have the hope that motherhood will provide true fulfilment, as will the security of knowing that they are safe within the boundaries of a 'normal' heterosexual life (see Ussher, 1997a).

This isn't merely an analysis of fairy stories, or of an outmoded script of heterosexual femininity that many women have rejected in their quest for a more autonomous or agentic life. It is one of the explanations put forward for why women stay in unhappy, neglectful or violent relationships with men (Dobash and Dobash, 1979), and arguably one of the explanations for why women internalise marital or family difficulties as depression, or as PMS (Ussher, 2003b). Women are taught to gain happiness through relationships, invariably with men. They are also taught that it is their fault if a relationship fails.

1.5.3   The level of the intrapsychic

Intrapsychic factors are those which operate at the level of the individual and the psychological: factors which are traditionally the central focus of psychological analyses of women's madness. This would include analyses of the ways in which women blame themselves for problems in relationships, and psychological explanations for why this is so, incorporating factors such as low self-esteem, depression, the impact of previous neglect or abuse, guilt, shame, fear of loss or separation, and the idealisation both of heterosexuality and of men. It would include an analysis of psychological defences, such as repression, denial, projection or splitting, as mechanisms for dealing with difficulty or psychological pain. For example, we see evidence of splitting in the way women see themselves, or their man, as all good or all bad, with no acknowledgment that everyone can exhibit both positive and negative characteristics at the same time, or in the way women blame themselves, or their bodies, for problems which they experience (Ussher, 2003b). It would also include women's internalisation of the idealised fantasy of motherhood, and of the expectations of being 'woman' in a heterosexual social sphere.

1.5.4 Integrating the material, discursive and intrapsychic (MDI)

The MDI model posits that a fluid and ongoing interaction of material, discursive and intrapsychic factors produces emotions, bodily sensations and behaviours which come to be diagnosed as 'madness', or as 'mental health problems' such as PMS or PND by the woman herself, or by a clinician. As noted above, a number of other multifactorial models, within a bio-psycho-social framework, have been put forward (Ussher, 1992; Walker, 1995). However, MDI does not position either psychological or biological aetiological factors as the point of origin of 'symptoms'; it develops the analysis of psychological processes involved in mental health beyond the cognitive-behavioural, and is the first to explicitly engage with constructionist and discursive accounts, through acknowledging the role of discursive representations of 'madness' in analyses of the development and course of symptoms. Whilst many constructivist critics dismiss mainstream theories and treatments, resulting in the absence of a discursive analysis from the sphere of intervention, the MDI model incorporates a critical cultural analysis into a framework that allows a detailed examination of the development, course and treatment of mental health issues, using a combination of methodologies.

In a number of recent studies the MDI model has been used as the theoretical framework. For example, a recent UK project compared psychological treatment with medical treatment (fluoxetine), and a combination of the two, in 108 women with moderate-severe PMS (Hunter *et al*, 2002). The researchers examined the subjective meaning of PMS, and the ongoing appraisal and negotiation of symptomatology, through narrative interviews and questionnaires pre- and post treatment. Three interrelated processes of appraisal and coping appeared to be central to the development and maintenance of premenstrual symptoms: awareness of psychological or physical changes, perceived ability to cope, or reactivity to others, premenstrually; expectations and perceptions of premenstrual changes; and individual responses and ways of coping (Ussher, 2002). Feeling out of control and unable to tolerate negative emotional or bodily changes, particularly in situations where there were demands from others, or other life problems, was the most common description of PMS given by women. The most problematic 'symptoms' were uncontrolled expressions of anger or irritation, followed by shame or guilt. Women attributed their symptoms to an external thing, PMS, even when alternative environmental explanations could be found. Thus, through a process of splitting, they disassociated negative emotions or behaviours from the self (Ussher, 2003a). It is posited that these accounts can be interpreted as difficulties in emotional regulation, resulting from premenstrual changes in arousal and hormones, combined with environmental stress (Ussher and Wilding, 1992), and relationship issues (Ussher, 2003b). These experiences are attributed to PMS in a process of 'subjectification' (Ussher, 2003a) through which the premenstrual phase of the cycle is discursively constructed as problematic (Ussher, 1999b). One of the questions that arises in the PMS literature is: why do some women negotiate and cope with premenstrual changes, avoiding a self-diagnosis or experience of PMS, and others do not? Ongoing research is using the MDI model as a means of addressing these questions, through examining the role of reflective functioning and emotional regulation associated with early attachment relationships, as well as self-policing, in the aetiology, management and prevention of PMS. The MDI model has also been used to examine women's experience of postnatal depression (Ussher, 2004) and of living with an alcohol-dependent partner (Ussher, 1997c).

In order to give a concrete illustration of how both women's madness and mental health symptoms can be conceptualised in the MDI framework, I will outline a brief description of a case of an individual woman positioned as 'depressed'. This is an actual case based on my own clinical work with women, with significant details changed in order to protect anonymity and confidentiality.

1.5.5   Understanding women's madness from a material-discursive-intrapsychic standpoint

Alison is 33 years old and has a son, Toby, who is two. She has recently been given a diagnosis of clinical depression, and is being treated with anti-depressants. She has been told that it is a reactive depression, and that the drugs will alleviate her symptoms, and allow her to get on with life like any normal mother.

Alison and Toby live in rented accommodation on a sprawling modern housing estate on the outskirts of Sydney. Alison separated from her husband, David, 18 months ago, and receives no financial support from him. She works three days a week as a shop assistant, spending the other two with Toby. David has custody of Toby every weekend, and for the early part of the week. Being without her son for four days is a source of great distress for Alison, and she finds that she is listless and depressed on the days she is alone. She sits and watches television, finding that anything of a remotely emotional nature will bring her to the brink of tears. She also has no appetite, and sometimes forgets to eat for a couple of days. Sleep is often elusive, and Alison can lie awake all night tossing and turning, feeling dreadful the next day. She often wonders whether it was her fault that the marriage didn't work, and whether she should give it another try. She wonders whether she was abnormal in finding sex with David painful and repugnant, and whether there is something wrong with her body. She's been told that some women like a dominant man who has his way whenever and wherever he wants with his wife, as David did.

When they were still living together, during the first six months of Toby's life, David showed no interest in his son, and offered Alison no support in caring for him. He expected his dinner on the table as soon as he returned from work, but would often demand that Alison take a shower before he would eat it, as he wanted his 'marital rights' as an appetiser. She eventually left him after an argument in which he locked her out of the house in her nightdress, to 'teach her a lesson' for not being more passionate in bed. As was common in their relationship, David called her 'good for nothing' and told her that he'd take Toby from her if she didn't 'buck up'. Alison didn't want to leave, but was persuaded to do so by a colleague at work, when she broke down and told her about the ongoing abuse.

Whilst she is now relieved to be away from her marriage, Alison finds life on her own difficult and lonely. She can't afford to run a car, and has no friends on the estate. She had to live here because it was the only place that she could afford within the Sydney metropolis. Alison would dearly like to return to Adelaide, where her family live, and where she could afford to live somewhere closer to shops and amenities, but David is insistent on staying in Sydney, so Alison has to stay too. David wants her to return to the marital home, and is confident that he can 'break her' by keeping Toby from her for half of the week. He has told her that he is considering fighting for full custody, as she isn't a fit mother because of being 'mad'.

Alison has been diagnosed and treated within a bio-medical model; even if familial factors are acknowledged to be part of the aetiology of her 'symptoms', drugs are being posited as the sole 'cure'. So how can a material-discursive-intrapsychic model, within a critical realist framework, help us to understand Alison's dilemma? We first need to recognise that Alison's distress is 'real': she is exhibiting clear signs of clinical depression, and at a subjective level experiences a high level of distress and hopelessness. However, the discursive construction of this distress as a biomedical illness, as a pathology, can be contested, and a case can be made for a clear interaction between material, discursive and intrapsychic factors in the development, and treatment of, her 'symptoms'.

There are clearly many material factors associated with Alison's distress. These include: the ongoing abusive relationship with David, manifested in past physical and psychological abuse, and current manipulation of Alison's access to Toby; economic difficulties due to being a single mother with no child support; social isolation due to being apart from her family, and living in an outlying housing estate; the inability to take on extra paid employment, or to undergo further training which might improve her economic prospects, due to only having access to Toby on the two days a weeks she isn't working. The materiality of the impact of depression – in terms of physiological symptoms (emotionality, disrupted sleep and eating patterns, tiredness) – is also a factor which needs to be acknowledged.

Discursive factors include: the positioning of Alison's distress as illness, with bio-medical treatment as the most appropriate cure; the stigma associated with 'madness' which puts barriers against Alison seeking psychological help, and precludes her gaining a more holistic form of intervention; hegemonic constructions of masculinity and femininity, and of heterosexual marriage, which legitimate David behaving in the way he does, and which prevented Alison from developing a sense of entitlement to respect and reciprocal care before the relationship deteriorated beyond a point of repair; the emphasis on heterosexual relationships as the centre of a woman's existence, leading to self-pathologisation of the woman who is not thus fulfilled; and recent constructions of fathering in the Australian context, which lead to equal custody being given to mothers and fathers after a marriage break-up, regardless of individual circumstances.

Intrapsychic factors include Alison blaming herself (or her body) for her problems, in concert with the exoneration of her husband, her low self-esteem, which was largely a product of ongoing abuse, her patterns of thinking which increased her feelings of hopelessness, her ways of coping (through withdrawal), and the psychic pain she experienced, which was labelled 'depression'.

Whilst each level of analysis can be described separately, Alison's 'depression' can only be understood as an interaction of all three; they are irrevocably interlinked. Her symptoms, which were undoubtedly real to her, were no more the product of her unhappy marriage or her husband's abuse than they were the result of the recent changes which had happened in her body at a biochemical or physiological level as part of her 'depression', or the fact that she had no money and no social support. Her symptoms resulted from the continuous interaction of all of these factors; given these circumstances very few individuals would not be 'depressed'.

But Alison is not 'mad'. She is not deviant, deficient or even necessarily in need of expert assessment or intervention. However, there are a number of suggestions which could be made to address her problems. Unfortunately, hers is not an atypical case history, so suggestions made in this context arguably can be applied more broadly in this sphere.

First, I would argue for a critical realist standpoint in any research to investigate problems such as Alison's, as was outlined above. Secondly, any clinical assessment should take on board the level of the material, discursive and intrapsychic, as should any intervention. Intervention could take place at a number of different levels: in individual, couple, family, or group therapy which allowed for the acknowledgment of these three inter-related levels of analysis; psychological intervention with her husband, to deal with the issue of abuse and his feelings about their relationship, and ongoing custody of their son; community intervention which focuses on the social environment in which Alison lives; facilitation of training, education, or employment to address her economic and psychological powerlessness; provision of alternative housing; facilitation of self-help strategies or of support from wider social networks.

Taking this approach to intervention does not blame Alison for her problems, or locate the cause of her symptomatology within her. It provides a framework for addressing her individual needs (which may be for individual psychological support, or for retraining at work), whilst also focusing on the wider social and discursive factors which precipitate and maintain her problems. It is implicitly multi-disciplinary – no one person could attempt all these interventions. However, Alison may have preferences about what type of support or help *she* wants. Her preferences should be guiding factors in what is offered, if anything is offered at all.

All of the above may seem a utopian analysis – it certainly requires greater resources than are often available in the field of women's health, but there is no reason why it should be utopian. If we look outwards, instead of confining ourselves within our own ideological or professional boundaries, we may surprise ourselves at what can be achieved.

1.6 Conclusion

'Madness' is a phenomenon experienced by individual women at material, discursive and intrapsychic levels; we cannot disentangle one from the other. Its meaning to women, and to the experts who research and treat it, has to be understood in relation to the specific historical and cultural contexts in which both are positioned. It is in the context of dominant cultural discourses associating femininity with madness, infirmity, and reproductive lability that psychological symptoms are interpreted or experienced as 'madness' – by the women who suffer from these symptoms, and by the experts who intervene. It is in the context of the positivist/realist tradition in the bio-medical and psychological sciences that madness is positioned as a real entity – as a syndrome or a disease. An epistemological shift to a critical realist epistemological standpoint, and a material-discursive-intrapsychic analysis allows us to incorporate these different layers of women's subjective experience, and the different types of expert knowledge about both 'madness' and mental health problems, into one framework. What may appear to be contradictions or irrevocable disagreements within either a positivist or realist frame are then transformed into different parts of the complex picture that is 'women's madness': a picture which makes sense only when all the different parts are considered together.

The shift from a positivist/realist approach to a material-discursive-intrapsychic approach is analogous to the shift from capturing the world through a pin-hole camera to capturing it on moving film. Neither provides a more 'true' vision of reality. The pin-hole camera is merely more simplistic and limited, and can only show one fragment of the world at any one time, whilst a whole range of experiences can be captured in all of their fluid complexity with the more sophisticated medium of moving film. A shift from positivism/realism to a material-discursive-intrapsychic model will serve the same purpose in exploring women's madness, both as a discursive construct and as a set of symptoms experienced by individual women.

Chapter 2
Beyond Reason: Social Constructions of Mentally Disordered Female Offenders[1]

Kathleen Kendall

2.1   The social construction of Aileen Wuornos

On the morning of 9 October 2002, a media frenzy surrounded the walls of Florida State Prison. Newspaper journalists and television crews had arrived the evening before, as Aileen Wuornos read the Bible and listened to an oldies radio station. Although they would not be direct witnesses to her execution, the media found it enough to be on site as the state took the life of the woman dubbed America's first female serial killer. For many journalists, Wuornos's death by lethal injection brought to a close a story which began in January 1991, following her confession to the murders of six men. In the 12 years between her arrest and execution, reporters and others attempted to make sense of the prisoner's actions by piecing together the strands of her marginal existence. Wuornos's own claim to have acted in self-defence while working along Florida's highways as a prostitute was buttressed by evidence exposing a life of abuse, violence, rootlessness and betrayal. Expert witnesses testified that Wuornos was mentally ill, and her lesbian relationship added a further salacious element to her story. However, these apparent facts lent themselves to competing interpretations. Depending upon the source, Wuornos was described as either a victim of society or an evil monster; an avenging angel or a madwoman. She was both ascribed full agency and stripped bare of it. Her crimes were at once contextualised and removed from the events circumscribing them (Hart, 1994; Kelleher and Kelleher, 1998; Kennedy, 1992; McWinney, 1993; Morrissey, 2003; Russell, 1992; Shipley and Arrigo, 2004).

Wuornos's own narrative changed course as attested to by film-makers Nick Broomfield and Joan Churchill.[2] Their two documentaries expose cynical attempts to profit from her story, an incompetent legal defence, corruption among the state police, high-level politics surrounding the death penalty and the pains of imprisonment. The films also illustrate the ways in which attempts to capture the truth of human actions and people's essence evade us. Until the months leading up to her execution, Wuornos steadfastly maintained that she had acted in self-defence. However, as her impending death neared, she insisted that the murders had been committed in cold blood. In response, Wuornos's lawyers challenged her execution on the grounds of mental incompetence. In turn, Wuornos fired them. Ultimately, psychiatric examinations concluded that Wuornos was mentally competent and fit

---

1   Enormous thanks to Bob Menzies for being such a patient and thorough editor and to Clive Webb for his support and assistance.
2   *Aileen: The Life and Death of a Serial Killer*, directed by Nick Broomfield, UK, 2003; *Aileen Wuornos: The Selling of a Serial Killer*, directed by Nick Broomfield and Joan Churchill, USA, 1993.

for execution and Governor Jeb Bush concurred. Nick Broomfield implies that Wuornos's change of story was the consequence of suicidal paranoia arising from both her earlier history and the more immediate pressures of death row. She claimed that prison officials were torturing her through mind control and attempting to make her crazy. After being told that the camera was turned off, when in fact it was still running, Wuornos confided to the film-makers that her murderous actions were in self-defence and that her change of story was a means of ensuring a swift execution.

In the wake of her crimes, public trial and death by lethal injection, Aileen Wuornos has become a fixture in popular culture. She features in a number of true-crime and academic books, many websites, a series of films, a comic book, trading cards, a song and even an opera. Despite the vast and growing amount of material attempting to unravel the truth behind Aileen Wuornos and her crimes, we are instead left with complexity, contradiction and confusion. The harder we try to pin down an explanation, the more elusive the answers appear to become.

Aileen Wuornos is but one of a small yet enigmatic group of women deemed to have transgressed both the law and reason. The intense interest and speculation surrounding mentally disordered female offenders like Wuornos rest in the fact that they embody three kinds of social deviance: madness, criminality and femininity. In addition, because criminality implies responsibility for one's actions and madness infers the opposite, the two categories appear incongruous. Similarly, the attributes associated with femaleness do not appear to fit with criminal deeds. Therefore, females deemed both mad and bad endanger the social order not only through their actions, but because they threaten to expose the fissures and failures within the myriad of methods designed to understand and manage society's miscreants.

A variety of discourses or systems of language for talking about mentally disordered female offenders have been established over time. Discourses create knowledge which informs how we think about and manage ourselves, others and our social world. Some discourses come to be regarded as 'truth', defining and limiting the terms within which something can be meaningfully discussed and understood. These dominant discourses reflect and reproduce power relations. Those occupying positions of power have greater resources through which to embed their own interests within the dominant discourse. At the same time, however, alternative discourses exist on the margins, often challenging and resisting taken-for-granted truths (Foucault, 1965).

This chapter provides an overview of the dominant discourses enveloping mad and bad women, focusing upon the 19th century, during which time criminal lunacy became entrenched as an officially legal category. Such examination will help us to understand how a problematic group of women has historically been understood and treated and, in doing so, will reveal the political rationalities and relations of power underpinning these psycho-legal constructions. Dominant discourses represent an attempt to contain, explain and manage what would otherwise appear to be beyond reason, reconstructing 'paradox as coherence' (Worrall, 1990, p 8). In these ways, belief in an ordered world can be maintained or restored and power relations preserved. At the same time, through deconstructing these dominant discourses, some of this veneer can be peeled away, revealing the tentative and brittle nature of accepted wisdoms. This process of deconstruction offers the possibility that marginal or alternative discourses will be heard and, through them, a change in power relations established.

I will argue that marginal discourses can indeed move to the centre and even become dominant themselves. However, in the case of Aileen Wuornos and others like her, the subversive elements have tended to disappear or be reconfigured in ways which have functioned to maintain rather than subvert power relations. Her story serves as an important reminder that the academic, clinical, legal and activist work we do has very real consequences. We are not situated outside of power relations and we bring our own knowledge, experiences and social position to our involvements with mentally disordered female offenders, as we do in other spheres. Therefore, we must remain unremittingly self-reflexive, and acknowledge the limitations and implications of our own social constructions.

Adopting a self-reflexive position does not mean, however, that we should be immobilised by relativism, or by a fear of where our actions and words may take us. Inaction has its own effects. Moreover, the people we study and write about, both historically and contemporarily, were and are real. To become completely lost in our own theoretical and ethical quagmire is to neglect the human subjects of our enquiries. Language and meaning are not isolated from the bodies we occupy or our broader physical environment. However we define 'madness' or 'crime', these constructs have very real consequences. The actions they denote sometimes disrupt, injure, and obliterate people as well as objects. This reality cannot be ignored. Similarly, femaleness is not only constructed but embodied. Our bodies are corporeal as well as sites of discursive production and consumption. Through them we experience physical as well as emotional pain and pleasure.

Following Ussher (Chapter 1, this volume; also 2000, p 208), I argue for a material-discursive-intrapsychic (MDI) approach. Such a position attempts to encompass the intrapsychic pain and defences experienced by females positioned as mentally disordered offenders, the material world in which they are situated and the discourses which envelop them, without privileging one of these spheres over another. Furthermore, the MDI perspective, as developed by Ussher, recognises the legitimacy of lay knowledge. That is, it regards women's own understandings to have equal, but not superior, status to expert knowledge about mentally disordered offenders (Pilgrim and Rogers, 1997). Although they have been silenced and muted by dominant as well as marginal discourses, female offenders labelled as mentally disordered have much knowledge, experience and insight to share. They are not simply passive victims, but rather actors who make choices and influence their own lives and the lives of those around them, albeit under constrained and often very restricted parameters. More importantly, as feminists, we must be mindful that we are attempting to understand and intervene in *their* lives. If we wish to propose a more astute and possibly emancipatory framework we must not assume that we can simply speak on their behalf, but equally important, we should not expect these women to provide us with *the* truth, given that they represent such a diverse and ever-shifting spectrum of conduct, experience and social position. Furthermore, like all of us, 'criminally insane' women draw upon available constructions to understand and shape their own identities. None of us remains untainted by discourse or unimpeded by power relations. Furthermore, we re-write our stories and ourselves over time. As Aileen Wuornos demonstrates, truths are always fractured, porous and elusive, yet, the people behind them are very real.

2.2 The social construction of criminal lunacy

This section provides a brief historical overview of the origins of criminal lunacy upon which the notion of mentally disordered offending is founded. In revealing the political and social factors which contributed to the development of criminal lunacy, its apparent naturalness becomes subject to challenge. Through this process, the possibility of interrogating current truth claims about mentally disordered female offenders opens up, allowing us to think differently about the present and future.

As Smith (1981) suggests, although there was a long western tradition of excusing criminals who displayed extreme forms of madness, 'idiocy' or delusion, the idea of 'criminal lunacy' was a 19th century invention. Prior to this time, the insanity defence was not commonly used and 'criminal insanity' did not exist as an official or separate category. Its establishment derived from attempts to apply both Enlightenment and liberal notions to the management of perceived social problems.

The transformation of western society that occurred during the 18th and 19th centuries as a result of urbanisation, industrialisation and immigration engendered widespread social anxiety. Reformers feared that such developments were inviting social chaos and decay. To help restore order, they urged that the methods used to understand, predict and control the natural world be applied to the social realm. This recommendation was informed by both the Enlightenment movement and liberal political philosophy. As I am using it here, liberalism refers to a particular style of government which avoids both under- and over-regulation, valuing the liberty of free individuals above all else. The liberal emphasis on individual autonomy partially evolved through capitalist economic relations which required the freedom to labour, produce and consume. Its exponents maintained that a free market economy was best achieved through non-interference with natural laws. At the same time, it was acknowledged that limited forms of government were necessary to ensure civility, order, and productivity (McCallum, 2001; Rose, 1988, 1999a, 1999b).

This latter assumption was embedded in the 'doctrine of the social contract', which posited that a bond between citizens and government held society together. It maintained that people were entitled to protection through laws but necessarily surrendered some of their individuality so that these laws could be administered and enforced for the common good. The natural rights and freedoms of independent citizens would therefore be protected, under the liberal state, through the 'rule of law' (Goff, 1999). A further notion, the 'doctrine of free will', maintained that all humans would freely and rationally accept the social contract and rule of law. Correspondingly, individuals who broke the law and breached the social contract were seen to deserve punishment (Goff, 1999).

Liberalism originated in the Renaissance, but gained a stronger footing through the Enlightenment movement which flourished in the 18th century. Enlightenment philosophy embraced the supremacy of reason over superstition, celebrated the liberty of individual citizens, and posited that human progress could be achieved through the ministrations of science and technology. It was thought that the scientific tools of observation, calculation and classification could be mobilised to reveal the general laws which underpinned social life. In turn, once these laws were known, they could be harnessed economically and efficiently to predict, contain and control all aspects of the material world. Since scientific investigation claimed to discover objective facts through empirical and value free means, policies emanating from social research were purported to be in the best interests of everyone in society (Douglas, 1992; Foucault, 1977, 1991; Rose, 1996, 1999a, 1999b).

Prior to the 18th century, understandings of criminality were generally informed by religious doctrine, and lawbreaking was thus understood as a submission to temptation or sin. Furthermore, the European monarchies depended on sovereign power to maintain social control. Punishment was meant to deter through terror, and was justified as a means through which individuals could be restored to a state of grace (Hay *et al*, 1975). It typically consisted of physical, overt and repressive measures such as shaming, flogging, execution, mutilation and banishment (Gamberg and Thomson, 1984).

However, Enlightenment liberalism challenged the authority of rulers and regarded 'human nature as essentially good, rational, and capable of self-government' (Halttunen, 1998, p 4). Reformers thus urged the application of humanitarianism and science to solve social problems. The rise of imprisonment, involving forced labour as well as religious instruction in an attempt to instil discipline and morality (Spierenburg, 1995), was one outcome of such endeavours. However, as a number of scholars have noted, the shift in punishment from public sanctions to carceral internment was a gradual process; penal bondage had been in use in a number of European countries as early as the 16th century (Garland, 1985, 1990).

Moreover, public executions and corporal penalties continued to be carried out even after the advent of the prison. Accordingly, in 18th century England a variety of punishments were in place, including fines and transportation to the colonies, as well as whipping and execution. Only a small minority of people were actually imprisoned, and most of these were incarcerated for minor offences such as vagrancy. Two types of institutions existed at this time: the jail, which theoretically was used to house debtors and felons; and the house of correction, which held those people who were sentenced for short terms. However, the distinction between these two penal sites was often blurred in practice. Different types of prisoners were, in fact, kept together (Garland, 1985, 1990; McGowen, 1995). Indeed, men, women and children often shared the same quarters. These regimes of compulsory cohabitation contributed to the abuse of women by men, and where females were segregated, their accommodation was often worse than that provided for males (Faith, 1993; Zedner, 1991, 1995).

Among the populations housed in jails and houses of correction were those people thought to be mad. Their keepers considered this group to be particularly disruptive and troublesome. However, there were very few other public facilities available within which to house such problem citizens (Moran, 2000).

As Porter (2002) suggests, the creation of establishments exclusively for the insane is a relatively recent development. For a long time, insanity was generally regarded as a domestic responsibility. Mad people who appeared to pose no danger were allowed to wander, while those considered seriously deranged were kept at home. While segregation began in the Middle Ages, often under the direction of religious patronage, purpose-built institutions for the mad were not widespread until the 18th century.

Social reformers looked to these establishments as both a source and a solution for many of the problems they considered to be plaguing society. They maintained that overcrowding, poor conditions and the intermingling of different types of deviants were contributing to social vice. Inspired by the humanitarianism and science of Enlightenment liberalism, reformers sought to extract order out of chaos by removing lunatics, criminals and paupers from the antiquated establishments of the ancien regime, and placing them instead in specialised asylums, penitentiaries and almshouses. These social engineers assumed that the new arrangements would bring the forces of reason and calculus of science to bear on the unique dangers that each class of deviants posed to the social order. Such methods of categorisation and division could, they believed, achieve efficiency and order as well as expose the causes of, and most efficient solutions to, the problem of human deviance (Foucault, 1977; Rose, 1996, 1999a, 1999b; Sim, 1990).

Consequently, with individual differences across nations, such institutions were variously established throughout the 18th and 19th centuries. At the same time, there followed further attempts to create more precise categories of human difference contained within each. These strategies relied on the emerging penal methodologies of observation, measurement, calculation and classification. The knowledge which emerged through such procedures was used to manage not only institutionalised populations, but citizens in many other domains of social life as well. These practices were accomplished as the state developed systematic means of gathering population data, and applying statistical calculations on this knowledge to establish averages or norms. People who did not measure up to the standards of the 'ideal citizen' were encouraged to reconstruct themselves, often with the advice or assistance of experts. Foucault (1977) argues that these methods of 'disciplinary power' increasingly came to replace 'sovereign power' which, as discussed above, had involved more overt, physical and repressive means of regulation and control. However, coercive measures did not completely disappear but, instead, typically came to be applied only against those who either would not or could not embrace established norms (Foucault, 1977, 1991; McCallum, 2001; Rose, 1996, 1999a, 1999b).

The shift from a religious to a scientific model of managing human conduct has traditionally been seen as the beginning of an ever-progressive and increasingly compassionate means of governance. More recently, however, revisionist scholars have argued that such developments can more accurately be understood as the replacement of one technique of social regulation and control with another, more covert and seemingly less brutal, one. Rose (1999a), for example, argues that these emergent forms of social governance allowed for populations to be managed in ways consistent with the ideals of liberal democracy. Rather than appear cruel and unjust, the new modalities remained largely invisible and were legitimated by claims to scientific neutrality, objectivity and rationality. However, the social reforms actually reproduced power relations in the interests of the reformers themselves, who were overwhelmingly white, western, middle-class males. These developments did not occur in a conspiratorial fashion simply at their behest, but rather arose idiosyncratically and pragmatically.

Rose (1988, 1999b) further argues that the psy sciences developed through reform efforts to monitor, measure and classify individual human beings. As the psychiatric and ancillary disciplines evolved, their practitioners purported to harbour unique and scientific knowledge about human beings. In particular, they claimed the ability to peer into people's minds and souls. As evidence of their specialist knowledge, they produced numerous data, charts, graphs, drawings, instruments and eventually photographs that ostensibly rendered an individual's mental processes or subjectivities concrete. Such intimate knowledge of citizens, Rose argues, allowed for people to be regulated through their minds as well as bodies, creating the conditions for self-governance along with force. As such, people could be governed through their 'freedom' in ways commensurate with the policies and practices of liberal democracy which were gaining currency throughout the 19th century.

However, the psy sciences did not expose the real, inner workings of the human mind. Rather, they fashioned an authoritative means of claiming to do so. At the same time, the knowledge produced by the psy sciences was inherently informed by and reflected power relations. In this way, as in other spheres of social relations, power and knowledge can be seen as inexorably linked: psychological knowledge was used to exercise power, and power created fresh objects of knowledge while generating new kinds of information about human mind-state (Cohen, 1985; Foucault, 1965, 1977).

While new knowledge about the mad and criminals had been established, and separate institutions erected to house them, there remained a class of individuals who appeared to fit into neither category, and who were simultaneously ill-suited for the establishments that confined them – namely, those deemed both 'mad' and 'bad'. As they had both committed crimes and harboured symptoms of insanity, such people were intrinsically liminal beings. Considered both unruly and threatening, they posed practical problems to prisons and asylums. Furthermore, they embodied a philosophical conundrum, since criminality implied responsibility for one's actions, whilst lunacy suggested a loss of reason and therefore absence of responsibility. Their contradictory status meant that opinion varied as to whether such persons should be punished or treated. In fact, they were often shunted between prisons and asylums or kept in separate, temporary, make-shift and hazardous quarters within each. Many feared that inmates feigned madness in order to escape the harshness of prison. At the same time, there was concern that brutal prison conditions created madness (McCallum, 2001; Moran, 2000; Smith, 1981).

Although they were small in actual numbers, such concerns necessitated that these 'criminal lunatics' received special consideration. However, the advent of separate establishments for their containment was not imminent. In England the real turning point occurred in the courts, with the proclamation of the Criminal Lunatics Act in 1800. This Act was informed by the high-profile criminal trial of James Hadfield, who was tried for attempting to assassinate King George III in 1800. An ex-soldier, Hadfield had been discharged from the military after suffering severe head injuries while in battle. He came to believe that his own death was necessary to prevent God from destroying the world. In the hope of provoking such an end, he shot at the King in order to secure his execution.

According to English law both then and now, persons can only be found guilty of a crime if they meet two conditions: they must commit a criminal act (*actus reus*) and have a criminal mind (*mens rea*). Since insanity affects the mind, the law contains the possibility of exculpation for those so afflicted. However, much debate surrounds the criteria for what constitutes criminal mind-state; moreover, legal understandings of the relationship between crime, responsibility and madness have changed over time.

At the time of Hadfield's trial, the English law subscribed to the 'wild beast' test of insanity. That is, criminal exculpability on the grounds of insanity could be granted only if the defendant was totally insane, with a complete loss of reason. Since Hadfield knew that he was breaking the law, he did not fit this definition. His lawyer, Thomas Erskine, therefore argued for a less stringent standard – the presence of delusion or partial madness. Erskine's tactic succeeded – Hadfield was acquitted and thus escaped the gallows.

The new test of insanity created the possibility that more people would be entitled to such a defence, yet there was no institutional accommodation for them. As chronicled above, prior to the 19th century, most criminals found to be insane were sent to jails. However, there was growing concern about the intermingling of disparate groups, and about the overcrowded nature of existing facilities. Furthermore, most criminals found insane and sent to asylums were released within 12 months (Reznek, 1997, p 18). While vagrancy legislation enacted in 1744 allowed for the detention of offenders deemed 'dangerous lunatics', the common law authorised their incarceration only until they recovered. As a result, 'lunatics' deemed still 'dangerous' were often discharged against the better judgment of their keepers during periods of lucidity (Reznek, 1997, p 18). The judge in Hadfield's case wanted him neither released nor simply placed in a jail. Consequently, Parliament hastily created and passed the Criminal Lunatics Act which provided for a verdict of not guilty on the ground of insanity, whilst allowing the possibility of indefinite custody for defendants meeting such criteria (Quen, 1974; Reznek, 1997; Smith, 1981).

It was through these measures that the category of criminal lunacy came to be invented in Anglophone jurisprudence. However, criminal lunatics were still not provided with their own quarters until, in 1815, authorities added criminal wings to Bethlem Hospital in London. Overcrowding at this facility subsequently led to the construction of a special wing at Fisherton House, a private asylum in Salisbury. It was not until 1863, with the establishment of Broadmoor, that an institution was created in England especially for criminal lunatics (Russell, 1997).

As time passed, other European and other western nations created various laws and establishments specifically targeting this category of insane offender. And while the timing of their implementation varied, the controversy they provoked crossed all borders. Over the intervening years, criminal lunatics have continued to represent both practical and philosophical dilemmas for those involved in their regulation and treatment, not only in the domains of law and the psy sciences, but in the public culture more generally (Mason and Mercer, 1999).

This brief historical overview has demonstrated that criminal lunacy is a social construction rather than a 'natural' phenomenon. It is a fairly recent classification which has arisen through the unfolding of a complex and contradictory political, cultural and psycho-legal history. As Hacking (1986) argues, the processes involved in 'making people up' inherently involve authority, ethics and power. Although the category of criminal lunacy is an invention, the fact of its creation had very real consequences for its human subjects, and for society more generally. Once criminal lunacy came into being, new possibilities opened up for thinking about and managing human conduct both within and beyond the courts, prisons and hospitals. These novel strategies reflected and upheld dominant power relations across gender, class and 'race'.

2.3   The social construction of criminal lunatic women

Before addressing the situation of criminal lunatic women in the 19th century, I will briefly outline some of the key debates regarding women's madness and criminality. Until recently, the accepted orthodoxy amongst scholars was that, while females commit far less crime than do males, they are much more likely to be mentally ill. In other words, while males are more commonly 'bad', females have a greater likelihood of being 'mad'. The weight of current evidence appears to support the first of these assumptions. That is, both recorded crime statistics and self-reports indicate that, across different nations, women and girls are much less likely to engage in criminal activities than are men and boys (Harvey *et al*, 1992; Heidensohn, 2002).

Daly and Chesney-Lind (1988) refer to this phenomenon as the 'gender-ratio problem'. The word 'problem' connotes the fact that the disparity is not self-explanatory. Rather, there are a number of competing explanations accounting for the under-representation of females as criminal offenders. Furthermore, commentators disagree about the degree to which a gender gap exists across various types of crime. The common adage that women commit much less serious and violent crime has been challenged, for example, by questions surrounding definition, methodology and social processes which may serve to mask and distort women's actual criminal involvements (Heidensohn, 2002; Walklate, 1995).

Finally, recent historical work suggests that the female share of crime has shifted across time. Some commentators contend, for example, that official records show women's share of crime as being far more equivalent to that of men at the beginning of the 1800s, but as subsequently declining through the 19th century (Boritch and Hagan, 1990; Feeley and Little, 1991). Others have argued that women's share of crime rose during the 1970s (Adler, 1975; Simon, 1975), or have interpreted recent growth in the female prison population as reflecting a more general increase in women's crime, especially among serious offences (Pearson, 1998). However, these propositions have met with caution and dispute because of problems inherent in the data sources as well as their interpretation (Burman, 2004; Deakin and Spencer, 2003; Gelsthorpe and Morris, 2002). Thus, while the general supposition that women's involvement in crime is not as serious as men's is broadly supported, it must be qualified.

The second half of the accepted wisdom, that females are more likely to be mentally ill than males, is more contentious. A number of scholars have claimed madness to be a 'female malady' (Chesler, 1972; Gove and Tudor, 1973; Ehrenreich and English, 1979; Russell, 1995; Showalter, 1987). Collectively, their use of official records, self-reports and cultural depictions appear to demonstrate both an historical and contemporaneous over-representation of madness among females. While much debate has surrounded the interpretation of this disparity, most scholars have accepted the discrepancy as fact (Busfield, 1994). However, as with the gender-ratio question around crime, a more careful examination of the evidence raises doubts and reveals a much more complex and diverse picture. For example, depending upon the sources of information and methods of calculation used, the statistics vary considerably. Re-examinations of various psychiatric records indicate a much less steep gradient of difference, as well as male dominance in some areas of madness and at certain points in history (Busfield, 1994; Houston, 2002; Kramer, 1977; Prior, 1999; Smith, 1975). Similarly, Busfield (1994) argues that gendered cultural representations of madness have shifted across time, and that some imagery is much more associated with masculinity than femininity. One example of the latter is the image of the criminal lunatic.

Although representations of the criminal lunatic have taken different forms across time, the most enduring and notorious of these is the male 'homicidal maniac', deformed in morality, mind and body (Busfield, 1994; Leps, 1992; Smith, 1981). While the available data suggests that more males than females were positioned as 'criminal lunatics', the crimes they were charged with committing were generally of a non-violent nature. For example, in his analysis of courtroom testimony involving insanity pleas at the Old Bailey in London between 1760 and 1843, Eigen (1998, p 412) found that offences of violence 'accounted for no more than one in eight crimes'. The use of an insanity plea for property-related crimes during this time is partially explained by the fact that many were capital offences and could result in execution. However, as Menzies (2002) argues, a vast body of historical and contemporary research reliably demonstrates the under-representation of homicidal insanity in both pre-trial and post-sentence forensic populations. Given this fact, why has the image of the 'homicidal maniac' persisted?

Enlightenment liberalism introduced fundamental shifts in how human nature was understood. In particular, the commonly accepted belief in innate moral deprivation and sin was eclipsed by the conviction that people were essentially virtuous, rational and responsible. Halttunen (1998) argues that the image of the 'homicidal maniac' helped to maintain this modern conceptualisation of human nature. The existence of a 'moral monster' provided a means of understanding criminal transgressions which appeared to flagrantly challenge the new belief system. That is, the 'homicidal maniac' allowed murder and other apparently inexplicable human behaviour to be explained away as the actions of a non-human 'Other'. Popular narratives of this figure have become deeply entrenched, precisely because they reinforce the moral distance between 'normality' and criminal deviancy (Colaizzi, 1989; Mason and Mercer, 1999).

It is not coincidental that the image of the 'homicidal maniac' is indelibly male. During the 19th century, in western nations, women became positioned as morally superior to men. Whereas pre-Enlightenment Christian philosophy had held females to be more evil and corrupt than males, owing in large part to the legacy of Eve's original sin, a new ideal of womanhood insisted that respectable females were nurturing, pure, passive and self-sacrificing. Through its implication that women belonged in the domestic sphere and in a subservient role, this construction of womanly virtue helped to maintain patriarchal power relations. Although male dominance was never complete, and expectations of femininity differed across class and 'race', the emerging cult of true womanhood contributed to female oppression (Cott, 1977; Hartman, 1985; Welter, 1966).

The enormously lofty moral expectations placed upon women meant that they had much further to fall when they transgressed. Although they, too, were threatening to cultural sensibilities and political rationalities, criminal deeds fit much more closely with prevailing notions of masculinity. In contrast, female offences, particularly violent ones, appeared to be entirely unfathomable. Therefore, those women who violated laws and committed acts of aggression were even more alien to human civilization than were their male counterparts. The relatively small numbers of females committing serious offences served only to widen the divide. The fact that women criminals violated not only the law but also gendered expectations meant that they were 'doubly deviant'. As such, they attracted a disproportionate degree of attention and loathing (Birch, 1993; Chan, 2001; Chunn and Menzies, 1998; Damousi, 1997; Jones, 2003; Knelman, 1998; Lloyd, 1995; Menzies and Chunn, 1999; Myers and Wight, 1996).

The invention of criminal lunacy therefore allowed for the emergence of its stock image, the 'homicidal maniac'. By accounting for serious male transgressions as the actions of a non-human, monstrous male 'Other', this cultural image helped to uphold emerging political and philosophical beliefs, yet his female counterpart came to be imagined as an even more horrendous and monstrous being, whose existence contained a host of social anxieties, and functioned to preserve emerging sexual politics. The rising dominance of medicine throughout the 19th century reinforced and lent scientific legitimacy to these popular representations of criminal insanity.

2.4   The medical construction of female criminal lunatics

As discussed earlier, the psy sciences helped to allow the governance of citizens to occur in ways commensurate with the tenets of liberal democracy. Rose (1999a, 1999b) argues that the instrumentality of these psychiatric and ancillary disciplines partially accounts for their growing dominance across the 19th century. The invention of criminal lunacy was also an important means through which alienists (physicians specialising in the treatment of insanity) and the nascent profession of psychiatry established their power (Foucault, 1977; McCallum, 2001; Parker *et al*, 1995; Smith, 1981).

During James Hadfield's trial it was established that criminal lunacy was not necessarily manifested by raving or complete madness, but could also be demonstrated through the presence of derangement or delusion. A 'lunatic' could thus appear normal for the majority of the time. Although this new legal category was generally informed by lay understandings of madness rather than any rigorous scientific theory, it encouraged medical involvement in cases of criminal lunacy (Halttunen, 1998; Reznek, 1997; Smith, 1981). As Eigen (1998) remarks, while medical men appeared in criminal trials prior to the 19th century, their testimony around issues of insanity tended to be uncommon and mundane. The broader definition of criminal lunacy allowed a wider set of behaviour to be classified as insane, and suggested that lunacy could be concealed. The possibility of its invisibility implied the necessity of expert involvement in the detection of criminal lunacy. It was here that alienists were to claim expertise.

While alienists had not yet made their mark in the courtroom at the beginning of the 19th century, they were carving out their profession within the asylums emerging across a number of western nations. Along with the practical management of institutional life, these nascent psychiatrists were explicating a new mental science. Their theories of insanity corresponded well with the new legal definition of criminal insanity (McCallum, 2001; Parker *et al*, 1995; Rose, 1988, 1996, 1999b). As Haltunnen (1998) states, alienists founded their emerging discipline on two main concepts: faculty psychology and somatisation. The latter of these identified insanity as a brain disease, while the former separated out different parts of the mind in such a manner as to allow one aspect to be damaged without disturbing the others. In this way, insanity could be represented as partial, as well as in need of medical knowledge to be fully comprehended.

Alienists used their knowledge of insanity to claim an expert role over criminal lunacy. Consequently, their presence in the courtroom increased over the course of the 19th century. However, the insanity plea was not initially invoked widely, and the testimony of mental scientists was often controversial, disputed and/or simply ignored (Ainsley, 2000; Smith, 1981). The reasons for these medico-legal tensions were complex and varied, but included the conviction held by some people that successful medical testimony prevented some defendants from receiving their 'just deserts' of execution. More generally, in accounting for human behaviour which violated liberal notions of 'free will' and the 'social contract', psychiatric explanations could also appear to undermine these same precepts (Smith, 1981).

Medical theories of criminal behaviour also seemed to fall short when alienists were asked to apply them to specific cases. The theories they built were founded upon invisible processes within the brain or mind, which often made their explanations appear circular, esoteric and pretentious (Smith, 1981). It was not until later in the century, as the psy sciences became more established, that visual measures and representations of mental processes were constructed (Rafter, 1997; Rose, 1988, 1999b). Furthermore, as White-Mair (2001) argues, expert opinion often competed unsuccessfully with the testimony of non-expert laypeople, and was most successful when it corresponded with common-sense understandings.

Although the invention of criminal lunacy helped to mobilise the entry of psychiatric power into the legal arena, its hold was uneven and incomplete, yet the medical construction of criminal lunacy went far beyond the courtroom. In portraying criminal lunatics as suffering a diseased mind-state, earlier notions of the monstrous Other were reinforced. Despite the contested nature of criminal lunacy as a psychiatric illness, its medical status lent it legitimacy at a time when science was becoming increasingly significant. The application of a scientific framework to otherwise incomprehensible criminal actions enabled citizens to believe that human nature was essentially self-governing, free-willed and moral. Furthermore, asylums and prisons in which many alienists worked provided the physical means by which miscreants could be safely removed and contained. The separation of the criminally insane from the rest of society further underlined their difference (Halttunen, 1998).

As the 19th century wore on, psychiatric explanations grew increasingly sophisticated and detailed, though perhaps no less contentious (Rose, 1988, 1996, 1999b). At the same time, the cult of true womanhood became further embedded in western cultures (Cott, 1977). Given these developments, evolving psychiatric explanations of criminal insanity were perhaps even more important in making sense of the behaviour of criminally deviant women. As Smith (1981) observes, for example, medical men had long been expected to give legal testimony in cases of infanticide. The existing role of these men facilitated the later acceptance of alienists as medical experts in the prosecution of mothers accused of murdering their own children. Furthermore, both lay beliefs and medical accounts of women's social position drew increasingly upon biological explanations. Females were conceptualised as being inherently closer to nature than males, and therefore their physiology became more important in explaining their criminality as well as other conduct. A burgeoning medical and popular literature already attributed women's insanity to their biology, and in particular their reproductivity (Ehrenreich and English, 1979; Faith, 1993; Laqueur, 1990; Mitchinson, 1991; Mort, 1987; Ussher, 1992). Both the earlier involvement of doctors in cases of infanticide and the sexual construction of women provided alienists with an important point of entry into the legal sphere. Although this process appears to have started slowly, it gathered increasing momentum toward the end of the 19th century (Baker, 1902).

Eigen's (1998) examination of insanity cases at the Old Bailey, London between 1760 and 1843 found that although medical men testified at the trials of both males and females, the evidence they gave was not gendered. There were no references to women's unique sexual nature apart from 'a few cases of puerperal mania, which focused on delivery, not eroticism' (Eigen, 1998, p 416). Further, women comprised 22% of the defendants alleging insanity, nearly the equivalent of those in the criminal population more generally. The crimes for which these women were tried spanned the full range of personal and property offences. Sixty per cent of women who pleaded insanity were acquitted, slightly exceeding the 50% of men who received a similar judicial ruling. However, among those convicted, females were much less likely to be executed than males.

These findings can be contrasted to Ainsley's (2000) examination of insanity pleas for violent crime trials in England and Wales between 1832 and 1901. She found that only 12% of women and 8% of men sought exoneration on the grounds of insanity. The majority of women's insanity pleas (77%) comprised murder charges, most of which involved child murder and a defence of puerperal mania. In contrast, only 15% of men's pleas were for murder offences. Females were also more successful in their cases: the courts accepted 87% of women's pleas, compared to 59% of men's pleas. Moreover, the proportion of women being acquitted had increased even further by the end of the 19th century. Ainsley suggests that this over-representation of women reflected unequal standards of judgment regarding responsibility, while the shift across time represented a growing tendency to account for women's actions through their unique biology. She concludes that both of these patterns were informed by the growing power and prestige of the medical profession within legal and other cultural domains.

The extant newspaper reports and legal records upon which Ainsley based her research were filled with deep descriptions of defendants' social circumstances. Poverty, tragedy and despair, rooted in complex webs of material and personal conditions, commonly circumscribed the lives of the men and women who found themselves in the courtroom. While juries often acknowledged the economic hardships encountered by women, they nonetheless tended to account for their crimes in medical terms. Women positioned as criminal lunatics were represented as victims of their reproductive system, and only to a lesser degree of their social circumstances. In contrast, the financial situation of males was rarely considered to be a mitigating factor. Overall, while women were under-endowed with responsibility, men were over-endowed with it. While these gender-based ascriptions of liability and blame saved a number of women from the gallows, they also stripped them of agency and placed their crimes beyond reason. Even when women spoke eloquently, demonstrating sharp insight into the nature of their crimes, they were deemed to be insane.

Prior's (1997) examination of records pertaining to the Criminal Lunatic Asylum at Dundrum, Dublin, between 1850 and 1900, found that women comprised 21% of the population. Poverty featured in most of the patient's lives and, perhaps not coincidentally, the majority of women's offences (31%) were property-related. These same crimes comprised 22% of men's overall offence total. One of the most striking findings was that, although 31% of females were tried for murder, none of the cases involved the killing of a man. In comparison, many of the 32% of men charged with homicide had killed not only their wives, but also other women in their households. Prior concludes that medical men were not a key feature in trial outcomes, since their testimony appeared to have had arbitrary outcomes.

The collective works of Menzies (2001, 2002), Chunn and Menzies (1998) and Menzies and Chunn (1999; see also Chapter 4, this book) illuminate the lived experiences of men and women positioned as 'criminally insane' in British Columbia, Canada, between 1872 and 1950. During this period, women represented only 12.5% of the 303 total admissions for 'criminal insanity'. Like their male counterparts, however, the women tended to be poor, disproportionately derived from ethnic minority groups, and already entwined in systems of social regulation. Although they were circumscribed by a multitude of medico-legal discourses and practices, the prisoners resisted these authoritative accounts in a variety of ways. The clinical records of these 'criminally insane' inmates, the authors observe, 'were brimming with examples of counter-discourse and claims to legitimacy and normalcy' (Chunn and Menzies, 1998, p 327).

Similarly, my examination of case files and other official records of the Rockwood Criminal Lunatic Asylum, Kingston, Ontario, between 1857 and 1877 showed that women resisted the constructions of deviance which were imposed upon them (Kendall, 1999a, 1999b). At the same time, the pains of imprisonment appeared to pose a serious threat to their physical health and mind-state. The treatment women received reflected the dominant somatic practices of the time – restraint, blood letting, enemas, blistering, sedatives, leeching – which frequently served to harm rather than help.

A review of research examining the historical experiences of women positioned as criminal lunatics suggests that the role of medical men in criminal trials increased over the course of the 19th century. This trend coincided with the establishment of various strategies and modes of practice which purportedly made human subjectivity, including insanity, visible. Furthermore, these methods appear to have made their initial entry into criminal hearings most effectively in the cases of female defendants. Both medical and popular notions of women's sexuality converged in such a way as to hold female reproductive systems responsible for women's seemingly inexplicable crimes. While this process sometimes served to save women from execution, it also positioned them as victims without agency and stripped their actions of meaning.

However, as the historical record reveals, the influence of expert testimony on the fate of individual women was uneven. The evidence that alienists brought into the courts was often contested, dismissed or overtaken by non-experts. Moreover, women defendants, prisoners and patients themselves often challenged the dominant medical, legal and sexual discourses and practices within which they were entwined, but the forms and effects of women's resistance were tempered, in large part, by the harsh and painful conditions of their lives both prior to and following incarceration. The choices that women made and the actions that they took were often profoundly constrained by myriad social, economic and political forces. In Reaume's words (2000, p 21), although women 'were not merely passive actors in this historical drama, they were not able to direct the scenes either'.

Over the course of the 20th century, the psy sciences experienced a remarkable growth in power and prestige. As Sim (1990, p 29) argues, practitioners managed to establish themselves over 'multiple surfaces of emergence'. Their reach extended far beyond institutional walls into the domestic sphere. Such success is at least partially due to the utility of psychiatric-related disciplines in allowing for the continued governance of citizens in ways commensurate with notions of liberal democracy, and later neo-liberalism. This role has been perhaps most evident, contradictory and controversial at the boundaries of law and medicine.

The 20th century, for example, witnessed a dramatic decline in the number of asylums and large psychiatric facilities, while at the same time the psychiatric net was cast more widely into communities (Cohen, 1985; Rose, 1996, 1999a, 1999b). Additionally, the size of the prison population in many nations is currently at an all-time high, and many commentators (Kupers, 1999; O'Brien *et al*, 2001) observe that increasing numbers of mentally disordered offenders, disproportionately female, fall within its ranks. Furthermore, the medical model of crime, which lost favour in the 1970s, is presently experiencing a renaissance.[3] Gender, 'race', class, ability and sexuality all intersect in varying ways across these multiple changes to contemporary psychiatric and penal regimes.

---

3 This resurgence is occurring through the 'What Works' movement, which rests on the psychological framework of cognitive-behavioural therapy. For a critique of this approach to therapy, see Mair, 2004.

Nonetheless, current representations of mentally disordered female offenders remain remarkably similar to the images of female criminal lunatics first constructed two hundred years ago. As the above-discussed case of Aileen Wuornos demonstrates, both medico-legal and popular discourse represent women who commit crimes – particularly crimes of a violent nature – as either evil monsters or passive victims (Birch, 1993; Lloyd, 1995). Not only their actions, but they themselves appear to be beyond reason.

Some commentators (Morrissey, 2003; Pearson, 1998) claim that this latter portrayal is a new construct, introduced into legal discourse by feminists but, as this historical review has demonstrated, the imagery of woman-as-victim is far from novel. The current manifestation of this stereotype has taken on some of the feminist issues and concerns regarding women's oppression, but feminism did not invent it. Nonetheless, it is significant that potentially subversive feminist discourse has become co-opted and re-configured in ways which maintain rather than challenge dominant power relations.[4] This experience should serve as a reminder that the work we do, from whatever our position, has real and often unintended consequences. We are located within traversing networks of power and bring our own social locations, knowledge and experience to our involvements with mentally disordered female offenders, whether we are academics, clinicians, activists, lawyers, or find ourselves positioned as mentally unstable criminals. As argued at the outset of this chapter, we need to be self-reflexive and to anticipate the consequences of our own social constructions, while avoiding immobilisation either out of fear that our actions may cause harm or from a sense of futility. To these ends, the material-discursive-intrapsychic approach suggested by Ussher (2000; Chapter 1, this book) adopts such a position, and offers a way forward. In the concluding section of this essay, I will briefly outline how such a framework might be usefully applied to the situation of women positioned as mentally disordered female offenders.

2.5 Applying a material-discursive-intrapsychic approach to mentally disordered female offenders

Ussher describes a material-discursive-intrapsychic approach as:

> a position where material, discursive and intrapsychic aspects of experience can be examined without privileging one level of analysis above the other, and within an epistemological and methodological framework that does not make *a priori* assumptions about causality and objectivity. (2000, pp 218–19)

As noted by Ussher, 'material discursive' approaches to theory and praxis have recently emerged within the discipline of psychology (Stoppard, 2000; Ussher, 1997b; Yardley, 1997). These integrative schemes for understanding human experience were born out of dissatisfaction with traditional psychology which generally neglects the discursive level, and with discourse analysis which tends to

---

4 For example, women prisoners who have been victims of violence are deemed risky in terms of re-offending and security. The greater the history of violence, the riskier they are thought to be (see Hannah-Moffat and Shaw, 2003). For feminist critiques of current manifestations of 'victim discourse' see Alcoff and Gray, 1993; Batacharya, 2000; and Armstrong, 1996.

ignore the material world. Ussher moves beyond a 'material discursive' approach, however, by incorporating the intrapsychic as well. Material factors include those at the institutional, corporeal or societal level, such as psychiatry, the body and social class. Discursive issues include the areas of language, culture, power, ideology and visual images. The social construction of femininity and masculinity unfolds within this discursive realm. Finally, intrapsychic aspects incorporate the individual and psychological elements of a woman's life, such as the strategies she adopts to cope with trauma or distress. Interventions must occur on all three levels and acknowledge their inter-relatedness. Finally, research operating from this multi-sited framework necessitates the involvement of lay people, recognising that lay knowledge is just as valid as, and sometimes more so than, that of experts.

It seems to me that the material-discursive-intrapsychic approach would be a productive framework to use in understanding mentally disordered female offending. For example, this chapter has documented how a number of factors operating at the material level – for example, poverty, gender, medicine, and the law – have combined to bring women into the medico-legal domain. Discursive elements have included, among others, the advent of Enlightenment and liberal democratic ideals, the ideal of normative womanhood, the image of the homicidal maniac, and representations of criminally insane women as 'mad', 'bad' and 'victim'. Finally, intrapsychic aspects have incorporated the emotional distress involved in some of women's 'criminally insane' actions, as well as the psychic pain associated with their imprisonment and harmful treatment regimes.

Finally, the historical overview presented in this chapter has, above all else, served to challenge the naturalness of the category 'mentally disordered female offender'. By engaging with history, we can draw lessons from the past that might facilitate the deconstruction of entrenched ideas about women's madness and criminality – and, at the same time, guide future theory, policy and practice toward more progressive, and even transformative, ends. And a material-discursive-intrapsychic framework which acknowledges both the reality and the elusiveness of women's lives, as well as competing discourses surrounding them, may offer a potential route forward. This chapter opened with the recent example of Aileen Wuornos, who is regarded as beyond reason because she continues to evade dominant social constructions. The essay will close with a similar historical case, the words of one 19th century female 'criminal lunatic', Grace Marks, as imagined by the novelist Margaret Atwood:

> I think of all the things that have been written about me – that I am an inhuman female demon, that I am an innocent victim of a blackguard forced against my will and in danger of my own life, that I was too ignorant to know how to act and that to hang me would be judicial murder ... that I am a good girl with a pliable nature and no harm is told of me, that I am cunning and devious, that I am soft in the head and little better than an idiot. And I wonder, how can I be all of these different things at once? (1997, p 25)

Chapter 3

The Boundaries of Femininity: Madness and Gender in New Zealand, 1870–1910[1]

Bronwyn Labrum

In 1885 Hannah W was committed to the Auckland Lunatic Asylum. She was described as 'excited, noisy, incoherent, restless and mischievous … Has been in the asylum on more than one previous occasion'. Her form of insanity was recorded as 'mania' with the cause unknown. John V was committed in 1870 because he was 'constantly pacing up and down excited and says there is something wrong in his head'. Doctors were also at a loss to explain his 'mania'.[2]

Hannah and John were just two of the patients I wrote about, over a decade ago, in an article about gender and the process of committal to one New Zealand institution. I became interested in their experiences in the context of a burgeoning historical literature about asylum patients that reflected both the growth of the history of medicine as a field and the impact of a revitalised social and cultural history. The majority of existing histories of mental illness (Foucault, 1989; Grob, 1973; Rothman, 1971; Scull, 1979, 1981) focused on state policy, the establishment of a network of institutions, and the doctors and their treatment were the focus of inquiry. Although they demonstrated that madness has a history and that, to a large degree, it has social origins and is socially constructed, the social significance and explanations behind the resort to asylums by people in the community remained obscure.

Since then, another wave of studies has taken up this challenge, basing their research, as I did, on patient casenotes. Using this rich and complex source, scholars have emphasised the social functions of commitment and the variety of people who sought to have individuals confined in psychiatric contexts. This patient-based perspective argues that the mad represented threats to persons, property, law and order and 'articulated moral norms' (Fox, 1978, p 152; Walton, 1985, p 132; see also Porter and Wright, 2003). As a result, community officials and policing agents figure in these accounts more frequently than do medical men. Elaborating on pioneering studies by Michael Ignatieff (1983) and Mark Finanne (1985), growing importance

---

1 This chapter appeared in an earlier version as 'Looking beyond the asylum: gender and the process of committal in Auckland, 1870–1910' (1992) 26 The New Zealand Journal of History 125.

2 Case 1287, Casebooks 1853–1911, Carrington Hospital Files (YCAA) 1048/4, p 153; Case 130, Committed Patient Case Files 1869–1910, YCAA 1026/2. Both sets of records are held at National Archives Records Centre, Auckland. As a condition of access to the records, names have been changed to preserve confidentiality.

has been placed on the role of the family in the committal process and on domestic and social crisis as catalysts for admission (Kelm, 1994; Wright, 1997; Forsythe and Melling, 1999; Brookes and Thomson, 2001; Coleborne and MacKinnon, 2003).

Studies which revealed that issues of femininity and femaleness lay at the heart of the detection of madness shaped my thinking considerably at the time. For example, Elaine Showalter argued that in 19th century England a 'feminization' of madness occurred; women came to be seen as the cultural exemplars of madness. Although she does not look at the process of committal, Showalter (1987, pp 7, 81) surmises that the female lunatics' talkativeness and their violations of conventional feminine speech were factors in their committal. An emphasis on the breaking of feminine proprieties is demonstrated in the work of other historians, including Anne Digby and Jill Matthews. Digby shows that, among other things, 'the rigid limitations imposed on the Victorian woman's role' may have produced either depression or rebellion. Moreover, women were particularly liable to be defined as mad because of mildly deviant and independent behaviour, or failure to be a 'paragon of domestic virtue'. None of the men in her analysis were pulled up by such strict behavioural codes (Digby, 1985, pp 96, 190). In 20th century Australia, Matthews (1984, pp 147, 172, 185) argues that women who were defined as mad had failed in the pursuit of femininity, specifically in the fundamental areas of sexuality (heterosexual, monogamous legal marriage), work (centred on the family and home) and mothering. In a similar vein, Stephen Garton (1998) found that in late 19th and early 20th century New South Wales, 'tensions in the construction of femininity' were apparent in the delusions of female patients, although they had to develop in a specific material and social context for committal to be warranted. In a manner that was new at the time, although it has been extended considerably since, I also drew upon the way that scholars in the new 'men's studies' related men's madness to problems and contradictions in the construction of masculinity (Garton, 1988, pp 140, 131; Hughes, 1990, p 56).

Subsequently, more detailed work on gender has complicated this equation of femininity and madness and focused more attention on the committal of male patients. Examining research in the United States, Nancy Tomes noted that such evidence has functioned to overturn 'certain assumptions about the gender-madness nexus, and to reject oversimplified notions of women's liability to mental illness and victimization at the hands of male physicians' (Tomes, 1990, p 171). As I found for Auckland, and Barbara Brookes confirmed for other areas in New Zealand, men were incarcerated *more* frequently than women (Brookes, 1998, p 20; see also Brookes, 1992), yet, as I show in this chapter, interpretations of behaviour that led to committal were still highly gendered.

The most recent cultural histories have focused on life inside the asylum walls as a 'physical and mental landscape'. Casenotes in these studies are used as 'complex cultural texts that both construct inmates as patients and work to cement forms of sexual difference within the gendered space of the asylum' (Coleborne and MacKinnon, 2003, pp 8, 18). Such a reading has not yet been applied to the equally important process of committal. The return to the asylum as an institution also reflects the new focus on colonialism and the asylum (Ernst, 1991; Mills, 2000; Coleborne, 2001). The 'functions of race for colonialism' (Keller, 2001, p 298) are emerging as a key area of inquiry in these new accounts of regulation and psychiatric institution building within settler colonies, but they seldom extend to the histories and experiences of indigenous patients entering or resident within asylums. My research provided a preliminary but very suggestive discussion of the experiences of indigenous patients at Auckland. At the same time, I noted how equally important it was to discuss society's attitudes towards the political issues surrounding indigenous people at this time. Although I did not frame it that way at the time, in that respect the issue becomes one of deconstructing 'whiteness' as a category of 'race' as much as focusing on indigeneity. Despite the current interest in these matters, they have yet to be more systematically explored on a broader canvas.

The paths patients followed to the asylum have continued to be a focus of current international research, yet few studies attempt to compare the experiences of both female and male patients as old frameworks linger and new concerns shift attention elsewhere. The experience of committal to the Auckland Lunatic Asylum between 1870 and 1910 still provides an important and, from the perspective of later studies, highly original case study of two important themes: shifting the perspective to the patient and looking at differences between the sexes. The period chosen encompasses the early years of the institution, when records are more readily available, until significant change in mental health law in 1911.

The Auckland Lunatic Asylum serviced a wide geographical area, and was used by both urban and rural districts. It was truly a provincial amenity, especially in its first decades, although its catchment area concentrated on greater Auckland in the north of the North Island. A few patients came from as far afield as Gisborne, Ruapekapeka and Wanganui in the middle of the island, reflecting the closure of smaller asylums at New Plymouth on the west coast and Napier on the east coast in the 1880s, and later the transfer of patients in an effort to solve the perennial problem of overcrowding.

Between 1870 and 1910, 4,037 cases were admitted (including readmissions). Just over a third of these (1,459) were women. Annual numbers fluctuated from year to year but rose steadily after 1900. In 1870 there were 62 admissions; the figure rose slightly to 67 in 1890, and to 201 new cases in 1910. More meaningful figures are revealed by the rate of committal, when admissions are compared to the provincial population. These calculations show clearly that there were fewer female than male patients. In 1871, 13 per 10,000 women and 22 per 10,000 men were committed; by 1911 it was down to eight and 12 respectively. The rate of Maori committal is most interesting and shows how explanations of committal in terms of colonial rule only begin to have salience in the early 20th century. In 1871, five per 10,000 Maori women and four per 10,000 Maori men were admitted, but by 1911 the number had risen to 14 and 23 respectively.[3]

I examined a random sample of 20 patient case records from each of the years 1870, 1890 and 1910, 60 in total. Because the majority of the total patient population was male – women formed around a quarter to a third of all patients in any one

---

3 All numbers were averaged across three or five years centred on a sample year. Annual Reports of the Lunatic Asylums, *Appendices to the Journals of the House of Representatives* (AJHR), 1871–73, 1890–94, 1911–13; *Census of New Zealand*, 1871, 1891, 1911.

year – I included five male cases for each year. The smaller sample of men's records act as a control group. Many of the variations in the casenotes were revealed only when considering women and men in relation to each other, providing a useful reminder of the way that gender is a comparative tool of analysis. Such a relational analysis is especially important in a mixed-sex institution like the Auckland Asylum. Sex-role stereotypes occur in relation to each other and socially approved models of behaviour are constructed for each sex. As RA Houston has recently argued about the 18th century, a 'symmetrical' approach of studying women and men together reveals that 'the word "mad" was not sex-specific, but it was certainly gendered' (Houston, 2002, pp 311, 324).

Focusing on the differences between the sexes at Auckland reveals that women were less vulnerable to committal than men and were committed for reasons that were often quite different. It is not just a case of adding women to an established framework of analysis, but attempting to understand why they are missing. As Charlotte Macdonald found with women's criminality, the detection of madness at Auckland in this period emerges as part of what has come to be called 'masculinism': 'the specific, historical reality into which men were socialised, and within which they lived their lives' (1989, p 10). By looking beyond the asylum, the reasons why women were committed, and equally importantly, why they were not, emerge more clearly.

3.1 The committal process

An understanding of the nature of the committal process is the key to a more complex interpretation. Patients were committed through formalised legal processes which involved two Justices of the Peace and, from 1882, the Resident Magistrate, assisted by two doctors. There were six main categories under which a person was declared insane: those defined as 'dangerous' lunatics; prisoners found to be insane; those declared lunatic by a jury; charged with indictable offences; lunatic 'drunkards'; and lunatics 'at large or insufficiently cared for'. Proceedings could also be initiated by friends and relatives of alleged lunatics. In all cases legal evidence consisted of, at the very least, an order for committal signed by the justices and the magistrate, and two medical certificates attesting to the individual's insanity. A thorough reading of all available legal and medical sources, not just the law or the reports of doctors, reveals that, while on paper the process was first of all a legal one, in practice medical men were more important. Moreover, because justices and magistrates were required to commit an individual on the basis of medical evidence, it was the family which was central to the process. The medical certificates and both family and medical histories recorded in later casebooks reveal that the certifying general practitioners made judgments on people who were often not their patients and whom they saw only once. The doctors largely confirmed, and gave legitimacy to, decisions already made by others. It was principally family, friends and neighbours who instigated proceedings or allowed them to continue.

The patterns in the reasons why these people were committed are, at times, ambiguous. Incomplete evidence is obviously a factor. The medical certificates of patients at the Auckland asylum were often filled out perfunctorily, to conform to bureaucratic standards rather than clinical needs. More generally, there was not the comprehensive examination of a patient's personal and social history that a post-Freudian psychiatry would consider necessary. There are also problems with assigning a single reason for committal. The case materials suggest the futility of such efforts and the arbitrary labelling and artificial simplicity in given reasons that must have resulted. Often, multiple pressures were involved. As a result, a range of committal grounds emerge, some of which were obvious, involving concerns over threats to property, threats to persons, varying manifestations of 'paranoia' and threats to articulated social norms. These were common to women and men, although a pattern of gender differentiation is apparent.

3.1.1 Threats to property

Of all the reasons cited, threats to property constituted a small number of both female and male cases, and among women these declined over time, as Table 3.1 shows. Such women most commonly attempted to destroy things around them: their clothes, bedding and books or, if in hospital, institutional bedding and crockery. Agnes E, a 26 year old servant, 'put her hand thro' one or two panes of glass' in her employer's house.[4] A smaller number of women abused things that were either not theirs or in their immediate environment. For example, Mary H believed her next-door neighbour had 'illegally taken possession of her late husband's property'. She was constantly giving her neighbour 'notice to quit ... and using violent means at night to gain admission into his house'.[5] Only one woman in the sample did not use violence; instead she removed objects intact. Blanche A, a 31 year old housewife was 'a great source of annoyance to boarders in the house taking possession of letters, telegrams etc'.[6]

Family members and neighbours considered that most of these threats were not criminal actions, although the conduct of the property trespasser came closest to the mark. Even the initiators of Blanche's committal put her deeds in context. Doctors recorded her letter-snatching as an additional, rather than as a primary, motivating factor for others to want to have her committed. Constables initially became involved because she went to them making 'extraordinary charges of persecution against certain people', not because she took the letters and telegrams.[7] For the most part, these women carried out their actions against property within a domestic situation and others deemed the activities a nuisance rather than as illegal or punishable by law.

Given the often nomadic and survival-based lifestyle of many of the male patients in this period, it is surprising that there was only one man who interfered with property in any way (nor were his actions violent). William N, a 59 year old unmarried clerk, lived with his brother and sister-in-law, and they told the certificating doctor in 1910 that he had 'a habit of carrying away articles and not

---

4   Case 1629, YCAA 1048/5, p 451.
5   Case 138, YCAA 1026/2.
6   Case 3970, YCAA 1048/11, p 276.
7   *Ibid*.

TABLE 3.1   Causes of committal among sample female patients, 1870–1910

Cause of committal	1870 % (No)	1890 % (No)	1910 % (No)
Threats to property	11 (5)	9 (4)	4 (2)
Threats to persons			
family	13 (6)	9 (4)	9 (4)
friends	–	–	2 (1)
strangers	2 (1)	4 (2)	9 (4)
self	4 (2)	11 (5)	9 (4)
general	4 (2)	4 (2)	–
Paranoia	9 (4)	11 (5)	13 (6)
Threats to social norms	7 (3)	9 (4)	11 (5)
self-expression	18 (8)	7 (3)	7 (3)
housework	2 (1)	7 (3)	2 (1)
marital	9 (4)	9 (4)	11 (5)
maternal	9 (4)	9 (4)	13 (6)

Source: Committed Patient Case Files, YCAA 1026/1–12; Casebooks, YCAA 1048/1–12. Numbers in this and the next table equal instances, not necessarily persons, and therefore, because one person can display a number of different reasons for committal, numbers total more than 45 women/15 men and percentages total more than 100%.

knowing where he has put them. Invariably he answers, when asked, that they are in the closet'.[8]

3.1.2   Threats to persons

The relative importance of the remaining grounds for committal differ clearly by sex. It is not surprising, given the domestic location of most women, that of all threats to persons, threats to family members were the most commonly cited single reason for committal among the female cases, slightly declining in importance by 1910. Some of the recorded reasons were brief. Doctors authorised the committal of Jane B, a 22 year old carpenter's wife, because she 'threatened to kill persons around her'; exactly whom was not specified.[9] In other cases there was more detail of the circumstances leading to committal. Twenty-eight year old Ellen L attempted to bite her father and threatened her sister with a knife. Only one woman in the sample expressed animosity towards friends: Paulina W tried to kill a neighbour.

Threats to self were the second most common single reason for committal after threats to family members, and they increased in frequency by 1910. Any tendency to suicide by these women was especially worrying to their families. Suicide attempts caused practical difficulties in terms of the preventive vigilance required by family members. Forty-five year old Olive B tried to drown herself. Not only did Paulina W try to kill her neighbour, but she also attempted suicide by eating matches and hiding knives under her pillow. However, these attempts were also clear indications in most people's minds of temporary, if not long-term, insanity (Luke, 1982, pp 26–27). Sane people did not threaten to take their own lives. By 1910, when case books had become standardised, entries always stated whether the patient was suicidal as well as dangerous or epileptic. Not all of these women went

---

8   Case 138, YCAA 1026/2.
9   Case 160, YCAA 126/3.

as far as attempting suicide. Family members had to personally restrain Frances F, a 45 year old settler's wife, to prevent injury to herself because she repeatedly struck her knuckles against the wall.

A smaller but increasing number of women threatened strangers. Many of these women were elderly. For example, Margaret L, who was married and in her sixties, wandered at night and threatened 'to do for people'.[10] According to one constable, 70 year old widowed Mary A had been a lunatic for the last six months and was dangerous to children.[11]

Finally, four of the 45 women in the sample cases made generalised threats and did not direct their behaviour at anyone in particular until attempts were made to apprehend or restrain them. In many cases, these women did not carry out their threats or preventive measures were taken in time. However, in 19 out of 35 cited instances of threats to people the violence was real, not just implicit. In a rather extreme example, 17 year old Taruke W 'smashed' a girl's face in a coach journeying to Waiuku.[12] The proportion of threats which contained varying degrees of violence remained fairly constant over time.

The issue of the degree of violence is crucial to an understanding of the reasons for committal. The women threatening violence appear to be in a different category from those deemed deranged or absurd. Why, then, were they not sent to prison? The experience of the only woman in the sample who was transferred from the prison to the asylum provides some clues. Bridget H, a 25 year old soldier's wife, served two prison terms in 1870 for being an 'habitual drunkard'. In jail she behaved very similarly to the other women described above. The warders related that she was 'very violent towards the Matron and would have done her some bodily harm', and that she used 'violent language, and threatened the inmates with personal abuse'.[13] This behaviour alone did not place her in the category of insane rather than criminal, although it certainly contributed to the process. Indeed, Bridget attempted to assault the matron a month before doctors examined her for signs of lunacy. Rather her 'delusions' – voices at night, spirits annoying her – sealed her fate.

The other cases demonstrate a similar pattern. Many women threatened (and some carried out) acts of violence towards others, but at the same time they heard, saw or believed things that their family and friends did not accept to be valid.

3.1.3 Manifestations of 'paranoia'

The second largest group of reasons for female committal involved 'paranoia'. Instead of making a nuisance of themselves, these women exhibited outlandish or unwelcome behaviour or dwelt on real or imagined misfortune. The distribution of these cases increased slightly by 1910. Thirty-four year old Rebecca J went to live with her sister and brother-in-law after her husband's death. According to one of her medical certificates, 'She has been a long time in a very excited state of mind in

---

10 Case 4116, YCAA 1026/12.
11 Case 1631, YCAA 1048/5, p 453.
12 Case 4075, YCAA 1048/11, p 381.
13 Case 125, YCAA 1026/2.

fact that it commenced about the time of late husband's illness ... I heard this morning that she will not get up out of bed, but is expecting her husband (who has been dead some months) to return every minute'. Rebecca believed that her sister had poisoned her husband and child. She also drank heavily and threatened her sister's children.[14] Four of these 15 women 'committed because of paranoia' had delusions regarding their children (Table 3.1). For example, Margaret L, a 60 year old housewife, believed that she had four children at home and that rats were threatening them.

Why other women were unacceptable victims is less apparent. Four of the 15 believed that they were being persecuted. The bullies mostly appear as 'everyone' or just 'others', but a 55 year old single dressmaker named the perpetrators. Catherine D claimed 'that she is persecuted by detectives sent by Mr Kettle and Inspector Cullen to prevent her being allowed to stay in any lodging house. She also stated that several people – Mr Brown of Onehunga and her late landladies – Mrs Webb and Mrs Mckenna repeatedly tried to poison her food'.[15]

The belief in poisoned food occurs repeatedly, and two women were admitted because they stopped eating. Agnes F informed her certificating doctors that voices told her not to eat as people were poisoning her. Before being committed to the Auckland Asylum, 15 year old Margaret Y resisted attempts to feed her for some months while she was in Auckland Hospital. Margaret said that she had orders not to take food.

3.1.4   Threats to social norms

Threats to articulated social norms comprise the fourth group of reasons for committal. A total of 12 women out of the 45 exhibited such behaviour in general terms, with numbers rising slightly by 1910. These actions included five women who persisted in going naked around the house and in front of the children. The employers of a domestic servant observed her 'pick up rubbish and even dirt and eat it'.[16]

Another five women made public nuisances of themselves. Martha L, a 40 year old pensioner's wife, bothered the police when they were on duty, repeatedly interrupted business at the bank and wandered about the roads 'talking aloud and gesticulating'.[17] Fifty-six year old Hannah W returned to the asylum in 1890 again after her arrest for 'behaving in an extraordinary manner in Queen St' at five o'clock in the morning.[18]

The perception of threats to articulated social norms also contained racial overtones. Police found Taruke W wandering at large, insufficiently clothed and 'caressing strangers on the street' (see fn 18). As well as being very dirty and not speaking any English, 'she catches hold of any person who approaches her and

---

14 Case 154, YCAA 1026/3.
15 Case 3974, YCAA 1048/11, p 253.
16 Case 1627, YCAA 1048/5, p 449.
17 Case 155, YCAA 1026/3.
18 Case 1624, YCAA 1048/5, p 446.

appears to be erotic'. Maori women were among the first to be condemned as naturally promiscuous, a judgment later extended to 'female defectives' (Pool, 1977, p 93; see also Anderson, 1981; Tennant, 1986). Not only did 40 year old Matua W attempt to burn down the *whare* (house) at her settlement, but she also offended settler notions of propriety by believing she was Queen Victoria. Doctors recorded this delusion first in all witness accounts, indicating that it was held to be as serious an issue as the arson.[19]

3.2   The committal of men

For men, however, the order of reasons for committal was mostly reversed. Equally small numbers of male patients threatened property. In the group of causes for committal labelled 'threats to persons', threats to self formed the largest single category, constituting three cases out of 15. For example, John V carried a scar on the right side of his neck as evidence of a previous suicide attempt.[20] County foreman Joseph T attempted suicide at least three times according to his brother, by cutting his throat with a razor, for example and jumping off Grafton Bridge.[21]

The high number of single men in the sample is reflected in the small number of male threats to family members. Both cases involved threats against a wife. John V, a 30 year old doctor, 'repeatedly threatened to kill her'.[22] Thirty year old farmer Denis C struck his wife 'with a bill hook' taking his violence further than any of the women involved in domestic disputes.[23]

Parallel with the women in the sample, only one man threatened a friend. Two men out of the 15 threatened strangers. In the latter cases, one man threatened unfamiliar persons in a more specific way that had no correlation among the

TABLE 3.2   Causes of committal among sample male patients, 1870–1910

Cause of committal	1870 % (No)	1890 % (No)	1910 % (No)
Threats to property	–	–	7 (1)
Threats to persons			
family	13 (2)	–	–
friends	–	7 (1)	–
strangers	–	7 (1)	7 (1)
self	7 (1)	13 (2)	–
general	7 (1)	7 (1)	–
Paranoia	20 (3)	13 (2)	7 (1)
Threats to social norms	13 (2)	20 (3)	27 (4)

Source: Committed Patient Case Files, YCAA 1026/1–12; Casebooks, YCAA 1048/1–12.

19 Case 4028, YCAA 1048/11, p 334.
20 Case 130, YCAA 1026/2.
21 Case 3982, YCAA 1048/11, p 288.
22 Case 130, YCAA 1026/2.
23 Case 176, YCAA 1048/1, p 229.

women. Police arrested 59 year old single gum digger Herbert R because he was wandering about frightening women. The certificating doctor commented that '[t]he women are leaving their houses when he goes wandering near them'.[24]

Although the sample of males is much smaller, the case records suggest that males exhibited a greater degree of actual violence, resulting, perhaps, from the fact that family and friends more frequently restrained women before they could carry out their threats. Alternatively, characterising the women's behaviour as less violent may reflect the greater sensitivity with which society regarded such actions by women. Because 19th century women were meant to be pious, demure and submissive, others found their deviations all the more noticeable and challenged them earlier. In contrast, they may have been more likely to see male violence as 'normal' and expected.

A greater proportion of men – nearly half – displayed paranoid behaviour. Only one distrusted food. He believed that he had lost part of his body and feared eating and drinking. The other six believed that they were persecuted or had 'unreasonable suspicions', the contents of which were never divulged.[25]

Threats to articulated social norms were more frequent in the male sample too, accounting for 11 of the 15 cases. Some features similar to the women's behaviour are evident. These men stripped themselves naked and wandered off. Two men's propensity to be alone in the bush indicated their insanity. Alexander S neglected his family and farm and roamed in the bush for two days. He was found six miles from home. A constable testified that Ray P, a 25 year old gumdigger, 'had been living alone in the Bush for some 2 or 3 years gumdigging. Refuses to answer questions & is very peculiar in his manner'. The police had been trying to catch him for some months.[26] These last two cases suggest that solitude in the bush was an archetypal malady for men. Jock Phillips (1987, p 27) reports that the lone man in the frontier situation was often regarded as 'more or less cranky' or a 'hatter' (from the phrase 'as mad as a hatter'). In New South Wales in this period many cases involved solitude, and it entered the popular literature of the period as a theme (Garton, 1988, pp 118–19).

The number of men committed because of public threats to articulated social norms increased over the period. It appears that '[w]ith the population increasing and larger cities appearing, respectable Pakehas [Europeans] became more intolerant of social disorder … Cities brought new expectations of order, routine and public decorum' (Phillips, 1987, p 49; see also Tennant, 1986). For example, the certifying doctors noted that a 57 year old gum digger talked a lot of nonsense. He believed he was the engineer of the world who would soon control the world, and that the British government owed him £32.2 million for use of his machinery. More importantly, he was also 'curious in his behaviour'.[27]

---

24 Case 4105, YCAA 1026/12.
25 Case 4129, YCAA 1026/12.
26 Case 1637, YCAA 1048/5, p 465.
27 Case 4129, YCAA 1026/12.

'Race' was a factor for men, too, but in a different way. Among the smaller number of male cases, Pakeha manifested inappropriate behaviour by believing in or supporting Maori systems of belief. Dennis C, who beat his wife, thought that his wife had 'makutu-ed him' put a spell on him (witchcraft). 'He was told that blood was necessary to remove the witchcraft so he beat his wife to produce the blood.'[28]

The case of Charles J is even more interesting for the light it casts on Pakeha views at a time when many believed that the Maori were dying out or facing complete assimilation (Belich, 2001). Charles called himself 'White Chief Tiger Snake' of the Ngati Porou tribe and wrote circulars championing Maori rights. After his admission he defended himself by saying 'his mere feeling of fairness induced him to say that he would throw in his lot with the Maoris were any attempt made to exterminate them'.[29] Being Pakeha at that time meant supporting white dominance, not sympathising with the Maoris' disadvantage and the discrimination and prejudice they faced.

3.3   Enforcing femininity

While notions of propriety and impropriety that were not sex-specific influenced perceptions of insanity, another set of factors, specifically linked to their having crossed the boundaries of acceptable feminine behaviour, ran through many of the cases involving women. Their deviance in this second respect was an integral aspect of their perceived abnormality, as important as other more obvious reasons. Sometimes it was the only ground for committal. Women transgressed codes of conduct in four areas: self-expression, housework, marital relations, and maternal behaviour. In each area these women did not behave in what others believed to be a feminine manner.

3.3.1   Self-expression

Many of the Auckland case files support Showalter's hunch about the importance of violations of female speech conventions. Committal certificates frequently comment on the violent and obscene nature of the women's language. Notions of piety and purity are explicit in the case of Agnes E, who 'used horrible language, having been up to that time a decent & even religious young woman, fully self-respecting'.[30] In the case of one woman who passed the test of rationality and was coherent with a good memory for recent and past events, doctors noted that she was 'very argumentative'.[31] Good women were supposed to be quiescent, decorous and meek, qualities which many women at the Auckland asylum clearly did not possess. Good women also readily complied with the wishes of others, but the female lunatics here were 'rather obstinate and inclined to be more so',[32] or repeatedly replied 'don't know' to questions at medical examinations.[33]

---

28 Case 176, YCAA 1026/3.
29 Entry dated 4 July 1890, case 1637, YCAA 1048/5, p 465.
30 Case 1629, YCAA 1048/5, p 451.
31 Case 3947, YCAA 1048/11, p 253.
32 Case 3974, YCAA 1048/11, p 280.
33 Case 145, YCAA 1026/2.

Informants and doctors associated femininity with a lack of ego. The certifying doctor described Rebecca J censoriously: as well as her immoderate laughter, referred to above, she spoke to him 'as if she were acting tragedy upon a stage'.[34] Similarly, doctors described Amy G in the following terms upon her release: '[m]entally with the exception of exaggerated egotism, shows no sign of insanity'.[35] Moreover, not all these women shared the sense of shame and repentance expected of them. Bridget H had 50 different convictions for drunkenness in a total of six and a half years. She was transferred from the jail to the asylum several times. Although she was always quiet and rational upon admission, she stated defiantly when brought up before the court on a vagrancy charge that 'she had been drunk for four years and would be drunk for four years more'.[36]

Such prohibitions did not apply to men's behaviour. Although doctors recorded 'raving', 'volubility', 'rambling' and 'muttering' as signs of abnormality, the informants did not view these deviations with the same degree of censure. They expected men to be assertive and vocal; they regarded some as strange because they were 'silent and retiring',[37] 'dull, morose and silent'[38] or 'very reticent'.[39]

3.3.2 Housework and marital relations

The second area of contention centred on women's role as homemakers. Others noted specifically that many women were 'unable to attend to [their] household duties'. The fact that this was a constant refrain throughout the casenotes suggests that it was a standard test of female normality. Indeed, Elizabeth M wrote a telling letter to the asylum superintendent after returning home. In a shaky hand, the note reads: 'I have improved very much in my health since I came Home and am quite able to attend to my Household Duties ... my Dear Husband was glad and happy to have back his cook and housekeeper.'[40] Judgment as to what constituted ability to perform household tasks could be quite exacting. Family members witnessed Albina C sewing on a patch of calico with cotton used for stockings, instead of ordinary thread.[41]

Women also overstepped boundaries in the marital arena. Feminist historians have observed that marriage was the 'cornerstone of femininity'. Good women were expected to see marriage as 'an essential part of every truly feminine woman's life plan', as natural and necessary (Matthews, 1984, p 112). Earlier studies argued firmly that, in colonial New Zealand, the imbalance of the sex ratio in favour of women gave greater opportunities for them to marry and 'put a premium on women as wives' (Dalziel, 1986, p 58). Most even regarded domestic service, the largest category of paid work for women, as a preparation for marriage (Elphick,

---

34 Case 153, YCAA 1026/3.
35 Case 57, YCAA 1048/3, p 47.
36 *New Zealand Herald*, 20 January 1868, p 4, cited in Anderson, 1981, p 77.
37 Case 135, YCAA 1048/1, p 99.
38 Case 176, YCAA 1048/1, p 229.
39 Case 4129, YCAA 1048/12, p 34.
40 Case 128, YCAA 1048/1, p 191.
41 Case 157, YCAA 1026/2.

1986), yet Charlotte Macdonald (1999, p 28) has recently shown that 'the number of settlers who experienced life in a highly unbalanced population was relatively small, and that such experience was relatively short-lived'.

At the same time, the laws surrounding marriage changed markedly in this period – and by 1910 there were improvements in women's legal position in regard to rights, property and participation in public life, including the Married Women's Property Act of 1884 – yet the underlying basis of the law remained the same. These changes took place because they were seen as compatible with women's traditional role of wife, mother and homemaker, and were campaigned for on that basis (Dalziel, 1986; Labrum, 1990).

Historians have argued that, despite the legal and ideological constraints upon women in 19th century New Zealand, migrant women experienced a greater sense of purpose, a feeling of usefulness and a greater degree of independence than they would have in Britain (Dalziel, 1986). Marriage became, in practice, much more of a partnership because husband and wife had to work together as an economic unit. When the pioneering phase ended, women responded enthusiastically to the new cults of domesticity and true womanhood apparent in the early 20th century, which gave them a similar sense of importance, dignity and purpose (Olssen and Levesque, 1978; Phillips, 1987). As Margot Roth (1980, p 88) has pointed out, however true these assertions may be, they are based on the assumption 'that women's lives are assessed by themselves and others in terms of acquiring a husband as a necessary prelude to housework and increasing the population' (see also Macdonald, 1990, especially Chapter 5).

The experience of the women committed to the Auckland asylum offers a different kind of testimony to that of the strong colonial 'helpmeet' ideal and supports other more recent and more nuanced accounts of 19th century women's lives. Many women did not behave as a respectful or satisfied wife should have. For example, after Susannah E attempted to escape her husband by ship in 1870, he committed her to the asylum. This was not the first time: she had been admitted twice in 1869. On the second occasion, she was 'still labouring under the impression that she requires another partner in order to be happy – states she did not live happily with her husband'. Unsurprisingly, when committed for a third time, 'she was rather depressed and bewails her fate most piteously'.[42] Helen C had, in the words of one of her certificating doctors, 'taken an ill will against her husband, and accuses him of ill treatment'. She had also been admitted three times, after either a birth or miscarriage. 'She talks incessantly about her home life, complaining of her husband. She states that he ordered her out of the house as a "bloody whore", after she had asked him for a drink of water. She states that her husband would kill her if he could. When she sees her husband she goes off at once in a violent attack of rage and raging.'[43] Even if outright hostility was not a factor, doctors noted other transgressions of behaviour. Elizabeth M, for example, 'parted from her husband with seeming indifference'.[44]

---

42 Case 101, YCAA 1049/1, p 172.
43 Case 4066, YCAA 1048/11, p 372.
44 Case 128, YCAA 1048/1, p 191.

Many women accused their husbands of ill-treatment or infidelity and there is no evidence of any acceptance of the truth of their statements. Jessie N believed her husband had tried to poison her, would not let her husband near her and charged him with unfaithfulness, an allegation that the doctor believed to be 'most unfounded', yet she would not recant, carried her action through to the extent of suing her husband for maintenance upon discharge, and requested the asylum superintendent for a statement of her condition and conduct, and as to whether her condition was the effect of her husband's ill-treatment.[45]

As with cases of men charged with wife-beating in court, it seems that doctors gave a woman's testimony favourable hearing only if she was clearly an innocent or 'genuine' victim. Women who did not live with their husbands, women in *de facto* relationships, and women who fought back were less likely to win their cases (Anderson, 1981, Chapter 10); in the case of alleged lunacy, it was women who fought back or who acted indifferently towards their husbands who lost. In contrast to the area of contention discussed next, where the problems related to a woman's performance in her maternal role, husbands did not seem eager to reclaim these truculent wives. It appears that confinement in these examples served as a kind of *de facto* divorce. In other words, it was a way of getting rid of troublesome women. Divorce in 19th and early 20th century New Zealand carried a very high degree of social stigma; there were a limited number of grounds under which it could be obtained; and until 1881 all petitions had to be heard in Wellington, the capital city. A 1907 amendment to divorce legislation related specifically to lunacy, and appears to have legitimated what was happening in practice, at least on the husband's part. It granted divorce if one of the spouses had been confined to an asylum for a total of 10 of the 12 years preceding the act of petition, and where there was little likelihood of recovery from lunacy. Objections during the reading of the bill reveal recognition of the potential to use the asylum in this way. Dr Grey Hassell, superintendent of the Auckland and Porirua asylums, argued that some men and women would conspire to keep their spouses in an asylum in order to qualify for divorce. Significantly, he believed men would do this more frequently than women (Phillips, 1987, pp 18, 38, 110–11).

3.3.3 Maternal behaviour

The final area of deviance concerned women's behaviour towards their children. From the beginning of colonisation in New Zealand, the family had been promoted as a source of social stability and a means of reproducing labour. However, it is argued that in a self-sufficient household, where women and men could both work in the family economy, there was a relatively flexible division of labour between the sexes (Dalziel, 1986, pp 60–61). By the end of the period of this study, the links between women and the family were being articulated in a more comprehensive and rigid fashion. As had already happened in England and North America, the cults of domesticity and true womanhood increasingly held sway. These cults emphasised almost exclusively the nurturant and maternal capacities of women, whose lives became even more dependent and privatised.

---

45 Case 1656, YCAA 1048/5, p 503.

The new wife-mother and her attractive home were promulgated as the fitting solution to problems apparently associated with urban growth: prostitution, destitution, illegitimacy, larrikinism and more general immorality and crime. Motherhood and housekeeping were increasingly professionalised, at a time when racial fitness and the supremacy of the British Empire were believed by some to be under threat (Olssen, 1981, pp 8–10, 21–22; Fleming, 1981, pp 9–10, 21–22). Belief in social Darwinism and eugenics, championed by the emerging medical profession and the state, compounded the pressures on women, for it was argued that women were biologically suited for the roles of having children and keeping house.

A number of the women committed to the Auckland asylum neglected, or behaved violently towards, their children and this complaint became slightly more frequent in the later case files. Mary O entered the asylum from hospital some weeks after giving birth. According to her certificate, 'she refused to see her children in the room and told him to take them away from her'.[46] Contemporaries expected women to want to be with their children at all times and to have a predominant interest in their welfare. Doctors censured Jessie N for the 'ready way she is satisfied with regard to her children ... Says she would like to be with her children but expresses the wish in a vague way and seems far more satisfied to be absent from them than a sane mother would be'.[47] Mothers in particular were supposed to be selfless and giving, servers not takers, not 'self absorbed' as another 'neglectful' mother was described.[48]

In contrast to the difficult wives, husbands more eagerly claimed these women back, sometimes before the medical superintendent thought they were ready. This degree of willingness to reclaim discloses women's function as an economic adjunct, a purpose which is revealed in other ways. Roderick Phillips (1981, p 79) has shown how advertisements at the turn of the century demonstrated the pervasiveness of economic criteria in a marriage, and employment agencies which catered especially for domestic servants also offered matrimonial introductions: a blatant indication of the similar functions and legal status of servant and wife. The following case indicates that their labour potential may have saved other women from confinement. Maria C was a 15 year old epileptic pupil at St Mary's Industrial School. The school's medical officer made much of the terror that Maria's epileptic fits produced in the other children and wanted her committed to the asylum. The provincial surgeon initially refused to declare her insane, finding Maria an intelligent girl, 'and the constant work in which she is engaged ... the best thing for her'. In his reply, the medical officer advised him that he wanted to send her to the hospital or Old Women's Institute instead, and emphasised the availability of Maria's domestic services.[49]

The changing importance attached to women as mothers, and indeed the many roles they had to live up to, demonstrate how ideals of femininity varied. Women

---

46 Case 132, YCAA 1026/2.
47 Case 1656, YCAA 1048/5, p 503.
48 Case 3997, YCAA 1048/11, p 303.
49 W Lee to Provincial Superintendent, 30 July 1874, AP2 1874/2538, Auckland Provincial Government Files, National Archives.

could never reach the ideal because it was always shifting. In this sense, the ideal of the good woman, wife and mother was internally contradictory, as Matthews (1984, pp 7–8) has argued, yet these roles, particularly that of wife and mother towards the end of the period, were extremely important because there were few alternatives. The casefiles show that women continued to strive for this ideal. Doctors admitted Mary P in 1870 after they found her 'following men with the idea they were going to marry her'.[50] Lydia Y, who was later diagnosed as mentally retarded, held 'delusions as to marriage, says she is able to cook and perform all household duties'.[51] It therefore comes as no surprise to find that 'disappointment in love' was a female-dominated diagnosis.

3.4 Domestic and economic crises

Along with the main reasons for committal – threats to persons, property, articulated social norms and paranoid attitudes – two further issues demand consideration. Again, these factors occurred in many of the cases and formed part of the multiple pressures operating in the process of committal. They are stresses that ran through all the cases but were not usually triggers in themselves. Recognition of these factors underscores the necessity for a different framework of interpretation, one which moves beyond the asylum walls.

First, the case records show that domestic crisis featured strongly in committal. Even if the cause of distress lay elsewhere, the abnormal behaviour and delusions associated with insanity played havoc with family life. For example, Ethel R, a 33 year old schoolteacher living at home, 'persistently [stood] and [would] not sit down even for food – which [had] to be spooned into her mouth makes no effort at conversation ... stands whining in the middle of the room with an appearance of abject depression and had an antipathy to anyone approaching her'.[52] This was less the case with the male patients because they most often came from non-domestic situations, but is apparent for those living with others. Robert T, a 19 year old married settler, 'got no sleep at night ... kept muttering to himself the whole time' and was 'occasionally very violent'.[53]

Contrary to what might be expected, the family's response was ambivalent. An all too human picture emerges which shows that families were both resistant to and the trigger for committal. Families resisted institutionalisation, despite the fact that superintendents frequently urged earlier admission.[54] Although the asylum had established its legitimacy in the eyes of both patients and families, as grateful letters to the staff testify, its standing was fragile and ambiguous. Despite what the authorities professed, families clearly saw the institution as a last resort, not helped by the stigma attached to recipients of treatment, the therapeutic limitations of

---

50 Case 134, YCAA 1026/2.

51 Case 1616, YCAA 1048/5, p 438.

52 Case 4123, YCAA 1048/12, p 28. Punctuation as in original.

53 Case 169, YCAA 1026/3.

54 See, for example, Report on the Lunatic Asylums of the Colony, AJHR, 1887, H-9, pp 1–2, and 1898, H-7, pp 3 and 7–8, also 1908, H-7, p 3.

asylums and other negative features of their development (Brunton, 1986, pp 49–50).

They admitted family members months and even years after they saw the first signs of abnormal behaviour, often because these events took a sudden turn for the worse. Inspector-General MacGregor noted in his 1904 annual report that 91 out of 580 admissions to all asylums had been cared for privately for the previous year. Only half were admitted within three months of their 'first attack' and some were only admitted after their 'second attack'.[55] Alicia H had 'been strange for twelve months past'.[56] Although she had been under the care of a private nurse for seven months, and had been suffering for two years before being committed in 1910, Ethel R's parents only relented when she became too much for the nurse to handle. Her sister wrote that '[m]y mother is very old and quite heart-broken about sending her little girl away'.[57] Jane B's husband informed the doctor that her attack occurred some 18 months ago, but that now 'she cannot be kept quiet at home'.[58]

Indeed, the decision often depended on how easy it was to care for the patient at home. Many of the individuals required constant watching. Emma G, a 30 year old housewife, had been treated before in Te Aroha, Wairoa and also at Hamilton Hospital. Her husband told the doctor that she 'required watching night and day that she would lie on the floor rather than in bed, goes without food for days together and has a tendency to incendiarism'.[59] It is easy therefore to see why many 'imbecilic', 'idiotic' and congenital cases found their way into the asylums, even though these institutions were not meant for incurable cases.[60] Families' resistance gave way. They also procrastinated because they needed women as housekeepers and their men as breadwinners.

Despite the avoidance of institutional care by families, it is also true, especially for the women in the sample, that in many of these cases of domestic crisis, the family also acted as a trigger. The combined effects of frequent childbirth, onerous household duties and making ends meet exacted their toll, although families and doctors were reluctant to acknowledge this. In the only case where they formally recognised this as the 'exciting cause' of insanity, it was clear from the 'impaired and thin' bodily condition.[61] Eight of the women admitted suffered from puerperal mania and ignored or tried to hurt a new baby or other children. One woman felt welcome relief at the chance to escape to the asylum. Admitted for the third time after the birth of her fourth child, 26 year old settler's wife Amy G, was 'perfectly cool and collected and rather pleased at being here where she says she will have

---

55 Report on the Mental Hospitals of the Colony, AJHR, 1905, H-7, p 2.

56 Case 1611, YCAA 1048/5, p 432.

57 Case 4123, YCAA 1048/12, p 28.

58 Case 160, YCAA 1048/1, p 218; 1026/3.

59 Case 1649, YCAA 1048/5, p 489.

60 The asylum was originally envisaged as an institution for the treatment of acute cases. In the 1870s there were unsuccessful proposals for separate facilities for the 'chronic and the incurable'. In 1889 the Inspector-General claimed that New Zealand asylums 'were being steadily converted into refuges for the mere safekeeping of chronic and incurable lunatics'. Report on the Lunatic Asylums of the Colony, AJHR, 1889, H-22, p l.

61 Case 1611, YCAA 1048/5, p 432.

better food than she has had lately'.[62] Other women used the condition of pregnancy as a lever to get out of the home, if not to go to the asylum. Elizabeth H, a 30 year old settler's wife, insisted that she was 'in the family way' and should be sent away.[63]

Amy G's attitude raises the question of whether some women used the rebellious, wilful role of the madwoman to advantage. As feminist historians have demonstrated, the sick role legitimated a withdrawal from domestic and conjugal duties and, in the eyes of the family, explained other embarrassing behaviour (Smith Rosenberg, 1986, p 98).

The role of economic distress is the second factor that recurs throughout the case records. The very frequency with which economic trouble of many kinds presents itself in the patient case histories, and the primacy it holds in some cases, indicates that individuals in 19th century New Zealand were not allowed to be poor and drop out of society. A strong social norm appeared to operate, which held that you should pull yourself together, persevere and courageously fight through. For example, George K, a labourer recently laid off, who was admitted in the winter of 1890, manifested delusions of grandeur, wealth and 'complete control over the world' coupled with a desire to 'make the streets of Auckland flow in blood and Mr JB Russell's blood should flow in it' (Russell was a prominent local businessman and holder of the mortgage on George's house).[64]

As in New South Wales, the itinerant, casual and unskilled workers constituted the bulk of the asylum population. These people most lacked resources to help them cope with illness or injury let alone the more common problems of relative poverty and hardship. An early inspector estimated that at least 60% of admissions were 'far gone in bodily diseases of all kinds'.[65] The sample women suffered from diarrhoea, bronchial catarrh, influenza, bedsores, rheumatic joints, leg oedemas and tuberculosis besides any supposed mental illness. Indeed, a Member of Parliament claimed in 1903 that 'the medical authorities will tell you that a large percentage of insane cases among women are due to physical weakness; they are not mentally diseased, their mental weakness is the result of want of food, excessive lactation and other physical causes'.[66] In particular, Amy G's case shows that 'it was often the wife and mother who made the sacrifices of food to ensure that the breadwinner and the children were fed and clothed' (Garton, 1988, pp 107–08). Although cure rates were not high overall nor consistent, they were higher for female patients. As the MP concluded, 'a majority would recover health after a brief period of rest and treatment'. Indeed, in this era before drugs, treatment mostly consisted of adequate rest and a good diet.

However, those involved in the committal process tended to ignore this kind of stress, particularly in the female cases. In contrast to some of the male cases, doctors did not commit any women directly because of economic hardship. Accounts of

---

62 Case 57, YCAA 1048/1, p 101.
63 Case 128, YCAA 1026/2.
64 Case 1648, YCAA 1044/1, p 4; 1048/5, p 489.
65 Reports on the Lunatic Asylums in New Zealand, AJHR, 1876, H-4, p 3.
66 *New Zealand Parliamentary Debates*, 123 (1903), p 159.

money or material hardship are absent from their casenotes and, in contrast to the male cases, they assigned the category 'domestic troubles' rather than 'money-related' as a cause of insanity. Studies of other types of delinquent women note that their actions were not seen to be prompted by economic motives but by psychological sickness, whereas delinquent men were perceived to be acting out of economic necessity rather than out of immorality (Anderson, 1981, p 47; Dalley, 1987, p 84; Robinson, 1983, p 59).

3.5 Conclusion

An examination of committal to the Auckland Lunatic Asylum demonstrates the centrality of the family and the fact that families were using the asylum for reasons different from those envisaged by asylum officials. Relatives often acted as both a site of resistance to institutionalisation and, for women especially, a trigger of committal.

Moreover, middle-class notions of respectability, stimulated by urbanisation and subsequent overcrowding, became increasingly important. These developments reduced tolerance for 'unproductive', 'inefficient' behaviour, such as public drunkenness and public loitering, and led to the establishment of institutions and professions devoted to the control of such conduct. This Auckland study shows that this model best fits the male experience and became increasingly important by the end of the period.

Nonetheless, specifically feminine notions of respectability are evident in this case study. Such assumptions related directly to patients' performance in the roles of wife, mother, and housewife, and in their behaviour as women. The existence of feminine notions of respectability affirms the importance of gender in studies of the committal of those deemed mad, yet, as more recent studies have argued, the experience of patients at Auckland points to a more complex situation. Auckland women were not labelled mad solely because of their failure in the pursuit of femininity. While expectations of appropriate womanly behaviour influenced contemporary definitions of madness, it was not a sex-specific problem.

The material conditions in which individuals and their families lived emerge as equally crucial factors which were interpreted in highly gendered ways. In addition, attention to the colonial features of New Zealand society in this period shows how 'race' strongly influenced perceptions of respectability, whether it was female Maori who were 'un-English' or who appeared to treat English institutions lightly and without due respect, or Pakeha men who sought to side with Maori. Gender was fundamental, but it was not the only category of definition and exclusion operating on the many pathways to the colonial asylum.

Chapter 4

Charlotte's Web: Historical Regulation of 'Insane' Women Murderers[1]

Robert Menzies and Dorothy E Chunn

4.1 Women, murder and madness

On an early autumn evening in the late 1940s,[2] in a medium-sized city located in the Canadian west coast province of British Columbia, 33 year old Charlotte Ross[3] severed her husband's jugular vein with a 14 inch carving knife as he sat sleeping in the living room of their fashionable duplex apartment. Awakened by the attack, the unfortunate Jimmy Ross managed to stagger a few feet to the centre of the room before collapsing in a pool of his own blood. Charlotte then turned the knife on herself, slashing her left wrist and throat and, in the process, half-severing the trachea. After an abortive effort to telephone the police, Charlotte slumped onto a sofa chair and gradually lost consciousness. It was not until hours later that Jimmy's son arrived at the apartment, stumbled onto the macabre aftermath of the attack, and called the police. As the press later reported, 'officers who first examined the death scene said the phone receiver was off the hook and a blood-stained butcher knife, believed to be the weapon, was lying on the telephone table'.[4] Jimmy was clearly dead, but Charlotte's eyelids were fluttering and she was moaning almost imperceptibly.

An ambulance transported Charlotte to the city's general hospital, where over the next two weeks she slowly recuperated from her wounds. Meanwhile, police charged Charlotte with capital murder,[5] and a string of local psychiatrists subjected her to a battery of mental assessments. When she was sufficiently recovered, Charlotte found herself in the city jail, alone in a cell, awaiting trial. Her dark voyage through the inner reaches of the state's criminal justice and mental health complex was just beginning.

Through the remainder of the 1940s, and across most of the following two decades, Charlotte Ross would find herself inextricably entangled in the byzantine web of psychiatry and law. In the aftermath of Jimmy's Ross' murder, Charlotte would come to experience the awesome powers of forensic justice in a more intensive and prolonged way, arguably, than any other woman in British Columbia history. Charlotte's troubled journey into the locked wards of the provincial asylum,

---

1   Many thanks, for their input and support, to Wendy Chan, Beverley Brown, and the professionals and staff of the British Columbia Archives, and the Research Advisory Committee and East Lawn clinical records service of Riverview Hospital.
2   To safeguard confidentiality, we withhold and/or alter dates and place names throughout the chapter.
3   Charlotte Ross, like all other names mentioned in the chapter, is a pseudonym.
4   Media sources are unspecified to protect protagonist identities.
5   On the history of murder and capital punishment in Canada, see, among others, Chandler, 1976; Elliott, 1996; Hustak, 1987; Leyton, 1996; and Strange, 1996.

and back through the malestream structures of crime control, affords a unique opportunity to chronicle the gendered operations of judicial and medical institutions during a critically transformative era in the history of socio-legal responses to women's, and men's, madness and criminality. The re-telling of Charlotte Ross' remarkable story shows how her crime, mentality and intransigence, her gender, and her very identity combined to propel Charlotte into recurrent conflict with the experts and officials who were striving to make sense of her – and to return her to what they considered a state of normalcy. In the process, we document how Charlotte's tribulations harboured critically important insights into the dominant cultural understandings that constitute women's normative roles in law, science and society.

Charlotte Ross was one of 38 women whose clinical files we surveyed in our recent historical project on the experience of gender, crime and 'insanity' in British Columbia's mental health system between the years 1888 and 1950 (Chunn and Menzies, 1998; Menzies and Chunn, 1999). This study of 'Order-in-Council' cases – women found unfit to stand trial, or not guilty by reason of insanity, or transferred from prison on account of mental disorder – was concerned with how medicine and law combined to pathologise the behaviours and being of women in conflict with the criminal justice system. Based on documentary analyses of medical and legal records, government reports and correspondence, media accounts and related archival materials, we tried to reconstruct the dominant images of docile, responsible, sane womanhood that framed the practices of psy experts in the British Columbia criminal courts – images which in turn reflected wider understandings of gender, rationality and order that circulated globally through the public culture, then and now.

From its inception in the early 1870s (Davies, 1987; Ferguson, 2002; Kelm, 1992; Menzies, 2001), the west coast province's mental health apparatus was a gender-stratified, and highly segregated, enterprise. In contrast to the feminisation of asylums that was transpiring in England and elsewhere during the second half of the 1800s (Busfield, 1994; Chesler, 1972; Geller and Harris, 1994; Ripa, 1990; Showalter, 1987), the Victoria Lunatic Asylum (1872–78) and its successors – the Public Hospital for the Insane (operating in the Lower Mainland city of New Westminster, commencing in 1878) and the Provincial Mental Hospital, Essondale (opened in 1913, to the east of the PHI in Port Coquitlam) – initially interned far more men than women. It was not until the middle of the 20th century that the numbers reached a comparative balance.[6]

Moreover, the public asylum worlds of female and male patients were separate spheres in virtually every aspect of their organisational structure and culture. As in other European, North American and Antipodean jurisdictions during the period under study (Brookes, 1998; Dwyer, 1987; Finnane, 1985; Geller and Harris, 1994; Labrum, 1992; Matthews, 1984; Prestwich, 1994; Ripa, 1990; Tomes, 1990), patients

---

6   The percentage of women in mental hospital admission registries and provincial census statistics were, respectively: 23% and 25.6% in 1881; 22.6% and 29.1% in 1901; 30.7% and 41.5% in 1921; 42.2% and 46.0% in 1941; and 45.7% and 48.6% in 1951 (Menzies and Chunn, 1999, fn 17; see also Labrum, this book).

spent their days in gender-exclusive wards and/or buildings[7] and engaged in forms of labour, leisure and treatment that reflected deeply entrenched gender identities and expectations. While female matrons and nursing staff may have been omnipresent in the lives of these patients, they did not question the overarching authoritative identity of medical, legal and administrative officialdom which was unremittingly male.

In their collisions with the British Columbia medico-legal system, 'Order-in-Council' women found themselves relentlessly drawn into these gendered realms of governance. On various levels of experience, their institutional careers paralleled those of other women mental patients. They inhabited the same wards, devoted themselves to the same kinds of dreary domestic institutional service, underwent equivalent regimens of treatment and regulation, and endured similarly protracted terms of confinement as did their civilly committed counterparts.[8] At the same time, however, their hybrid status as both criminal and 'insane' conferred unique qualities upon these dually mad and bad women. Their ascribed attributes both singled these patient-offenders out for intensive expert scrutiny, and earmarked them as particularly troubling creatures who posed distinctive threats to an androcentric social, juridical, and scientific establishment. Such 'criminal lunatics' were, in Carlen's words (1983, p 155), 'outwith' women who dwelt beyond the reaffirming paradigms of medicine and law. 'Ordinary' madwomen might be (re)constructed as the objects of pity, or dismissed as pathological monstrosities or nonentities, or incorporated into reigning narratives of feminine frailty and somatic inferiority, but those rare women who transgressed criminal as well as mental boundaries were in direct violation of gender identity standards of mind and action. As such, in the eyes of authorities, they required extraordinary measures of conceptual and systemic domestication.

Notably, the crimes of most 'criminally insane' women were then, and remain today, relatively minor. Among the 38 British Columbia cases in our study, 30 (80%) involved non-violent offences.[9] The most common precipitating charge (9 in total) was for vagrancy, which for women was typically associated with participation in the sex trade. Other crimes ranged from public intoxication to incorrigibility to defamatory libel to public nudity to causing a disturbance. Only six 'Order-in-Council' women during this period were charged with or convicted of murder. All killed family members, which is 'typical' of women who commit homicide. All except Charlotte Ross had taken the lives of their own children, thereby inciting cycles of pathologisation and pity that typically yielded comparatively lenient responses from the courts, and often diversion out of the criminal justice system

---

7   During the early 1900s, the PHI facilities were reserved exclusively for women. The gendered deployment of patients shifted again in 1930, with the opening of the Women's Chronic Building (later East Lawn) at Essondale.

8   Through the first century of British Columbia's public mental health operations, the vast majority of individuals entered hospital as involuntary civil commitment patients, under the province's Mental Hospitals Act, following an application by a family member, other citizen or authority; certification by two physicians, and ratification by a magistrate or justice of the peace (Davies, 1987; Kelm, 1992). See the 1897 Hospitals for the Insane Act [61 Vict, c 101], renamed the Mental Hospitals Act in 1912. Amended in 1940.

9   There was also a case that involved self-injury and an attempted suicide charge.

altogether (Backhouse, 1996; Bernier and Cellard, 1996; Ward, 1999; White-Mair, 2000; Wright, 1987).

In statistical terms, therefore, Charlotte Ross was an uncommon forensic specimen. However, her rarity aside, in the wider context of gender and power relations that infused mid 20th century life, it is scarcely surprising that her case became by far the most infamous of these 38 'criminally insane' women in British Columbia through this 62 year period (generating some 1,000 pages of clinical records during her more than two decades of contact with the provincial mental health system). The 'black widows' (Skrapec, 1994) who, like Charlotte, murdered their husbands or male lovers were the embodiment of intimate danger in both public culture and forensic discourse.

Historically, in England, a woman who killed her husband was liable to be indicted for petit treason and, if convicted, was subject to more severe punishment than was a man who murdered his wife (Gavigan, 1989–90). With the repeal of the petit treason law in 1828, wives were governed by the same homicide law as husbands (Gavigan, 1989–90) but, as various feminist historians and commentators have remarked (Allen, 1987; Chan, 2001; Harris, 1989; Hartman, 1985; Jones, 1996; Knelman, 1998; Lloyd, 1995; Myers and Wight, 1996), from the Victorian era to the present, women who kill their men have continued to precipitate reactions that are out of all proportion to their miniscule numbers, and to the minimal risk that they actually pose to men, civil society, and the state. While reactions might have varied across jurisdictions and cultures (Harris, 1989), more than any other category of criminal womanhood these violent females evoked outrage and uncertainty that resonated with their multiple transgressions against already fragile boundaries of femininity, rationality and deference. The black widow's inherently liminal, polymorphous deviance was her defining attribute in the eyes of the community, science and the law. While she might be mad (ultimately, there was no other way to register such alarming inversions of gender standards), her insanity also expressed itself in calculated, manipulative, 'cold blooded' crimes that seemed at their core to be neither entirely male nor female, willed nor compelled, crazy nor sane. According to many official interpretations of criminal responsibility standards (MacKay, 1995; O'Marra, 1994; Verdun-Jones, 1980; also Moran, 1981; Walker, 1968), many of these women knew right from wrong and were therefore legally accountable. Others, like Charlotte Ross, seemed to inhabit an interstitial mental zone between culpability and blamelessness, and arguably were all the more dangerous for their marginality. As with the forensic category of 'psychopathy' that became increasingly prominent as the 20th century progressed, the urge to punish these women seeped through the medicalising languages and practices of modern psychiatry. Knelman writes, relative to women murderers in England, that 'judges and juries, recoiling at the havoc wreaked by furious women, saw to it that they suffered for the indulgence of their passions' (1998, p 87).

Like other murderous women in Canadian history (Atwood, 1996; Bernier and Cellard, 1996; Kendall, 1999a, 1999b; White-Mair, 2000), Charlotte Ross was acting against nature, or rather against the hegemonic, naturalising images of a docile, nurturing and subservient femininity. However, in contrast to impoverished immigrant women like Anna Balo, who strangled her baby on the outskirts of Nanaimo, British Columbia in 1896 (Backhouse, 1996), or Angelina Napolitano, who retaliated with an axe against a sadistic husband in Sault Ste, Marie, Ontario, 15 years after Balo's case went to trial (Dubinsky and Iacovetta, 1991), Charlotte's external conduct seemed indefensible. Her inner motives, as viewed through the objectifying lens of science, were utterly opaque.

As we chronicle below, Charlotte Ross' suicide attempt in the wake of her husband Jimmy's murder, along with an emerging record of prior psychiatric involvement, did bring her mental capacity into question and justified the medical interventions that followed her arrest, but from the outset Charlotte seemed, to most observers at the time, the antithesis of a prototypical victim. Jimmy had never physically abused her, and was a reliable 'breadwinner'. Moreover, he had been recently diagnosed with colon cancer. Instead, Charlotte's notoriety derived largely from her positioning as a morally questionable and recalcitrant woman whose crime could not be attributed wholly to mental disease or defect. 'The most sensational murderesses,' writes Knelman (1998, p 121), 'were spirited women who were a threat to the social order. Men and women alike were fascinated by [their] audacity and aggressiveness.' Throughout the many years of her entanglements with the state's medical and legal apparatus, Charlotte Ross was, for all intents and purposes, on trial for moral turpitude. Her criminal and mental status were subsumed within, and inextricably latticed to, gender-laced attributions regarding the quality of her character, and her worth as a woman. Her forensic travails were mainly attributable, in Warren's words (1987, p 60), to 'money, sex and trouble'. In these respects, however 'atypical' her case, the arc of Charlotte Ross' forensic 'career' retraced the all-too-familiar contours of women's archetypical experiences with the criminal justice and mental health systems.

4.2   The making of a femme fatale

Charlotte Ross grew up on a farm on the Canadian prairies, the first-born daughter, and the sixth-eldest overall, of fourteen children. Her father was a carpenter – a 'short-tempered, aggressive, independent man ... a rigid man with deep religious convictions'. According to the Essondale clinical records, compiled after her admission to that institution, Abner Ross 'could be physically violent ... and dominated his passive ineffectual wife'.[10] Charlotte's childhood was austere, arduous and short-lived. Like many young women of her era, Charlotte was 'obliged and expected to terminate her schooling [at age 13] to help her mother look after the younger members of the family'. These were hard times for the entire family, as they struggled to survive the onslaught of the Great Depression.

By the age of 15 Charlotte had left home, but she continued her domestic service, finding work as a housekeeper. While still in her teens, in the mid-1930s she met a man with whom she relocated to the Canadian west coast. In the later-recorded words of Charlotte's clinical biographers at Essondale, her companion was 'apparently a drug addict, a dealer in narcotics, and a procurer of women [who] is supposed to have seduced her'. Upon arriving in a small British Columbia coastal

---

10 Unless otherwise indicated, all passages quoted in the chapter are taken from Charlotte Ross'
   Essondale clinical record.

town, this worthy directed Charlotte to a local address which turned out to be the site of a 'house of ill repute'. The proprietors seized her belongings, and some time evidently passed before Charlotte managed to effectuate her escape from this ordeal of sexual servitude. She then took up employment as a waitress in what physicians described as 'one dive after another' in the Chinatown of a nearby city.[11] As expressed through the moralising discourse of her clinical file contents, during that period in the latter years of the Depression 'her dealings with men were on the basis of pick-ups and she indulged in some prostitution'. She received treatment for venereal disease, became pregnant, and obtained an abortion.[12]

Charlotte Ross was entering adulthood at an especially critical juncture in the history of Canadian working women. From the early 20th century through the tumultuous years of the Great Depression and World War II, women like Charlotte, who penetrated the public realm through either choice or necessity, inevitably found themselves face to face with the gendered forces of moral regulation. The reigning state and civil agents and institutions of social purity, mental hygiene, eugenics, citizenship, education and other associated causes combined to construct the single, independent 'working girl' of questionable repute as the quintessential risk to normative Canadian family life (Myers, 1998; Sangster, 2002; Stephen, 1995; Strange, 1995). As integral as they were to the country's economy (increasingly so after 1939), such women were also seen by many to represent an ominous trend in 20th century gender, race, class and sexual relations. For those who decried the alleged assault on traditional values of femininity, family, homeplace and nation, the 'occupational wanderer',[13] the 'factory girl', the 'pick-up girl' and their ilk (Freund, 2002; Roach Pierson, 1990; Stephen, 1995; Strange, 1995) were the collective source of innumerable evils that ranged from the decline of the British imperial order, to the emasculation of the labour force, to all manner of social pathologies including crime, public drunkenness, mental illness, venereal disease and the mixing of the races. In the early years of World War II, public panics targeting the evils of female promiscuity reached a crescendo in cities like Vancouver, where the newly-elected social democratic mayor Lyle Telford zealously unleashed yet another in a decades-long series of anti-vice campaigns (with predictably feeble results). And as Michaela Freund (2002) argues, it was not so much the professional sex trade workers, but rather the liminally transgressive and disrespectable women like Charlotte Ross who were the main targets of these moral enforcement sorties. In these respects, Charlotte's tale is highly representational of Canadian women's experience – or, at least, of those who breached the frontiers of normative family life – as the century approached its midpoint.

---

11 On racialised images of white women living and working in Chinese communities, and efforts to regulate them, see Anderson, 1991 and Backhouse, 1994. On the events and aftermath of the 1924 Janet Smith case, which involved a Chinese 'houseboy' falsely accused of murdering his white female co-worker, see Kerwin, 1999, and Macdonald and O'Keefe, 2000.

12 See Chunn and Menzies, 1990; Sangster, 2002; Stephen, 1995; and Strange, 1995 on the moral regulation of young Canadian women during this era; Freund, 2002 and McLaren, 1987 on campaigns against prostitution; Cassel, 1987; Chunn, 1997 and Mawani, 2002 on venereal disease control; and McLaren, 1993 and McLaren and McLaren, 1997 on abortion.

13 This term originates with the prominent Ontario psychiatrist, medical professor and mental hygienist CK Clarke (Stephen, 1995).

However, in so many other ways Charlotte Ross' story is utterly unique. For one thing, as the years passed, Charlotte proved herself to be a talented and, for a time, eminently successful entrepreneur. Extricating herself from her marginal life of waitressing and part-time prostitution, Charlotte managed, in the retrospective discourse of the Essondale social worker, to 'improv[e] herself as she went along ... [She] worked hard, saved her money and played the races', and took on a succession of jobs as a clothing store clerk, jeweller's assistant, and practical nurse and companion. One of her nursing assignments (later described uncharitably by authorities as a 'sugar daddy' experience) involved an elderly salesman whom Charlotte tended through a protracted and eventually fatal bout of cancer. In partial recompense for her services, the gentleman subsidised Charlotte's urban apartment, and partially financed a coffee shop which Charlotte owned and operated through the war years.

Charlotte's life course took yet another directional shift when, toward the end of World War II, she met the prosperous and well-connected local businessman Jimmy L Ross[14] – a seemingly sympathetic man, in his late fifties, whom Charlotte's brother would later affectionately describe in court as 'a prince'. At first, Charlotte was a hired employee, assisting Jimmy in running his household and repairing his leisure boat, but soon they were cohabiting, and within two years Jimmy and Charlotte married while on vacation in the western United States. From the outset, family and friends on both sides regarded the relationship with suspicion. During subsequent interviews with social workers, Charlotte's siblings depicted her as an aggressive and mercenary manhunter who had 'been pursuing this wealthy man for a considerable period of time'. In her sister's words, Charlotte 'felt that she had made a "good catch" in Mr Ross and was rather inclined to look down on the rest of the family'. For their part, Jimmy's business associates considered Charlotte a 'gold digger' who had 'taken in' their ingenuous, lovestruck friend.

Then, only weeks after the wedding, two shattering revelations punctured this already overwrought domestic setting. First, Jimmy divulged that he was suffering from cancer of the bowel, and required immediate treatment to save his life. Secondly, while Jimmy was in hospital, Charlotte learned (from her own family members) that Jimmy had been leading two utterly discrete private lives. Contrary to his many reassurances over the three preceding years, Jimmy had never finalised the divorce from his first wife. Furthermore, to Charlotte's astonishment Jimmy had an adult son who was living just a short distance away from the Ross' home. When confronted with the truth, Jimmy claimed that he was no longer in communication with his first wife. He pleaded with Charlotte not to leave him. For the time being, a conflicted Charlotte acquiesced.

It was at this precise moment in time that Charlotte's immersion into the mental health system began. Displaying a quite stunning talent for compression of experience, the Riverview authorities later reported simply that 'after Mr Ross' first hospitalization she became ill, requiring three or four hospitalizations'. Charlotte precipitated her first therapeutic encounter by presenting herself at the city police station and endeavouring to lay an attempted murder charge against her own

---

14 By coincidence, Charlotte and Jimmy shared surnames.

brother. During her subsequent 10-day confinement on the psychiatric ward of the local general hospital, Charlotte expanded her circle of persecution, accusing Jimmy and her other siblings of participating in a plot to poison her for her money. While under observation, she threw her $1,500 diamond ring, a gift from Jimmy, down a ward toilet. During this and subsequent hospitalisations over the ensuing months, while Jimmy continued his protracted cancer treatment, Charlotte endured insulin shock therapy and was eventually declared to be stabilised. While one of her brothers had advised that Charlotte be committed involuntarily to Essondale, Jimmy allowed that 'I would not send a dog there'.

The culmination to this ever-escalating calamity arrived six days after Jimmy's release from yet another hospital stay, which on this occasion had lasted a full month and eventuated in a radical colostomy. By this time, Charlotte had determined to leave Jimmy for, in the subsequent phrasing of the Essondale social worker, 'she could no longer place any trust or confidence in what he said'. Moreover, after several days of nursing Jimmy and daily driving him to hospital, Charlotte's mentality was evidently deteriorating. On the morning of Jimmy's death, Charlotte's brothers had visited the home, both later reporting (at Charlotte's preliminary hearing) that she had appeared 'a wee bit sick mentally' and 'seemed very strange at the time [and] she kept saying sarcastic remarks'. That same evening, after shepherding Jimmy through a further outpatient treatment session, Charlotte finally disclosed her intention to leave. According to the clinical files, 'an argument ensued, and she claims that she has no other recollection of what happened'. When Charlotte next awoke in a hospital bed, Jimmy was dead, her slashed wrist and throat were stitched and bound, and her life was in tatters.

4.3   At the Lieutenant-Governor's pleasure

Following her discharge from hospital, Charlotte Ross spent nine weeks in the women's wing at Oakalla, the province's largest prison and detention centre, located in the Vancouver suburb of Burnaby (Anderson, 1993). Pending her murder trial scheduled for the spring Assizes, Charlotte became the object of an intensive psychiatric inquiry, involving three different medical experts, aimed at determining her criminal responsibility at the time of Jimmy's homicide, along with her mental fitness to undergo the upcoming trial (see Eaves, Ogloff and Roesch, 2000; Menzies, 1989; Ogloff and Whittemore, 2001).

Charlotte Ross' legal predicament was clearly desperate. Charged with capital murder, and with all evidence pointing to her guilt, Charlotte faced the very real prospect of execution by hanging (Anderson, 1982; Chandler, 1976; Hustak, 1987; Strange, 1996). While a short-lived unofficial moratorium on the capital punishment of women had prevailed earlier in the century, by the 1940s Canadian women murderers were again, albeit with infrequency and selectivity, being condemned to the scaffold (Dubinsky and Iacovetta, 1991; Greenwood and Boissery, 2000; Kramer and Mitchell, 2002). For Charlotte, then, the availability of medical expertise would have ostensibly been a godsend. A demonstration of irresponsibility, incompetency, or other mental ailments or shortcomings might function to mitigate the charge or sentence, to divert Charlotte out of the judicial system altogether, or, should the worst case scenario unfold, to support an argument for commutation of the death sentence.[15]

However, as so many observers have cautioned (Arrigo, 2002; Coleman, 1984; Menzies, 1989; Pfohl, 1978; Sjostrom, 1997), the introduction of psychiatric expertise into the courts does not, in practice, dilute the power of criminal law. To the contrary, by conferring a legitimising set of scientific discourses and practices upon penal sanctions, the forensic professional serves as a medium for the mutual immersion of medicine and justice into a hybridised control network that is far more potent than either in isolation. The scientific veneer of impartiality and precision becomes a legitimator and catalyst for the invoking of penal outcomes. Far from being 'diverted' out of law's reach, those defendants deemed 'mentally disordered' find themselves channeled into polycentred realms of regulation where their characters and mentalities are as much on trial as their criminal deeds.

Moreover, above and beyond the pervasive effects of social class, race, ethnicity, generation, sexuality and (dis)ability, the conduct and outcome of these 'mental health' evaluations for the courts are intensely gendered (Allen, 1987; Chunn and Menzies, 1990; Kendall, 2000; Menzies, Chunn and Webster, 1992). In ostensibly being 'saved from law' (Smart, 1989, p 47), the woman defendant collides with a malestream system of forensic judgment that potentially imperils her freedom, her state of mind, and her very identity. Moralisation and medicalisation combine to intensify legal sanctions. The 'dually deviant' female forensic patient (Lloyd, 1995) encounters an intensity of medico-moral scrutiny that often far exceeds that experienced by her male counterparts – a process whose outcomes reverberate back into the criminal courts and further exacerbate already potent legal sanctions.

Of the three medical authorities who visited Charlotte Ross in Oakalla, two were Crown appointees, and the other was commissioned by her defence. Regardless of affiliation, however, they returned virtually identical renderings of Charlotte's mind-state in their written reports and subsequent trial testimony. These assessments systematically rehearsed Charlotte's prior encounters with mental health professionals; her 'paranoic' stance toward family, legal and medical authorities; and the bizarre circumstances of Jimmy's death. These themes would become indelibly inscribed into Charlotte's official record, and would register recurrently through her subsequent encounters with institutional psychiatry. The conclusions of one assessor – one of the province's most eminent and respected psychiatrists – was typical. In the wake of three examinations (the first of which Charlotte rebuffed by remaining stonily silent), he wrote:

> ... I am of the opinion that Mrs Ross possesses delusions of a persecutory character which unfits her to stand trial from a mental standpoint as these delusions create such a personal fear that she seemed ... duty bound to protect herself against such further occurrences.

---

15 From Canadian Confederation in 1867 through to the abolition of capital punishment in 1976, the federal cabinet in Ottawa undertook an automatic review of all capital sentences, commuting about half of these cases to life imprisonment (Strange, 1996; Swainger, 1995).

Prior to the commencement of Charlotte's scheduled Assize trial for capital murder, the presiding judge convened a hearing before the appointed 12-member jury to determine her fitness to stand trial. The three medical experts who had evaluated Charlotte in Oakalla gave testimony at the hearing. The Crown and defence psychiatrists were unanimous in declaring that her delusional condition rendered Charlotte unfit to stand trial. Their opinion likely gained support, in the minds of judge and jury, by the fact that Charlotte had discharged her lawyer on the very eve of the trial. Learning of this development, the judge hastily summoned a substitute attorney from a local law firm, although the hearing was already in progress when the latter finally arrived. The jury deliberated for all of 10 minutes before finding Charlotte unfit to stand trial. Her automatic disposition under the Canadian *Criminal Code* was transfer to psychiatric facilities as an 'Order-in-Council' patient, under an indeterminate Lieutenant-Governor's Warrant (LGW), until she regained her fitness and could return to court to stand her trial.

Charlotte's own memories of these events, conveyed to an Essondale physician two months following her admission, are worth reproducing at length. They reveal much about Charlotte's own experience of the trial process, along with her ultimately abortive efforts to assume some measure of control over her trial and to fend off a psychiatric commitment:

> I discharged [my first] lawyer on the ... Sunday evening and my trial came up on the [Monday], so I had an idea that this is what they were trying to do, to send me to this place ... so trying to stop that I used my own knowledge of what I knew of the law, if I discharged my lawyer they wouldn't go on with the trial and I would be able to get another lawyer and have a trial, but apparently they still went on with the trial ... Of course at ... my trial ... [my lawyer] got up and said he was discharged a few hours beforehand, and according to law they have to adjourn for 24 hours notice for discharge. Anyhow there was Dr D and Dr M ... and several other people ... and he said how he had attended me from the middle of October and up until now and he was discharged a few hours ago, and that well, I was waiting for the judge to nod to me and say something to me to give me an opportunity to speak, I didn't want to jump up – I didn't know just the procedures to go through, which naturally I just sat there. Well then the Judge spoke to the clerk there and one of the other men ... and asked him to get in touch with [law firm]. [The new lawyer] was kind enough to come down to the court, and of course the Judge asked Mr L if he was informed or hired by me and he said he hadn't. I didn't say anything. I should have said well I hire him now. I didn't know the procedures. Well the Judge asked Mr L to look over [former lawyer's] papers and then they went on. You know the usual procedures of the court, and several times I had the opportunity to say something if I had known the right thing to say. Anyhow the jury went out and that was that.

Equally illuminating were Charlotte's reflections on the trial's aftermath, extracted from an Essondale case conference convened around the same time. 'I didn't see [my lawyer] after my trial and I never saw him for seven weeks previous,' Charlotte disclosed to the assembled hospital physicians and staff members. Further:

> ... all the time I was staying at the Oakalla Jail in custody he has never come to see me. He corresponded with me several times. Other than that he didn't come up to see me, so when I went back over to ... stand my trial the next morning, he came up to see me about 9:30 in the evening and before he arrived Dr [ ] came up and said hello to me, and that was the first time I had seen him for seven weeks. He said that I was looking very

well and a few things and then left. He met [lawyer] in the hall and had a few words together, then [lawyer] came in to see me and proceeded to say what was going to happen.

When one doctor ventured, 'Were you satisfied with that arrangement or would you have preferred to have gone to trial?' Charlotte's reply was an emphatic, 'Well I would have preferred to have gone to trial for several reasons'. 'Could you give me any reasons?' continued the examiner. 'No, not now,' was Charlotte's interview-ending retort.

From a retrospective reading of these selected exchanges, it is clear that Charlotte had incisively gauged the implications of her medical 'diversion' to Essondale as an 'unfit' criminal defendant. For Charlotte, this consignment to medico-legal limbo was an unwelcome intrusion that she deeply resented. Charlotte's unrelenting protests against her mental confinement, her steadfast claim to be fit for trial, and her inexhaustible demands for access to the law rapidly emerged as the *leitmotivs* of her mental hospital experience. As Charlotte confided to her ward physician shortly after admission, commitment to Essondale was:

> ... the very thing I didn't want to happen at my hearing ... If I'm going to stand trial there is no reason why I can't stand now. [Coming here] is the very thing I didn't want to happen ... If I'm going to stand trial there is no reason why I can't stand now. Why didn't I stay in [jail] and get my lawyer? If I was able to stay in [jail] for nine weeks altogether, do my knitting, help the girls there, I don't know why I have to come here for treatment.

4.4 Into the belly of the beast

Charlotte Ross' 13 years spent on the wards of the Essondale Women's Chronic Building passed slowly. Like other women psychiatric inpatients in British Columbia and beyond (Davies, 1987; Geller and Harris, 1994; Labrum, 1992; Kelm, 1992; Mitchinson, 1987; Reaume, 2000; Ripa, 1990), Charlotte found herself enclosed in a highly-regulated medical surround where the hierarchies of doctor-patient relations were readily apparent to all, and where gender figured prominently in every minute detail of daily life. Women's experiences as Essondale inmates followed the tightly orchestrated institutional rhythms and configurations of time, space, labour and leisure. For many, isolation from the world beyond the walls was total. Moreover, particularly after the arrival of women psychiatrists at Essondale in the late 1940s, only rarely did a male presence punctuate the gender-segregated milieu of the East Lawn wards. Contact between physicians and patients was sporadic at the best of times. As Charlotte observed in one letter intended for her mother, but confiscated by staff, 'we had gotten so many Doctors in such a short time it was rather difficult to get an appointment with any of them'. A few years later, in a staff conference Charlotte recollected that, '[a]s far as I know I have never seen a doctor in our ward, even in our dorm, other than if a patient has been sick'. Contributing to her dilemma was the fact that Charlotte's 'criminally insane' designation necessitated special security arrangements which consigned her to a locked ward, restricted her comings and goings, debarred her from grounds privileges, and no doubt greatly inhibited her interactions with ward physicians. As Charlotte wrote in the same letter to her mother, 'I am an Order of council, and ... I can not[16] get a Doctor that will stay long enough to get interested in my case'. In contrast to her tenuous and often hostile relations with medical staff, however, Charlotte clearly took pleasure in the company of other women patients, and benefited from the feminine culture that prevailed on the wards. 'The ladies are very nice and very considerate,' Charlotte opined in one case conference, 'because we realize we are all in the same boat so to speak, we are all rowing for one thing, and that is to get well physically and mentally and be able to live what is considered a normal life on the outside.'

Charlotte's experience as an 'Order-in-Council' patient at Essondale pivoted around the continuing efforts of medical authorities to appraise her mental competency and responsibility; to reconstruct her moral biography of pathology and violence (Allen, 1987; Carlen, 1983; Chunn and Menzies, 1990); and to ascertain the syndromes and afflictions that had propelled her into hospital. As many feminist researchers and authors have observed (Becker, 1997; Bordo, 1988; Caplan, 1996; Lerman, 1996; Raitt and Zeedyk, 2000; Stubbs and Tolmie, 1999), the imputation of psychiatric classifications is an intensely gendered process that concerns women's moral transgressions, and their violations of normative femininity, as much as it does their implied mental aberrations. In Charlotte's case, physicians arrived at a diagnosis of 'Schizophrenic Reaction – Paranoid Type'. 'It is evident,' they reasoned, 'from her evasions and occasional blocking in her speech that she has systematized a delusional formation beginning at least as far back as the time of her marriage and involving ideas of jealousy, the police, and the idea that someone is after her money.' These clinical conclusions derived from recurrent sessions of psychological testing; from the observations of individual physicians based on their conversations and interviews with Charlotte, and inscribed into 'progress notes' and reports; and from regular 'case conferences' comprising assembled teams of hospital staff.

First, since the 1930s, psychological testing had been an integral part of the evaluation repertoire available to Essondale professional staff. Charlotte was the subject of recurrent psychological assessments throughout her confinement, involving such instruments as the Rorschach test, the Wechsler Bellevue intelligence test, the Draw-a-Person test, the Thematic Apperception Test (TAT), the Minnesota Multiphasic Personality Inventory (MMPI), and the Rosensweig Picture-Frustration test. Her results, as interpreted by the staff psychometrists, inevitably compounded and confirmed the multiple psychiatric pathologies that had already been inscribed into Charlotte's ever-expanding clinical file. The following excerpt, extracted from an evaluation conducted in the mid-1950s, was typical:

> The W-B [Wechsler-Bellevue] shows that although potentially of high average ability Mrs Ross is quite incapacitated by thought disturbance. The projective tests show strong evidence of a thought disorder. The Rorschach is full of deteriorative, malignant anatomy responses. In this type of picture one would expect sexual preoccupation with deviant thoughts; projection; and inadequate control of acting out behavior … this appears to be the record of a paranoid schizophrenic who is incapacitated by use of projection and repression and inability to think in abstract terms. She is at the moment

---

16 We reproduce all excerpts from letters and other documents verbatim, with no corrections of spelling or grammar errors.

functioning in the dull normal range of intelligence. Her attempts to use rigid controls to inhibit her psychotic thoughts breaks down very easily and she would be expected to act out in a frustrating situation.

Second, interviews with individual psychiatrists, many of them transcribed verbatim into the clinical case file, were regular features of Charlotte's Essondale experience. Charlotte plainly took exception to the confessional, mind-probing qualities of these one-to-one encounters. Charlotte especially objected to physicians' overt and furtive efforts to elicit legally relevant knowledge that, in her judgment, had no bearing on her medical status. The following exchange with her first ward physician, who (not incidentally) had testified at Charlotte's fitness hearing, occurred shortly after her admission. It offers telling insight into the dynamics of these diagnostic 'consults':

Q What do you think is the next thing for you, what is in the future for you?
A What do you mean?
Q What do you plan? You have arrived here and now what do you think is going to happen?
A I just sit and wait on what you doctors say.
Q You are quite content to abide by the decision of the doctors outside to have you here?
A I certainly am not. There isn't anything I can do. I have fought and fought and everything I did – what did they do on Saturday – rushed in and said you are going and here I am. I fought about coming to this place ever since they started.
Q The only way in which your present status can be altered is to talk to people on just what your future is.
A If it didn't help me when I was there, how is it going to help me when I'm in here?
Q It may not help you but it is the only possibility you have.
A No. I did all I could to keep from coming in here. Now I'm here anyway. I don't see any sense in my taking up your time.
Q If there is anything you want to tell me about it at a later date you let me know and I'll be glad to talk with you.
A That is very kind of you.

Third, in periodic 'case conferences', physicians, psychologists, social workers, nurses and other staff members congregated to conduct communal inquiries into Charlotte's mental and legal status. These group endeavours to 'open up' the patient invariably ended in frustration. The collective exertions of the assembled experts notwithstanding, Charlotte remained resolutely silent about her alleged crime. Claiming the protections of legal process, and citing the unhappy experience of her fitness hearing, she disputed doctors' claims to be working in her best interests. In one such exchange, extracted from a conference held a few months after her admission, Charlotte showed that she was more than a match for the assembled professionals. Stymied by her continuing intransigence, an exasperated head physician finally resorted to a thinly-veiled threat – an ominous expression of his ultimate power to determine Charlotte's fate:

Q All we are interested in is your own health, your mental health and physical health. We have no interest in the legal aspect of your difficulties, it is only in your personal health we are interested so if I ask you any question you would rather not answer you don't need to answer. I'll try to ask no question like that. In any case it is merely between ourselves from a doctor and patient angle … Would you care to give any statements to me?

A I can't very well.

Q What transpires here is a confidence between doctors and patients and is never broken.

A Pardon me for saying so, Dr [ ] said that to me and he is a doctor – it isn't that I doubt any doctors it has just made me a little wary of that fact.

Q It makes it when you are not willing to discuss and talk freely with us very difficult for us to come to any conclusions to be of assistance to you. You can see that point?

A Maybe. On the other hand I don't need any assistance.

Q Well, you need assistance at least to get out of here.

A Yes, I understand that.

Q Well how are we to determine your present mental state if you close up like a clam all the time?

A I am sorry if I close up like a clam as you put it, but you understand my position, I can't say anything more than I have, and probably if I hadn't said as much previous to this I probably would not be here …

Q Naturally I would take it quite frankly that as long as your attitude persists, it is the attitude of a person who is mentally unwell, that would be my reasoning. You will have to change that idea that I have got …

A I talked too much apparently before and I still came here, and I keep on talking and I still stay, so what am I to do?

Q You tell me what you would like to do? What would you like us to do for you?

A Well, naturally I guess you are going to laugh at me, I would like to be left alone, let me go out and stand my trial and attend to my own affairs … What point is my staying here? How long am I going to stay? Is there ever a chance of going out, or what is it?

Q You will have to stay here until we say you are ready to leave here … And yet as you sit here not talking to me you are making it difficult for me to arrive at that conclusion are you not?

A Not in the way I look at it … As I said before I talked to Dr [ ] and he said he was going to help me and I still came here. I told him then and I told Dr [ ] then. I still came here.

Such intransigence could not go unchallenged. At Essondale, as in other such closed settings, practitioners typically interpreted women's refusals and oppositions as 'pathologies of female protest' (Bordo, 1988, p 87) and as symptomatic of the mental aberrations that underpinned their resistance to medical authority. Undoubtedly, Charlotte defied the interrogatory gambits of her psychiatric interlocutors at her peril. Following the above interview, for example, the attending clinicians resolved to diagnose her with paranoia and to recommend insulin treatment. In a ward note written after this exchange, the physician wrote:

Mrs Ross remains anxious to be considered fit to be discharged and to conduct her own defence … she has always refused to answer my 'leading' questions – that is questions which are concerned with the circumstances of her thinking and behaviour immediately prior to and including the day of her husband's death, for which she was charged. She will not, she says, answer those questions except in the presence of a lawyer. Her general attitude towards the staff and Hospital authorities is a persecutory one – that is she is being unfairly detained here and has never been given a chance to defend herself of the charge made against her … She understands that she is here on an O-in-C, but believes that in various ways this entitles her to special attention – which it does but not in the ways that she thinks.

By every indication, Charlotte dreaded these conferences. 'She … relates,' observed one physician, 'how distasteful her previous appearance at conference proved to be when the decision was never in her favour and she was returned ... to be given ECT and detained on a closed ward for years to come.' Charlotte was keenly aware, therefore, of the price she paid for failing the conference test, and for refusing to assume the deferent patient role in these contexts. In persistently refusing to address her charges and trial, because '[t]hat is legal, and that is personal', Charlotte confirmed clinical impressions about her 'paranoic' personality and 'ideas of reference'. Following one such encounter, the presiding psychiatrist concluded that 'she … successfully retreats behind the defense that her lawyer had instructed her not to divulge this material as it pertains to the legal and not to the medical issues involved', and that 'her defenses of denial and projection are inadequate methods of dealing with her difficulties'.

Besides her strategic use of silence, and her spirited invocation of rights discourse at every opportunity, Charlotte showed herself capable of deploying other creative means of contesting medical authority. Indeed, over the course of many years, Charlotte's unruly, 'chronically' transgressive in-hospital conduct violated nearly every aspect of the prescribed woman patient's role. She retained a lawyer. She wrote innumerable letters to governmental officials and potential advocates outside the hospital. She accused staff physicians of impeding the discharge of patients through their 'professional and political influence'. Understanding the currency of her status as an alleged knife-wielding 'murderess', she was not above mobilising her reputation to advantage by approaching ill-favoured doctors and offering to cut their throats (as her ward physician allowed after one such outburst, '[h]er threats, in view of her past history and this evidence of her extreme aggression and hostility, should not be taken lightly and she must remain under close supervision').

From Charlotte's vantage point, the medical men were her sole adversaries. 'It is funny,' she confided in one conversation, 'but I have never got mad at the patients or staff in hospital – it has always been doctors.' For the latter, Charlotte's resistance to medical authority represented nothing more than psychotic pathology – or, perhaps, 'arrest in psychosexual development', and 'latent homosexuality', as one physician surmised. And as much as they would have preferred to dispense with this ongoing irritant to the institutional routine, the hospital staff were powerless to act. As the Essondale Medical Superintendent reasoned in the mid-1950s:

> We can't remove the Order-in-Council because her sentence has not expired as she has not been sentenced, and she is not fit to stand trial, therefore I don't see how we can alter her personal status … She is paranoidal. She is suspicious. She is hostile. She has no regrets for anything she has ever done. This woman would be a menace to be at large. If through some mistake, inadvertently she was sent to the Court, the charge, I think would be removed … I would say the prognosis would be extremely poor, very very unlikely she would ever clear sufficiently.

In their efforts to manage Charlotte, and to relieve her mental afflictions, the Essondale medical authorities relied mainly on the somatic 'therapies' that were dominating institutional psychiatric practice in Canada and elsewhere through the post-War era. In the second summer of her detention, Charlotte endured more than two months of daily insulin injections. These 'treatments' induced 58 separate comas lasting several hours each morning, after which Charlotte returned daily to the ward sewing room for afternoon 'occupational therapy' sessions. The effects of the insulin were immediate and profound. After one week of injections, Charlotte addressed the following letter to a friend on the outside, which physicians proceeded to confiscate (alarmed as much by the scarcely recognisable scrawl, no doubt, as by the contents):

> Dear [ ] since I have been taken treatment this past week I don't believe I have had a letter from you or have I written any. I really have been too sick this past week for the first time since I have arrived here. I was doing very well on my own so to speak, and everyone has been so surprise to see me on treatment, they say they don't understand because I was the last person they expected to see taken these treatments. As far as I can make out it is Dr [ ] that is earning himself a red feather by having me on. And apperetly it will take untell early this fall before I am through taken them. I am taken these treatments every morning that that is all I know. And feel far worse since I have been taken them. I don't mind so much if they were doing me some good ... I only know a little of the other side and can understand a bit, that is all. So would be pleased to see you any time you can get away. Your Loving Friend. Charlotte.

However, Charlotte's treatment regimen had scarcely begun. Medical staff introduced rounds of electroconvulsive therapy (ECT) during Charlotte's fifth year in hospital, and repeated them intermittently thereafter. During one typical course of ECT, Charlotte underwent 21 induced grand mal seizures over a seven-week period. 'All this shock,' as Charlotte described it, was clearly devastating. In one note conveyed to the Essondale Medical Superintendent, nine years after her admission, Charlotte declared that 'the word "Shock Treatments" or "ECT" makes me ill to my stomach ... I'm off my food can not sleep, also have lost weight'. Three years later, after countless more ECTs, the ward physician surmised that Charlotte had incorporated ECT into her 'paranoid' belief system, voicing the opinion 'that electroshock was a criminal procedure and ... that it had its beginning some way that was not acceptable'.[17] Despite her protests, the shocks continued. When the first generation of antipsychotic medications became available in the mid-1950s, doctors forthwith placed Charlotte on heavy doses of largactil. When her blood pressure began to plummet dangerously, they shifted to 400 milligram dosages of riserpine daily. Afterwards, they reported that 'she works in the laundry and is much more amenable'. In Charlotte's case, it seemed that patient docility was the main arbiter of a successful treatment regimen.

If amenability and compliance were the measures of psychiatric recovery for women like Charlotte, they also presented the fastest, and arguably the only, available escape from the locked hospital wards. Whether induced by electricity, chemistry, burnout or a genuine mental reformation, Charlotte's conduct change by the late 1950s was conspicuous. Incrementally, in response, medical staff began to confer previously withheld privileges, such as bimonthly 'comfort' payments of $50 (supplied by the Attorney General's department), along with supervised walks, picnics and games of tennis on the hospital grounds. Correspondingly, in

---

17 Charlotte had a point. Ugo Cerletti pioneered the ECT after witnessing how electrical shocks had a calming effect on pigs in an Italian slaughterhouse. On the origin of ECT see, *inter alia*, Breggin, 1993; Frank, 1978; Friedberg, 1976; and Valenstein, 1986.

perceptible gradations, the psychiatric assessments began to shift in substance and tone. 'Mrs Ross,' observed one physician, 'has taken very responsible jobs in working in … the kitchen, helping recreation to supervise grounds picnics and she had free access to the gardens and to the picking of flowers to decorate her ward and the dining room. She has talked to me about the "poor patients" and she has told me how some of the patients are confused as to whether she is a patient or a staff member.' Then, near the decade's end, Charlotte finally earned her transfer to an open ward. Her long-awaited emancipation from Essondale was apparently within reach, at long last.

4.5 A preference for law

For Charlotte Ross, as for those in similar predicaments elsewhere, the law was a potential redeemer, and a much sought-after alternative to the psychiatric purgatory which had entombed her for more than a decade. Charlotte was strikingly aware of the inequities she faced in being denied access to the courts. As the above chronicling of her hospital experience attests, Charlotte evinced much resourcefulness and resolve, throughout the course of her confinement, in her efforts to enlist the protections of law. For Charlotte, establishing her mental competency before the courts was her sole route to liberation from the asylum system but, as ensuing events would affirm, Charlotte poignantly failed to fathom the full extent of psychiatry's penetration into the criminal justice apparatus. In the labyrinthine world of medicine and law, mental competency was no panacea. For the 'mentally disordered offender', legal due process was far from being a guarantor of freedom.

Even toward the end of the 1950s, Essondale physicians were still resisting Charlotte's return to court. One psychiatrist opined, following yet another extended interview, that 'Mrs Ross … had not looked at the six months of her life prior to the alleged attack and that her refusal to discuss this with anyone but her lawyer was part of her ineffective defences of denial and projection'. The doctor considered that 'in her present state of health … her personality would disintegrate in the court setting', and he reminded others that Charlotte faced execution should she be convicted on the capital murder charge. Moreover, even should Charlotte proceed to court and somehow be acquitted, another physician advised that she would nonetheless require further inpatient treatment under mental health law. According to the case file notes, when Charlotte remonstrated angrily against this suggestion, 'Dr M told her that her response indicated that she may be ill still'.

Nonetheless, as the 1960s dawned, the Riverview staff physicians, under unremitting pressure from Charlotte and her lawyer, and perhaps impressed by her improved conduct on the wards, at last recommended that she 'had recovered sufficiently from her psychotic condition to be returned to court to stand trial' (rather disingenuously, they also recommended that, for the sake of her mental health, Charlotte 'not become involved in any civil litigation following her discharge'). So advised, the provincial Attorney General lifted Charlotte's warrant and she returned to Oakalla prison pending her Assize court trial scheduled for the spring.

The trial unfolded in a legal milieu that far pre-dated the advent of the *Canadian Charter of Rights and Freedoms*[18] along with the assorted statutory and case law reforms[19] that, in subsequent decades, came to offer some measure of procedural protection to 'mentally disordered' persons in conflict with the law. In such cases during the early 1960s, prosecutorial discretion was wide-ranging; the influence of medical expert witnesses was immense; the Crown retained the right to raise the issue of criminal responsibility and adduce evidence supporting it; the potential for double jeopardy outcomes (unfit and guilty, unfit and criminally insane) was ever-present; and defendants found not guilty by reason of insanity faced an automatic disposition of indeterminate psychiatric internment, with at best tenuous options for review, under warrant of the Lieutenant-Governor.

Charlotte Ross' murder trial rapidly mutated into a media circus for the local press, a field day for participating psychiatrists, and a topic of titillation for a captivated public. As with Judith Knelman's Victorian murderesses (1998), Charlotte was the personification of the crazed and lethal black widow temptress whose warped mentality and morals were seen to have exploded into ineffable mayhem (Shipley and Arrigo, 2004; Skrapec, 1994). All context and nuance purged from her narrative, Charlotte found herself reduced to a cipher for the objectifying cautionary tales that issued forth on all available fronts – in the courtroom, through medical discourse, and within the public culture – about the dangers and disorders of femininity gone appallingly wrong.

After the jury's double negative declaration that Charlotte was 'not unfit to stand trial' (despite her diagnosis by three prosecution psychiatrists as a paranoic schizophrenic), the trial proper began. Under the headline 'Hidden Fears Beset Once-Happy Woman', one journalist's account described 'a comely brunette on trial for her life' who 'look[ed] haggard and drawn after nearly three days in the prisoner's box, the last two listening to testimony surrounding the … knife-slaying of city car dealer Jimmy L Ross'. According to this rendition, 'Mrs Ross sat with downcast eyes as one of her brothers described her sudden change of character … how she suddenly became transformed from a cheerful, happy, normal person to an individual beset by nameless fears and suspicions – an individual who secreted a gun in her bedroom and who obtained cartridges to fit it'. Charlotte's union with Jimmy was now reduced, in her brother's testimony, into a 'supposed marriage' to a 'common law husband' (an invalidating theme that both prosecution and state-appointed psychiatrists subsequently reinforced). Then, medical witnesses for both defence and Crown advanced a litany of evidence attesting to Charlotte's mental state at the time of the killing, and her resulting incapacity to distinguish right from wrong under the Canadian Criminal Code's version of the McNaughtan rules.[20]

---

18 Constitution Act 1982, RSC 1985, Appendix II, No 44. Enacted by the Canada Act 1982 (UK), c 11.

19 For a general appraisal of the 1992 reforms to the mental health provisions of the Canadian Criminal Code, and the three pivotal Supreme Court of Canada cases *R v Chaulk* (1990), *R v Swain* [1991], and *Winko v British Columbia (Forensic Psychiatric Institute)* (1999), see Eaves, Ogloff and Roesch, 2000.

20 On Canadian adaptations of the cognitive 'knowing right from wrong' test derived from the 1843 McNaughtan case, and still enshrined in s 16 of the Criminal Code, see Eaves, Ogloff and Roesch, 2000; Ogloff and Whittemore, 2001; O'Marra, 1994; and Verdun-Jones, 1980.

One expert testified that 'she was ... upset by the prospect her common law husband was jilting her, or about to jilt her'. Another psychiatrist, who had treated her two months prior to the murder, revealed that Charlotte had 'thought her food was poisoned by Jimmy Ross. She had said "they wanted to kill me because I was not good enough for the social position"'. Yet another witness reported that Charlotte 'thought her husband had hired an Indian to kill her'.

On the fourth and final day of the trial, Charlotte took the stand herself. 'Dressed in black, with black and white gloves,' as one newspaper recounted, 'she hesitated before answering questions from counsel, and gave her replies quietly. During her testimony, the spectators in the public gallery were so quiet the rustle of counsel's gowns sounded unnaturally loud. She denied any recollection of events leading up to the death of Jimmy Ross.' Unsurprisingly, Charlotte's version of events did not go unchallenged. 'Crown prosecutor,' the reporter continued, 'submitted Mrs Ross to a searching cross-examination of her life leading up to the time she met Jimmy Ross and went through a form of marriage with him in [the United States].'

After the trial ground to a merciful close, the Assize court jury deliberated for all of 34 minutes before rendering a verdict of 'not guilty by reason of insanity'.[21] Initially, Charlotte was mightily relieved to hear the presiding judge order her returned to Oakalla prison. In a subsequent visiting room conversation with her protestant minister brother-in-law, recorded by the prison matron, Charlotte confided that 'she had asked to be sent back here, as she felt that she just could not face Essondale again, and her lawyer had told her that she would only be here for about a week'. Further, whereas the trial had been 'horrible and very gruesome, resulting in one lawyer collapsing during the hearing', Charlotte expressed satisfaction with her treatment at the hands of the criminal court: '... everyone ... was very kind to her ... the RCMP[22] and the Judge both stopped the TV people and press from taking her picture, and after the trial was over, they told her it was better to stay there and relax for a few days ... the matron was very nice to her and took her to a quite place on the beach, where she was able to lie down and relax without a crowd.'

It was with all the more shock and disbelief, then, that Charlotte learned about the provincial Attorney General's decision to issue a second Order-in-Council, which ordered her sent back to Essondale for yet another indeterminate term of confinement. For Charlotte, this double jeopardy outcome was in every way the worst-case scenario. When the Oakalla prison matron broke the news, the latter reported that Charlotte 'raved about [Attorney General] Mr [Robert] Bonner, said she came her at the Lieutenant Governor's pleasure and Mr Bonner had stepped in and taken over and he was doing everything to suit himself'.

---

21 It is possible that the jury decision was influenced by the knowledge that a guilty verdict might lead to a capital sentence for Charlotte Ross.

22 The Royal Canadian Mounted Police assumed jurisdiction over provincial-level policing, supplanting the British Columbia Provincial Police (BCPP), in 1950 (Marquis, 1993; Stonier-Newman, 1991).

4.6 Aftermath

In the wake of her insanity acquittal, Charlotte, now 48 years old, incredibly found herself back on the closed wards of Essondale. At first defiant, she 'refused physical examination' at readmission 'on the grounds that she no longer came under the jurisdiction of the hospital authorities'. Before long, though, the grim actualities of her plight began to penetrate. Even the institutional authorities acknowledged the folly of Charlotte's continuing confinement, at the same time as they took pains to emphasise the pathological roots of her enraged reaction. 'She presents a most difficult problem,' wrote her presiding psychiatrist, 'in that her very real and justified resentment at being detained in hospital indefinitely is difficult to distinguish from her morbid state of paranoid schizophrenia.' Ambivalently, the physician and his colleagues petitioned provincial Attorney General Robert Bonner to vacate this new Order-in-Council, but the redoubtable long-time politician rebuffed their efforts. Meanwhile, Charlotte began to deteriorate again, with the consequence that, during the following winter, doctors subjected her to two months of prolonged sleep therapy[23] followed by another protracted course of chlorpromazine.

One more year elapsed before authorities at last deemed Charlotte Ross sufficiently recuperated to exit hospital one more time. Charlotte began to earn leaves of absence from Essondale, commencing during the Christmas holiday season, but it was not until the following spring that Bonner finally consented to an extended leave. Charlotte took up work on the outside, first as housekeeper for a motel owner, then as a waitress. Still, the long arm of the indeterminate Order-in-Council followed Charlotte into the community and, true to form, Charlotte continued to resist. As her caseworker complained in May of that year: 'After Care appointments and visiting as a part of hospital service were dismissed scornfully as she has "never received any treatment or service". ... She repeatedly said she would not be "snooped upon" ... and that I must not show my face around the motel again.' In the face of their repeated reproaches, Charlotte continued to evade social workers and miss appointments until the exasperated Essondale administrators finally placed her on AWOL and notified the police. A month later, on an early summer morning in the mid-1960s, Charlotte found herself once again in Essondale. Describing her as a 'well-groomed, well preserved woman with an erect carriage, very decisive manner and a somewhat harsh voice', physicians once again reaffirmed Charlotte's diagnosis of 'schizophrenic reaction paranoid type', and she spent another three months on the wards still 'Waiting to get my final release from the Attorney General'.

That release came at last during the following autumn, when Attorney General Bonner grudgingly consented to lift Charlotte's Lieutenant-Governor's Warrant. Three days later, a relieved Riverview Hospital[24] medical staff discharged Charlotte and closed her case. On this occasion there was no follow-up, for, in the words of the discharging physician:

---

23 Historical accounts of prolonged sleep therapy and other somatic 'treatments' include, in Canada, Collins, 1988, and elsewhere, Breggin, 1993; Schrag, 1978; and Valenstein, 1986.

24 In the wake of revisions to the British Columbia Mental Hospitals (thereafter Mental Health) Act, the Essondale Provincial Mental Hospital became Riverview Hospital in 1964.

Mrs Ross is so evasive that it is almost a physical impossibility to keep in touch with her. Her employment has been sporadic and the hours irregular and she will not make an effort to arrange appointments. She has not once given a change of address. We know of no community agency who would give service to so unreasonable and paranoid a client. Mrs Ross functions by being highly manipulative, which tends to play one discipline against another and inhibits maximum team cooperative effort ... This hostile manipulation has also destroyed her relationship with her siblings and indeed has destroyed relationships between siblings so that Social Service time and effort has been wastefully used in dealing with their recriminations.

Even then, however, Charlotte Ross' encounter with medico-legal authority had not ended. One further admission occurred, this time voluntary, toward the end of the 1960s. Charlotte's employer, for whom she was working as a domestic, had reported to police that she was voicing delusions. By now considered a hopeless case, Charlotte received short shrift from hospital staff: 'Despite an attempt to dissimulate and play the role of a normal person,' doctors wrote, 'she betrayed her basic condition and personality on several occasions evidencing extreme verbal hostility with slight provocation.' Charlotte's continuing truculence also earned her a new label as a 'Personality Pattern Disturbance – Paranoid Personality'. 'Mrs Ross,' they wrote this time:

... seems unable to deal with people except at a level of manipulation and object relations. There seems a total absence of feeling for the other person's point of view or the needs of others. The ability to deal with people beyond a strictly transactional relationship is absent and one doubts at this rate, that it will ever be gained.

Moreover, Essondale doctors seemed increasingly inclined to generalise the pathology to Charlotte's entire family: 'Somehow, [her siblings] seem to get some perverse satisfaction out of her playing field marshall in the various rivalries that exist within this large family ... This would ... appear to be almost more of a family problem than a mere individual one.' They rapidly discharged Charlotte, ironically enough, back into the arms of these same relatives.

Sadly, Charlotte's life continued to spiral inexorably downward after this last official encounter with the provincial mental health system. As late as the early 1970s, a public health officer in another region of British Columbia contacted Riverview Hospital, requesting information about a new patient, Charlotte Ross, who was eking out a marginal existence, living alone in a farmhouse on a $104 per month income of unemployment insurance. According to the inquiry, the patient was afflicted with 'many problems, both physical and mental'. From there the trail finally goes cold. The files contain nothing further about Charlotte Ross' subsequent fate, although a check of the provincial Vital Events records[25] reveals that she was probably still alive as of the early 1980s.

In the end, it can perhaps be argued that Charlotte's web was at least partially of her own weaving. Certainly, from the standpoint of medico-legal officialdom, Charlotte's downfall was best understood as a cautionary tale about the ravages of a disordered mind, the perils of a woman's promiscuity, and the fate that awaited

---

25 The site URL is www.bcarchives.gov.bc.ca/textual/governmt/vstats/v_events.htm.

those misguided or diseased female mental patients who failed to yield to the reasoned ministrations of therapeutic science.

However, such an account – replicated again and again, with endless overtones, throughout the historical clinical files of female mental patients in British Columbia, as elsewhere – represents at best a partial and refracted rendering of women's experiences with the state's institutional psychiatric apparatus. In the case of Charlotte Ross and others like her, the attribution of legal troubles to a woman's internal medico-moral deficiency was a convenient means of explaining, and explaining away, publicly and privately aberrant conduct that, in various ways, threatened to sunder the gendered social fabric. In this sense, the psy experts contributed to the pacification of women, as they continue to do in this new century (Becker, 1997; Chesler, 1972; Raitt and Zeedyk, 2000; Russell, 1995; Ussher, 1992), by segregating women's troubles from the world that engulfed them and fueled their anguish. In endeavouring to obliterate context, and therefore meaning, from the erratic, subversive, violent thoughts and deeds of these dually mad and bad women, professional knowledge workers played a crucial role in the perpetuation of the gender hierarchy (as they did with other axes of racial, ethnic, class, generational and sexual stratification).

At the same time, Charlotte Ross' melancholy tale graphically reveals just how tenuous, and open to challenge, were these psychiatric lines of demarcation between defect and reason, madness and sanity, good and evil. Indeed, if Charlotte did leave behind a legacy, it resides in the fallacies, hypocrisies and contradictions that she managed to expose in the state's relentless efforts, through its public mental health enterprise, to domesticate 'criminally insane' women such as her. That she ultimately spiraled downward into a near-certain oblivion in no way diminishes Charlotte Ross' exceptional capacity – despite her status as a reputed 'madwoman' and 'murderess' – to contest the androcentric, normalising practices of constituted medico-legal authority throughout those many lost years.

Chapter 5
Women's Misery: Continuing Pigeonholes into the 21st Century
Hannah Lerman

5.1   Introduction

Some time within the past 20 years, the part of the practice of psychotherapy that is a business has changed radically. Today, we must do more than simply respond to whatever distress or trauma our clients bring to us. In order for them to receive reimbursement for their treatment we must also provide a diagnosis to the powers that be (insurance companies and Health Maintenance Organizations (HMOs)), whether or not this knowledge is relevant to our immediate relationship to the person we are seeing. The diagnosis must be one formally listed in the most current version of the Diagnostic and Statistical Manual of Mental Disorders (DSM) published periodically by the American Psychiatric Association since 1952. Currently there is DSM-IV (published in 1994 and re-issued, with minimal text revisions and no changes in diagnostic nomenclature, as DSM-IV-TR in 2000), and we are looking ahead to DSM-V (scheduled for release by 2010).

Diagnosis as it has evolved in the mental health field refers to the process of classification and labelling in determining whether an individual is suffering from a specific disorder. There is an implication that the diagnosis will, among other purposes, help the clinician determine appropriate treatment. The process of assigning labels depends on the assessor who evaluates facts about the person being examined and then arrives at conclusions based on some set of suppositions. We know from history that professional assumptions have often been based on beliefs that do not have a factual basis and that have not considered the context of gender and other cultural factors (Lerman, 1996). Those who have formulated the system, primarily men, are often far removed from and ignorant about the context and lives of the persons to whom they assign labels.

Although mental health diagnosis has been around in one form or another since the beginning of recorded history, the practice has only been well systematised and formalised in the United States since the middle of the 20th century. The definition of women by men has long been a major component within diagnostic systems and has only recently been challenged in any major form. The current status of women, although still far from perfect, changed drastically during the twentieth century but many carryovers from past views remain entrenched within mental diagnostic systems.

This chapter provides a brief overview of mental diagnostic systems through a feminist lens. I begin with a discussion of the DSM and how feminists have both challenged and attempted to rework this diagnostic tool. I then describe and assess the potential usefulness of other classification systems.

5.2 The DSM and mental health diagnosis

To get back to our current clinical situation, our client's distress may be major or minor. It may respond to therapeutic listening and other techniques over a brief time frame, and it may even fall within what we personally would consider to be the normal range of emotion and experience but, of course, no one really knows what normal is, how it relates to the context of any person's life (ie, what is normal for them) and, perhaps more importantly, whether our vantage point (life experience, professional experience, mode of interviewing, individual biases and prejudices) actually brings us even close to appropriate information.

We mental health professionals thus work within a paradox. We have to describe and diagnose whatever deviates from the mythical normal, yet there are many definitions of what normal is (Lerman, 1996). The current thinking in American psychiatry, incorporated into the DSMs, is that abnormality has something to do with the experience of distress along with some degree of dysfunction in some aspect of functioning (Wakefield and Spitzer, 2003). In DSM-IV-TR, the definition of mental disorder is 'clinically significant behavior or psychological syndrome or pattern that occurs in an individual and is associated with present distress or disability (in areas of functioning) or with a significantly increased risk of suffering, death, pain, disability, or an important loss of freedom' (American Psychiatric Association, 2000, p xxxi). The authors of DSM-IV-TR recognise, however, that distress and some degree of disability can exist without a disorder. Even psychiatrists understand that people may come to a therapist to deal with something, such as grief, that can involve both distress and disability, but which everyone agrees is *not* a disorder. In addition, some labelled disorders may involve neither distress nor disability.

These two factors, however, do contribute a major part of the definition used in DSM-IV-TR. This manual is the bible of the mental health field, now used as well in medical, psychiatric, insurance and forensic arenas. Much has changed since the original publication of DSM-I in 1952, most importantly the greater inclusion of behaviours and proliferation of diagnoses, as well as the elimination of psychoanalytic conceptualisations about etiology. During the past 50 years, we have also accumulated some greater degree of knowledge about human behaviour (although still only a dropful in a bucket) and our society has changed some of its attitudes about mental disorder. These developments have affected diagnosis in many ways. Meanwhile, the usage of diagnostic labels has expanded far beyond the mental health system itself.

A psychiatric resident once replied to my questioning something he had said about a patient in the Los Angeles County Hospital Psychiatric Unit, where I then worked, with 'Freud said ...', relying on this invocation as religious fundamentalists do on the Bible. More recently, I have heard psychologists refer to the diagnoses of the DSM-IV-TR in a similar fashion, indicating that because a particular person (usually a woman) meets three out of four or two out of three criteria listed for a diagnosis, she *is* A Schizophrenic or, more usually in the current climate, A Bipolar. This unreflective labelling process can perhaps be sometimes excused as shorthand for communication purposes, but I think that too often it reflects a mechanistic view of the world that does not recognise individuality and the context of the person involved.

If there is no other value to knowing the history of diagnostic classifications, and how diagnosis and the conceptualisation of mental illness have evolved over time (Lerman, 1996), one can learn that diagnoses are human devices (often literally man-made) which are changeable and subject to myriad influences, errors and political pressures. There are not and never have been any external criteria against which a diagnosis can be measured. Do the paranoid thoughts of a criminal gang member or refugee from terror constitute a mental disorder or are they the normal, even expected, behaviours for these circumstances? The answers to these and other similar questions are always culturally, even politically bound. There is no way to answer them in a so-called objective scientific manner, although the creators and proponents of the DSMs pretend to do so.

The DSM-IV-TR was designed to be atheoretical and the descriptions of most of the disorders listed in it deliberately say nothing about etiology (one exception is the diagnosis of Post Traumatic Stress Disorder, which will be discussed later). Although psychiatrists tout the reliability of the disorders listed (Kendall, 2002), others disagree (Kirk and Kutchins, 1995; Kutchins and Kirk, 1997). Many other aspects of the diagnostic classification system have also been questioned, such as the overlap and specificity of diagnoses, but seldom has the question of who defines the presence of distress and/or disability been made or posed.

In my book about the impact of psychiatric classification on women's misery (Lerman, 1996), I indicated that the authority of the examiner was the first (and I think, most important) filter through which diagnoses are made. Since the examiner is the primary source for interaction with many aspects of society (regardless of the actual diagnostic system used), what happens at the examiner level deserves much more attention than it has heretofore received. Other feminists (most recently Suyemoto, 2002; Webster, 2002) have observed that the person and authority of the examiner are significant factors in the application of diagnostic schema, but this dynamic does not appear to be acknowledged within the classification mainstream. Although gender and ethnic/racial biases in diagnosis have also been noted (Kaplan, 1983; Landrine, 1992; Loring and Powell, 1988; Pavkov, Lewis and Lyons, 1989), these elements have rarely been considered by those who work on diagnostic classification.

A recent article by Kim and Ahn 'demonstrated strong converging evidence that despite the fact that they have a well-known atheoretical manual, clinicians nonetheless use their own theories when reasoning about mental disorders' (2002, p 471). In other words, the person who does the diagnosing with all the educational, personal, gender, hierarchical baggage that he (used advisedly) carries is the primary instrument through which diagnoses are made. We have not yet come to terms with the fact that the actual diagnoses given depend upon the person giving the diagnosis and, therefore, depend in large measure upon the mental schema held by psychiatrists and psychologists, most of whom implicitly if not explicitly accept the patriarchal mental health structure. In some senses, then, the changes in labels from one DSM to the next are somewhat irrelevant because most diagnoses are individually, even idiosyncratically, based and are practically never challenged or subjected to any reliability check.

According to Blashfield and Draguns (1976), labels are necessary for five general purposes. First, one must be able to share a common language in order to communicate with other professionals. Jargon, in any field, is a shorthand way to communicate. Secondly, Blashfield and Draguns suggest that labels facilitate information retrieval. In the present day, in which searching is done by computer, a common language in the form of keywords makes information sharing easier. Thirdly, labels at least theoretically enable us to describe similarities and differences among people. Fourthly, under ideal circumstances (although only rarely in mental health practice), different labels may lead to different treatments, and labels can be made part of the predictive process. Fifthly, labels are assumed to be useful in theory formation. While Blashfield and Draguns argue that changes in classification lead to better theory, we see little evidence of this effect in the mental health arena.

After I looked at Blashfield and Draguns' list of purposes, I suggested three others (Lerman, 1996). I asked that a classification system have clinical usefulness. This criterion is difficult to gauge. Perhaps it is even difficult to implement. As previously mentioned, clinicians in reality seem to use their own entrenched systems (Kim and Ahn, 2002) rather than what is in the next newly developed manual. I also suggested that labels have great usefulness in communication with third parties (Lerman, 1996). The need for diagnoses by insurance companies, among other institutions, is a very good example of this application, although the current system does not facilitate communication among groups of mental health professionals from different backgrounds and theoretical orientations.

I did note, however, that labels contribute to the comfort levels of professionals. This factor is rarely acknowledged but I think that it is a very important component of the need to label (see Nunnally, 1975 for an early discussion of this point). When you can label, you can, if you have a mind to do so, separate yourself from the 'sick' person. One of the most important things that clinical professionals need to recognise – and unfortunately they often don't – is that a person is a person first, long before (s)he acquires a label, as well as afterwards. Feminists, in general, seem to have a better grasp of this idea than do others. Laura Brown (1994) eloquently discussed the individual human qualities with which the best feminist therapists approach the need to diagnose (*not* label) their clients in order to help them deal with their distress.

Feminist clinicians have relied heavily on the Post Traumatic Stress Disorder (PTSD) diagnosis since DSM-III was published by the American Psychiatric Association in 1980. The advent of PTSD enabled us to identify and make sense of the distress our clients presented to us without having to pathologise the women themselves, since it was (and is) the only major diagnosis that could be used for normal people reacting normally to abnormal circumstances. PTSD is the only major diagnosis that mentions etiology. It is diagnosed as a result of extreme external stressors and trauma on an individual. Its symptoms can be quite variable, including depression, anxiety, dissociation and personality changes which are sometimes indistinguishable from the disorders with these specific labels. In order to differentiate its symptoms from those of other diagnostic labels, one must learn about the person's contextual history. In recent years, the relationship between chronic abuse, both personal and cultural, and the development of personality as it is supposedly exemplified in the Axis II diagnoses (see below) is finally being explored and studied (Carlson *et al*, 2001; Friedman *et al*, 2002; MacMillan *et al*, 2001; Naar-King *et al*, 2002; Roelofs *et al*, 2002; Roy, 2002; Sansone, Gaither and Songer, 2002; Soloff, Lynch and Kelly, 2002; Van Houdenhove *et al*, 2001). Many feminists, among them Judith Herman (1992a, b), have discussed the problems raised by diagnosing women with those labels.

A side note about the Axis II diagnoses, first established in DSM-III (American Psychiatric Association, 1980), is in order here. These diagnoses are supposed to represent longstanding characterological aspects of behaviour rather than symptom disorders. The number of such personality disorders listed, and their respective names, have varied somewhat through DSM-III, DSM-III-R, DSM-IV and DSM-IV-TR (American Psychiatric Association, 1980, 1987, 1994 and 2000). Feminist clinicians battled against the proposed incorporation of Masochistic Personality Disorder (later Self-Defeating Personality Disorder) (Caplan, 1987a; Carmen, 1985; Rosewater, 1987) into DSM-III-R. In addition to arguments that the listed characteristics could result from undiagnosed abuse (ie, questions not asked) and from self-effacing behaviours that are well socialised into women's psyches, Lenore Walker (1985) also disputed that the behaviour in question was characterological. As Walker observed, the behaviours changed when women's situations changed (ie, women who might fit this diagnosis when with abusive domestic partners would frequently act differently once they were on their own).

The Borderline Personality Disorder (BPD), however, is the most problematic of all those listed on Axis II, especially as a diagnosis for women. Of the many diagnoses, BPD is the most stigmatising. The focus for therapists (and examiners) is on the difficulties of helping those highly labile emotional women who react unpredictably to persons who try to work with them. When a history of abuse is not considered, these women are often seen as different from their examiners, as making therapists' lives difficult and as being generally unlikable and obnoxious. If, in contrast, practitioners could recognise that these women are reacting to traumatic histories, they might then see these women as distressed and attempting to cope with their abusive experiences. As a result, they may be less inclined to react judgmentally and separate themselves from these women. The patients and their symptoms could be placed along an abuse continuum that could even include some more minor abuse experienced in the lives of potential helpers. The women would be viewed as being more human and their behaviour understandable and, therefore, more accessible to being helped.

Not for any of the reasons mentioned above, but instead primarily because of the difficulty in clearly distinguishing the symptomatology of one personality disorder from another (First *et al*, 2002), there is some movement in psychiatric circles to do something about the Axis II personality disorders for DSM-V, although it is not yet clear what forms these changes might take.

Trying to work within the DSM framework, Lenore Walker (1986) first suggested a category of disorders she envisioned as falling somewhere between the Axis II personality disorders and the PTSD diagnosis. She suggested a category of abuse disorders, which she saw as more pervasive than PTSD but connected less to what could be called core personality than are the personality disorders themselves. She tentatively suggested that persons with these situationally derived disorders:

could be seen to have disturbances in the nature of the reinforcement (ie, blunted affect, dissociation so as not to feel pain, disturbance in sexual pleasure, etc), in the reinforcement source (ie, self-mutilation, uncontrollable sexual abuse from father, love from father, uncontrollable physical abuse from husband, love from husband, abuse of others) and different instrumental styles such as passive, active, or mixed types which could produce passivity in some battered women, aggression in abusive mates, or aggression in battered women who abuse their children or abusive partners (Walker, 1986, p 17).

Walker (1986) suggested that pervasive and seemingly enduring symptoms would be apparent as long as the individual faced the threat of potential danger.

Laura Brown (1987) took these ideas even further. She advocated a category of oppression artifact disorders, which she thinks is needed to:

take into account the life-time learning experiences of living in a sexist, racist, homophobic, ageist, and otherwise oppressive cultural context. Most individuals who are not securely ensconced within a culturally valued group (eg, white, upper-middle class heterosexual able-bodied young males) will have repeated exposure throughout their lifetime to the overt expressions of such oppression. Depending on the particular context, the penalties for failure to respond correctly can vary from annoying (being verbally harassed on the street for simply being female) to life-threatening (being raped for simply being female). Women, people of color, sexual minorities, disabled people, and elders all may experience a social and interpersonal context of forced choice in which the adoption of certain patterns of response, and certain perceptions of self allow for an easier fit with an oppressive society (Brown, 1987, pp 12–13).

Feminist thinking about diagnostic issues has not ceased since these proposals have been raised. Critiques of existing theories and systems continue to be made. Suyemoto (2002) summarised the criticisms thusly:

1 They use male norms, goals and ideas of health.

2 They examine and evaluate the individual in relative isolation from the social context.

3 They fail to adequately recognize social influences and socialization.

4 They fail to recognize the influence of external systemic and structural forces and the effects of power, privilege and oppression.

5 They frequently fail to attend to the sociohistorically situated aspect of theory development (eg, the basic acceptance of the inferiority of women) and address changes in time and context.

6 They fail to address cultural influences and relativity. assuming an ethnocentric stance of universal applicability (p 71).

Ballou, Matsumoto and Wagner (2002) also have recently described a comprehensive theory of human nature which, while not related directly to diagnostic classification, nevertheless encompasses the many realms that impact on an individual's experience. They view their system as an ecological one. In building their system, they considered many sources, including feminist psychology, feminist therapy, critical psychology, liberation psychology, multiculturalism, and ecopsychology. The dimensions they describe (Macro, Exo, Micro and Individual) include subdivisions which parallel (although they greatly elaborate upon) the six physical and five socioemotional factors I have previously elucidated (Lerman, 1996). Figure 5.1 describes the factors I described (Lerman, 1996), the convoluted intertwined mixture I see them caught up in, and the effects of the passage of time on how psychopathology is diagnosed.

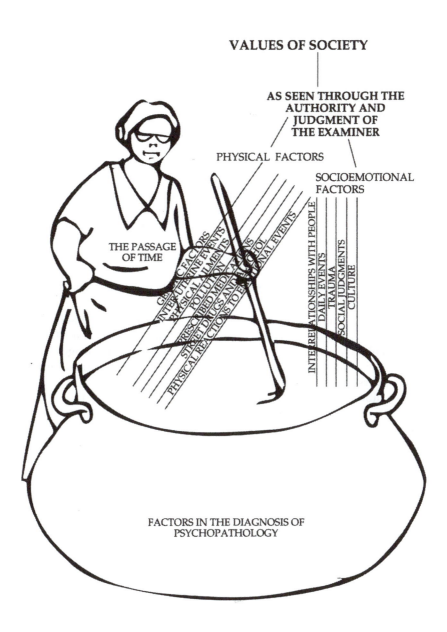

FIGURE 5.1

In my book, I provided more detailed descriptions of genetic factors, intrauterine events, physical ailments, the effects of living in a polluted world, the effects of medications, street drugs and alcohol, and of physical reactions to emotional events – as well as the fact that we are affected by our inter-relationships with people, daily events, trauma, social judgments, culture and the passage of time (Lerman, 1996). I see all of these factors as affecting our behaviour. At this moment, we still do not know enough about the extent and degree to which any of them are involved in any particular case. It is eminently clear, however, that all of those listed under socioemotional factors, as well as those factors that impose the values of society by means of the authority and judgment of the examiner, have previously been insufficiently emphasised, explored, or perhaps even named.

Figure 5.2 is from Ballou, Matsumoto and Wagner (2002) and in a multi-dimensional way deals with similar factors.

The DSM-IV (American Psychiatric Association, 1994) was not a radical departure from the DSM-III-R (American Psychiatric Association, 1987) and therefore generated relatively little direct comment. As noted above, since its publication, and its revised release as DSM-IV-TR in 2000, plans are now underway for development of the next edition (DSM-V) which is due to be published before 2010. To that end, the American Psychiatric Association has published *A Research Agenda for DSM-V* (Kupfer, First and Regier, 2002). Although this book contains many proposals for actual changes in diagnostic format – and even conceptualisation of diagnostic classification, and occasionally some sensitivity to the concerns which feminists and others have raised (see, for example, Rounsaville *et al*, 2002) – our words do not seem to have penetrated far into the world of American diagnostic classifiers.

Indeed, from all such discussions, one generally would be unable to glean that we actually know comparatively little about mental illness and, for that matter, about psychological functioning in general. With increased knowledge of the brain and new brain imaging techniques, especially what has been learned through our growing understanding of how certain medications affect the brain, we have come to know a little more than we previously did. The pendulum which had swung from physical causation in the early 20th century to psychoanalytic conceptualisations shortly thereafter is now, in this new century, largely swinging back to accounts of mental illness that emphasise its physiological underpinnings – albeit with a difference. We now know, for example, that traumatic psychological events have the potentiality of physically altering aspects of the brain, and thus that nature/nurture is not a dichotomy but, instead, a very intricate interaction and feedback system. In the interest of completeness, therefore, context – broadly defined – must be included in every aspect of every discussion of diagnosis and classification.

5.3 Alternatives to the DSM

The mental health disorders system formulated by American psychiatry does not represent the only classification system available. Among others is a system developed by nursing (Schultz and Videbeck, 1994), one developed within social work (Karls and Wandrei, 1992, 1994a, b), and several proposed by psychologists.

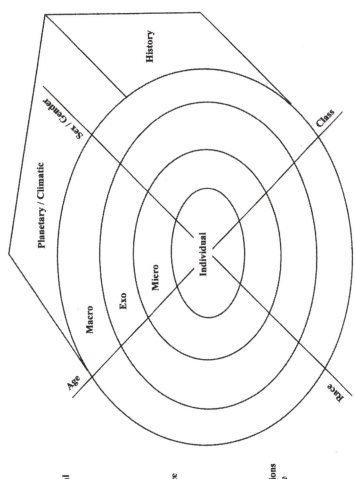

Macro — Global
- Political / Economic
- Environmental
- Distribution of Resources
- Values
- World Views
- Ideologies

Exo — Regional, State, National
- Educational / Political Systems and Structures
- Social Institutions
- Legal / Economic Systems
- Professional / Disciplines
- Religion
- Culture
- Ethnicity

Micro — Immediate face to face interactions and influences
- Family
- School
- Work
- Church
- Neighborhood
- Friends

Individual — Multiple dimensions of the self interacting over time
- Biological
- Emotional
- Cognitive
- Creative
- Social
- Sexual
- Intuitive
- Spiritual

FIGURE 5.2

The North American Nursing Diagnosis Association (NANDA, 1994) saw nursing diagnoses as defining altered patterns of human functioning or problems that could be dealt with by nurses independently but in accord with the medical diagnosis. They developed nine patterns of potential difficulty: (1) exchanging, (2) communicating, (3) relating, (4) valuing, (5) choosing, (6) moving, (7) perceiving, (8) knowing, and (9) feeling. Many of the subdivisions under these patterns relate to physical or potentially physical issues, especially those under exchanging and moving, although some of the moving categories can have psychological/ psychiatric implications (such as activity intolerance, fatigue, sleep pattern disturbance, diversional activity deficit, feeding self-care deficit, bathing/hygiene self-care deficit, dressing/grooming self-care deficit and relocation stress syndrome). All the other patterns deal almost exclusively with at least potentially psychological, environmental and/or social issues. The only subdivision listed under (2) communicating, for example, is impaired verbal communication. This item does not indicate the cause, which, like many other patterns in the system, depends upon the particular medical diagnosis, but could be related to either psychological or physical factors.

Similarly, as noted above, social work has developed a separate system for classifying the problems that are their primary focus. Social workers involved in its formulation wanted their system to provide:

1 common language for all social work practitioners in all settings for describing their clients' problems.

2 a common capsulated description of social phenomena that could facilitate treatment or amelioration of the problems presented by clients.

3 a basis for gathering data required to measure the need for services and to design human services problems and evaluate effectiveness.

4 a mechanism for clearer communication among social work practitioners.

5 and between practitioners and administrators and researchers.

6 a basis for clarifying the domain of social work in the human services field (Karls and Wandrei, 1994a, p 7).

The originators call their basic idea Person-In-Environment (PIE). It describes human behaviour as a result of intrapersonal and interpersonal forces in interaction. They see these forces as originating in 'social performance expectations' arising out of an individual's personal life experience or social context.

PIE is a four-factor system. Factors I and II focus primarily on the social functioning of an individual. Factor I, entitled Social Role Problems, includes provision for listing various social roles, which are grouped into four major categories: family roles, other interpersonal roles, occupational roles, and special life situation roles. Under family roles are six subgroupings: parent, spouse, child, sibling, other family, and significant other. Interpersonal roles include lover, friend, neighbour and other. Occupational roles include five categories: worker-paid, worker-home, volunteer, student and other. The special life situations role subgroupings include consumer, inpatient/client, outpatient/client, probationer/parolee, prisoner, immigrant-legal, immigrant-undocumented, immigrant-refugee and other. For all of these roles, nine types of problems might arise, including power, ambivalence, responsibility, dependency, loss, isolation, victimisation, mixed and others. Each of these can be measured according to severity, duration and level of coping skills.

Factor II, entitled Environmental Problems, uses five subsystems: economic, educational, legal, health, and social and affectional. These also can be rated for severity and duration. Factor III, Mental Disorders, is used to report diagnoses on axes I and II of the DSM. Factor IV, entitled Physical Disorders, reports information gathered from relevant medical sources (Karls and Wandrei, 1992).

PIE is problem oriented and it does not, in itself, label. It deals very explicitly with the context of the individual being diagnosed, without preconceived ideas about etiology. It is purely descriptive. I think it has a great deal of potential beyond the field of social work and I would like to see it more widely used. It is my understanding that it is routinely taught to social workers in the United States but that it is not often used in clinical settings.

The profession of psychology itself has made sporadic attempts to develop its own official classification system. For a variety of reasons, not least among them the vast scope of the subject and the difficulty of persuading different theoretical camps to agree, no attempt has gotten very far and most have been quickly aborted. The fact that the issue resurfaces regularly, however, is one sign of the fact that psychology is dissatisfied with the psychiatric DSMs. Psychologists in general have expressed the most displeasure with the atheoreticality and lack of true operationalism in the DSMs.

However, individuals and groups of psychologists have proposed alternative systems. These include the Five Factors Model of Personality (FFM) which has garnered some recent attention (First *et al*, 2002) and Lorna Smith Benjamin's Structural Analysis of Social Behavior (SASB) (Benjamin, 1974). The theoretical underpinnings of FFM are not new. It is based on the early work by McDougall and Thurstone on personality traits, but was brought into the current era by McCrae and John (1992) and Digman (1994). Much of the work on this model has been based on the interpretation of factor analyses, where personality is viewed in terms of five dimensions: neuroticism (N), extroversion (E), openness to experience (O), agreeableness (A) and conscientiousness (C) (Digman, 1994). Its proponents believe they have discovered the basic dimensions of personality and that it:

> could provide a common language for psychologists from different traditions, a basic phenomenon for personality theorists to explain, a natural framework for organizing research, and a guide to the industrial/organizational, and clinical psychologists (McCrae and John, 1992, p 177)

Research (Widiger and Costa, 1994) has demonstrated that neuroticism is more closely related to personality dysfunction than any other attribute. For none of the other traits does an extreme score automatically imply a personality disorder. In addition, the relationship of Axis I disorders to personality remains equally clouded (Widiger and Trull, 1992). The Five Factors Model has a mathematical rather than individual basis and the information it yields about persons seems too limited to be clinically useful. What value it may have seems to be limited primarily to research.

SASB has its roots in the theories of the neo-psychoanalysts who focused on the interpersonal realm. Originally, the concept of interpersonal diagnosis was advanced by Timothy Leary (1957), who developed the Interpersonal Circle, a circular array of behaviour variables built around two axes (love-hate and dominance-submission). Using this and other related models, Lorna Smith Benjamin (1974) developed a system consisting of three grids, within each of which the horizontal axis is affiliation (love-hate) and the vertical axis is interdependence. The diamond shaped grids in Figure 5.3 below relate to three levels of functioning. Two relate to the interpersonal world, one focusing on view of others and the other on view of self. The third applies to intrapsychic aspects of behaving. Assessment is made via self-report or report by significant others. Each spot on a grid represents a point somewhere on a dimension between two poles with a total of 108 categories possible. The long-form grid can be collapsed into a shorter, less elaborate structure.

Benjamin, who functions as a clinician as well as academic, has been developing her system and accumulating data for over 25 years. She believes that the model has useful therapeutic applications and the capacity to deal in a somewhat dimensional fashion with the categories in the DSMs. Her work had some impact upon the descriptions of the Axis II personality disorders in DSM-IV (Benjamin, 1994). Although feminists in general have not studied this system, the idea of dimensionality rather than rigid category seems consonant with feminist thinking, and this system therefore seems potentially useful.

Also interesting is the concept of relational diagnosis (Kaslow, 1996) which is being tentatively considered for inclusion in some fashion in DSM-V (First *et al*, 2002). This system encompasses four broad categories of disorders: disorders of relationships, relationship problems associated with individual disorders, disorders that require relational data for their validation, and individual disorders whose evocation, course, and treatment are strongly influenced by relationship factors. Proponents of this system come primarily from a family therapy background and have concluded that the DSMs are extremely limited when viewed from their perspective. This approach bears watching as its concepts are more fully fleshed out.

We must also remember that, although the American diagnostic system is increasingly being used worldwide, other countries and cultures often formulate diagnosis differently (see Lerman, 1996, for examples).

5.4 Conclusion

Notwithstanding the development of alternative systems, however, few are as comprehensive as the DSM. The prominence and expansion of the DSM into more and more aspects of society, and across cultures and nations, have inhibited the growth, development and usage of these other systems. Whatever their potential may be, at present these various options do not offer any practical alternatives to the diagnostic system that pervades our mental health institutions, except for the degree to which aspects of them may become incorporated into the DSM itself.

Feminists need, however, to maintain their pressure on mainstream psychiatry through thoughtful analyses, critiques and development of alternative theoretical

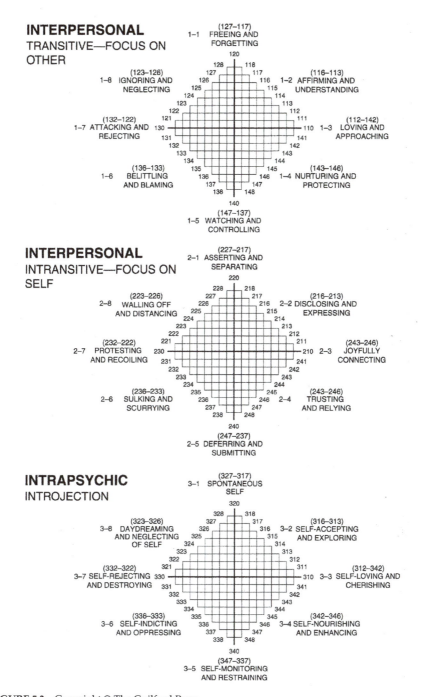

FIGURE 5.3   Copyright © The Guilford Press

systems. I particularly recommend an upcoming discussion of the challenges facing feminist therapy by Mary Ballou (in press). It is not sufficient to work on sensitising members of the mental health professions to gender issues, as we have been doing for many years. Feminists must also work on increasing our representation in the seats of power of our various professions, so that we can influence the official system that is usually devised by the most conservative among us. Simultaneously, we must maintain our own efforts to popularise the alternate systems which do exist, while continuing to build and refine our own thinking on diagnostic matters.

Chapter 6
Sex Bias in Psychiatric Diagnosis and the Courts[1]

Paula J Caplan

6.1   Introduction

Despite the efforts of Second Wave feminists since the late 1960s to eradicate sexism, North America remains profoundly sexist in significant ways. In a sexist society, anything that *can* be used against women *will* be used against women (Caplan, 1993), and the legal system is rife with manifestations of sexism. In this chapter, I shall provide examples of this sexism as they relate directly or indirectly to criminal matters in particular, although some domestic matters will be mentioned, especially when they also include criminal aspects. It is important to do this because the widespread belief that sexism has been eradicated can blind one to the power that bias against women still has in the legal system. As illustrations of this, examples of the operation of sexism within some actual criminal cases, including juvenile crimes, will be given, and the matter of sexism's relationship to failures to bring certain charges or to prosecute will be addressed.

Intimately intertwined with this sexism is the matter of psychiatric diagnosis, for it is often (though of course not always) through the ways that psychiatric categories are created, named, and used that sexism takes its devastating effects. Feminist psychologist Phyllis Chesler's courageous book, *Women and Madness*, was a pioneering revelation of the ways that virtually any kind of behaviour, when enacted by women, had been considered evidence that women warranted labels of mental illness (Chesler, 1972). Unfortunately, the essence and much of the substance of this book remains relevant today. In this connection, it is important to know that, for decades, the whole process of creating the 'Bible' of mental health professionals, the diagnostic manual called the *Diagnostic and Statistical Manual of Mental Disorders* (DSM), has involved a great deal of art, intuition, and political expediency but little high-quality science (Caplan, 1996). This is the case despite the aggressive, well-financed marketing of each of the frequent new editions of the DSM as scientifically grounded that is done by its publisher, the American Psychiatric Association. As in so many arenas, an unwarranted aura of science in fact provides fertile ground for the growth and development of all forms of bias, including sexism (Caplan and Caplan, 1999; Caplan and Cosgrove, 2004).

---

1   Some portions of this chapter are slightly revised versions of an article in *The Journal of Trauma Practice* (Caplan, 2004a).

6.2 Case studies of sexism and psychiatric diagnosis in the courts

6.2.1 Some pertinent research

A study that I conducted with colleagues a quarter-century ago at the Toronto Family Court Clinic (TFCC) (Caplan *et al*, 1980) offered evidence regarding a clear pattern of the effects of society's prescriptions and proscriptions with respect to violent and other 'deviant' behaviour. In cases referred to the clinic by the Toronto Family Court, significantly higher percentages of girls than boys found themselves charged for status offences or other crimes in which no one but the offender was hurt; examples of such offences were truancy, drug use, and prostitution.[2] In contrast, significantly higher percentages of boys than girls faced charges of theft or breaking and entering. This result was consistent with the stereotyping and role-prescription for females to direct aggression against themselves rather than against others while boys were allowed, and sometimes even encouraged, to express aggression rather than turning it inward.[3] This pattern was also reflected in the information gathered using the symptom checklist which was the standard intake form used at the initial interview for adolescents who were referred to the clinic (Caplan *et al*, 1980); that is, with respect to a wide range of behaviour other than that for which they had been brought to court, the girls were more likely than the boys to show symptoms that were harmful only to themselves and the boys to show symptoms that were harmful to others or to property. It is important to note that, even in the population studied, which was considered to be doubly atypical (some would say 'deviant'), in that they were both charged in court and also referred to the clinic because they were suspected of having family or individual psychological problems, the power of sex-role expectations was persistent and great: even within their atypical behaviour, these teenagers tended to be conforming rather than deviant with respect to behaviour considered sex-appropriate. This study is some years old but, in cases since then, I have usually found this pattern to persist.

The results of the TFCC study are also consistent with the important, qualitative study of women prisoners undertaken by Evelyn Sommers (1995). Sommers found that the women in prison, each of whom she interviewed repeatedly, had had relationships with their parents or caregivers that were troubled, sometimes even abusive. These early relationships left the women emotionally vulnerable, with the result that they often tried to find ways to feel better or more empowered that were feminine-stereotypic, such as trying to appeal to others by offering them gifts that they had stolen. Many, after being abused and abandoned as adults, became addicted to drugs or alcohol, and their desperate need for these substances was often what led to the crimes for which they were imprisoned. Like the girls in the TFCC study, their crimes tended to be, solely or primarily, harmful only to

---

2   A larger *number* of boys were referred for status offences, but a higher *proportion* of girls than of boys received these charges.

3   Caplan (1973) discovered that people found it more disturbing for girls than boys to display acting-out behaviour. Caplan (1977) reported that withdrawn behaviour in boys and acting-out behaviour in girls were considered cause for concern more so than the reverse, probably because withdrawn behaviour is inconsistent with the traditional masculine sex-role, and acting-out behaviour is inconsistent with the female sex-role.

themselves. Thus, the reasons for their entry into criminal activity, and the forms that activity took, were part of the fabric of sex-role stereotyping.

Another manifestation of sexism in relation to criminal activity is that people tend to make very different kinds of judgments about victims of within-family violence when the victims are women than when they are men. Caplan and Walton-Allen (1984) found that, whereas women battered by their husbands are likely to be assumed to be masochistic or to have done something to deserve the attack, such a victim-blaming assumption does not tend to be made about men who are described as having been battered by their wives. This difference in assumptions about motives can lead to very disparate standards of prosecution for domestic violence and for crimes committed in self-defence against such violence, depending on the sexes of victim and perpetrator. Related to this, it has been deeply troubling to see how the courts have usually dealt with women who have been repeatedly abused, often over many years, and who finally use more force than is being used against them at a particular moment, in an attempt to ward off what she reasonably believes is an imminent assault by her abuser. It has often been difficult to persuade judges and juries that these women were acting in self-defence (Chan, 2001, pp 108–49; see also Comack, 1993).

In a recent criminal case of killing in self-defence,[4] a woman with a lifelong history of being sexually, physically and emotionally abused – who had no record of criminal activity, and who had a history of doing all she could to care for her children and to acquire an education in the field of human services – was charged with first-degree murder for killing the man with whom she had been living and who had repeatedly abused her in various ways. It was clear from the records that the woman had a history of serious emotional problems and that she psychologically 'snapped', going into a psychotic state, when the man appeared about to attack her yet again. Further, the records confirmed that she acted in self-defence, grabbed a knife that was near her in the kitchen as she tried to fend him off, and stabbed him once. The knife hit his femoral artery and, despite her three immediate, frantic, pleading phone calls to 911, he bled to death before help arrived. The woman remained utterly out of touch with reality for a long time after his death, and indeed a psychiatrist who saw her in prison diagnosed her as psychotic, as did subsequent therapists she saw. In spite of all of this, the prosecutor charged her with first-degree murder and offered a plea bargain of 20 years in prison.

In another case, a highly publicised civil child custody dispute in Ontario,[5] a divorced couple was involved in a battle over custody of their children, and the mother said that her ex-husband had severely abused her in front of the children. She gave this as one reason why he should not be awarded custody of them. The psychologist who conducted the assessment for this case wrote that the abuse occurred because the woman was a masochist (somehow, presumably, 'needing' to be hurt), and thus the fact of his having abused her was not even questioned and was deemed irrelevant to a decision about his having custody of the children. This case, then, was an example of a situation in which the man was acknowledged to

---

4   For reasons of confidentiality, I cannot give a citation for this case.
5   *Sherrett v Sherrett* (1987) 6 RFL (3d) 172 (Ont CA).

have been abusive but was not criminally charged, and even in the civil case, the importance of his assault on his ex-wife was minimised. Courts often conclude in custody cases that evidence that a man has abused his spouse/partner is irrelevant to the assessment of his parenting abilities, although, in 1990, Peter Jaffe, David Wolfe, and Susan Wilson compellingly demonstrated the utter fallacy of that assumption (see also Caplan, 2000; Boyd, 2003).

6.2.2 Mental health experts' sexism becomes a rights issue

The case of *Sherrett v Sherrett*[6] is important from another standpoint as well. To oversimplify somewhat (but not very much, in fact), in the realm of psychology and psychiatry there are two kinds of theories. One kind tends not to be supported by logic, by responsible interpretation of clinical cases, or by well-done research. The other kind tends to be supported by any or all of these three. With respect to the unsupported theories, it is not surprising that they are often seriously biased against one or more groups – for the advancement of a theory, in the absence of evidence of its soundness, allows ample room for biases to operate. Such is the case with the widespread myth that women enjoy suffering, that they are masochists (Caplan, 1987a, b) – an 'explanatory' concept that is heavily biased against women and used far more often to excuse abuse of women than abuse of men. The excuse is on the grounds that 'masochists' allegedly bring suffering on themselves, consciously or unconsciously, by somehow making other people treat them abusively. There is no solid evidence that anyone enjoys suffering; there are other, well-supported explanations of what leads to the abuse of women and others.

In *Sherrett*, the judge effectively rubber-stamped the psychologist's recommendations that the children be split, with custody of two going to the mother and custody of two going to the father. This case, then, represents a situation where, in the Canadian context, the woman's rights under the Canadian Charter of Rights and Freedoms were infringed.[7] The dismissal of the husband's violence as a concern would probably never have occurred had the sexes been reversed. Consequently, discrimination on the basis of sex was clearly in evidence. Furthermore, no criminal charge was brought against the ex-husband for his assault in this Ontario case. Had the case occurred in the United States, I submit that, according to United States law as well, the woman was denied equal protection, a right that is enshrined in the Bill of Rights of that country's Constitution. According to the US cases of *Loving v Virginia* (1967) and *Palmore v Sidoti* (1984), the courts cannot give legal effect to the kind of prejudice that the court revealed in this case, as other courts have shown in many others like it.

---

6 *Ibid.*

7 According to s 15(1) of the Canadian Charter of Rights and Freedoms, 'Every individual is equal before and under the law and has the right to the equal protection and equal benefit of the law without discrimination and, in particular, without discrimination based on race, national or ethnic origin, colour, religion, sex, age or mental or physical disability.' Constitution Act 1982, RSC 1985, Appendix II, No 44, enacted by the Canada Act 1982 (UK), cl 11.

There are many kinds of cases in which these kinds of constitutional arguments with respect to deprivation of equal protection on the basis of sex could apply. A US case, somewhat different from the Ontario child custody dispute discussed above, involved a mother who had already lost custody of her children. The judge had decided that her wish to homeschool her children was a sign that she was an overinvolved mother. That basis for his decision would not have been likely to be applied to a father who wished to homeschool his children himself. The reason is that even giving care and attention to children, traditionally 'feminine' though those activities are often thought to be, has frequently been pathologised as overinvolvement when carried out by mothers but praised when carried out by fathers (Caplan, 2000).

To the best of my knowledge, this kind of equal rights argument has not been used in this way in court, and it is not clear why. It is to be hoped, however, that such arguments will begin to be made, for the combined power of the mental health system, the public's tendency to be in awe of therapists, and the court system have created an enormous barrier to judges', attorneys', therapists' and laypeople's view of this serious and deeply biased infringement of human rights. Whereas, for instance, it is at least fairly difficult for employers to fail to provide reasonable accommodation for employees who have serious psychological problems, it has been very easy for discrimination against people on the basis of category memberships such as sex, race, or age to go unnoticed as long as it is mediated by mental health experts. Attorneys tend to attack psychologists' and psychiatrists' testimony on a variety of grounds, including specifics of assessment situations or conflicts of interest, but even when they attack on the basis of unsubstantiated claims, the equal rights arguments have not been made. This is a major and serious omission.

6.2.3   Sexism and child sexual abuse

Another manifestation of differential thinking about criminal acts, depending on the sex of victim and perpetrator, has appeared in patterns of public response to news about the sexual abuse of children. When the Second Wave of the feminist movement gave courage to many women who had been victims of child sexual abuse (CSA) to break their silence about the abuse, at first it was fairly widely acknowledged that these stories were, by and large, true – that indeed it was painful to speak up about such things and, for the most part, those who came forward did not do so lightly or without justification. Second Wave authors and activists (eg, Armstrong, 1982; Butler, 1978; Masson, 1984; Rush, 1980; Walker, 1979) not only encouraged people who had been sexually or physically abused or assaulted as children or adults to disclose their experiences but also encouraged mental health professionals to take seriously the frequency and impact of these hidden forms of interpersonal violence (although even now, hardly anyone talks about psychological abuse: Caplan, 1998; Evans, 1993). The overwhelming majority of survivors of CSA are girls and women, and so it was particularly heartening that their reports of abuse were not immediately dismissed as the products of hysteria. However, there was soon a backlash, impelled in no small part by a group that called itself the False Memory Syndrome Foundation (FMSF), which claimed that therapists were misleading large numbers of patients into believing they had been abused as children. This group invented the term 'False Memory Syndrome' and unwarrantedly presented it as though it were a proven psychiatric disorder, even though the existence of this alleged psychiatric entity has never been proven (Caplan, 1994; Freyd, 1996; Olio, 2004).

The False Memory Syndrome Foundation did a great deal of work aimed at discrediting people who said they had been CSA victims. The FMSF made a stunning impact on the public and on the so-called 'justice' system's approach to child sexual abuse. For one thing, the media jumped on the FMSF bandwagon, and soon women (and men) who truly had been abused as children were again afraid to talk about it. Stanton (1997) reported a major shift in the way that sexual abuse was portrayed in four of the most widely read and influential magazines in the US – *Time, Newsweek, People,* and *US News & World Report*. Stanton noted that, while in 1991 more than 80% of coverage in these publications was about stories of sexual abuse survivors, by 1994 more than 80% was about allegedly false accusations. This public questioning of the honesty and integrity of victim/survivors (V/Ss) has had a silencing effect. As lawyer Phillip Zylberberg has observed, for a few years, one had heard in lawyers' discussions and judges' chambers that women and children who said they were sexually abused were probably telling the truth. Suddenly, however, such comments became rare. Lawyers began pouring in droves to seminars about how to use 'False Memory Syndrome' to defend clients who were alleged to have abused children (Zylberberg, personal communication, 1993). Parents began to sue their children's therapists, alleging that the therapists had created 'false memories' of abuse in their patients' minds (Olio, 2004).

Recently, there has come a powerful tide of reports of CSA being committed by priests. It is consistent with the robust health of sexism that these reports have been questioned little or not at all by the same groups and individuals who regularly trashed women who reported CSA (Caplan, 2004a). Naturally, abuse victims of any sex deserve supportive and respectful treatment, but the cases of abuse by priests that have received the vast majority of public (including media) attention have been those involving male survivors. It seems scarcely coincidental that men's reports of having been abused are more likely than women's to be believed (Caplan, 2004a). It is worth noting, too, that homophobia may be a major force that impels the more intense concern about priests' male sexual abuse victims than of their female ones.

The disbelieving of what women say has reached such an alarming level that many family law attorneys with whom I have worked, in both Canada and the United States, have said that they dread having a woman client in a child custody dispute express a fear that their ex-husband might be sexually abusing their children. The reason for their dread is their awareness that many courts give custody to fathers when ex-wives report suspected abuse by those fathers. Such a judicial bias may seem counterintuitive, but the usual reason given is that a woman who accuses her ex-husband of abusing their children is just venomous and is trying to alienate the children from their father (Armstrong, 1982, 1994; Caplan, 2004b). In fact, the late Richard Gardner made a career of testifying to this effect in court after he thought up the term 'Parental Alienation Syndrome' (PAS) and, in essence, claimed that it applied to the kind of situation just described (see, eg, Gardner, 1998).[8] This fabricated entity became a virtually knee-jerk defense for men accused of abuse in the context of a child custody or access dispute. In court cases, mothers are more likely to be alleged by their ex-husbands to have 'PAS' than are fathers by their ex-wives.

This is a particularly disturbing phenomenon in light of research by two Canadian law professors who found that allegations of physical or sexual abuse of their children by mothers were actually *less* likely than such allegations by fathers to be found by courts to be intentionally false: Bala and Schuman (2000) reviewed judges' decisions and found that just 1.3% of female-initiated allegations that their children's father had abused their children were deemed by civil court judges to be intentionally false, compared with 21% when the man initiated such allegations against the children's mother. This pattern is all the more important in light of the finding that mothers were far more likely than fathers to make these allegations (Bala and Schuman, 2000).

The other alleged psychiatric disorder attributed to women in these situations is 'Munchausen's syndrome by proxy', which is described as a pathological need for attention, usually from medical professionals, that leads the person to make false claims that her child is hurt or ill, or even actively to hurt the child or make the child ill and in need of medical care (Allison and Roberts, 1998). When Munchausen's syndrome by proxy is invoked it, too, is used as a defence against claims of the father's abusiveness, on the grounds that the mother is imagining or causing a problem and that the child has not actually been sexually abused.

Thus, as a result of bias against women, not only have many abusers escaped being charged (or even investigated) for sexual abuse, but also the focus has often switched to the mothers of abused children as the alleged source of trouble. The effect is a troubling combination of intermittent invisibility and hypervisibility for women when CSA is involved: on the one hand, women survivors are silenced and rendered invisible because they are so often accused of lying,[9] but, on the other hand, the mothers of child victims of CSA become hypervisible, cast into the spotlight as alleged troublemakers.

In one of the most serious Canadian cases of the latter kind,[10] a woman named Gail Bezaire lost custody of her children because she had substantial evidence that their father was abusing them and said so. After losing custody, Bezaire was so upset about what she feared they were going through that she kidnapped them. Subsequently, she was criminally charged, convicted for the abduction of her

---

8 Despite intense effort on Gardner's part, 'Parental Alienation Syndrome' was never officially recognised by mental health associations as an actual psychiatric syndrome, or included in major diagnostic manuals. Increasingly, United States courts have determined that this concept fails to meet the Daubert rules for scientific evidence (Caplan, 2004b).

9 In Canada, mothers who make complaints about child sexual abuse in custody and access disputes often are disadvantaged by the so-called 'friendly parent rule' that requires a custodial parent to facilitate access of the non-custodial parent to the children.

10 *Bezaire v Bezaire* (1980) 20 RFL (2d) 358 (Ont CA); see also Boyd, 2003, pp 111–12; Crean, 2000.

children and sentenced to probation.[11] Although Bezaire was not jailed, as in many cases of this ilk, it was the mother who became the target of concern about the children's welfare.

Indeed, in the United States, the radical right has used the legal system and the media to create and perpetuate the notion that the most important thing about children and women who report abuse by intimates or strangers is that they have sick needs to portray themselves as victims (eg, Doe, 1993; Freyd and Goldstein, 1998a, b; Hill, 1998). As noted in the beginning of this chapter: *In a sexist society, anything that can be used against women will be used against women* (Caplan, 1993). According to Louise Armstrong (1994), author of one of the two earliest books about incest, *Kiss Daddy Goodnight* (Armstrong, 1982), it is no accident that the backlash swelled when large numbers of white, middle-class men found themselves accused of incest. As illustrated above by the generally respectful, unquestioning response to male victims of CSA by priests, nothing like this large-scale imputing of psychopathology to victims has ever been done to men who are victims of violent, even sexually violent crimes (Caplan, 1987b).

6.3   Reprivatising abuse: out of the courtroom, into the therapist's office

There is another important factor that has drained away much of the energy that earlier went into holding accountable the perpetrators of intimate violence. This factor is the psychologising and even pathologising of the V/S. The squelching of public discussion about the kinds of trauma discussed above, in an important sense, pushed the discussion out of the legal system and back into the private sphere, including into the offices of therapists. What has not been much addressed is the troubling side of what I shall call the current reprivatising of abuse (see also Armstrong, 1994).[12]

It was probably inevitable that in a society as steeped in psychological concepts as ours, intimate violence would come to be regarded as part of the psychotherapist's purview. Of course, some therapists have been helpful to some victims of violence, but why is the reprivatising of the effects of trauma due to abuse a cause for concern? It is because it takes society's focus off the perpetrator, off prevention, and off the political and social factors that lead to these kinds of trauma. Increasingly, even when reports of intimate violence are both true and believed, no charge is filed by police or prosecutors, the perpetrator's culpability is typically ignored, and the focus swings to the victims' real or alleged emotional disturbances. Most of the energy, time, and money used for dealing with the effects of trauma are poured into analysis and treatment of what is regarded as the victim's 'mental illness'. As a result, psychotherapy acquires paramount importance, and one fails to focus on the responsibility and culpability of the abuser (except to note

---

11 'Toronto woman guilty on 5 abduction counts for hiding her children' (1987) *Globe and Mail*, 10 June, p A15; 'Hid children, mother gets probation: outside court, enraged father denies abuse' (1987) *Globe and Mail*, 19 June, p A17.

12 This trend occurred historically as well. For instance, Linda Gordon (1988) has documented the 'reprivatization' of incest in the early 20th century in the US.

when abusers have had difficult childhoods (Caplan *et al*, 1984; Watters *et al*, 1986)), on the abuse of power, on the betrayal of the victim's trust, and on the social arrangements that make abuse so common. In addition, it becomes harder to keep in mind that abuse of children or domestic partners *is a crime*.

Two psychiatric diagnoses have probably been the ones most commonly applied to trauma victims, although the lack of regulation of diagnosis makes it impossible to know for sure (Caplan, 2004a). These are 'Post Traumatic Stress Disorder' (PTSD) and 'Borderline Personality Disorder' (BPD). Many feminist therapists were pleased by the description of PTSD in the DSM-III-R (American Psychiatric Association, 1987), because it included the specification that it was caused by an experience that would be traumatic for anyone, paradoxical though it was that an implicitly 'normal' response would be listed as a mental disorder in a manual of mental disorders. It seemed to be understood that trauma victims could have suffered extreme psychological consequences but not be 'sick' in the sense of having had bizarre or inexplicable reactions, that the focus of PTSD was on the traumatic events and their effects rather than on alleged intrapsychic problems of the individual (Brown, 1994; Carmen, Rieker and Mills, 1984; Courtois, 1999). It was indeed helpful in normalising the flashbacks, hypervigilance, difficulties in concentrating, and so on that so many victims of violence had, and many conscientious therapists accordingly diagnosed V/Ss with PTSD.

Unfortunately, in the next edition of the DSM-IV (1994, 2000), it was specified that traumatic experiences could only be considered to have caused PTSD if 'the person experienced, witnessed, or was confronted with an event or events that involved actual or threatened death or serious injury or a threat to the physical integrity of self or others' (American Psychiatric Association, 2000, p 467). This definitional shift is troubling, because: (1) the criteria seem to exclude people who have experienced verbal and emotional abuse, no matter how severe it might have been; (2) in many instances of sexual abuse the victim's 'physical integrity' was not threatened; and (3) the judgment of what constitutes a threat to physical integrity would be subjective. Becker (2004) has expressed concern that the use of this label in particular detracts 'from the impetus to attack the problem of male-to-female violence on a socio-structural level (Becker, 2000)'.

The 'Borderline Personality Disorder' (BPD) label has often been applied to people who have endured extreme, usually ongoing abuse (Becker, 1997, 2000; Goodwin, Cheeves and Connell, 1990; Herman, Perry and van der Kolk, 1989; Ogata *et al*, 1990; Surrey *et al*, 1990; Weaver and Clum, 1993; Zanarini *et al*, 1989). The BPD diagnosis tends to carry extremely pejorative connotations. It is applied more frequently to women than to men (see Adler, Drake and Teague, 1990; Becker and Lamb, 1994; Fish, 2004), and women diagnosed with BPD are often treated worse than people with other diagnostic labels (Stefan, 1998). In 30 years of clinical experience, I have frequently heard colleagues remark that when they see someone with BPD coming, they want to run fast in the opposite direction. Kaysen (1993) reports that after she discovered that she had been diagnosed with BPD, a psychiatrist told her that BPD 'is what they call people whose lifestyles bother them' (pp 150–51).

Although it is not unusual for people who have been severely abused to be difficult to work with, because they are so often deeply ambivalent about forming relationships and maintaining them, it is not helpful for clinicians to regard these difficulties as though they had sprung, unwarranted, from their patients' heads rather than as understandable responses to victimisation. And clinicians know that it is not only more humane and responsible but also more effective to focus work with troubled people on specific, known causes of their problems – such as abuse – than on presumably somehow individually-produced psychopathology. When clear explanations for the etiology of allegedly individually-produced pathology are not available, the knee-jerk, but often inappropriate and inaccurate, response of too many clinicians has been to assume that the patients' mothers are to blame (Caplan, 2000).

6.4   Why does this happen?

Volumes would be necessary to address the question of how sexism in general arose and why it persists, but suffice it to say that sexism continues to pervade the world of crime and the courts. As society becomes more complex – and as it also becomes increasingly psychologised and psychiatrised, with people expecting that scientific and technological experts will find solutions to everything – judges have increasingly come to rely on scientific evidence as the basis for their decisions. This trend is particularly evident in those most painful cases that involve family violence and child custody. In light of this context, Tobin's (1989) findings – namely, that family court judges in Toronto accepted and implemented 97% of recommendations from psychological assessments in child custody disputes – are therefore scarcely surprising. Further, my experience as an expert witness suggests that these high rates of acceptance are in evidence today in other jurisdictions as well. Mosoff (1995) has observed this tendency not only in Canadian courts but also 'American law that explicitly suggests judicial deferral to psychiatrists in mental health cases' (p 129). It is one thing to ask medical researchers to testify, for instance, about adequate precautions chemical manufacturers ought to take to protect their workers, but it is quite another thing to treat psychological and psychiatric assessments of those charged with crimes, or involved in child custody disputes, as though they were scientifically-based and objective statements of truth.

The two-part problem is that mental health professionals, being human, cannot ever be free from biases, and that many of our methods of conducting both assessments and research are deeply flawed (Caplan and Caplan, 1999). These factors make it all the more important for mental health professionals and social science researchers to be straightforward and forthcoming about our biases and the imperfections in our work (Caplan and Wilson, 1990; Caplan and Caplan, 1999). But such admissions can be disconcerting. After I gave a talk to the Canadian Institute for the Administration of Justice (1993) in which I described these kinds of limitations, one of the most respected law professors in the country looked shaken and asked me: 'If this is true, then how are judges supposed to make their decisions in these kinds of cases?' That was an interesting and important question, because it exposed the way that judges often shift the burden of making judgments onto the shoulders of mental health professionals and social science researchers. Judges want to believe that we can find the truth, because then they can be more confident in making their judgments, but when systematic and systemic biases such as sexism are involved in the ways that such expert witnesses operate, it is particularly important to make these biases transparent.

Although not all mental health professionals introduce bias into judicial decisions in significant ways, it is important to be aware of how they *can* do this. The following is a very recent example from a case in which I was involved.[13] A judge ordered the parents of a toddler to undergo a psychological assessment because each was demanding custody of the child, and because the mother had provided some information supporting her concern that the father might be sexually abusing their daughter. In this case, as in many, no criminal charge was brought against the father, in spite of persuasive evidence that he had committed this abuse. Indeed, here is what the psychologist did: he administered a huge battery of psychological tests to the parents and had them scored by a company that used a computer program to produce a very large number of analyses and interpretations of the psychological functioning of each parent. He wrote a lengthy letter to the court, in which he included many statements that came straight from that company's report to him. In the report, not only did the concern about the father's possibly having committed the crime of child sexual abuse become almost invisible but, in fact, the mother's grounds for concern about this abuse were transformed into evidence that she was a bad parent for 'overreacting', being 'hysterical', being 'manipulative', and so on. Nothing in the psychologist's report even began to address seriously the question of whether or not the father *might* possibly be abusive. In fact, nearly everything he wrote about the father was good, and nearly everything he wrote about the mother was bad. Had the psychologist's report gone to the judge, and had the psychologist been allowed to testify without there being any scrutiny of the basis for his report, the judge would quite likely have granted custody to the father. Indeed, the psychologist was known to be a favourite of judges, to the point where attorneys for clients who were negatively portrayed in his reports were reluctant to challenge him on cross-examination.

In the case in question, however, the mother's attorney asked that the psychologist produce the report from the computer-scoring company, as well as both parents' answer sheets and test scores. Brief examination of this material showed the following: many of the parents' scores on various test scales were virtually identical and, as a result, many of the computer company's interpretive statements for the two parents were identical. However, the psychologist had reported those interpretive statements only in relation to the father when the statements were positive and only in relation to the mother when they were negative. Without the mother's lawyer's careful scrutiny – something that is unfortunately all too rare for busy attorneys – the psychologist's report would have led away from any potential trail of criminal investigation of the father, not to mention leading toward him for purposes of granting custody.

13 For reasons of confidentiality, I cannot give a citation for this case.

Referring to the great vulnerability in child custody disputes of mothers who have been psychiatrically labelled, Canadian attorney Judith Mosoff (1995) has written that:

> Women [who have been classified as mentally ill in the mental health system] tend to lose their children on the basis of psychiatric opinion. Because the legal model of a child protection proceeding is somewhat peculiar, and the disciplines of psychology and psychiatry so pertinent, judges tend to defer to the opinions of psychiatrists on the substantive matters and intervene where the authorities appear to have flagrant disregard for legal process. In effect, judges share their decision-making with psychiatrists by largely accepting psychiatric opinion on the substance and retaining the power to rule on breaches of procedure. Where the mother retains or regains custody the order almost always includes the condition of the ongoing watchful eye of a psychiatrist.

> In trying to maintain or regain custody of their children, women with a psychiatric diagnosis are faced with an implicit presumption against their fitness ... As a result, women with mental health histories continue to lose their children to the state through some combination of moral suasion, legal process, consent, and threat, all woven with the opinions of particular mental health personnel (p 142).

6.5 Where to go from here

Sexism – like racism, classism, ageism, heterosexism, and other forms of bias not addressed here – is so embedded in North American culture that it often goes unnoticed. Sometimes it may not occur to us that, in the system we charge with protecting us and ensuring that justice is done, there may be powerful biases at play. When we do become aware of such bias, it can be a painful and frightening experience, but awareness is the foundation, the *sine qua non*, for change. Therefore, it is essential for mental health professionals, social science researchers, judges, attorneys, police officers, and laypeople to be on the watch for signs of bias, to raise it as an important subject for discussion, and to search for ways to make its operation more transparent so that it can be challenged and, ideally, eradicated.

Chapter 7
Homelessness, Mental Disorder, and Penal Intervention: Women Referred to a Mobile Crisis Intervention Team[1]

Daphné Morin, Shirley Roy, Marielle Rozier and Pierre Landreville

The last 20 years have seen dramatic changes in the social response to conflicts that often appear in urban public space, straddling the line between madness and dangerousness. Among these changes are the appearance of poorly defined problems, responses by new categories of professionals, and new intervention strategies developed in the heat of the action. Intervention to deal with 'boundary' problems crosses fields of expertise, normative frameworks, and symbolic universes, as witnessed by the numerous hybrid classifications for disorders (eg, the antisocial personality, in which correctional and psychiatric aspects are intertwined); 'catch-all' psycho-social nomenclature (social maladjustment; social dysfunction; lack of cognitive, behavioural or emotional skills, etc) (Otero, 2000, 2003); and even collective urban representations of risk (the homeless former psychiatric patient, the junkie, the street kid, etc).

At the junction of different fields, the tensions evoked are often laid at the psychiatry-justice boundary, whereas what distinguishes the groups involved in these conflicts is their extreme poverty, social isolation and homelessness. The prevalence of this orientation can be explained by a set of changes operating in conjunction: transformations in the representations of mental illness and its treatment, causing a shift in the living environment of people formerly cared for in psychiatric hospitals (Brown, 1985; Castel, 1981; Comité de la Santé Mentale du Québec, 1997; Dear and Wolch, 1987; Dorvil, 1988, 1997; Sicot, 2001; Steadman and Morrissey, 1987); major reforms to the laws governing involuntary civil commitment, marked by a tendency to base enforcement of the law exclusively on the criterion of dangerousness (Barreau du Québec, 1998; Dallaire *et al*, 2001; Hiday, 1988; Holstein, 1993; Robertson, 1987; Warren, 1982); and changes in the role of the state, including cuts to health, housing, and employment assistance budgets (Castel, 1995; Ulysse and Lesemann, 2004). The community, so often invoked in these reforms, is seen as both means (the response of choice; the caring, restorative community) and end (membership, inclusion), but it is crumbling or becoming inaccessible for social groups rendered increasingly vulnerable as a result of these transformations.

Against this backdrop, both the opportunities for confrontation and the visibility of the conflicts increased, with a significant number of these situations being placed

1 This research was supported by a grant from the Fonds pour la formation de chercheurs et l'aide à la recherche (FCAR) under its 'Soutien aux équipes de recherche' (support for research teams) programme. We would like to thank all of our collaborators: the UPS-J team of the CLSC des Faubourgs for their commitment to this project, and, in particular, Louise Riopel and Hélène Brouillet for their wise comments and their confidence in us.

at the psychiatry/justice system junction. Because of their availability and their enforcement power, the police found themselves playing a major role in referral of these cases, but the available options appeared increasingly limited and inadequate: the homeless housing network, hospital emergency services or criminalisation (Borum *et al*, 1998; Cardinal, 2001; Laberge, Landreville and Morin, 2000a; Laberge and Morin, 1995; Menzies, 1987; Teplin, 2001; Watson, Segal and Newhill, 1993; Way, Evan and Banks, 1993). New intervention models then emerged throughout the Anglo-American world: models situated at the interface between psychiatry and the justice system, and targeting isolated, vulnerable, destitute groups. The earliest of these models claimed to offer an alternative (diversion)[2] to the criminalisation of mental illness. More recent ones have extended their reach by viewing the problem in an intersectorial perspective (Badger *et al*, 1999; Laberge, Landreville and Morin, 2000b; Schnapp, Nguyen and Johnson, 1996; Lamberti, 1999). Acknowledging how systems functioning independently from each other[3] help to maintain the 'revolving door' between hospital psychiatric wards and the agencies of the criminal justice system, these models have proposed integrated collaborative practices designed to provide responses better suited to the complex situations they are called upon to address.

With these new intervention strategies, the avoidance of authoritarian system responses (criminalisation, involuntary civil commitment) does appear to work for a certain number of people. For others, however, the proposed alternatives do not yield the anticipated results. Despite individual goodwill and efforts to work collaboratively, individuals continue to be trapped in the spiral of exclusion, and the situations in which they find themselves do not fit the mandates of the agencies whose job it is to respond. Should this unintended reform outcome be seen as resulting from fragmented services, overspecialised responses, competing visions of the phenomenon, excessively ad hoc collaborations, and/or collective disengagement? This chapter addresses these questions by examining the social mechanisms that operate at the junction of diverse social problems (mental illness, extreme poverty, homelessness, isolation, addiction, HIV/AIDS, troubles with the criminal justice system, etc) when problem situations of this kind appear, resulting in the intervention of specialised agencies.

To grasp the orientation and responses adopted in these circumstances, we have restricted our field of study to the cases of a group of women referred on multiple occasions to a Montreal mobile crisis intervention team, Urgence psychosociale-justice (UPS-J). Homelessness, marginality, and social exclusion characterise the trajectories of these women. Difficult to label, they could be placed in any category of deviance, but truly fit into none of them. These are the 'multi-problem cases', the 'hard core', as they are called in certain circles. We have chosen to study 'boundary' cases in order to map more precisely the complex processes involved in defining

---

2 The notion of diversion refers to a variety of practices whose essential goal is to avoid criminalisation, or incarceration. It has been widely used in intervention practices in the area of psychiatry-justice (Brinded *et al*, 1996; Brown, 1999; Cohen and Tsemberis, 1991; Draine and Solomon, 1999; Fennell, 1991; Finn and Sullivan, 1989; Frisman *et al*, 2001; Greenhalgh *et al*, 1996; Hoff *et al*, 1999; James and Hamilton, 1991, 1992; Joseph and Potter, 1993a, b; Laberge, Landreville and Morin, 2000b; Steadman, Cocozza and Veysey, 1999).

3 Wolff (1998) uses the term 'intersystem parallelism' to refer to this phenomenon.

and referring situations that challenge the practices of the agencies involved in these cases. By documenting events that give rise to these interventions, how the cases are routed through the resource networks, the strategies of the actors, and the institutional approaches, we will gain a better grasp of the limitations and dead ends associated with certain management practices.

7.1 Montreal's Urgence psychosociale-justice (UPS-J)

During the 1980s in Quebec, the problems posed by hard-to-define groups at the interface of various social institutions, grappling with difficult access to care and services, began to emerge (see the work of Montreal's consultation committees (*tables de concertation*) on mental health, justice, and homelessness, among other examples). In 1989, Quebec's health and social services ministry and its public security ministry signed a protocol recognising the rights of prisoners and those under the courts' jurisdiction to health care (MSSS and MSP, 1990). This was an important event, because it signalled a recognition that certain groups who are bounced back and forth between the two systems encounter persistent difficulty in having their needs met. The 'psychosocial emergency' concept arose out of this context in 1992 (Laberge and Morin, 1992). UPS-J was set up at the CLSC des Faubourgs[4] and opened four years later, in October 1996.

As a 24/7 mobile emergency intervention service, UPS-J's task is to provide round-the-clock intervention for individuals defined as being: (1) affected by 'persistent, severe mental health problems'; and (2) involved in events which are liable to result in police intervention, criminalisation, or involuntary hospitalisation. Its mandate is: (1) to prevent criminalisation or incarceration and keep the situation from deteriorating; and (2) to do this by setting up collaborative practice among the various services. UPS-J establishes contact not only with the individuals targeted by interventions restricted to the 'psychiatry-justice' domain, but also with resources and services that play a role in criminal justice diversion and community responses. Its mandate thus includes activities to promote interfacing and collaboration between institutions, facilitated by the establishment of a consortium of partners.[5] Recognition of the problem of collaboration among the various services shaped the UPS-J referral process: only the police, the courts, and health and community resources can contact the Montreal resource.

During the period of the study, the UPS-J team was made up of 12 professionals from backgrounds in different disciplines (criminology, psychology, nursing science,

---

4   In Quebec, first level health and social services are generally provided at a private clinic or at a public clinic known as a CLSC (abbreviation for Centre local de services communautaires, or local community service centre). Each CLSC is designated to serve the population of a given territory. Some, like the CLSC des Faubourgs, have developed a range of specialised services to meet precise needs or handle particular problems within a territory, such as UPS-J.

5   The partners include representatives of the Montreal city police force and the Quebec correctional service; Crown prosecutors at the Court of Quebec in Montreal; community resources such as the Le Transit crisis centre and the Dollard-Cormier detox centre; and institutional health services (Centre de psychiatrie légale de Montréal, Notre-Dame Hospital psychosocial services, UPS-J intervention team).

sexology, social work), who had experience in a variety of professional settings (health, social intervention, correctional services) when the service opened. Its activities can be segmented into three intervention modes: (1) responding to emergency calls;[6] (2) providing support for agents of the courts (the Montreal municipal court and the Court of Quebec, criminal and penal divisions), by performing assessments and researching options to permit diversion, prevent the extension of pre-trial detention, or avoid prison sentences; and (3) promoting the UPS-J programme, engaging in an exchange of expertise with partners, and raising public awareness regarding the problem of the criminalisation of mental illness.

7.2 Methodological approach and population of the study

In this chapter, we use data taken from a study on the practices of UPS-J,[7] including data on a cohort of women for whom UPS-J received at least three intervention requests between 15 October 1996 and 30 April 1998, with an update of UPS-J's intervention requests as of 30 June 1999. The study is thus a cohort analysis covering a 33-month period during which 970 individuals were referred to UPS-J, generating 1,553 intervention requests (calls). Women make up 30% of the total population and account for 32% of the requests.

Whereas UPS-J receives one call, or a maximum of two, for most individuals, a tiny group within the population generated repeated intervention requests which seem to have no satisfactory outcome. This phenomenon was slightly more marked among women, of whom 14% (ie, 38 women out of a total of 284) generated 40% of the requests received by the service.[8]

We are interested in the phenomenon of multiple returns[9] in the framework of UPS-J's practice. As Table 7.1 shows, these cases involve a very small number of individuals but, paradoxically, they mobilise the service and its partners to a considerable extent. Moreover, this phenomenon embodies the greatest challenges for the intervention milieu: they require the most indepth expertise and the most complex networking activities, with no guarantee of results. One must be prepared

TABLE 7.1   Number of Service Requests to UPS-J: Female Population

Requests to UPS-J	Number of Women	%	Number of Calls	%
1	199	70.1	199	40.6
2	47	16.5	94	19.2
3 or more	38	13.4	197	40.2
Total	284	100.0	490	100.0

6   The response generally involves a visit to the site of the event, an assessment, a matching process, and short-term follow-up.
7   Two of the authors (Pierre Landreville and Daphné Morin) have been connected with the UPS-J project since its inception. They were in charge of the evaluation on the break-in period in 1996–97, and Morin is a member of the Consortium, in the capacity of expert researcher.
8   In the case of men, 13% (ie, 90 men out of a total of 673) generated 36% of the requests.
9   In this text, a 'multiple return' refers to at least three intervention requests.

to settle for modest – even extremely modest – successes. These situations illustrate the difficulties and tensions that exist in practice at the junction of diverse social problems (involving mental illness, extreme poverty, homelessness, isolation, multiple addictions, HIV/AIDS, and troubles with the law): tensions between organisations designated to manage these types of conflict, tensions between the world views of different disciplines, tensions between community and institutional circles, and so on.

In this chapter, we have opted to examine case studies generated by this cohort of women for whom UPS-J has received multiple requests (three or more).[10] The subjects selected are obviously not representative of all cases referred to UPS-J, but they do represent the most difficult cases. This methodological approach lets us do a closer analysis of the social processes underlying the handling of these cases when UPS-J is called in, track the development of these dynamics over time (a period of nearly three years), and identify the dominant management patterns.

The analyses were carried out on data from two main sources: (1) the file from CLSC des Faubourgs, the institution to which UPS-J is attached; and (2) the penal file. The CLSC des Faubourgs file contains data on all intervention requests to UPS-J: precoded information as well as open fields, with clinical notes written by the UPS-J team and other professionals at the clinic (social workers, psychiatrists, physicians and nurses). The penal file is made up of data collected systematically from two official sources of judicial information: DACOR (the Quebec correctional service database) and the CPIC (Canadian Police Information Centre, under the Forensic Information Services of the Royal Canadian Mounted Police). Three types of data were compiled: (1) prior convictions at the time of each UPS-J intervention (this information varied from one UPS-J intervention to the next); (2) new brushes with the law occurring subsequent to the first UPS-J intervention (gathered as of 4 October 1999); and (3) incarceration sequences (pre-trial detention and prison sentence) subsequent to the date of the first UPS-J intervention.

There is no UPS-J intervention unless an event or 'problem situation' is reported to UPS-J. We use the notion of a 'problem situation' to mean a set of ways of acting or being that infringe norms, for which there are various possible interpretations and responses. 'A problem' – often qualified as being 'a mental health problem' – is identified on the basis of socio-interactional criteria (incoherence, inability to get one's bearings in space, totally inappropriate speech or behaviour, talking to oneself, dangerous behaviour, etc). The main characteristic of these criteria is their reference to the deemed inappropriateness of the behaviour. When attributed to an individual, 'problem situation' implies a normative reference and postulates the likelihood of an intervention designed to make the problem disappear.

Before presenting the case histories, we will give a quick outline of the cohort of women examined in our study, and the problem situations underlying the multiple interventions addressed to them.

---

10 Other articles dealing with UPS-J practices have been published (Laberge, Landreville and Morin, 2000b; Landreville, Morin and Laberge, 2003) and more are forthcoming, specifically addressing the social construction of the 'unclassifiable' category.

7.3 'Unclassifiable' street women

The cohort contains 25[11] women, who generated 147 intervention requests to UPS-J. These women are the 'multi-problem cases', the 'unclassifiables', those who, almost unanimously, radiate a feeling of powerlessness. They present a panoply of inter-related problems: homelessness, history of psychiatric problems, substance abuse, numerous brushes with the law both before and after the intervention of UPS-J.[12] They exist outside the sphere of normalised inclusion.

Most of the events are reported by the homelessness resource network and the police. In most cases, at the time of the service call to UPS-J, the woman had no fixed address or was living in a shelter; some were shuttling between apartments or rooms and the street. Only four of the women were in self-contained apartments at the time each of the calls concerning them was made, and they seemed to be in vulnerable situations.[13] In very rare cases, links with a social network were mentioned.[14] These women's world is the street: they live in public space.

Visibility is another central dimension of the events reported to UPS-J, and one that conditions the probable responses. The following characteristics contribute to an event's visibility: (1) it occurs in public space (or private space with public access);[15] (2) the woman is circulating in group living space;[16] (3) the event mobilises key emergency responders whose power to act, or authority, is symbolically very salient (uniform, intervention equipment, etc);[17] and (4) the woman is making a non-standard use of the public or private space she is occupying.[18]

One revealing feature of the problem situations reported to UPS-J is their banality from a penal perspective. Indeed, the events most often reported are suicide threats or attempts, requests for support during eviction from a resource, and requests for accompaniment and prevention. Other, very rare, events involve family conflicts,[19] aggressive behaviour towards strangers, and, finally, incoherent behaviour.

While minor from a penal law perspective, in psycho-social terms these problem situations are desperate. Their emergency, crisis character is marked, and they reflect tremendous deterioration in these women's social circumstances. While the situations are seemingly diverse, the trigger or problem that needs solving is that of

---

11 We excluded from this cohort a group of 13 older women whose profile and treatment were different. For an analysis that includes this group, see Landreville, Morin and Laberge (2003).

12 We will use the terms 'post-UPS-J criminalisation' and 'post-UPS-J penal contacts' to refer to the portion of the penal history subsequent to UPS-J's intervention.

13 For instance, all events show conflictual relations with the neighbourhood that create opportunities for expulsion: one involving prosecution for repeatedly setting off the fire alarm in the building where the woman is living; another involving prosecution for death threats addressed to the superintendent of the building where she is living.

14 Presence of a child, marital or family conflict, ejection from the couple's residence, reports from family or friends.

15 Street, subway, bus, bus terminal, bridge, highway, store, shopping centre, CLSC, hospital.

16 Housing resource in the homelessness or mental health network, detox centre, prison.

17 Police officers, ambulance attendants, firefighters.

18 Urinating on private property, needlessly setting off the fire alarm in the building where she lives, shouting in the street, etc.

19 These cases involve fellow residents or workers at resources the women frequent.

shelter – and this, more often than not, appears insoluble. Possible interventions are complicated and limited by these women's extremely difficult relationships with institutions. These conflicts appear at the root of the intervention requests to UPS-J. Because the institution is providing the woman with shelter, rapid resolution of the crisis is understandably crucial. There isn't much time available: many calls are received in the evening. UPS-J must often deal with women who are in crisis or distressed by the difficult situation they are experiencing or likely to experience. Shelter must be negotiated with resources that know these individuals and have often blacklisted them. In most cases, the file does not indicate the reason for the conflicts or problems an institution encounters with an individual. The very absence of explanation indicates institutional practices that tend to decontextualize the events to make them fit the institution's category and definition.

Without being explicitly termed 'ejections', a fairly high number of requests to UPS-J arise in a service termination: ie, discharge from hospital, the end of a stay in a housing resource, etc. This is a sensitive point for efforts to implement the principle of continuity of service: a mandate that is a huge challenge in the case of this cohort of homeless women, who meet with refusal pretty much everywhere.

The repetitive or similar nature of the situations is another central dimension, even though it is rarely mentioned in the file. In those cases where it is noted, the repetition can have the effect of exacerbating tensions between resources in the community, or between resources and individuals who make multiple returns, because a repeat case is seen at first glance as a failure. At the opposite extreme, this could be the trigger for greater attention and result in a mobilisation of actors. Whatever the case, the repetitive character undoubtedly illustrates the great complexity of the situations and the difficulty of finding a lasting solution.

Like the other studies examining the management practices for emergency situations at the 'psychiatry-justice' junction, our research illustrates three main outcomes of UPS-J interventions: 'informal' management (by far the most common, at least two-thirds of cases);[20] referral to hospital; and criminalisation. For this cohort, the most frequent outcome is 'no follow-up' (indicated as such in the file): either no resource is available, or the woman declines the offer of service. Referral to hospital is relatively infrequent – but, that being said, it can be noted that in nearly one case out of five, hospitalisation does occur during the period the UPS-J file is open.[21] As for criminalisation, 11 of the events reported to UPS-J (involving eight of the 25 women) were referred to the courts for various offences: shoplifting (in two cases); food fraud (one); refusal to leave the premises (three); mischief involving setting off a fire alarm in the building where the woman was living (one); mischief against private property (knocking on doors and urinating on private land); attacks and threats (two). The fact that there were victims or complainants (in 10 of the 11 events) and the repetitive nature of the situations (in seven of the 11) may have influenced the decision to criminalise these cases.

---

20 'Informal' management refers to different sorts of management: homelessness network, relatives, neighbourhood, or any other actions or consequences, spontaneous or planned.

21 A file is closed when the UPS-J workers deem that they have transferred the case; they verify this transfer through calls to the services involved.

While criminalisation of events reported to UPS-J is generally rare, examination of the cohort's penal history shows it to be a very common management practice for this group. Upon entering the cohort, 19 of the 25 women already had criminal records. At the end of the period studied, this was true for 24 of the 25. The number of brushes with the law (arrests, prosecutions with or without convictions) is another indicator of the severity of the penal treatment received by these women.[22] Most cases concerned minor offences, involving public order disruptions (disturbing the peace, traffic violations, infringements of municipal regulations or the Highway Safety Code, and, finally, a false alarm). While the penal file does not provide context, comparison of the judicial events and the UPS-J events reveals a similarity: the remarkable banality of these cases from the penal law standpoint. Nonetheless, this banality was insufficient to protect these women from incarceration,[23] a measure which should be reserved for other types of situation,[24] according to sentencing principles under Canadian criminal law.

This preliminary description permits certain general observations about the nature of the events – including the important role played by the street – and about the various categories of actors involved and the main orientations, but this analysis remains inadequate. To understand the recurrence of these situations, the dynamics that are set in motion, and how they evolve through dialogue and the adoption of various approaches, we have constructed three case histories. Each is presented in two sections: a brief description of the route taken through the resource network and the relations among the actors involved in definition and referral, followed by an analysis of the processes and dynamics that came into play in the management of these cases.

7.4 Cases that call practices into question

7.4.1 Case 1: intensive mobilisation, as an interlude between episodes of incarceration

Hélène[25] is 43 years old, with no fixed address. From the first call, she is described as a suicidal individual who has an alcohol problem in addition to homelessness, psychiatric difficulties, and troubles with the law. Hélène expresses her need for help by asking to see a psychiatrist or go to the hospital. She is seen by a psychiatrist and a diagnosis of manic depression is recorded. She actively seeks help, voluntarily, and an intense mobilisation can be observed, involving numerous actors, with jointly organised initiatives. There is a will to define a shared line of

---

22 Thus, over the 33 months of the study, these women had 83 contacts with the criminal justice system, for an average of 3.3 per person; 16 of the 25 women had three or more contacts with the criminal justice system.

23 Over the 33 months of the study, 22 of the 25 women amassed a total of 67 prison sequences, corresponding to an average of three sequences per person. As a group, they totalled 1,120 days in custody (figures unknown for three of the women), for an average stay of 17.5 days.

24 The growing tendency in Canada to imprison women, especially since 1996, raises questions for numerous female observers (Bertrand, 2003; Frigon, 2002).

25 The names are fictitious.

conduct and an intervention plan that goes beyond emergency response. As the weeks go by, however, disagreements can be observed as to solutions; viewpoints change, as reflected by the disengagement of key actors.

Hélène is the subject of 12 service requests to UPS-J in five months. These requests come between episodes of incarceration. In fact, when the first service call is made to UPS-J, Hélène has just been released from prison; she already has five convictions, four of them for offences against persons; the first dates back three years. During the series of calls of concern here, Hélène spends five months in the community without troubles with the law: periods spent in two homelessness network housing resources alternate with several hospital stays and admission to a supervised apartment. One month after the last call, she is incarcerated again for a period of 57 days, for an assault conviction; two and a half months later, she will be imprisoned again. Numerous actors are involved in her case. Two, in particular, are seen to be consistently present: the attending psychiatrist, who provides follow-up at the hospital, and a worker from a community follow-up programme. They operate in liaison with UPS-J, the housing resources for the homeless and the mentally ill, and the crisis centres.

All of the calls come in an emergency context. The events involve threats (in the majority of cases) and attempted suicide (one case). This is a woman who fears committing acts of aggression against individuals ('scared of hurting someone') or destroying objects (breaking windows) – or hurting herself (expresses suicidal ideas, 'verbalizes desire to self-mutilate'). In certain instances, she has put these threats into action (attacks against other residents, altercation with a male friend; suicide attempt by slashing her wrists).

At the times of the calls, Hélène is living in a shelter (eight out of 12) or a supervised apartment (one out of 12), or has no address at all (one out of 12). The requests to UPS-J come from two housing resources in the homelessness network (short-term and shelter) and the mental health network (supervised apartment). There are two exceptions: one call comes from the police and one from a community follow-up resource. Most of the calls (nine out of 12) come after 4 pm or during the night, which may accentuate their crisis or emergency character and restrict the possible responses. Visibility is a feature of these events, because they occur in group living spaces.

When the first request is made to UPS-J, the worker from a community follow-up program describes the individual as presenting multiple problems. The request to UPS-J is preventive in nature. It is an attempt to establish liaison among resources, and, above all, to find someone at the housing resource willing to take responsibility for the case. These requests suggest a 'heavy' case: no event or problem situation has occurred; instead, the goal is to define a sort of intervention plan in advance. The UPS-J is being informed that Hélène will be released from the women's prison and housed in a community resource in the homelessness network; UPS-J is asked to intervene should the situation deteriorate. UPS-J agrees to act as backup.

In a number of the calls, the request arises because Hélène is being ejected from a housing resource: she is threatening to kill herself; or she attacks another resident and displays agitated behaviour. The worker wants to know where to refer her. When the intervention results in her being admitted to hospital, the response is very short-lived (a few hours, one night) and after her hospital stay, Hélène cannot be readmitted to the housing resource.

In two cases, UPS-J deems that the request does not fit its mandate: in one instance, she is redirected to the regular emergency service (911), and in the other there is no follow-up. In the first case, UPS-J is being asked to accompany the client to hospital; they are informed that she has lost consciousness 10 times in 24 hours. In the second, the request is to accompany the client after her discharge from hospital but, that same day, UPS-J receives a call from the police notifying them that the housing resource is not readmitting Hélène and the other resources refuse to take her.

7.4.1.1 Comments

The first call, from the community follow-up programme, can be seen as an attempt to establish co-operation among the resources involved. There is a relatively explicit request for the designation of someone responsible for the case, to open up access to the homelessness network's housing resources, and also to facilitate access to care if other, more serious types of intervention (such as hospitalisation in a psychiatric facility) should prove necessary.[26]

What follows – ie, the series of repeated calls concerning suicide threats and attacks – would indicate that the two housing resources are unable to cope. The sequence of calls shows the case being passed back and forth.

Recourse to hospitalisation apparently corresponds to turning points which highlight the gravity of the situation (suicidal ideation, threats of self-injury or aggression, etc) and provide an opportunity to fall back on other resources.

The hospitals' brief response appears to be perceived as inadequate by the housing resources for the homeless, which are short on means to deal with this kind of difficulty. The question, then, is which system should respond: the health system? Homelessness resources? The criminal justice system? UPS-J's responses could also have been seen as a lack of collaboration by the various resources. These episodes could be an illustration that, while attempts at collaboration do exist in the field, these efforts remain unsatisfactory.

This route through the resource network could illustrate conflicts in the ways the resources concerned – particularly the hospitals and the housing resources for the homeless – interpret the individual's needs and the services that can be offered.

Two key actors are observed in this case, who remain in contact throughout the episode. They adopt a shared approach: helping the individual identify ways of managing her frustration to avoid becoming disorganised; not responding systematically to her demands for attention unless she is in physical danger; criminalising if she acts out, to make her take responsibility. However, in the end,

---

26 This is common practice in the psychiatry-justice resource network. Before admitting a new client, most resources require that the individual be receiving psychiatric care; in other words, that there be a psychiatrist to take responsibility should hospitalisation become necessary, a medication problem arise, etc. In actuality, this condition has often been evoked as a barrier preventing these groups from gaining access to resources: few psychiatrists are willing to undertake this commitment; many clients would refuse care. In the case described here, UPS-J shoulders the responsibility with the psychiatrist.

their collaboration breaks down. At the last contact, the attending psychiatrist is described by the other worker as 'not very cooperative; he thinks the client isn't making an effort. He won't see her more than once a month and no longer sees the point of trying hypnotherapy. He is more in favour of criminalisation and incarceration to make the client take responsibility'.

7.4.2 Case 2: putting collaboration to the test

Doris is 38 years old at the time of the first call to UPS-J. Her history shows many previous convictions and a substance abuse problem (heroin, cocaine). Survival prostitution is mentioned at the first contact with CLSC des Faubourgs. She has been homeless for about two years and her drug use and homelessness are reflected in her health condition: HIV/AIDS, hepatitis C, cirrhosis, diabetes, abscesses, trouble walking, fatigue, pain, wounds, edema, etc. On occasion, it is noted that she is not clean, that her clothes are dirty and she smells of urine. In terms of her mental health, the focus is on behaviour problems, aggressiveness (screaming, yelling, etc), infantilism – things that are not perceived as being psychiatric problems: she is not suicidal, shows no decompensation, delirium, or hallucinations. Over a year and a half, UPS-J will receive eight intervention requests in connection with Doris. Four new convictions and four prison terms are noted over the period of the study. Most of the service networks have been approached or gotten involved, but she is regularly refused, rejected, ejected, or admitted for a single night, with conditions, as a stopgap measure. There is little mention of her expectations or needs. Where such references do occur, they indicate that she wants to eat, wash, sleep; she is asking for tranquilisers, body lotion, cigarettes; or else she is threatening to resume her intravenous drug use and refusing proposed treatment.[27]

Doris's trajectory features many brushes with the law. Her first conviction dates back to 1984, when she was 26. Before UPS-J's intervention, Doris had 25 convictions, for offences against property (16) and against persons (two), public disturbance charges (three), system infractions (three) and other offences (one). She has also been handed 16 prison sentences, but brief ones, suggesting that the offences were relatively minor.[28] This relation with the criminal justice system has not failed to leave its mark on Doris's identity, contributing to her stigmatisation as a delinquent and a drug addict.

The events reported to UPS-J form three sequences: a single call in June 1997; six calls four and a half months later; and a last call 11 months after that. The time between the first two sequences features a hospital stay and a period of incarceration lasting nearly three months. The second sequence of calls covers a few weeks. The events involved include a series of ejections and brief admissions (for one night or a weekend) to different resources: hospitals, crisis centres, detox centres. Finally, the last sequence consists of a single isolated event, separated from the others by a period of 11 months: a request for a medical assessment, from a *bas*

---

27 Ejection from a city hospital detox ward; admission to a detox centre for one night; stay in a high-support, low-demand homelessness-addiction-HIV housing resource.

28 There are at least three additional convictions over the period of the study, for very minor offences: system infractions (breach of obligation) and traffic and highway code violations.

seuil (high-support low-demand) AIDS/homelessness housing resource where she was living. Four years later, she was said to be in the terminal phase of AIDS and still living on the street.

Of the events reported, all but one involve relatively explicit refusals, on the part of the institutions approached, to take charge of Doris: ejection or discharge from hospitals after very brief stays, postponing the initial problem by a few hours or days in each case. In four of the events, Doris's behaviour is described in terms of rudeness (yelling in the street, insulting people, screaming in the emergency department); disorganisation; crisis; improper drug use (taking her medication quickly, in combination with cocaine, and asking for more); and manifestation of physical symptoms (palpitations after taking medication and cocaine).

Doris is well known to the networks, and she suffers the consequences. Comments about her are negative (she is aggressive, arrogant; doesn't follow the resources' rules; is excluded because they know her too well; doesn't seem to be aware that she is exhausting the resources; 'all she's done is to perfect her multiple demand techniques').[29]

The calls are always placed in emergency circumstances: Doris is in crisis or will be discharged in a matter of hours, or the next day, thereby setting up conditions that favour a new crisis because of her homeless predicament.

Three of eight calls in crisis situations come from the police; these are similar. She has no address. The events occur on the street, making them highly visible and placing them in the emergency category. In the first case, the police are about to criminalise because (among other reasons) no resource is prepared to take her. The eighth call features an element that undoubtedly has a decisive effect on the intervention: she has an address. She is living in a housing resource, and while there is a crisis, she is not ejected as a result; an expert consultation is requested.

After crisis situations, most of the calls are requests for liaison[30] or for information sharing in a search for temporary solutions. None of the resources seem to consider a more long-term intervention. The approach is ad hoc: it's a matter of responding to emergencies: transfer from hospital to crisis centre; weekend admission by a crisis centre as a stopgap measure; one night in a detox centre while waiting for someone else to take over. In short, Doris generates tensions; the resources foresee a crisis, which they want to avoid at all costs: 'if we keep this person in the department any longer, the entire hospital staff will quit.'

7.4.2.1 Comments

In terms of the intervention, both the ejections and the short-term, temporary admissions create an emergency, crisis situation, because the consequence is the

---

29 These are the words of a crisis centre worker who knew her 10 years earlier when he was working in a resource for the homeless.

30 They include requests for: (1) emergency housing, because Doris will be ejected from the hospital in the morning; (2) information sharing with a hospital (discharge for a weekend in a crisis centre is being considered); (3) information sharing with the crisis centre for an assessment of Doris for a weekend stay; (4) information sharing with a detox centre (search for the organisation responsible for the client).

street.[31] In at least five of the eight events, Doris is ejected from a hospital or rapidly discharged after being seen by a doctor.

Information exchange does not mean co-operation. In Doris's story, the number of resources involved is striking (four hospitals, police, ambulance attendants, a crisis centre, a detox centre, a *bas seuil* homelessness-addiction-HIV housing resource, and numerous housing resources in the homelessness network), as is the range of sectors mobilised (homelessness, addiction, and HIV/AIDS resources, hospitals, CLSCs, community groups, family), but all of these contacts, information exchanges, and liaison requests do not imply the development of an action plan. Instead, repeated interventions on a case-by-case basis, in emergency conditions, give the impression that no viable long-term solution is available or conceivable. While the file shows traces of attempts at collaboration, what mainly emerges is the wearing down of the resources. The arrival of the AIDS network on the scene coincides with the longest admissions recorded in the file. Is this because a fresh network is involved, or because her physical condition has deteriorated further? Also, implementing co-operative practices presupposes a set of conditions, one of them being that the 'client-patient' authorises the release of information.

Doris is rejected by every resource except the prisons. The fact that no resource is willing to take her on indicates how difficult it is to intervene with this individual. Her homelessness, the temporary nature of the responses, and the difficulty of working co-operatively all tend to orient responses in the direction of the criminal justice system, despite the diversion policies that have been adopted and the resources devoted to implementing them (UPS-J in particular).

Conflicts between institutions are apparent. The first call is an instructive example of conflict in the management of problem situations, with the police and the ambulance service tossing the case back and forth. After four ejections from the same hospital emergency department in one day, the event is on the point of being criminalised, but ultimately Doris is hospitalised in another of the city's hospitals. This situation definitely illustrates tensions between the three institutions. The repeated ejections can be seen as the hospital's way of disclaiming responsibility, shunting it onto the ambulance service and the police. In situations deemed to be outside their jurisdiction (ie, those that are the concern of psychiatry rather than the criminal justice system), the lack of co-operation by hospital emergency departments can mean an uncertain outcome. Moreover, when a hospital admits an individual who has already been ejected four times from another emergency room, confusion may result: given the hospitals' divergent interpretations of the situation, what will guide the decision the next time around? The articulation of disciplinary frameworks and areas of intervention, distinct or overlapping, looms as a real challenge.

---

31 At the time of each of the service calls to UPS-J except the last, Doris has no address.

7.4.3 Case 3: Inconsistent responses in a conflict over the use of public space

France's story can be read as a conflict over the use of public space, in which the resources involved in the negotiation lean first in one direction, then in another. The management practice here is characterised by inconsistency.

France is a 31 year old homeless woman who has been living on the street for some years now. Over the period of the study, UPS-J receives 12 intervention requests concerning her. At each call, she is reported as having no address, even though she is known to have an address in a Montreal suburb. There are indications of a diagnosis of schizophrenia and regular follow-up by a psychiatrist in an outpatient clinic for at least the last five years. All of the interventions are very short-lived (less than one day in response to 11 of the calls and one day for the twelfth). The calls form two sequences, with a period of a year and a half between the first call and all of the others.

The first sequence comprises a preventive call from her lawyer (no problem situation occurs). France is in pre-trial detention and the lawyer asks UPS-J to provide follow-up for his client so that she may be released. France has made a suicide attempt on a city bridge, on which occasion she was prosecuted for mischief. She has been hospitalised for a month and is to be discharged from a forensic psychiatry hospital in Montreal. She is to appear in court the next day and may be discharged if the defence lawyer's negotiations are successful. At the time of the call, an outreach team is familiar with France and she is being seen at a psychiatric outpatient clinic. UPS-J undertakes to refer France to the outreach team so that the follow-up requested by the lawyer is guaranteed. No trace of this liaison between UPS-J and the outreach team can be found, leaving some ambiguity as to the required character of the commitment. Nonetheless, the referral is formalised in the decision of the court: suspended sentence with a probation order including an obligation that France submit to psychiatric follow-up. Two conditions are imposed: follow-up with the attending psychiatrist and follow-up in the community by the outreach team. At this stage, the file shows the parties' low expectations as to the benefits of this process: there is agreement on the 'limited' objectives of the intervention.

A year and a half later, 11 service calls are placed to UPS-J over a four-month period, some of them in rapid succession, separated by a few hours or days. The problem situation is the same each time: it involves a woman who has settled on the outdoor air grids of a downtown Montreal shopping centre, whom they claim to be 'forced to move'. Most of the calls (nine out of 12) come in the evening. In this series of calls, the first two are placed directly by the shopping centre's private security agents; the subsequent ones come from the police. Most of the calls mention that they don't want to criminalise, they're looking for solutions, they want to offer services but they don't know 'what to do' with this homeless woman. Many of the calls stress her passive resistance to order: France 'refuses to budge'; 'after several warnings she still refuses to leave the premises'; 'she hangs onto the grid and refuses to talk'; 'she's in the same place again and refuses to leave'. While all of the events are similar, three will be criminalised; one will result in referral to hospital as a result of a police request for a psychiatric assessment; and the other calls generate no follow-up.

Regarding the court order, the file shows agreement between the outreach team and France at their first meeting. Both parties agree that France will come in for a brief meeting once a week, but only seven meetings will actually take place, marked by disagreement between the parties: at each meeting with France, and during discussions of the case among members of the outreach team or with the attending psychiatrist, the outreach team reiterates the formal nature of the contact, ie, the outreach team's legal obligation to take charge of the follow-up.

7.4.3.1   Comments

One salient characteristic of France's story is the persistence of the situation, and France's consistent attitude under the circumstances. In event after event, she is occupying space that is either 'public' or 'private for public use', from which there is an effort to dislodge her. She refuses to budge, just as she refuses the intervention that is offered to her or imposed upon her. Her resistance is passive: she misses appointments despite threats of criminalisation, or she applies the force of inertia. Is this the only power she wields in her relations with others? Is it also a way of maintaining a distance from the intervention? Could this resistance account for the vacillation in the response?

We note tensions between the various actors, but also a certain alliance between the outreach team, the court, the defence attorney, and the attending psychiatrist. For instance, the outreach team expresses its surprise regarding the order for mandatory follow-up. In actual fact, the order is twofold, as it applies to both France and the outreach team.[32] The agreement between UPS-J and the defence attorney to propose to the court that a condition of this kind be included in the probation order seems to have been seen as a unilateral, authoritarian decision by the outreach team.

In the file, the outreach team's intervention seems essentially focused on the necessity of maintaining contact with France, which is actually in line with the court order. The outreach team demands no modifications to the probation order and undertakes to enforce it. It recalls the nature of the bond between them, the legal obligation to maintain regular contact, but the ambiguity associated with the assignment of this legal mandate allows a certain degree of ambivalence to appear in the course of action undertaken. For instance, two and a half months after the order is issued, France still hasn't come to her appointments. When the members of the outreach team accidentally run into her, they tell her they are going to contact her attending physician to notify him that she is not complying with her probation conditions – which they do in fact do. They repeat this process two and half months later, contacting not only the attending physician but also the defence attorney. While these measures seem to indicate a willingness to criminalise France's behaviour, the outreach team agrees to consider an informal meeting at the team's offices as a formal appointment (of the kind stipulated in the order). Over the next

---

32 It probably applies to the attending psychiatrist as well, but we do not have access to that information.

month, France keeps her appointments with the outreach team but, after that, the file notes that she does not come regularly. Although she does not comply with the order and the various institutions are informed of this, no prosecution for breach of conditions ensues. Should this be seen as tolerance? Vacillation? Ambiguity? An intervention strategy? Can the mandate, as defined by the court, with its obligatory character, give way to something else? Is a concerted intervention plan possible in a situation where the third party charged with carrying out the order does not seem to have been consulted?

Two events suggest tensions between the police and the applicant (ie, the shopping centre and its security agents). When the police arrive on the premises in response to the seventh call, they refuse to intervene, deeming that it would be inappropriate for them to act. And on the twelfth call, the police detect a strategy of systematic reporting: every morning at the same time, the police receive a complaint. Pressure is brought to bear on them to force them to act. Sometimes they opt for a penal approach, sometimes not; the response is seemingly random. The three instances of criminalisation appear to be a sidelining strategy to deal with a situation where, if nothing is done, the problem (and the pressure on the police) will 'persist'.

One notable feature of the interventions is their interchangeability. Whereas the response varies from one event to another (criminalisation, psychiatrisation, no follow-up), the situations are remarkably similar: the underlying logic proceeds from a sidelining strategy. France is in public space, it's late, she's causing a disturbance and her presence here cannot be tolerated. What might appear random is actually a set of variations on the same theme.

The two sequences differ in the responses that are proposed. In the first case, actors are mobilised around France's situation; in the second series of events, they are not deployed: on some occasions an appeal is made to the kindness of those around her while on others, it is suggested that she needs to be criminalised to make her take responsibility.

7.5   Three distinct management patterns: mobilisation, abdication, vacillation

Based on these case histories, we have constructed three distinct patterns that are adopted by the various categories of actors in managing these recurring problem situations: mobilisation, abdication, and vacillation. While each of these responses may appear to describe the management of one case in particular, what should actually be borne in mind is that they can alternate, marking periods in a trajectory.

Mobilisation is characterised by the involvement of various actors in the search for a shared solution and position, a pattern that is reaffirmed with each new intervention. Another feature of mobilisation is that the contacts with UPS-J are concentrated in time. The underpinning for this pattern is a belief in the therapeutic benefits of the course of action adopted. However, mobilisation may continue for only a brief period of time, restricted, among other things, by the frequent confinements and other absences with which these trajectories are studded. At the end of the five months of mobilisation in Hélène's story, for instance, certain actors showed signs of demobilisation. How should her return to the prison setting at the end of this period be interpreted? And when she is released, what will become of the mobilisation? Will it be reactivated, or replaced by abdication or vacillation?

The second pattern, *abdication*, is also characterised by a consistent response, but one with no action plan, in a constant state of emergency. At each request, it's back to square one, in stopgap mode, with a new ad hoc response. No one really gets involved, but it is sometimes difficult to extricate oneself completely. Responses are proposed while stressing that the individual doesn't fit the resource's mandate. Each call reconfirms the lack of an intervention plan, and reveals actors devoid of resources, who do not believe in the effectiveness or the possibility of other types of intervention.

The last pattern is characterised by *vacillation*. Sometimes things are left as they are; sometimes criminalisation is chosen; sometimes hospitalisation in a psychiatric facility. These solutions are interchangeable and applied in alternation. There is no clear idea what to do; sometimes there is an appeal to tolerance, sometimes to the importance of instilling a sense of responsibility by criminalising, or to the need for care.

7.5.1 Correspondence and discrepancy between expectations and orientations

In mobilisation, there is a fit between the request and the proposed intervention. In other words, the individual expresses a request for guidance and seeks out workers in the system, asking to be helped and protected against him- or herself. The range of responses corresponds with what the person is asking for and with the orientation chosen for the intervention. In abdication, the requests are unacceptable to the resources approached. Doris wants to eat, sleep, wash; they want to detoxify her. She screams, takes offence, cries, becomes aggressive; they want her to calm down and follow the rules. The same merry-go-round can be seen in the relations between services. Someone wants to send her to the psychiatric hospital but she's too intoxicated; someone wants outpatient psychiatric follow-up for her but she is offered a few hours of emergency consultation; someone wants a place for her in a housing resource but she is offered an escort to emergency; and if alliances between the intervention sphere and Doris seem to be impossible, so are alliances between the actors involved in the intervention. Care plan, planned exit from a resource and implementation of follow-up are all irrelevant concepts here. Everyone is operating in isolation. Finally, in the vacillation pattern, nobody knows what to do. France's position is explicit and reaffirmed over time with the same assurance, but her position is unacceptable. She cannot stay where she is. In this open but silent confrontation, she raises doubts, issues challenges.

7.5.2 The homeless person: patient, victim, delinquent, subject

The mobilisation pattern requires a committed and willing client. Hélène embodies such a 'good' client. She is the victim of an illness; her deviant behaviour is attributed to psychiatric problems, so alcohol plays a less important role. She agrees to follow the workers' instructions, even though recurrence of the same scenarios may lead to weariness and disengagement.

In the abdication pattern, the individual is assigned responsibility for his or her own state and relations with others. He or she is not targeted by any institution. Doris is refused by every resource: 'The problem remains: what should we do? Neither psychiatry nor detox can take her.' Doris has no psychiatric problems and she is not suicidal. She is arrogant, offended, and aggressive, and she refuses treatment. She has little motivation to embark on a detoxification cure, and the HIV/AIDS problem is not brought to the fore. This pattern clearly illustrates that merely being recognised as having an addiction problem does not make one a target for this field of action. An additional condition must also be met: the individual must want to recover and stop using the substance. The development of high-support low-demand resources indicates a shift in the definition of addiction, but such changes are part of a long process characterised by various types of resistance.

In the vacillation pattern, the homeless woman is an enigma, even a paradox: is she a victim or a subject? Sitting on the sidewalk, refusing to communicate, France is nonetheless highly 'intelligent' and exercises her rights as a citizen (she institutes a legal proceeding to have her rights respected by the intervention milieu). Using inertia as a force for resistance, she lives on the street, but apparently has an address. In short, this woman successfully casts doubt on the relevance of the various actions. She confronts the intervention world, never formulating a single request (passive refusal of any form of assistance), but challenging each one of us with her homelessness. Should she be constrained? If so, to what?

7.6 Conclusion

Our analysis demonstrates the central role of the street as a condition of these 'hard core' women's lives, and in the management practices adopted. Of course, these are socially isolated women with no fixed address, whose life universe is the homelessness network. Visibility, emergency, crisis, and available options are all directly conditioned by the street. Recourse to the criminal justice system and incarceration measures thus remains a frequent response in dealing with matters that are minor from the standpoint of penal law.

Although we saw intense mobilisation around certain cases, it is generally short-lived or generates extremely limited responses which are used repeatedly. The attitude of refusal, flight, withdrawal or evasion the women adopt towards the institutions with which they have come in contact is undoubtedly a significant dimension in this dynamic. This attitude, often mentioned in their files, may give the institutions a reason for abdicating in the face of these women. Careful thought should be given to this characteristic, and it should be analysed in the light of the women's life and past experience with these institutions. Unfortunately, this is rarely the case. From the institutions' point of view, this 'characteristic' renders them 'unfit' for intervention. From the woman's own perspective, her relations with these institutions conceal a host of issues related to her physical reality (safeguarding her personal effects, getting back to her hideout, servicing her johns to pay for her dope, etc); freedom of movement; relationships (protecting her network); safety; and identity (protecting herself against the effects of stigmatisation). When the encounter occurs (ie, the UPS-J event), the woman is negotiating her identity, and flight (withdrawal, etc) can be interpreted as a refusal to be lumped into a social category that doesn't correspond to one's own image of oneself. In the case of women marked by life stories that are often dramatic, and whose mental health problems may be worsened by living on the street, institutions may frequently be portrayed as a major source of danger (Koegel, 1992).

The women in this group and the management practices favoured undoubtedly illustrate an important paradox. These 'unclassifiables' with their multiple problems offer a variety of handles that all of the social practices can grasp but, at the same time, these handles provide an escape, a way of dumping the problem next door: not disoriented enough, and too intoxicated, for psychiatric treatment; too sick to be in housing for the homeless; not dangerous enough to be locked up, but too threatening to be admitted anywhere else; and so on. This paradox is at the heart of the negotiation game that kicks in to deal with these problem situations, and the referral process that is triggered.

When a problem requires several types of very high-level expertise, how does one go about bringing them all together in one place, or devising effective networking practices? How does one rally a profound understanding of homelessness (survival strategies, stigmatisation, identity transformation, desocialisation, etc); vital pharmacological expertise (concerning, among other things, the effects of combining substances such as antidepressants, alcohol, cocaine, PCP, and antiretroviral agents); extensive competence in 'street medicine' (skin and foot diseases, respiratory disorders, traumas of every sort, alcoholism and other addictions, HIV/AIDS, etc) and penal law (legal proceedings and sentence management); and so on? Should the dominant public policy be the targeting of indigent populations with its baggage of specialised mechanisms, knowing that this may tend to exacerbate differences and lead to exclusion and stigmatisation? Or should we strengthen co-operative practices to promote the use of general services, knowing that this response may prove totally inadequate?

In recent years, much effort has gone into developing innovative intervention and co-operation practices to take into consideration the specific features of these 'clienteles', recognise the multiple barriers that exist, and propose responses that are more satisfactory from an individual and a group standpoint. One paradox has been underlined, however. One of the reasons for setting up these models or mechanisms, such as UPS-J, was to facilitate the use of the regular public services but, in the process, they tend to create new social categories and develop specific forms of expertise that may justify referral to this new intervention milieu, effectively shortcircuiting the initial objective. The present study would indicate that not all of the obstacles have been overcome. The responses to the women in this group raise profound questions about the social processes that have led them to the street and those that keep them there. In the more serious situations, the three patterns identified here reveal the limitations of the interventions brought to bear, but they also show the innovative potential of the practices developing in these new spaces for collaborative action.

Chapter 8
Gender, Murder and Madness[1]
Wendy Chan

Psychiatric decisions play a key role in the outcome of a homicide case. Particularly where defendants are diagnosed with a mental illness, psychiatric considerations are significant for the verdict and subsequent disposal of the case. As many feminist and legal writers have pointed out, however, these considerations are mediated by gendered assumptions of how madness[2] is constituted and the effects it has on the defendant's behaviour. This chapter examines the connection between gender, murder and psychiatric decisions by focusing on homicide cases in England and Wales where defendants have been diagnosed with a mental illness. In such cases, the defendant typically enters a plea of diminished responsibility, which, if successful, reduces a charge of murder to manslaughter.

Examining how mental illness is constructed for female and male defendants highlights gender differences in their construction, as well as the different legal effects produced by psychiatric advice and evidence for men and women. By focusing on defendants diagnosed with a mental illness, the concern is not so much with whether women are more likely to be found mentally ill than men, but rather on how psychiatric assessments determine and shape issues of intent, motive, and criminal responsibility which, it is argued, rely on a gendered and individualistic understanding about the causes of madness.

8.1   Contextualising gender and psychiatry

Claims that the psychiatric profession treats men and women differently have been the subject of much discussion by feminist writers and researchers. One of the major themes in the literature has been the question of medical control over the lives of many women. Feminist writers have argued that the medical profession exerts control over the physical and psychological health of many women through the manipulation of their health problems to reinforce their subordinate position within the dominant social order (Ehrenreich and English, 1979; Procek, 1980; Russell, 1995; Ussher, 1991). Barrett and Roberts claim that the medical profession has been able to assert control through a number of techniques which include: denying the importance of paid work to women; viewing women's worries as 'vague and

---

1   Adapted and abridged from Chapter 4, and pp 43–47, in Chan, W, *Women, Murder and Justice*, 2001.

2   The terms 'madness' and 'mental illness' are used interchangeably throughout this chapter. My claim is that mental illness has a socially constituted element, but it is also a legitimate condition, containing behavioural characteristics ranging from insanity to everyday unhappiness. Hence, the concepts of madness or mental illness refer to both the psychological and physiological notion of mental illness and the socially constructed categories defining such illness.

spurious' (in other words, psychosomatic rather than genuine); and adopting a decidedly unsympathetic approach towards women's complaints when they were viewed as stemming from social circumstances (1978, pp 45–46). They argue that nowhere have these practices been more prevalent than in the psychiatric profession. The psychiatrists they came into contact with in their research were 'more blatantly superior and patronising than the GPs in the way they referred to their middle-aged female patients' (1978, p 46). Procek confirmed Barrett and Roberts' claims, and added that the designation of the label 'sick' was not always an evenly negotiated process (1980, p 27). Manipulative strategies, such as pathologising women's resistance, could potentially be employed by psychiatrists to enforce the definition of 'sick' in a situation where there was disagreement between the woman and doctor.

Although Barrett and Roberts' article was published in the late 1970s, their main points continue to resonate in current analyses. They show how the hierarchical nature of the relationship between women and the medical profession allowed doctors to exercise control over their female patients' perceptions of their problems and situations. Current writings on women and the psychiatric profession maintain that this type of relationship persists. The interaction between present conventional medical practice and the patient is such that women still have very little input into selecting the type of treatment they receive or into determining the root cause of their health problems. Women's perceptions of themselves and their behaviour continue to be influenced by the medical profession's perception of them. As Hudson's (1987) research on the uses of psychosurgery demonstrated, the treatment was used mostly on women whose behaviour was regarded as problematic and undesirable by their relatives, psychiatrists, and even themselves, and hence, required modification.

Feminist writers have also argued that psychiatric practices have been sexist. Miller and Rose (1986) point out that feminist critiques of psychiatry have significantly challenged conceptions of both institutional and community psychiatry. The critique of psychiatric sexism has found support in: women's higher rates of referral to psychiatrists, psychologists and therapists than men (Briscoe, 1982); differential levels of diagnosis (Chunn and Menzies, 1998); and the greater likelihood of women being prescribed psychotropic drugs and of being given ECT (electro convulsive therapy) than men (Cooperstock, 1976, 1978). Feminist writers have asked whether women are genuinely mad or just diagnosed as mad according to associations made about their femininity (Kimball, 1975; King, 1975; Roth and Lerner, 1982; Ussher, 1991; Walker, 1993).

Some writers have suggested that the sex bias by the medical profession accounts for the existence of different attitudes towards the mental health of women and the mental health of men. Early studies conducted by Ehrenreich and English (1979) claimed that the image of women as 'mentally ill' is socially constructed. For example, married women who expressed unhappiness in a traditional marriage, where they assumed a passive, subservient role, had a higher risk of receiving a psychiatric diagnosis. Similarly, Broverman et al (1970, 1972) demonstrated a double standard of mental health operating where psychiatric descriptions of healthy adults independent of sex closely matched those descriptions of healthy men but not those of healthy women. Mental health professionals regarded a healthy woman as one who was more submissive and less independent than healthy men (Broverman *et al*, 1970, p 75).

Marcia Kaplan's (1983) study challenges the definitions of psychiatric categories and concepts for their supposedly gender-neutral interpretation and application. Her investigation of the most widely used manual for psychiatric diagnosis, the DSM-III-R (Diagnostic and Statistical Manual of Mental Disorders),[3] reveals how sex-role stereotyping and different attitudes to the mental health of women and men can result in women being more likely than men to be diagnosed as having personality disorders. She states that, 'via assumptions about sex roles made by clinicians, a healthy woman automatically earns the diagnosis of histrionic personality disorder' (1983, p 789). Similarly, Russell claims that psychiatric interpretations of mental illnesses do not emerge from medical theory, but are based on broad value judgments. She argues that a diagnosis of a mental disorder can simply be the result of a clash of values between the patient and psychiatrist, with the psychiatrist conforming to patriarchal values (1995, p 33). One example of this situation has been the historical view of lesbian relationships which psychiatrists have regarded as a mark of mental disorder (Hart, 1994; Penfold and Walker, 1984). Therefore, a serious weakness with the DSM-IV is its failure to acknowledge and clarify the values operating in discussions about the categories of mental disorders.

Literature on women's mental health has also disputed medical conceptions which tend to attribute madness in women to a biological cause (Busfield, 1983, 1986, 1989, 1994; Ussher, 1991; Burns, 1992). Feminist writers, in particular, have sought to emphasise madness in women as the product of cultural rather than natural forces. For example, Ripa argued that the mental health problems of unmarried women have been the result of emotional and mental loneliness rather than of some 'natural' cause (1990, p 55). Similarly, Russell (1995) asserted that many women's mental health problems were due to the weight of domestic, emotional and socio-economic situations rather than to inherent physiological problems.

Finally, feminist writers have also upheld the idea that the field of mental health sciences is actively gendered, producing different outcomes for women and for men. Jan Burns (1992) points to the imbalances in criminal and psychological statistics as the starting point for her contention that gender differences do exist. She takes as a given that these statistics, which represent women as less likely to be incarcerated for a crime yet more likely than men to be diagnosed with a mental disorder, are unproblematic. Her position resonates with the 'functional equivalence thesis' mentioned by Carol Smart (1976) which posits that deviant behaviour in men is identified with criminal behaviour whereas deviant behaviour in women is identified with mental disorder. The problem with this argument, however, is that there is no suggestion that the statistics may be interpreted differently, that the mental health and criminal justice systems can be so easily dichotomised, or that the statistics may not be an accurate reflection of what is actually happening. Therefore,

---

3   Since the publication of Kaplan's book, DSM-IV succeeded DSM-III in 1994, and a text-revised edition, DSM-IV-TR, materialised in 2000.

it is arguably premature to claim the presence of institutionalised gender differences which go beyond the presented statistics.

Burns goes on to argue that since there are fewer women than men detained under ss 3 and 37 of the Mental Health Act 1983,[4] even though there are more women diagnosed as having mental disorders, it must be the case that the few 'mad' men who exist must also be dangerous. Furthermore, based on these statistics, she formulates her argument as to how these differences are perpetuated. Examining the work of Lombroso and Pollak, Burns critiques biological explanations by reinforcing the assertion that biological and misogynistic explanations of women's criminality have been the starting point for women's inclusion in criminological writings. She concludes with the argument that gender imbalances are the result of a 'gendered understanding of behaviour that is all-pervasive' and of 'the intractable and static discourses of medicine and psychiatry' (1992, p 124). Such a conclusion, however, throws doubt on the possibility of transforming the interactions between women and psychiatry to open the path for an alternative relationship.

However, not all feminists would agree that sexism is an inherent feature of the institution of psychiatry. Joan Busfield, for example, contests the view that women are more liable to be identified as mad than men. She claims that there has not been sufficient evidence to make the claim that madness is exclusive to women. Instead, she argues that madness has taken on many forms, some of which are strongly linked to women and femininity (1994, p 275; see Allen, 1987). However, some forms of madness are also linked to men and masculinity. Ussher (1991) also argues that although there are certain psychiatric disorders that women are more likely to be diagnosed as having than men, the reverse is also true. Therefore, while a woman with depression may receive prompt treatment for her illness, for example, another woman with an alcohol related illness might find difficulties obtaining treatment.

Certainly an understanding of the gendered nature of psychiatry, or any other institution, necessarily involves moving beyond an unproblematic reading of statistics and explanations rooted in patriarchal interest-serving terms. That is, it is necessary to question how statistics and explanations about women and psychiatry are generated, and whose interests they are promoting. Jordanova rejects the idea that women are more mad than men, since it is her belief that engaging in a discussion about the quantity of madness is to 'render mathematical the suffering and unhappiness of many women' (1981, p 112). She opts instead for an examination of how women's mental illnesses are expressed *differently*. This difference is grounded in a critique of the assumption that women are characterised as more emotional and uncontrolled than men. As Jordanova states, 'the point

---

4   Section 3 of the Mental Health Act 1983 in the UK states that an individual can be detained in hospital for treatment, and s 37 states that if you are charged with or found guilty of an offence that could be punishable by imprisonment, then it is possible for the court not to record a conviction. Instead, they can make a hospital order for treatment or a guardianship order. This is not possible if the offence you committed carries a sentence that is fixed by law (murder). If the court makes an order under this section then it is in lieu of going to prison, being put on probation, or being fined.

would not necessarily be to reject the idea, but to show how this sexual polarity was sustained in specific historical cases' (1981, p 111). Therefore, examining the idea of mental illness as actively gendered moves beyond statistical differences, to a broader context of mental illness which, for example, includes the forms of emotional expression of both sexes. This inevitably undercuts the idea that an organic mental disorder always 'exists' and gives greater emphasis to how the external, social environment can also influence mental health as well as how mental illness is a social construction or effect that is constituted in social processes.

As this brief discussion demonstrates, tensions exist amongst feminists over how best to understand the role of psychiatry in women's lives. These issues become even more complex when considered in the context of a criminal case where there are major implications for the defendant. Psychiatric assessments not only affect how we understand men's and women's mental health problems, but they also occupy a key role in determining the criminal responsibility of the defendant. In Britain, where defendants are diagnosed with a mental illness, they can enter a plea of diminished responsibility.[5] However, as the following sections indicate, interpreting the meaning of diminished responsibility is not without its own set of difficulties.

8.2   The defence of diminished responsibility

In England and Wales, all murder defendants receive a pre-trial psychiatric assessment. If a mental disorder is discerned, then the defence can consider putting forward a plea of diminished responsibility, as introduced through s 2 of the Homicide Act 1957. A successful plea has the effect of reducing a murder conviction to manslaughter. The defendant can then be subject to a range of psychiatric dispositions, including hospital orders and restriction orders. Section 2 states:

> (1)   Where a person kills or is a party to the killing of another, he shall not be convicted of murder if he [sic] was suffering from such abnormality of mind (whether arising from a condition of arrested or retarded development of mind or any inherent causes or induced by disease or injury) as substantially impaired his [sic] mental responsibility for his acts and omissions in doing or being a party to the killing.
>
> (2)   On a charge of murder, it shall be for the defence to prove that the person charged is by virtue of this section not liable to be convicted of murder.
>
> (3)   A person who but for this section would be liable ... to be convicted of murder shall be liable to be convicted of manslaughter.

In R v Byrne[6] the Court of Appeal defined an abnormality of mind as 'a state of mind so different from that of ordinary human beings that a reasonable man [sic] would term it abnormal'. In deciding whether an abnormality of mind exists, the court must consider the medical evidence as well as the facts and circumstances of

---

5   In other western industrialised countries such as Canada, a similar defence of diminished capacity is available.

6   [1960] 3 All ER 1.

the homicide. An abnormality can encompass all aspects of the mind's activities to include 'not only the perception of physical acts and matters and the ability to form a rational judgment whether an act is right or wrong, but also the ability to exercise will-power to control physical acts in accordance with that rational judgement. The person does not have to be born with the abnormality'.[7]

The defendant's inability to exercise control is regarded as diminished responsibility but, where the defendant has difficulty in controlling physical acts which are regarded as controllable (for example, jealous behaviour), the decision on whether his/her responsibility is diminished will be made by reference to the standard of the reasonable person.[8] This acknowledges, however, that measuring degrees of difficulty in controlling impulses cannot be conducted through scientific measure, thus requiring a broad 'common-sense' approach. The Butler Committee pointed out in their 1975 Report that 'mental responsibility' in s 2 of the Homicide Act 1957 is not a clinical question on which doctors have expertise, but a legal or a moral question.[9] The presence or absence of 'mental responsibility' is, as Dell (1982) confirms, not the result of a medical assessment, but doctors have to confront it nonetheless. It is not surprising, as a result, that where psychiatrists disagree on the issue of diminished responsibility, it is not over the medical aspects but the moral aspects of the case.

The availability of the defence is limited to pathological disorders rather than other factors that may affect the functioning of the mind such as revenge or greed (Williams, 1990). However, this raises the problem of how to classify and categorise difficult psychiatric conditions. Medical opinions differ over categories like 'depression' (Zimmerman, 1988). In addition, it is not unusual to find that psychiatrists may agree on the presence of a mental abnormality, but disagree over whether it was substantial enough to diminish the defendant's responsibility (Dell, 1982, p 813).

The *Sanderson*[10] decision by the Court of Appeal suggested a movement towards providing greater guidance over what constitutes an 'abnormality of mind', yet clarification over aetiology can have unintended consequences. The opinion provided in *Sanderson* is that an abnormality of mind can be 'induced by disease or injury' which refers to 'an organic or physical injury or disease of the body including the brain', but that such an understanding of 'disease' is not synonymous with 'disease of the mind' as set out in the McNaughton Rules. Furthermore, functional mental illnesses are also a permissible cause of an abnormality of mind, but are regarded as 'inherent causes' rather than as 'diseases'. As MacKay (1999, p 122) notes, in attempting to clarify concepts like 'disease' or 'injury' in s 2(1) of the

---

7 Cited in Williams (1990, p 183). See *R v Gomez* (1964) Cr App R 310 (CCA).

8 Many feminist legal scholars have pointed out that the reasonable person standard has traditionally been interpreted in favour of how a reasonable man would respond, but not how a reasonable woman may respond in a similar situation.

9 Home Office, DHSS, *Report of the Committee on Mentally Abnormal Offenders* (1975), Cmnd 5698. Debate surrounding the moral issue concerns whether or not defendants' inability to control their behaviour ought to constitute a lack of mental responsibility and mitigate their crime(s).

10 (1994) 98 Cr App R 325.

Mental Health Act 1983, it may become more difficult for mercy killers and women who kill their spouses to prove that they were operating under diminished capacity. The problem is that if 'injury' is to be of an organic or physical nature, then 'injury' of a non-organic nature like psychological 'injury' in the form of reactive depression caused by emotional trauma will have greater difficulty falling within the notion of abnormality of mind as provided in *Sanderson* (MacKay, 1999, p 123).

The inconsistent legal and medical opinions arising from these disagreements and the lack of clear guidance over the precise meaning of concepts such as 'inherent', 'injury' and 'disease' have led some commentators to argue for the abolition of the defence.[11] Fraser states:

> ... lawyers are unhappy because of the incursion of psychological babble and mumbo-jumbo into the relatively clear and simple area of *mens rea*. Psychologists and psychiatrists are unhappy because legal notions of *mens rea* are unscientific and simplistically fail to deal with the complex understanding of the human psyche developed by the sciences of psychology and psychiatry (1991, p 115).

He convincingly argues that the defence of diminished responsibility is problematic because of the apparent contradiction between 'diminished' and 'responsibility', and between 'psychiatry' and 'law'. He claims that this contradiction has resulted in a unified strategy of social protection through 'creating' and 're-creating' the subject (the defendant) (1991, p 116). That is, the marginalisation of diminished responsibility, where the focus is on individual not social problems, allows for the creation of a renewed subject – someone who 'is not only the author of his [*sic*] acts (the author responsible in terms of certain criteria of free, conscious will), but is linked to his [*sic*] offence by a whole bundle of complex threads (instincts, desires, tendencies, character)' (Foucault, 1977, in Fraser, 1991, p 253). This view of the defendant denies the 'social' factors relating to responsibility and 'mental illness'. As a result, the defence of diminished responsibility does not shift the blame or explanation for the criminal act from the individual to the social but, rather, it reconstitutes the legal subject into a hybrid species who is both mad and bad (Fraser, 1991, p 118). For women defendants, prevailing stereotypes about female criminality make them particularly vulnerable to such reassignments by legal and psychiatric institutions.

Fraser's argument highlights the many contradictions that permeate the defence of diminished responsibility. The moral, political, social, ethical and practical implications of making a plea of diminished responsibility are complex. Whether or not it will be possible to remove the defence from the mire of contradictions within which it is stuck remains unknown. As opinions[12] such as those found in *Sanderson* illustrate, the debate continues over how best to interpret the application of diminished responsibility.

---

11 Both the Butler Committee and the CLRC have proposed a re-wording of s 2 of the Homicide Act 1957. See Home Office, *Report of the Committee on Mentally Abnormal Offenders* (1975), Cmnd 6244, and the Criminal Law Revision Committee, *Fourteenth Report: Offences Against the Person* (1980), Cmnd 7844.

12 See also *R v O'Connell* [1997] Crim LR 683.

8.3 Gender, psychiatry and the legal system: case studies

The original database that yields this study comprises 50 (25 male and 25 female) files[13] involving 'intimate homicide',[14] drawn from Crown Prosecution Offices in five different regions of England and Wales (Cheshire; West Midlands; London South and Surrey; Avon and Somerset; and West Mercia). These files were randomly selected, to the extent possible, from lists of homicides which the Home Office Research and Statistics Department provided for each region for the years 1985 to 1991.[15]

Defendants in 25 of these homicide cases, nine women and 16 men, were diagnosed with a mental illness. The majority of the defendants submitted pleas of diminished responsibility.[16] Depressive illness was the most common diagnosis defendants received. In the nine cases of female defendants, psychiatrists diagnosed six women with depression and in the 16 identified cases of male defendants, they diagnosed 12 men with a depressive illness. There were eight cases involving defendants who were considered to have a serious mental illness warranting, in some cases, a hospital and restriction order under ss 37 and 41 of the Mental Health Act 1983. The sentences for defendants diagnosed with a mental condition varied considerably, especially in cases involving male defendants where the possible outcome ranged from probation orders to life imprisonment. The defendants' diagnoses and the verdicts of these cases are listed in Tables 8.1 and 8.2.

8.3.1 The 'abnormal' defendant

Psychiatrists view the presence of pathology (whether psychological or physical) in the defendant as critical evidence of the defendant's mental state. While a minority of both male and female defendants were noted as having a history of mental disorders, a larger proportion of defendants were reported to have pathological or abnormal personality traits where depression was the most common diagnosis. This tendency was most noticeable amongst male defendants although there were several female defendants who were also labelled with abnormal traits. These characteristics include being described as 'socially isolated', 'over-controlled', 'vulnerable' and 'obsessional'. For female defendants, psychiatrists regarded their abnormalities in relation to their inability to cope with their circumstances:

---

13 The main body of documents gathered from the homicide files includes case summaries prepared by junior counsel, briefs for the Prosecution, investigating officers' reports, transcripts of police interviews with the defendant, psychiatric reports, disclosed and unused witness statements, bail notices, instructions and legal correspondence, and law clerks' notes. Except for minor discrepancies, these documents were accessible in almost all the homicide cases examined.

14 The categories of relationships selected were based on the Home Office Criminal Statistics delineation of categories of relationship between offender and victim. They include: spouse; cohabitant; former spouse; and former cohabitant. The category of spouse incorporates both marriages and common-law relationships.

15 For more detail on the file selection process, data contents and general methodology, see Chan, 2001, pp 43–47.

16 There were minor exceptions in the cases of two female defendants who made pleas other than diminished responsibility and two male defendants who made joint pleas of diminished responsibility and provocation.

TABLE 8.1 Female defendants diagnosed with a mental illness

DEFENDANT	OFFENCE	CONVICTION	PLEA	DIAGNOSES	SENTENCE
Cathy	Murder	Manslaughter	Diminished Responsibility	Depression due to a history of neurotic disorder	hospital order (s 37) – MHA* 1983
Gail	Murder	Manslaughter	Diminished Responsibility	Early dementia, depression and chronic anxiety	3 years' probation and outpatient treatment
Jean	Murder	Manslaughter	Diminished Responsibility	Depression	2.5 years' imprisonment
Maureen	Murder	Manslaughter	Diminished Responsibility	Schizophrenia	hospital order (s 37) and restriction order (s 41) – MHA 1983
Marlee	Murder	Manslaughter	Diminished Responsibility	Depression and anxiety	2 years' probation
Pat	Murder	Manslaughter	Diminished Responsibility	Anxiety state and chronic alcoholism	4 years' imprisonment
Tina	Murder	Manslaughter	Diminished Responsibility	Expected severe grief reaction	3 years' probation and psychiatric treatment
Susan	Murder & GBH (s 18)	Manslaughter	Not guilty to everything**	Obsessional personality traits with histrionic traits and intermittent episodes of depression	3 year probation order
Paula	Murder	Manslaughter	Provocation	Depression, acute situational stress, severe emotional disturbance, anxiety	diminished responsibility accepted instead of provocation; 2 years' probation with 12 month residence

* Mental Health Act

** Defendant refuses to plea to manslaughter on grounds of diminished responsibility

TABLE 8.2 Male defendants diagnosed with a mental illness

DEFENDANT	OFFENCE	CONVICTION	PLEA	DIAGNOSES	SENTENCE
Andy	Murder	Manslaughter	Diminished Responsibility	Depression and organic brain syndrome	hospital order (s 37) and restriction order (s 41) – MHA* 1983
Ben	Murder	Manslaughter	Diminished Responsibility	Depression and abnormal personality	7 years' imprisonment
Cecil	Murder	Manslaughter	Diminished Responsibility	Depression	life imprisonment
Colin	Murder	Murder	Diminished Responsibility	Morbid jealousy and irresistible impulse	life imprisonment – min 18 years
Donald	Murder	Manslaughter	Diminished Responsibility	Depression	hospital order (s 37) – MHA 1983
Jack	Murder	Murder	Diminished Responsibility and Provocation	Reactive depression	Life imprisonment
Jake	Murder	Manslaughter	Diminished Responsibility	Depression	3 years' probation
Kevin	Murder	Manslaughter	Diminished Responsibility	Pathological jealousy	6 years' imprisonment
Lloyd	Murder × 2	Manslaughter × 2	Diminished Responsibility	Paranoid schizophrenia	hospital order (s 37) and restriction order (s 41) without limit of time – MHA 1983
Mark	Murder	Manslaughter	Diminished Responsibility	Depression	3 years' imprisonment
Mike	Murder	Manslaughter	Diminished Responsibility	Depression	7 years' imprisonment
Roger	Murder	Murder	Diminished Responsibility	Depression	life imprisonment
Roy	Murder	Manslaughter	Diminished Responsibility	Depression	hospital order (s 37) and restriction order (s 41) – MHA 1983
Tom	Murder × 2	Manslaughter	Diminished Responsibility	Schizophrenia	hospital order (s 37) and restriction order (s 41) – MHA 1983
Tony	Murder	Manslaughter	Diminished Responsibility and Provocation	Over-controlled personality and depression	3 years' imprisonment
Trevor	Murder	Manslaughter	Diminished Responsibility	Depression	2 years' probation

* Mental Health Act

The psychological consequences of this deprived upbringing was the development of a shy vulnerable adolescent who expected emotional maltreatment and had no effective response to the occurrence.

(Psychiatrist #1 interviewing Gail)

The defendant's intelligence is low-average to borderline mentally subnormal. She thus has poor intellectual reserves to cope with the stresses that she was experiencing.

(Psychiatrist #1 interviewing Marlee)

It is likely that many of her symptoms can be explained by a neurotic reaction in a previously socially isolated personality who was unable to cope with the change in her lifestyle and family composition.

(Psychiatrist #3 interviewing Susan)

Female defendants' reactions to their circumstances are not treated as valid. Their lack of response and their powerlessness to alter their circumstances are construed as the result of an internal pathology, which is then translated into a symptom of a mental illness. What is also suggested here is that female defendants do not act, but only respond to the events that occur in their lives. Hence, the presence of abnormal characteristics speaks not to their actions, but to their reactions – to their coping abilities, their responses, rather than the choices they make for themselves. For defendants like Marlee and Susan, although they suffered violent abuse by their partners, psychiatrists viewed their responses as abnormal because, unlike Paula or Jean discussed in the following section, the violence they experienced was not as severe in quality or quantity. Hence, the expectation is that they should have been able to respond to and control the situation. That they seemingly did not appear able to manage suggests the presence of pathology.

For male defendants, psychiatrists take the opposite approach. Male defendants' pathological personalities do not diminish their choice-making activity; they simply place limits on how well they can make these choices. Unlike the reports in cases involving female defendants, psychiatric reports of male defendants provide lengthy lists of the defendants' symptoms and how they acted during their mental illness, stressing what they *did or could not do* rather than *what happened* to them:

He noticed he was losing his sense of humour, wanted not to mix so much and was snapping at people. He became irritable and did not want to work with the apprentices. He would be over cautious at work because he was fearful of making a mistake through lack of concentration. His sleep started to become fitful and he would wake up not feeling refreshed in the morning.

(Psychiatrist #2 interviewing Tony)

In the one month prior to the killing he asserts, and this is supported by witness statements, that he was suffering from sleep disturbance, dysphoria (ie, a state of variable unhappiness and sadness, impairment of appetite with weight loss of over a stone and impaired concentration and sexual drive).

(Psychiatrist #2 interviewing Cecil)

In addition, a large majority of the reports cite male defendants contemplating or planning to commit suicide after the homicide event – an issue which is hardly discussed, if at all, in female defendants' reports. Psychiatrists tended to provide more information about why and how the male defendant attempted to commit suicide in comparison to female defendants where the only information provided is a one-line statement indicating that a suicide attempt had been made. Again, this reinforces the view of male defendants as having agency – the ability to decide for themselves what happens to them or those around them – even if it is considered the wrong choice by psychiatrists. Their actions are rational, and it is their mental illness in the form of a pathological personality which contributes to their inability to exercise good judgment. Female defendants' actions are rarely accorded such rationality. Rather, they are viewed by psychiatrists as victims of their circumstances:

> [she] fulfilled the role of the powerless victim who is unable to change or escape from distressing circumstances.
>
> (Psychiatrist #3 interviewing Gail)

> The relationship between the defendant and her husband was one in which she was the victim of his alcoholism and his violence.
>
> (Psychiatrist#1 interviewing Marlee)

As a result of being victimised, female defendants' actions are not regarded as rational. Since they are acted upon rather than actors making choices, it is not their judgment which is questioned by psychiatrists, but their behaviour that is scrutinised. Their actions prior to the homicide and the homicide itself are deemed irrational, the product of a mental state caused by their victimisation and their abnormal personalities. Within this context, female defendants' suicide attempts become one of many symptoms of their victimisation.

Feminist writers have strongly critiqued this view of male defendants as active agents and female defendants as passive victims. They argue that psychiatrists are stereotyping women and women's mental illness in accepting these images. That is, psychiatric ideologies identify the problem differently – for a woman the problem is with *who she is* – seen here in the construction of women's mental illness as comprised of her irrational behaviour and in the portrayal of her as a victim of violence – whether it is in the form of violent abuse or as a victim of a homicide. As Elinore King (1975, p 22) notes, while men are associated with the positive qualities of courage, independence, leadership and rationality, women are ascribed negative qualities of being masochistic, narcissistic, weak, dependent and illogical. In the context of a domestic homicide, these stereotypes consequently allow psychiatric professionals to identify the mental illnesses manifested in female defendants as a pathology of their inner state of being, while male defendants' mental illnesses are embodied in their actions, their external state of doing.

8.3.2 *Violence and the victim*

One of the most noticeable themes in the psychiatric reports of the homicide cases discussed in this chapter is the frequency with which the issue of violence attracts attention in both male and female cases. In cases involving female defendants, psychiatrists place importance on determining whether or not the defendant has been abused by her partner prior to the homicide. However, with male defendants, they raise the opposite concern. That is, the emphasis by psychiatrists is on whether or not the defendant has been violent towards the victim prior to the homicide. The following statements exemplify the detailed attention paid to the problem of violence by the psychiatrist interviewing the defendant:

Although their relationship was 'alright at first' it soon deteriorated as [Gail's husband's] drinking and the consequences of that behaviour became apparent.

When he drank heavily, [he] became violent. 'He was horrific'. She was not only frightened by her husband's behaviour, but she was disturbed by the sense that it was reminiscent of her 'mother's' cruel behaviour. 'With drink he is evil'.

[Gail's husband] assaulted his wife two or three times each week. He would hit her where it would not show, eg, upper arms, torso. When he was sober he could not recall the abuse, and would often apologise for this drunken behaviour.

[Gail] tolerated the violence for fourteen months, at which time she left her husband. They were apart for a year, before he persuaded [Gail] to return, promising he would be different.

It was not to be. The physical abuse continued. He would hit her on the shoulders and chest, stamp on her arms and knee her in the back. Twice she went to hospital with her injuries (with an injury to her arm and when she had difficulty passing urine following a kick in the back), but she did not reveal that she was being abused. She told nobody of her plight, for she was scared of her husband. While she was intimidated by him, fearful of further beatings, at other times (when he was sober) he was pleasant and 'quiet'. [Gail] described her husband as a 'Jekyll and Hyde character'.

While he was courteous to others, at home when drunk he was domineering, loud and would use foul language. Not only did he insult his wife, he would also verbally abuse his step-son who had come to live with them in 1985 following a road traffic accident. In accordance with his mother's wishes, however, he kept himself to himself, avoided his step-father whenever possible and never became involved with [the victim] when provoked.

For [Gail], one of the worst insults was to be called a 'bastard' by her husband. She had told him of her upbringing and he would use it against her when drunk. Again this behaviour stimulated unpleasant memories from her past, reminding her of her lonely, insecure childhood. She was especially upset when [her husband] called [her son] a bastard.

According to [Gail] the drunken beatings continued after her son moved in, but he would abuse her when [her son] was out or upstairs in bed. [Gail] was, after years of abuse, subservient to the dominating will of her violent husband.

(Psychiatrist #2 interviewing Gail)

In contrast to the specific discussion of violence taking place in female defendants' cases, psychiatrists raise the issue of violence in male defendants' cases by focusing on the likelihood of the defendant behaving violently towards his spouse. Instead of discussing the presence or absence of violence in the relationship, the psychiatric reports emphasise the defendant's character, with a particular focus on his temper, in determining if the defendant is prone to violent behaviour. Hence, while women defendants are assessed for how much risk they were confronted with, male defendants are assessed for the type and level of risk they posed to the victim prior to the homicide. For example:

There is no clinical evidence to suggest he is a violent person. He has a normal development of conscience, has shown over the years that he is concerned at the effect of his behaviour on others and that he can learn by experience. There is again no clinical evidence to suggest that he has psychopathic traits in his personality or that he is given to irrational outbursts of temper and rage.

(Psychiatrist #2 interviewing Roger)

[Donald] describes himself as someone with no temper problems and who, on the whole, is quite easy going.

(Psychiatrist #1 interviewing Donald)

For his part he seems to have been a highly controlled man, never answering back, never losing his temper and only slapping her twice in a controlled manner because of the way she treated the children.

(Psychiatrist #1 interviewing Cecil)

The discussion of violence in the psychiatric reports highlights the importance placed on how the issue of violence reveals information about the defendant's mental health. Psychiatrists rely on external factors such as demonstrations of violent behaviour for an understanding of male defendants. For female defendants, it is the internal factors which influence psychiatrists' assessments.[17] The presence of violence in women's lives is regarded as a sign of a dysfunctional relationship which operates as a contributing factor to the onset of a mental illness.

In six of the nine cases involving female defendants, violence had been reported in the relationship. The degree and frequency of violence inflicted on the *defendants* varied, as did the turbulent nature of the relationship more generally. In these cases, psychiatrists tended to identify the violent abuse as the cause of the defendants' mental illness. In the following discussion of Jean and Paula's cases, which involved long and/or violent periods of abuse, their reports illustrate how psychiatrists theorise the role of violence in their lives for assessing their mental condition.

Jean claimed that she lived in constant fear of physical violence because her husband would assault her on many occasions for no apparent reason. Her husband had threatened to shoot her, her children and members of her family. She stated that she occasionally left him after he had violently assaulted her, but she would be forced to return when he caught up with her and made threats to her and others. One psychiatrist acknowledged that Jean had 'lived with a severely violent and sadistic man who submitted her to verbal, physical, and sexual abuse amounting to terrorization'. The psychiatrist did not believe that there were any reasons for treating Jean medically, thus recognising that it had been her domestic situation which resulted in her mental health problems. Once Jean was no longer in a violent and pathological environment, the belief was that her mental condition would improve.

For Paula, her marriage was reported by the prosecution as 'a turbulent business'. They recognised that Paula had been subject to 'an inordinately lengthy and vicious course of abuse over many years by her husband'. Paula stated that, prior to the killing, she had consulted her GP because she felt she had become depressed. As one psychiatric report noted:

She stated that 'normally, I'm resilient, even cheerful – I don't know how I do it, but I do', but that her resilience had now deserted her, she felt depressed, had found herself 'bursting into tears, even while peeling the vegetables' because 'I could no longer

---

17 Hilary Allen's (1987) study of gender and psychiatric decisions found similar results in that psychiatrists typically focused on the external, observable behaviour of men in locating their mental 'disorder'. In contrast, the site of women's mental 'disorder' is located in their inner events and feelings.

pretend there was any excuse for what he did to me' (referring to the totally inexplicable bottling of her face) – 'I was confused and unhappy and tearful' – something that she had 'never been before'.

(Psychiatrist #1 interviewing Paula)

The psychiatrists who interviewed the defendant stated that her husband's unfaithfulness caused a 'significant emotional trauma' which was exacerbated by the many years of violence she had endured. They state:

the realisation of her husband's blatant utilisation of her absence from home (due to injuries inflicted by him) was a very significant emotional trauma which, being added to the accumulated traumata of many years of violence produced an abnormality of mind.

(Psychiatrist #1 interviewing Paula)

the cumulative distress of many years of cruel treatment, together with the psychological injury brought about by [the defendant] suddenly learning that her husband had engaged in sexual intercourse in her house had given rise to such an abnormality of mind resulting in an irresistible impulse.

(Psychiatrist #2 interviewing Paula)

The homicide and Paula's mental condition are the direct results of the 'trauma' the defendant had endured. For female defendants who have been subjected to abuse and violence, it has been their role as targets of violent abuse by their spouses which has caused their mental illness. As these two cases illustrate, it has not been unusual to find that female defendants' mental illnesses have been a response to their dysfunctional social environment. Their attempts to manage the problems in their relationships have led to the deterioration of their mental health.

These two cases contrast with the following two cases of Ben and Mike. Ben was charged with the murder of his wife. The investigating officer stated that 'throughout their five year marriage, there was severe domestic turmoil, resulting in the deceased being assaulted frequently by her husband'. In the psychiatric interviews, one psychiatrist stated that Ben claimed he had become obsessed about his wife leaving him and being unfaithful. Ben told the psychiatrist he had become increasingly depressed a few months prior to the murder. Ben was diagnosed as suffering from a depressive illness. As the psychiatrist stated:

He is an irritable, temperamentally unstable man with an aggressive streak. He copes with stress badly and is subject to mood swings, when he is liable to intemperate outbursts and his feeling of aggression can be expressed in words or physical violence. He is a quarrelsome man who draws sharp distinctions between his own conduct and that of others ...

... He was obsessed with the thought of his wife leaving home and being unfaithful to him. He was not sleeping well, not concentrating well, not eating well and had lost about half a stone in weight, and was generally feeling very irritable and low in mood. His behaviour had become very erratic. He had sought help from his General Practitioner. This is a clinical picture of a depressive illness.

(Psychiatrist #2 interviewing Ben)

The psychiatrist maintained that, at the time of the killing, it was Ben's 'reactive depression, his personality, the relationship within the marriage, his wife's problems with alcohol, her relationship with [her lover] which amounts to an abnormality of mind'.

In Mike's case, it was reported that his partner had been living with him for the past four to five years when the relationship deteriorated, and she left him. Her family members gave evidence that Mike had frequently abused his partner, causing black eyes, cuts and bruises to her body. At the time of the murder, Mike claimed that he had taken his partner up to a bedroom because he wanted to speak to her in private. An argument had occurred, and Mike admitted that he had stabbed her. The prosecution believed that Mike's partner had left him because he was abusive towards her, and that Mike's attack against her had been premeditated.

Mike went through six psychiatric examinations where three psychiatrists diagnosed him with a mental illness, two psychiatrists claimed that he was not mentally ill, and one psychiatrist offered no medical opinion. The psychiatrists who diagnosed Mike with a mental condition stated that he had an abnormal personality and was suffering from a depressive illness. As one psychiatrist states:

> ... he could be construed as suffering from mental impairment and an order made under section 37 of the Mental Health Act on ground of his low intellect, limited social competence and recurrently violent behaviour.
>
> (Psychiatrist #5 interviewing Mike)

Hence, exhibiting symptoms of violent behaviour along with 'limited intellect' and 'emotional disturbance' leads psychiatrists to a diagnosis of a mental illness.

These cases indicate how, in psychiatric explanations of the defendant's behaviour and mental state, violence in male defendants' relationships with their partners occupies a different role than in female defendants' cases. Men's abusive behaviour towards their spouses is perceived as a sign of individual pathology and a symptom of mental disorder. However, for female defendants, it has been the violent abuse that caused their mental disorder. Unlike male defendants, however, in four of the six female defendants' cases referred to here, the development of their mental illness is not pathologised but rather regarded as 'normal' and 'acceptable' given the circumstances these women experienced. Since these female defendants did not have a history of mental illness, psychiatrists regarded the violence they suffered as a significant contribution to the deterioration of their mental health. As one psychiatrist notes:

> This woman does not suffer from mental illness nor from any other mental disorder specified within the terms of the formal provisions of the Mental Health Act 1983. Indeed I think that she is a reasonably normal person from the psychiatric viewpoint and she is certainly fit to plead. Admittedly her personal circumstances over the last seven or eight years have been rather chaotic and the two important relationships which she has had during this period have turned out to be quite disastrous. The first one with her husband ended up in divorce and the second one with [the victim] ended with him being killed during the course of a violent dispute between the two of them.
>
> (Psychiatrist #1 interviewing Tina)

For these female defendants, developing a mental illness was a 'normal' response to an 'abnormal' and stressful circumstance.

In considering the role of the victim in determining the defendant's mental state at the time of the homicide, as I have argued, psychiatrists attribute the cause of women's mental illness to the victim's behaviour. However, in male defendants' cases, it was not so much the victim's behaviour but rather the victim herself – that is, who she was in some cases – which contributed to the development of a mental illness. Note the following remarks made:

> [the victim] was an under-controlled over-emotional somewhat egocentric woman who would verbally abuse him and hit him at times ...
>
> (Psychiatrist #1 interviewing Cecil)

> ... the problem of a lady with neurotic traits recovering from an illness of this nature and having to come home. The accused felt he could cope with the situation but close questioning – and I have no reason to disbelieve him – shows that the [victim] was demanding and fussy ...
>
> (Psychiatrist #1 interviewing Trevor)

> ... further, the situation where a somewhat dependent man who feels himself sexually inadequate is married to a domineering and sexually rejecting wife ...
>
> (Psychiatrist #3 interviewing Kevin)

In the attempt to garner sympathy for the defendant's situation, one of the techniques used by psychiatrists is to cast a negative portrait of the defendant's partner to demonstrate the difficulties the defendant experienced in managing his relationship and how this contributed to the development of the defendant's mental illness. Since the stressful nature of his circumstance and his response is 'understandable', we can comprehend how he developed symptoms of a mental illness. What differentiates this view of female victims when compared to male victims is that, in the latter, the victim's behaviour is accentuated but, in the former, it is who she is as a victim which is given attention. Her transgression of gender norms, whether it is the result of being 'egocentric' or 'domineering', allows psychiatrists to scapegoat the victim as the cause of his mental illness. Furthermore, in contrast to the portrayal of female defendants as behaving 'normally', women victims are pathologised for not adhering to accepted boundaries of feminine conduct.

8.3.3   The problem of male jealousy

If violent abuse is a common theme found in female defendants' circumstances, jealousy is a common thread found in male defendants' cases. In half of the male defendants' cases, psychiatric reports cite jealousy as a factor in the deterioration of the defendant's relationship with his partner. In two of these cases the defendants were diagnosed with morbid or pathological jealousy (although for both, psychiatrists disagreed over the appropriate diagnosis, an indication perhaps of the ambiguous role that jealousy occupies in the context of a homicide).

Modern conceptions of jealousy view this emotion as a series of vices with little or no virtue, and are characterised by the adoption of reason as a determining factor in an individual's behaviour. Mullen notes how jealousy, as an emotive response, is riven by contradictions:

> At one extreme it embodies a longing for an ideal in human relationships and a cry of protest at the loss of that dream of sustained commitment and fidelity. At the other, it has always been contaminated by the attempt to impose the desires and priorities of one person upon another. (Mullen 1991, p 593)

As a result of attacks by 19th century psychologists and psychiatrists, reactions to jealousy were increasingly emphasised as defects in a person's character. Exhibiting jealousy was something to be avoided, and if avoidance was not possible, then treatment had to be considered, resulting in the view of jealousy as pathological. The pathologising of jealous behaviour contributes to the perception that any ensuing violence is a deviant social act associated with conceptions of madness, and that punishment should be mitigated.

Mullen (1991) notes that modern day English society is likely to see a jealous killer advance a defence of mental instability because of the stress of infidelity. Not surprisingly, as a mental illness, jealousy is a highly controversial diagnosis. The cases of Kevin and Colin in this study are two examples where defendants' jealous emotions are deemed, although not without controversy, by some psychiatrists as sufficiently pathological to warrant a reduced conviction. However, in most cases, where jealousy is mentioned as a contributing factor to a deteriorating relationship, defendants are not diagnosed with morbid or pathological jealousy.[18] Rather, their jealous behaviour is regarded as one indicator of the defendant's mental illness. For example, consider the following remarks:

> [Donald] has always been a quiet, withdrawn sort of person who has found it hard to confide in other people or express his feelings. He had been morbidly jealous of his wife, unfortunately his worst fears started to get confirmed ... while suffering from depression during the course of the marital row he ended up taking his wife's life.
>
> (Psychiatrist #2 interviewing Donald)

> There are pronounced traits of immaturity and dependency in his personality, such emotional immaturity being consistent with his intellectual backwardness and due to retarded development of mind. I believe [Mike] was extremely dependent on [the victim] and found her behaviour towards him exceedingly difficult to understand and accept. He had long had doubts about her fidelity and even concerning the paternity of his children. He had been dejected on the previous occasions when she had left him and on the final occasion had done all he believed possible to persuade her to return. He has an abnormally low inability to cope with such stresses and would act inappropriately and become anxious and depressed or blame others for his predicament.
>
> (Psychiatrist #2 interviewing Mike)

Given the cultural expectation that individuals are required to control their jealous emotions, as the cases here suggest, jealousy is more likely to be seen as a symptom of a mental illness than as an illness itself. Although there is acknowledgment that the presence of jealousy exists, disagreement exists over the extent to which the defendants' jealous emotions destabilised his ability to control his behaviour at the time of the homicide. These disagreements highlight the tensions that can exist over the issue of jealousy and the uncertainty of its role within homicides. In the context of a murder trial, being able to demarcate clearly what comes to be understood and defined as morbid or pathological jealousy is crucial. However, understanding the role of jealousy in homicides between partners is fraught with uncertainty about where the division between revenge and mental illness lies. Since the conditions giving rise to the problems of jealousy between partners are the result of complex social, emotional, and psychological circumstances, the range of legal outcomes in

---

18 Morbid or pathological jealousy constitutes a subtype of delusional disorder where the person believes, incorrectly, that his/her partner is unfaithful.

such cases reflects the need for more clearly established guidelines about how to consider the defendant's lack of control arising from jealous emotions.

8.3.4 Mental illness and legal responsibility

The legal outcomes of these cases reflect the divergent views of what causes madness for male and female defendants, and of the role that the defendants' mental condition plays in the homicide. Although psychiatrists may diagnose a defendant with a mental disorder, the extent to which the law accepts that a finding of mental illness mitigates the homicide varies significantly. In some cases, a mental disorder exonerates the defendant's legal responsibility; in others it plays a minor role in the final outcome of the case. As a result, the 25 defendants discussed here received a range of sentences from probation orders to life imprisonment or hospitalisation under the Mental Health Act 1983.

A comparison between female and male defendants demonstrates that, for female defendants, their diagnoses have been helpful in obtaining a lenient sentence.[19] Only two defendants, Cathy and Maureen, were committed under s 37 of the Mental Health Act 1983.[20] Both defendants had a history of mental illness and Maureen's diagnosis of schizophrenia was considered serious enough to also warrant a restriction order under s 41 of the Mental Health Act 1983.[21] None of the other female defendants were given sentences of more than four years imprisonment. In fact, five out of nine defendants received probation orders for their offences. This suggests that, despite having committed a violent crime, these female defendants are not regarded as a danger or risk to society:

> The defendant does not pose any danger to the public in the future. The court will wish to bear in mind that the defendant is currently pregnant and has three children, who would be severely disadvantaged if she were to receive a custodial sentence.
>
> (Psychiatrist #1 interviewing Jean)

> The stabbing of her husband occurred in special circumstances when she was seriously disturbed mentally, the severity of the disturbance not having been recognised or having been misunderstood. The attack on him reflected her despair at the prospect that he of whom she was very fond was going to leave her. Circumstances like these are unlikely to recur. She has not shown any tendency to violence otherwise. It is unlikely that she will ever again be a danger to others.
>
> (Psychiatrist #3 interviewing Susan)

However, three female defendants, although they received probation, were also recommended for short-term psychiatric treatment even though their psychiatric

---

19 Many feminist scholars would argue that the criminal justice system has not gone far enough in recognising women's different experiences of homicide. The system continues to criminalise women whose actions are arguably self-defensive in nature. Also, while many women may receive a light sentence, their pleas of diminished responsibility continue to render their behaviour as pathological. See, for example, Comack, 1996.

20 See note 4 above.

21 Section 41 of the Mental Health Act 1983 refers to the powers of higher courts to restrict discharge from a hospital and is used in conjunction with s 37. If the defendant, who is under a hospital order, is seen as posing a serious risk of harm to the general public, a Crown Court can impose a 'restriction order'.

reports stated that they did not have a serious mental illness. Thus, the argument made by some feminists that the institution of psychiatry has had a 'heavy-handed' role in women's mental health is worthy of continued investigation. However, despite the recommendation of treatment, the sentences for female defendants were generally lenient when compared to those of male defendants. Hilary Allen (1987, p 91) suggests that this may reflect an attempt by the courts to suppress or deny the criminal intent of the defendants, thereby reinforcing a more stereotyped view of female behaviour as harmless. Chunn and Menzies (1990), in contrast, argue that women are not being treated more leniently than men by the psychiatric profession. Rather, psychiatrists assess each individual with the assumption that all their clients have some form of deficiency. The appearance that women defendants may be receiving more lenient treatment than men is tempered by the view that although they are 'disordered', they are still mentally stable enough to stand trial and have their behaviour judged (Chunn and Menzies, 1990, p 50).

In comparison to their female counterparts, male defendants in this study received a broader range of sentences (see Tables 8.1 and 8.2) extending from a hospital and restriction order and life imprisonment on the one hand, to two years probation on the other. Among the categories of identified mental illnesses, the broadest range of sentences has been where male defendants were diagnosed with depression. Unlike cases of female defendants diagnosed with depression, most of whom received two to three years probation, there was a lack of uniformity in the sentencing of male defendants. In cases where psychiatrists cited violence in the relationship, female defendants received short-term sentences while most of the male defendants received longer sentences. This contrast reflects the circumstances of the case whereby female defendants are identified as *victims* of abuse while male defendants are the *perpetrators* of abuse. In cases where male defendants had a history of mental illness or were diagnosed with schizophrenia, like female defendants, they were committed under s 37 of the Mental Health Act 1983.

The sentencing of defendants discussed here reflects the gendered nature of psychiatric assessments. Female defendants are subject to risk assessments which see them as lacking criminal intent. Therefore, they are not fully responsible for their crimes because they were acting irrationally as a result of their mental illness. From the psychiatric perspective, these are not dangerous offenders, but rather women who were caught in unfortunate circumstances and fatally wounded their partners. However, their behaviour as women does not escape psychiatric scrutiny for they are still held accountable for their actions. The implication here is that they contributed to their circumstances by failing to live up to acceptable standards of feminine behaviour. This could account for why more women than men received recommendations for treatment and counselling. The view of male defendants is more mixed. Their sentences reflect the court's view that although they may be diagnosed with a mental disorder, the courts are more likely to recognise their decision-making and behaviour as rational when compared with female defendants. As a result, men are seen as more culpable for their actions although these differences between male and female defendants are, as previously mentioned, moderated by the recognition that psychiatrists view all the defendants as responsible to some extent for their actions, and deserving of legal sanctions.

8.4 Conclusion

As this chapter has highlighted, there are many complex issues arising from an examination of the psychiatric assessments of homicide defendants diagnosed with a mental illness.

First, the discussion here points to the way in which the defence of diminished responsibility gave psychiatry a powerful role in the homicide case whilst also allowing for a blurred distinction between diagnosis and compassion. The wide use of this defence in domestic homicides is evidence that the law does grant concessions where a discriminating and compassionate response is required. However, as the legal disposal of many male defendants' cases illustrates, the law is equally capable of marginalising psychiatric diagnoses where a stiffer penalty is desired. Some writers suggest that, in homicides involving intimate partners, diminished responsibility is the plea of last resort given the doctrinal restrictions on self-defence and provocation (Bacon and Lansdowne, 1982; Leader-Elliott, 1993). Although research on this point is inconclusive, the current study does indeed lend legitimacy to this claim, in that half of the 50 randomly selected intimate homicide cases involved a plea of diminished responsibility. Indeed, in two cases involving female defendants, the courts accepted a plea of diminished responsibility even though the defendants did not put forward a case for diminished capacity.

The tendency to invoke mental illness for women defendants is evident in the increasing acceptance of expert testimony on the battered woman syndrome (BWS) in the United States and Canada. While the introduction of the battered woman syndrome in England has been more sporadic, the acceptance of diminished responsibility pleas by the courts for female defendants parallels the view and logic in the United States that women who have been victims of domestic violence are psychologically disabled (Leader-Elliot, 1993, p 406). The problems with the courts accepting this view is that women defendants are dichotomously seen either as 'legitimate' victims of violence or as cold-blooded murderers. What is bypassed is the possibility for a more complex understanding of the defendants' actions and the circumstances leading to the homicide.

Secondly, the cases examined here highlight the way in which dualistic thinking by psychiatrists affects how diagnoses of mental illness are constructed, and how they are constructed differently for male and female homicide defendants. Indeed, missing from these reports are explanations of the defendants' mental health problems that adequately acknowledge the social manifestations of madness as well as individual pathology. Alan Norrie (1993, pp 187–88) argues that the accent on individual explanations hides the social significance of madness by decontextualising social action and agency. As the psychiatric reports in this study illustrate, such an emphasis on identifying the defendant's mental illness with her abnormal personality, her inability to adequately cope with her circumstances or her longstanding mental condition effectively removes society's responsibility for the mentally ill criminal. Particularly in cases where women have been abused by their spouses, explanations of women's mental illnesses based solely on individual factors are inadequate if they do not consider the social elements as well. Giving greater emphasis to social as well as individual psychiatric factors in diagnosing defendants may allow for a broader understanding of how mental illness can emerge.

Furthermore, consistent with the claims made in the literature about women's mental health, the institution of psychiatry relies on negative and stereotypical gender assumptions in constructing and labelling female defendants as mentally disordered. They are portrayed as irrational, their crimes are viewed as aberrant acts unfitting a 'normal' woman, and their diagnoses of mental disorder explain their behaviour. The few instances where women are able to escape such labels occur in circumstances such as those of Jean and Paula in this study, where psychiatrists are able to rationalise their behaviour as appropriate given the history of violent abuse they suffered. For women who do not fall within this latter category, the former view prevails. What is missing from this portrait of female defendants is a more multi-dimensional understanding and explanation of women's mental condition. Without denying that women are indeed victims in many cases, we also might ask what other possible explanations exist for their actions. Hence, rather than immediately pathologising women's minds and bodies, we might ask how the cultural construction of femininity, which imposes strict standards of gender norms and conceives women's madness as 'normal and internal' (Astbury, 1996, p 30), has affected the ways in which women respond to stressful events as well as how we interpret their responses. Such a view would recognise the plural and multi-faceted approaches women take in negotiating femininity. And as the discussion in this chapter has shown, for women, becoming a homicide defendant is part of this negotiation.

Chapter 9
Reclaiming Women's Agency: Exposing the Mental Health Effects of 'Post-Abortion Syndrome' Propaganda

Eileen Fegan

9.1   Introduction

... from the notion of the feckless, uncontrolled woman comes our disapproval of the 'easy' abortion – the hundreds of thousands of morning-after pills sold over the counter; the walk-in clinics; the swelling numbers; the lack of guilt. Women must be *made* to confront what they've done (Gerrard, 2001, p 5, emphasis added).

Much has been written about abortion and women's mental health since the mid-1980s when claims that abortion may cause 'post traumatic stress disorder' (PTSD) were first made by anti-abortion proponents in the United States (Rue, 1995, p 20). Subsequent literature details symptoms which, it is argued, constitute 'post-abortion syndrome' (PAS) as a specific form of trauma deserving of psychiatric diagnosis, treatment and, ultimately, of a legal response (Rice, 2003).[1] Though neither endorsed by professional medical bodies nor legally recognised, PAS has crept into public and individual consciousness with potentially deleterious effects for women, their partners, families and abortion providers. Most North American pro-choice work on PAS has taken a defensive position to prevent liberal abortion laws being overturned or having access to services otherwise restricted.

Here I revisit the issue, drawing on the testimonies of women describing their various responses to unplanned pregnancies for the purpose of refocusing this highly polarised debate. Contemporary understandings of the relationship between language and social power (Fairclough, 1994; Thompson, 1984) are enlisted to analyse the stories of 15 women,[2] all residing in Vancouver, Canada, in the late 1990s. Paying attention to the language used by women themselves may be fundamental in addressing feminist concerns about the effect of pseudo-scientific, anti-choice literature upon women's mental health. The stories and analyses below challenge unqualified assumptions about the existence of PAS made by dubiously

---

1   According to Lee (2001, p 2), anti-abortionists 'have attempted to suggest [PAS] is so frequent and so severe that abortion should be legally prohibited or, at the very least, women should be discouraged from having abortions, and warned through counselling that they are likely to suffer psychologically if they do so'. Legislative requirements in some US states (eg, that women undergo counselling, followed by mandatory waiting periods before accessing the procedure and parental notification and consent requirements for teenagers) are indicators of their legal success.

2   See 'Appendix' at the end of this chapter for a summary of relevant biographical information. First names are those volunteered by the women themselves and are not all pseudonyms, some being willing to use their own names in an academic project.

qualified experts, located primarily in the United States and actively working to overturn *Roe v Wade*.[3]

Specifically, this chapter situates claims of PAS in the various contexts within which I believe they need to be understood: contexts framed by medical, scientific and religious discourses, right-wing political agendas, and gender-biased cultural norms. Informed by this understanding and by a theoretical framework that prioritises women's agency, I examine the narratives of my research participants with a view to uncovering concrete and latent strategies to resist the effects of PAS propaganda upon post-abortive women and those contemplating abortion, as well as law and public consciousness.

9.2 The context

Though my interview study and the law upon which it reflects is confined to Canada, where PAS is not currently central to abortion discourse, the framework of analysis, findings, theoretical and strategic recommendations is relevant to other jurisdictions.[4] One caution is necessary, however. Culturally, Canada is one of the most permissive and progressive societies in the world.[5] In this respect, the arguments made here about the effect of PAS could have even greater significance to cultural contexts (eg, Irish) in which dominant anti-choice ideology, religious and medical discourse have succeeded in keeping abortion illegal in all but life-threatening circumstances and access to it precarious even then (Fegan and Rebouche, 2003). This said, however, feminist strategies to counter the effects of PAS upon law and medical practice in any culture must be sensitive to the likelihood of support for such claims within these and the 'psych' discourses.[6]

PAS must first be understood in the wider context of 'syndromisation' – the transformation of issues concerning women into medically defined and legally recognised mental states. 'Battered women's syndrome' (BWS) was developed by psychiatrists in response to the inadequacy of the law (on provocation) to accommodate women's experiences of cumulative domestic violence (O'Donovan, 1993). Feminist lawyers introduced expert evidence of the psychological effects of battering to defend women who eventually killed their batterers, reducing murder convictions to manslaughter on the grounds of diminished responsibility. A new psychiatric condition was thereby incorporated into and reinforced by law, some argue to the detriment of long-term feminist goals. Schneider (1986, p 198) suggests syndromisation creates greater problems for all women than it solves for individuals. By implicitly defining their actions as 'unreasonable' reactions to the most extreme, violent provocation, BWS reproduces oppressive images of women

---

3 *Roe v Wade* 410 US 164 (1973).

4 The stories span a 34-year period, coinciding with three different Canadian abortion regulation regimes: criminalisation (pre-1969), legislative therapeutic exceptions (under the Criminal Code 1969–88) and legalisation (1988–present).

5 Recently (July 2003), the first gay marriages were celebrated in British Columbia, the second Canadian province to grant legal status to same-sex partnerships.

6 See, eg, Sheldon (1993), discussing the negative constructions of women facilitated and reinforced by medical discourse in the formulation of the GB Abortion Act 1967.

as irrational and requiring psychiatric explanation insofar as their behaviour differs from men's.

More recently, 'False Memory Syndrome' (FMS) has evolved in respect of sexual assault and child abuse (Bjorklund, 2000). Although not yet explicitly accepted by the courts, its underlying assumption – that women's mental suffering may lead them to imagine sexual abuse – has introduced another dangerous female stereotype into the trial. It is arguably more difficult to expose and challenge the impact of pseudo-scientific ideas than of blatantly sexist notions implicating the complainant's clothing or sexual history in assessing *her* innocence. Just as FMS does not need legal backing to undermine the credibility of female witnesses before a jury, PAS has already begun to invert the abortion/mental health link in law.[7] Lawsuits launched in the UK, US and Australia[8] may have failed so far to make abortion providers liable for women's psychological distress, but it is worrying that these cases reached court in the first place, given their unsupported and often incredulous claims. Therefore, although not yet explicitly accepted in law, PAS has indirectly shaped judicial opinion in granting legal standing. In this discursive shift, the use of language in creating a PAS-sympathetic legal culture should not be underestimated.

9.2.1 The role of language

Although the incidence of abortion has increased in the last 30 years and become, 'bit by bit, more publicly acceptable, the language with which we talk about [it] has remained stubbornly the same' (Gerrard, 2001, p 1). As Gerrard argues, the emotional and judgmental vocabulary of shame and guilt is directed almost exclusively at the woman: 'to have an abortion is "the lesser of two evils"; a woman has been "careless" or "irresponsible" or "selfish"; *she* "should have known better; *she* shouldn't have got carried away; this will be a lesson"' (Gerrard, 2001, p 1, emphasis added).

Recent developments in social, legal and feminist theory highlight the role of language or 'discourse'[9] in social development. Sociological theorists have emphasised the ways in which language is used in everyday life to create 'meaning (or signification) ... serv[ing] to sustain relations of domination' (Thompson, 1984). This has important implications both for feminist theorists concerned with the construction of women in dominant discourses such as law (Smart, 1989, 1992), religion, psychiatry (Fegan and Fennell, 1998) and the 'psych' discourses that have

---

7   Psychological evidence was originally used to liberalise prohibitive abortion laws, on the grounds that pregnancy/motherhood was damaging to a particular woman's mental health (Sheldon, 1993).

8   See Lee (2002) for a discussion of the most recent British case. A woman sued the NHS, claiming that medical staff failed to warn her about possible adverse psychological effects of the procedure. The case, like its Australian predecessor in 1998, was settled out of court. Though the terms of both settlements remain confidential, the providers' negotiation of these claims is indicative of a regrettable defensiveness.

9   See Fegan (1996) for an exploration of the meaning of 'discourse' as inspired by the work of post-modernist forefather Michel Foucault and, in particular, how it differs from the Marxian concept, 'ideology'.

more recently gained institutional and social power (Mosoff, 1995). It has specific resonance for feminists in the context of current anti-choice methods to restrict abortion through claims that 'abortion hurts women'.

9.3 Deconstructing PAS

Ellie Lee (2001) sees PAS as constructed through discourse, arguing that 'our understandings of abortion, women and mental states ... are social products and as such their meanings change over time ...' (2001, p 1). It emerged in the US in the early 1980s (and later in the UK, Australia and Switzerland) when the anti-choice movement recognised its own 'limited success in convincing those involved in law and policy making, and the general public, that they should oppose abortion ... on moral grounds alone' (Lee, 2001, p 3). Having failed to convince judges, legislators and the public that 'abortion is murder', health-based claims putting the woman rather than the foetus at the centre of the debate became more attractive to the 'pro-life' cause. The new, subtler message reflects the increasing sophistication in anti-choice politics and their reliance upon language to win over public consciousness. Despite their success in spreading awareness of PAS, there is little agreement upon or standardisation of diagnosis among the professional psychiatric community.

9.3.1 Examining the evidence

As Lee (2001, p 3) argues:

> ... the diagnostic criteria given shift from a definition of the 'symptoms' of PAS where the proposed comparison with PTSD is made clear, to a much broader collection of 'symptoms' that could perhaps more accurately be described as negative feelings.

While this is problematic for women experiencing 'natural sadness' at ending a pregnancy (Lee, 2001), the scientific disagreement and shifting boundaries help to expose the political nature of PAS. Beyond the recognised symptoms,[10] it has been associated to varying degrees with sexual dysfunction, increased smoking, alcohol and drug abuse, eating disorders, divorce and chronic relationship problems, repeat abortions and of course 'denial' (Reardon, 2000, p 1). With such all-inclusive 'criteria' it could be argued that most people (men included) suffer PAS at some stage in their lives! However, Lee adds that, as the criteria become broader, it is easier to claim that many women suffer from this 'syndrome' (2001, p 3).

Despite the fact that neither US professional bodies[11] nor an earlier government-backed commission[12] have found evidence of a causal link between abortion and

---

10 Unlike PAS, PTSD has been accepted by the American Diagnostic and Statistical Manual of Psychiatric Disorders (DSM) as involving re-experience of the traumatic event (flashbacks), avoidance of the subject (often causing lost memory), denial and impacted grieving (Lee, 2001, p 3).

11 The American Association of Psychiatrists and the American Medical Association.

12 In 1987 President Reagan set up a commission under former Surgeon General (and anti-choice sympathiser) C Everett Koop to investigate the issue, but even he refused to issue an official report on the grounds that the available evidence did not warrant any conclusion. See Lee (2001) and Wassom (1999) for alternative analyses of the problems in research on PAS.

psychiatric illness, a link has nonetheless formed in public and some women's consciousness, problematising their experiences and undermining support for the pro-choice position. In Canada, Dr Philip Ney argues a negative connection from a variety of angles. He alleges that abortion has 'no psychiatric benefits' but does not compare this claim against evidence of the effects of denying abortion (Ney, 2003, p 83). Many countries still have the mental health exception to the criminal prohibition (legislatively in Great Britain and at common law in Northern Ireland). Under such regimes, women must demonstrate a risk to their mental health 'greater than if [the pregnancy were] ... terminated'[13] or a 'real and serious, permanent or long term ... adverse effect on [their] mental health',[14] in order to access abortion. Similar restrictions have led several young Irish women to threaten suicide – one in the face of an injunction restraining her from leaving the jurisdiction to access abortion in Great Britain.[15] Such regimes and cases surely contradict Ney's claim that 'being pregnant and having children are known to protect women against suicide' (Ney, 2003, p 84).

Interestingly, Ney relies on professors from Irish medical schools who state that 'no medical condition requires abortion' and adds, 'no evidence supports the claim that abortion in cases of rape or incest benefits the woman' (Ney, 2003). Ironically, when he blames legal abortion for (men's propensity to) rape itself, Ney supports the pro-choice argument that control over women is the ultimate concern of the anti-choice movement, which PAS is used to regain:

> Up against women's awesome power to decide who lives and who dies, men feel both impotent and angry. That sense of helplessness can result in sexual impotence ... [which] coupled with rage, can combine to cause rape (Ney, 2003, p 90).

In light of such statements it is tempting to give the anti-choice lobby 'enough rope' to expose their deep distrust of and desire to control women without the need for feminist intervention! Certainly, post-abortion women, those making abortion decisions and the public must be made aware that claims of PAS by psychiatrists (and other vaguely labelled 'scientists'[16]) such as Ney are made against this backdrop. Pro-choice activists and academics can encourage people to question not only the motivation behind the PAS research, but also the credentials of those conducting it. While it is difficult for laypersons to judge between pro-choice and pro-life claims of research bias, women still must negotiate unplanned pregnancy, make abortion decisions and deal with their post-abortion feelings within this confused and fearful context.

---

13 In Great Britain, as defined by the Abortion Act 1967, s 1(1)(a).

14 This common law formula was reinforced by the Northern Ireland High Court in *The Family Planning Association NI (fpaNI) v The Department of Health, Social Services and Public Safety (DHSSPS)* (2003).

15 *Attorney General v X and Others* (1992). For critical feminist commentary see Fox and Murphy, 1992.

16 Though Ney is described as 'a physician, child psychiatrist and psychologist', Dr David C Reardon, the most prolific writer for the anti-choice Elliot Institute in the US, provides no details of his PhD qualification.

9.3.2 Exploiting women

Both sides in this 'war of words' have argued that women are being exploited. Anti-choice medics and lawyers say that when women are not warned of PAS in advance of abortion they are being treated without informed consent (Ney, 2003, p 83), yet to what ends would abortion doctors deliberately keep women in the dark – especially given the growth in litigation for psychological distress in medical and other fields? Abortion is hardly a celebrated, highly profitable or safe career for any physician. Only doctors committed enough to risk their own lives to improve women's lives get involved at all.[17] Rather, exploitation under the guise of 'help' is practised upon women most 'at risk of serious distress'[18] when they are 'diagnosed' with PAS. They are encouraged by anti-choice, conservative religious organisations, pursuing right-wing and gender-biased political agendas, to 'bring their negative feelings to the surface' (Lee, 2002, p 1). 'Healing' is often conditional upon trying to dissuade other women from having abortions by admitted 'stealth' (Reardon, 1998, p 1).

While many anti-choice activists and post-abortive women defend these tactics as saving others long-term anguish, their denial of women's agency contradicts the historical evidence which, in many societies, has overturned abortion prohibition: women have *always* been prepared to take enormous risks to exercise reproductive control.[19] There is dubious benefit therefore in 'educating' them about the psychiatric risks. Rather than further research into 'Post-Abortion Trauma Syndrome', what is needed is a full exploration of the impact upon women worldwide of denying or restricting access to abortion – what I call 'No Abortion Trauma Syndrome'! Up-to-date research into the negative effects of PAS claims upon women through reduced abortion availability, similar to those upon women living under restrictive or prohibitive abortion regimes, would help expose the purpose of this propaganda in currently liberal jurisdictions. Canadian abortion discourse has so far remained free from PAS intrusion and, as my empirical research will show, women there reveal other factors accounting for their problematic post-abortion experiences. However, there is a need for feminists in Canada to be pro-active in informing the public about the lack of substance in PAS claims emanating from the US, as health fears are more likely to have an impact upon women than moral or religious arguments in a pro-choice dominant culture.

---

17 William F Harrison is one American doctor (2002, p 15) who told the British Columbia Pro-choice Action Network that he was led into abortion provision when, before legalisation, a patient told him upon confirming her pregnancy: 'I was hoping it was cancer.'

18 According to Erin Mullan, Director of the British Columbia Pro-Choice Action Network (PROCAN), an estimated 10% of the women she counsels fall into this category, and for 60% within this group, the distress is related to 'something else' (interview, 2002, 25 July). For them the abortion is a 'trigger experience ... a doorway the old pain walks through'. Pro-choice organisations such as National Abortion Federation (NAF – USA) and the Canadian Abortion Rights Action League (CARAL) also admit that a small percentage of women suffer psychologically for a variety of reasons, most pre-dating the abortion.

19 Mullan (interview 2003, 13 July) relates how Latin American women often come to the free-standing abortion clinic (in Vancouver) thinking it will be dirty, dangerous and even life threatening, 'and they come anyway'.

9.4 The theoretical framework

Before exploring Canadian women's narratives in relation to PAS, some discussion of the theoretical framework of my analysis and its strategic implications is necessary. Carol Smart's earlier work has shown how reliance upon experience 'as though it were concrete reality' can backfire against women whose experience does not conform to the feminist political agenda (1989, pp 77–81). The constructed nature of what we understand (and take for granted) as 'experience' has also been exposed. Joan Scott has shown how critical analyses founded on the assumption that nothing could be truer than a subject's account of what he or she has lived through actually decontextualise the subject. Such analyses ignore fundamental questions about how subjects themselves are constituted – and thus also about how one's vision is structured through language (or discourse) and history (Scott, 1992).

Elsewhere I have argued that although (all) our lives are conditioned by external forces, we still possess a discernible agency[20] and consequently a never-ending potential for empowerment. Seeing women's abortion-related experiences as shaped by pre-existing interpretive frameworks therefore is not to deny their role as agents in constructing them, nor their possibility for reconstruction according to newly identified needs and desires. This is where insights from *other* women's narratives are important, both personally in helping women contextualise and renegotiate their own experiences, and politically in producing strategies of resistance to constructions of abortion as an indicator of mental illness.

9.4.1 Agency and consciousness

> Women are rarely credited with having any real knowledge, even knowledge of themselves. (Sommers, 1995, p 3)

My framework of analysis of the stories below does *not* claim to access any transcendent truth about how women experience abortion or how they are affected mentally by it. I do not use the women's stories as 'proof' of any position, but rather to explore the influences upon them in making abortion decisions and processing post-abortion feelings. I am therefore *not* arguing that women[21] who have experienced symptoms claimed as indicators of PAS are falsely conscious (Fegan, 1996, 1999). Nor do I deny the authenticity of their suffering – women feel what they feel regardless of why they feel it. It is for this reason that I consider PAS a public health issue, despite its dismissal in pro-choice and professional literature. Not all women have access to these largely academic sources. Most are likely to come into contact with the greater volume of anti-choice literature dominating the

---

20 See Fegan (1999) where I argue that within the formation (and the reformation) of identity, agency is that aspect of human consciousness responsible for deciding which (of many possible) discursive constructions to identify with, enabling individual, diverse responses to the ideas currently prevalent in our societies.

21 Undeniably, several of the stories are in line with anti-choice literature describing PAS. A focus upon agency, however, turns our attention to the particular factors described by the women themselves as contributing to oppressive or undesirable after-effects. None of them point to abortion *per se* or alone as the cause.

worldwide web[22] and often the mainstream media.[23] For this reason alone it must be taken seriously as a threat to women's mental health.

My analysis focuses upon the women's own constructions as a way of exploring the meaning *they* attribute to personal experiences of termination, the importance of legalised abortion and the effect of anti-choice discourse in an intimate area of their lives where there is a constant struggle for control over meaning. One purpose is to enable women having difficulty with past abortion decisions to become more conscious of the effects of PAS propaganda upon their own suffering and the effects of their participation in efforts to use it as a method of restricting other women's access to abortion. Another is to expose the role of legal, religious, psychological and psychiatric discourses in constructing women as incapable of protecting their own welfare and to undermine their authority in establishing yet another 'syndrome' which devalues women's agency.

9.5 Exploring PAS through women's stories

Having first informed the interviewees of my purpose in assessing the effects of social, cultural and legal representations of abortion upon their experiences, I asked them about the circumstances of their unplanned pregnancies. I then used open-ended questions[24] to elicit their thoughts and feelings during the decision-making, afterwards and at time of interview.

9.5.1 Owning the process

9.5.1.1 Emotional support

Paramount to each woman was the need to feel that the decision was *hers* and that she was supported emotionally in it. Sharron, 48, did not want to abort and was traumatised (12 years previously) when told by her physician that prescribed medication may have harmed the foetus. Even though he refused to give 'a definite answer', she remained deferent to his 'professional' opinion, but eventually made her own decision to proceed with the pregnancy. She described her needs in that situation:

SB: It might have been good to have some kind of *personal* counselling. Someone I already had a relationship with possibly, someone I *trusted* to help me work through what I needed to and come to a conclusion I *thought was my own*.

EF: When you say trust, in what sense do you mean?

SB: Well, um, I'm not as intellectual as *emotional* based, so I would know very quickly whether I trusted someone or not.

---

22 One site, www.lifenews.com, associated with the National Life Center, urges that 'nine short months of pregnancy is a relatively small cost to pay in light of a lifetime of potential physical and mental health problems. Think about it'.

23 See, eg, www.afterabortion.org, which dominates searches of various engines using the term 'post-abortion'. It contains a plethora of papers claiming proven links between abortion and psychiatric illness, suicide and breast cancer. Most papers are authored by Dr David C Reardon, see above, note 16.

24 My questions (where reproduced) are indicated by the initials 'EF' and the responses by the initial(s) provided by the interviewees. All emphasis in the transcript material is mine.

Sharron's story shows the capacity for making difficult decisions and instincts of self-protection, yet she emphasises 'trust' as the most important value in receiving information and counselling in such vulnerable circumstances. In the fearful and confusing climate to which PAS has contributed, pro-choice workers must both encourage women to trust and protect themselves from exploitation and empower women by giving them space to express their emotions.

9.5.1.2 Pressure and resistance

Catherine, a University Women Students' counsellor, 'really familiar with [her] options', educated and empowered with information, had no problem owning her decision, nor in resisting her doctor's suggestion that she 'think about' continuing the pregnancy because she was married:

EF: But you didn't get the abortion before this 'semi-counselling'?

CP: No, I *had to* listen to that. I got a couple of questions from her. But they were very brief and I think it was *very clear to her that I didn't want to entertain those questions and she stopped.*

Catherine also experienced very different treatment from Jandyra, who was not married but 'dreamed of having a child'. Rather than being counselled on continuing the pregnancy, she was pressured by her doctor, her family and the 'father' to have an abortion. As a woman living with long-term health problems and unemployment, she felt 'controlled and overpowered all [her] life'. However, she resisted this pressure, bore and raised her child happily despite lack of emotional support and financial difficulties. She then fell pregnant again:

JW: I couldn't face my parents with this one because my father had asked me to have my tubes tied after my first. But then I realised the child had died.

EF: You miscarried?

JW: Yeah, I guess that little soul realised that *I would not make a good mum.*

EF: But you already were?

JW: I would not be able to have the energy to do it for two children and still keep myself and I felt like that *child released me and it was hard.*

EF: But you had a good experience with your first?

JW: Yeah, but … I needed more support to be able to do it.

Although Jandyra never had an abortion, she expressed the same wisdom and responsibility in respect of a child's needs as several women who did. Describing abortion as 'releasing' a child from a life of difficult circumstances respects that wisdom and is much more compassionate than violent anti-choice language, imagery and tactics. Re-framing pro-choice discourse along these emotionally sensitive lines could have beneficial effects upon the mental health of aborting (and miscarrying) women in what many admit to being a 'hard' time. At the very least it may help them resist the negative impact of PAS propaganda.

9.5.1.3 Resisting PAS

In order to gauge how women's mental health might be affected by the information available to them, I asked Catherine, who now had two children:

EF: A lot of the literature says that once a woman has had an abortion and later goes on to have children they feel the loss then. Is that something you experienced?

CP: Well, nobody really talked to me about loss or anything ... for me *I didn't have a great feeling of loss ... I felt just so good, I mean that I can get back to my life* and got that over with.

Catherine had refused to be fed negative suggestions about her abortion decision, largely as a result of her upbringing:

CP: My mother said to me when I was in my early twenties, 'you know, if you ever get pregnant and don't want to have the baby' she said, 'just go and have an abortion and not tell anybody'. I thought it was a good piece of advice, she didn't seem to think it mattered whether I was married or not. That stuck in my mind and gave me some *freedom*. Because of my work, I knew how incredibly *accessible* it was, even though *the media seemed to tell us that it wasn't*.

Her story shows the importance of knowledge in empowering women in a climate hostile to that freedom.

9.5.1.4   PAS: exploring 'where it comes from'

While Catherine emphasised privacy as beneficial to her processing of the abortion decision, it did not have the same effect upon Sue, who was raised with a very different 'message':

ST: I was thinking, 'I have this little secret that no one knows about, but God knows about it and he is going to *punish* me for it'. It was the kind of vengeful God I grew up with that is going to get you if you don't do everything right or repent ... I see a lot of women now who are Catholic and they *really believe* that they're going to burn in hell and how do you undo that?

Sue's story most resembles claims of PAS made by anti-choice psychiatrists and social scientists. She suffered most of the symptoms they characterise as mental illness *caused by* abortion. However, her description of the messages lingering from her evangelical upbringing and her admitted pre-existing lack of self-esteem would suggest that her 'symptoms' were less a result of the termination than of dormant feelings – including anger and disappointment in life – that it brought to the surface.

Given the intensity of suffering described, it is not surprising that many women with similar experiences turn to religious-based organisations[25] to find relief. Using their pain in the anti-choice war against all women's reproductive freedom is often the 'price' of the forgiveness so elusive to Sue. She described going to church after the abortion:

ST: I was just so distraught I just couldn't function and I thought maybe I would find some kind of peace there, but I didn't, it was just *terrifying*. You know, when it comes to religion it's like this stuff is all so based on *fear*.

EF: But isn't there also a religious image of God as forgiving?

---

25 Such as 'Rachel's Vineyard', an American Life League project (the largest US 'pro-life' educational organisation) – see www.rachelsvineyard.org and the 'Silent No More' campaign launched by the Elliot Institute this year to mark the 30th anniversary of *Roe v Wade*.

ST: That isn't what *sinks in*, it's the scary stuff, you know, '*you're* not going to be forgiven, *you're* going to hell'. *Even though I didn't believe that*, you know you hear ministers speak – it just blocks people – their *language* is so unforgiving and so rarely forgotten. They are on some kind of *power* trip.

Given her exposure to this language, it is perhaps not surprising that Sue suffered so badly after her abortion that she saw a psychiatrist 'for about *nine months*':

ST: I thought I was going to die ... and the psychiatrist told me I wasn't actually going to die – but *I was, my life* was. *I couldn't live my life. I just created a hell on earth for myself* ... So the psychiatrist helped me realise that, got me talking about my *feelings* and then I was able to function again.

Sue eventually set up her own post-abortion support group to share her experience 'as somebody who had been through it and *grown* from it' with other women in crisis. Sharing of such stories is an invaluable tool in resisting PAS, strategically and personally. Sue's story shows women needing forgiveness how to find it most powerfully, permanently and unconditionally within themselves, as an expression of their agency:

ST: You know what I think ... that there is a part of us that *rebels* against that and says 'I'm not going to do justice to some *male figurehead*'. I couldn't care less whether he forgives me anyway ... I have *forgiven myself*.

9.5.1.5   Abortion as a growing experience

I too was inspired by Sue's story of overcoming her post-abortion mental health problems, in particular by what she told me about the positive influence the healing experience had upon her whole life:

ST: It wasn't just from the abortion. The healing was from this *lack of self-esteem*. Now I think 'I am OK, I deserve to be happy and I am going to do what I need to for myself'. After abortion it's like a *pain* forces you to make a choice: 'am I going to live the same life and be miserable – just taking the next man that comes along? Or am I going to go out there and find out what really makes me happy and do that?'

Sue's words speak for themselves and help qualitatively illuminate Russo and Zierk's (1992) empirical research on post-abortive women reporting increased self-esteem:[26]

ST: You have to go really deep to find that out. It would be so much *easier* to go on believing that, 'oh I deserve to suffer and I'm just going to have this pain for the rest of my life'. But really the trick is to move through the pain and to know that there's a *reason* for it and know 'I'm going to be in a better place because of it'.

Jodie also described her abortion as:

J: ... a *character defining* moment. Thinking about it, which I don't do very often, made me think 'phew, how did you get through that one? You can get through anything'.

---

26 Russo and Zierk's (1992) study claims that a single abortion contributes to self-esteem, but women who had a history of more than one abortion had a lower average for self-esteem scores, which could arguably be an indication of reasons for their repeated unwanted pregnancies.

Both Sue and Jodie's comments could not be further removed from anti-choice claims that abortion is not only an exclusively negative life experience, but also one that causes severe mental health problems. However, according to most literature, not even such positive accounts contradict the incidence of PAS. Rather, they are seen as evidence of particularly bad suffering – as evidenced by their *extreme* denial.

9.5.2 Denial and responsibility

> Those who appear to have no qualms whatsoever about the decision may well be evincing an inability or unwillingness to honestly assess her own emotions. (Wassom, 1999, p 827)

As Joyce Arthur[27] suggests, anti-choice claims of 'denial' against women reporting positive or no feelings after abortion are 'non-falsifiable' and therefore unworthy of serious response. The argument that aborting women suffer mentally even if they are not aware of it covers all bases politically, as well as empirically. If no woman can escape psychiatric illness after abortion, there remains little therapeutic justification for the procedure. Rather, it is arguably a threat to public health of epidemic proportions given the millions of abortions carried out globally each year. Anti-choice assertions of 'denial' as a symptom of PAS are tantamount to early philosophical and religious proclamations that women have no independent agency or awareness of themselves.[28] Since this belief is still so pervasive in mainstream religion, it is unsurprising that those suffering understandable feelings of loss or sadness (Lee, 2001) may 'buy into' PAS discourse, particularly if pressured by circumstances or others into their abortion decisions.

9.5.2.1 Desperate decisions

As Christa's story highlights, when motherhood is not always an equally available choice – for whatever reason – feelings of helplessness and need for support can be paramount:

> C: I was hoping there would be somebody at the clinic that would say 'hey, you don't have to do this, you don't have to go through the abortion'. They go through the procedure like as if it's an *everyday thing*. I mean it is for them, but *for me it wasn't*.

Christa demonstrates the difficult dilemma abortion providers face between showing respect for women's agency and assessing the needs of women in desperate situations – for which she shows understanding: 'there isn't much anyone could say'. However, her description of what would have helped in her situation is revealing:

> C: ... longer, *more personal* treatment, more in tune with how you *feel* when you go there. If you're really confused, you need a *helping hand* ... more *emotion* could enter it. I don't know if that is *allowable*?

---

27 Director of the British Columbia Pro-Choice Action Network (PROCAN), interview 15 July 2003.

28 For example, in the work of Aristotle and St Thomas Aquinas. See Bridgeman and Millns (1998) for a discussion of the religious and philosophical origins of law's constructions of women as passive, emotional, weak and lacking in reason.

Christa's comments are indicative of pro-choice detachment from the emotional side of abortion, perhaps understandably, in response to anti-choice PAS campaigns. The unfortunate result is that 'pro-life' organisations are offering women with post-abortion emotional needs a forum they have not found elsewhere. Fortunately, Christa was recommended to an independent counsellor who helped her 'see where that feeling of "you don't deserve to be happy" *comes from*'. Had she fallen upon an anti-choice organisation, she may have become one of their 'statistics' in the PAS fight against abortion rights, rather than realising: 'it's OK, the way I feel is sort of *natural.*'

Christa's story shows the importance of sensitivity to women's individual needs in relation to abortion. According to Mullan,[29] it is a priority of the pre-abortion session to ensure a woman is comfortable with her decision before proceeding: 'the vast majority are absolutely clear ... my job is to look out for the ones that aren't.' She told me sometimes women are angry when asked to come back for a specific decision-making session, but this ensures that 'abortion clinics prevent more unsure women having abortions than anti-abortionists ever do'.

The fact that PAS propaganda has affected even women who are very sure is evidenced by the increase in questions such as: 'how will I feel afterwards?' Pro-choice counselling and literature therefore must respond not only to the cultural and religious concerns of women, but also to anti-choice efforts to make all women feel bad about abortion. As one commentator notes: 'women of all religions and spiritual practices have abortions. And women with different political beliefs have abortions; not everyone who has one is pro-choice ... And not everyone who is pro-choice has an abortion with no afterthoughts' (Salter, 2002, p 3). This point was illuminated for me in the stories of two women who were working in abortion provision and post-abortion counselling at the time of interview.

9.5.2.2   How choice helps

Cheryl described herself as an 'avid anti-choicer probably right up until grade 12 as a result of my limited experiences and schooling'. By the time she fell pregnant in university she had taken on 'more progressive ideas', yet she felt 'a certain degree of *shame and embarrassment*' about being pregnant and not wanting to be. It was really *terrifying*, such a feeling of *vulnerability*'. It is easy to see how in such situations women's feelings can swing either way depending to a large degree upon the sources of information they come into contact with. She described her experience at Planned Parenthood:

> CD: It was wonderful, to be able to just talk *openly* and get *non-judgmental* advice ... it really shocked me because I'd never had a discussion about abortion in that context. It made me realise there was *a way out* and it was the *start of me being in control* again ... though it was not easy to access the clinics, but that she could *even just say* 'yes it can be done and it can be safe'.

Cheryl's story is instructive on counteracting the effects of anti-choice propaganda. All women deserve clear, non-directive information, presented in a manner that

---

29 See note 19.

demonstrates, as her counsellor did, that 'this is something women deal with in their reproductive lives, it's not unusual'. When Cheryl went to a doctor to confirm the stage of pregnancy as required by the US clinic at the time (similar to the Canadian Criminal Code), she had a very different experience:

CD: I felt very disempowered. I felt that I had to *act a certain way*, be *requesting*, be a little bit *junior* ... even *contrite*, but *still be firm* about not wanting to continue the pregnancy so I could just get that letter he was in control of writing.

I asked Cheryl to elaborate on the effect of the legal requirements upon her. She explained:

CD: You had to sort of *pump it up*, you couldn't just say you know: 'I really am clear and I don't want to have this pregnancy' and smile about it. You had to look sufficiently *guilty* or embarrassed so that so they would *sympathise* or have enough *pity* on you or whatever to write this letter ... but *I wasn't being earnest*, because I really didn't want the pregnancy.

With a long history of abortion regulation that requires women to display guilt and contrition (whether they feel it or not), it is hardly surprising that some women interpret feelings of stress or sadness as evidence of PAS. Cheryl cried during the interview – in response to remembering the trauma *this* experience caused her as a young woman. While anti-choicers would interpret her display of emotion as 'regret', Cheryl's story provided very positive insights on resisting, both materially and discursively, their efforts to construct abortion as harmful to women's reproductive capacity:

CD: It was done in a 'family planning' sort of clinic, which wasn't just providing abortions, it did other things – pre-natal services. I remember feeling a sense of relief that *'this must be OK as it is in this context'*.

EF: That wasn't upsetting in any way?

CD: No, not at all. I was thinking 'this is OK, this is *part of that'*. I don't have to feel ashamed, because *I can do that too.*

Although all women may not feel comfortable having the procedure in this setting, it is important that women are given a choice of environments and the reassurance that abortion and future motherhood are not mutually exclusive – thereby counteracting PAS literature which has raised many women's fears about an unproven association between abortion and infertility.[30]

Skye, who worked in abortion peer-counselling, also cried during the interview, having experienced psychological problems after her third abortion. She attributes her response to the environment, method and lack of post-procedure counselling:

SS: I had the first one under general anaesthetic and I felt nothing, *no guilt*. I felt *relieved*, like I had *a new lease of life* ... and I thought I would feel the same way after this pregnancy.

---

30 Sue, who suffered the most severely psychologically, added: 'for many years after it I thought I would never be able to have a child, I didn't deserve to have a child.' Christa also believed initially that she had lost her 'only opportunity' for motherhood.

Due to the later stage of the pregnancy, her third procedure was performed under local anaesthetic at the clinic in a women's hospital after a four-week waiting period. Skye attributes her stress in part to this delay: 'I found myself *dissociating* from my body a lot during that time.' She describes the experience as:

SS: *extremely* traumatic. I can't emphasise that enough. It was the *hardest*, though it was the first time I had any counselling beforehand ... the appointment was the day before the procedure. That seemed like such a waste of time to me ... it doesn't make you *emotionally prepared*, there's a bit of a *psyching up* you want to do before anything like this.

On the two previous occasions Skye had been helped by the presence and emotional support of partners. Not feeling supported or prepared (having separated from her boyfriend), Skye was more vulnerable to distress both during and after the procedure.

SS: I had a really hard time. The *fact that it bothered me so much bothered me*, because I was emotionally stable. I felt *overwhelmed* to the point where I felt I was going to scream.

Her comments directly replicate anti-choice literature describing the symptoms of PAS, yet she described a medically induced abortion some years before as:

SS: an experience to me like a miscarriage. I've never had a miscarriage, but in my mind that's how I considered it ... because it was at home. I was in my comfy clothes and my blanket, it was nice and comfy. I was on my recliner. I *highly recommend it* ... I think it's the *easiest* way to do it.

Despite the intensity of her suffering, Skye did not blame abortion *per se* and was keen to relate the positive elements of different procedure methods. Her previous experiences and the space provided by the interview to articulate her feelings enabled Skye to identify the *reasons* for her suffering as related to the procedure itself (drugs given made her feel 'out of control'), the material surroundings and the inadequacy of the counselling:

SS: It was almost like it was something that I *had to do for the sake* of getting the abortion. It *wasn't for my sake*. If they had asked me when I called, 'when would you like to see a counsellor?' I would have said 'as soon as possible', to get all those things, all my *worries and concerns* about *what it would be like*, out of the way.

Skye's story demonstrates profoundly how women benefit from control over the process of termination itself, respect for the significance of the decision to them and professional recognition of the possibility of after-effects – for *whatever* reason. The need to counteract anti-choice PAS propaganda has left abortion providers in danger of neglecting these aspects of individual women's experiences.

9.5.2.3   Empowerment: information and education

When Jodie sought an abortion after her husband was killed in a road accident, her doctor falsely told her she was not pregnant,[31] though her pregnancy was

---

31 She explained: 'Later on, years later (in my 30s) I saw him in the paper and he was an anti-abortionist and I didn't know that when I went to him. He was just a GP out of the book.'

well-established and the reason for her marriage at 19! This and other unscrupulous tactics are used to delay the procedure, making it legally, physically and emotionally more difficult or impossible. Young North American women who, unlike their predecessors (such as Cheryl), are unskilled in negotiating abortion illegality and restrictions, must be well equipped to protect themselves from anti-choice manipulation at a stage of life where:

J: You're so *trusting* of doctors. You don't realise ... you think that they just do their job and they keep politics and personal things out of it. At the time, I must admit I was confused and I look at it now and think 'now I get it'.

As a result of her own experience Jodie has been vigilant in informing her teenage daughter with knowledge of abortion politics and validating the idea of the choice for her: 'I say "some women make these choices, some women make those choices".' Overcoming the effects of PAS claims requires not only this type of reinforcement of women's agency discursively, but also *trusting women* in practice.

9.5.2.4 Trusting women

Joan received much concern for her psychological wellbeing when she had an abortion at 17, though she '*really* was OK', due to a well nurtured sense of confidence and self-esteem. The manner of supporting women is even more important now that psychiatric, psychological and medical discourses have been hijacked in anti-choice constructions of abortion as inherently problematic for all women:

JC: My family were very concerned about my welfare, how I was dealing with it. I don't know if *I relieved them*. Because I have always been a very strong, confident person on the outside, they may have felt 'is she actually all right?' But I *actually felt that way* on the inside as well.

Disbelief that a woman may have very positive feelings about an abortion, without suffering any loss (natural or induced) was also raised by Cheryl's story:

CD: It actually turned out to be something I was *happy* about. I remember afterwards phoning my brother and saying 'this was so wonderful, wait till I get home and tell you about it.' *I spoke like that and most people would be just shocked* at that kind of response, but that's how I felt.

She was acutely aware that this language is not the most popular way of talking about abortion. Cheryl's story highlights the need to establish abortion as a normal part of reproductive experience – especially for those women described by Mullan[32] as 'super-fertile'. Since abortion has traditionally been understood within medical and legal discourse as anomalous and exceptional, many women understandably keep it secret. However, the isolation of secrecy leaves post-abortive women in most danger of interpreting their feelings as problematic and symptomatic of PAS.

A feminist discourse that recognises and reinforces the variability of women's abortion experiences, in defiance of past legal and current anti-abortion norms,

---

32 See note 19.

provides a framework for all, particularly religious,[33] women to reinterpret and reconcile their own feelings. Moreover, because the way women talk about their experiences is not inspired by what arguments are likely to succeed in the Supreme Court, their stories offer multitudinous insights from which to inform social and legal understandings of abortion in preparation for the PAS-led attack on choice.

9.6 Implications for feminist strategising

Hearing real women tell their own stories brings *all* the issues around abortion and mental health to the fore. Despite disparities in claims and conflicting research on the psychological after-effects of abortion, PAS has become a 'live' issue as a result of the *censure* (including women's self-censure) that still surrounds the decision to terminate, even in jurisdictions where it is legal and a constitutionally protected freedom. Feminists need to continue informing the public with real examples of how women have negotiated difficult abortion circumstances and feelings for the benefit of women like Sue and Christa, and to defend reproductive freedom for all women.

9.6.1 *Counselling*

Acknowledging the variety and complexity of women's feelings can contribute to feminist strategies to resist PAS. One counselling organisation, 'Exhale', allows women space to deal with their more complex emotions (Salter, 2002). As co-founder Aspen Baker explains:

> the moment women allow themselves to be vulnerable about their feelings after an abortion, it becomes an emotional minefield that can be manipulated. [Our aim is] to take off our armour and be faithful to our true selves. That is where empowerment lies. (Salter, 2002, p 3)

While many pro-choice organisations have been hesitant to focus on post-abortion counselling for this reason, the stories above confirm that women from diverse political, cultural, and religious backgrounds have either benefited or expressed a need for support. Skye, Sharron and Christa identified a more personalised approach in pre-abortion, and the availability of post-procedure counselling through the clinic as measures that would have helped them negotiate negative feelings. These suggestions invoke material improvements in service provision as necessary, in addition to pro-choice counter-discourse, to protect women from a burgeoning PAS culture. According to Skye:

> SS: The counselling office is all nice tones, but they had my post-abortion session in, like, one of the medical supply rooms – it was like a storage room, with metal shelving and sharp edges. It conveyed to me that now that the procedure was over, I was *no longer a high priority client*. I was *hurt by that* and the counsellor kept

---

33 Support for a compassionate approach that trusts women is forthcoming from religious leaders, such as Doubet King: '[F]aith is not a rigid structure of ideas to be imposed and protected, but an active trust in God, women and families to make wise decisions according to their own consciences' (2003, p 1).

looking at her watch. I felt *rushed*. She made no offer for me to come back, just
gave me a directory of support groups and counsellors. It was just so radically
different from the pre-abortion session.

North American abortion clinics operate under conditions of financial and physical
insecurity, due to anti-choice politics, violence and intimidation. Without their
commitment and dedication women's lives would be immeasurably worse. While
they are not responsible for women's post-abortion suffering, the issues raised
above are indicative of why *some women* turn to anti-choice agencies or sue abortion
providers, resulting ultimately in increased political pressure and further decreases
in funding. Because their work is fundamental to women's freedom and equality,
they must make women central to the delivery, assessment and review of their
services – as the anti-choice lobby has done in pursuit of its own ideological agenda.

Extra-legally, pro-choice organisations must continue producing and publicising
empirical evidence to counter anti-choice claims and to expose their right-wing
agendas and misogynist underpinnings. It is crucial now to inform women of the
underlying principles and goals of the growing number of post-abortion
counselling programmes and the manipulative tactics used by anti-choice agencies
to 'heal' women suffering PAS. While all women are free to acquire support –
psychological, spiritual or religious – that choice will be a more empowered and
conscious exercise of their agency if they have access to a variety of sources of
information.

9.6.2 Legal consequences

Despite denial by professional medical bodies and the failure of civil action lawsuits
in the UK, US and Australia (Lee, 2002), PAS already exists in public discourse and
legal understanding, undermining respect for women's agency and threatening
their reproductive freedom. As anti-choice academic Brian Wassom (1999) notes, no
legal question is ever truly 'settled' in the abortion context. Given that many
women's abortion freedom world-wide is accessible only through 'health'
(including psychological) exceptions to legal prohibition, mediated by the medical
and psychiatric professions, any receptivity in law towards the idea that abortion
harms women's mental health risks making their access to it more regulated and
vulnerable in the long run.

As demonstrated in the US, where in November 2003 President Bush signed into
law the 'Partial-Birth Abortion Ban Act', PAS propaganda has helped effect the first
federal abortion ban in US history, by portraying (at least later term) abortion as
more psychologically damaging to women than its denial. Constitutional challenges
planned by several groups[34] to the ban will, in all likelihood, be heard before a
future unsympathetic Supreme Court. Feminist interventions in these cases will
have potentially long-ranging effects upon legal and social understandings of
abortion, both in the US and elsewhere. It is critical, therefore, that they reinforce

---

34 These include the American Civil Liberties Union, The Centre for Reproductive Rights and
Planned Parenthood. See 'President Signs Controversial Abortion Bill: 3 Groups Challenge',
www.guttmacher.org, 5 November, 2003.

constructions of women as agents capable of assessing information, making moral decisions and accepting responsibility for them. Although PAS evolved in response to positive legal and cultural changes for women in North America, there are indications that it is being used to undermine or prevent such developments in other countries. In the Canadian context, the women's experiences above provide concrete insights from which pro-choice organisations can develop culturally responsive and effective strategies of resistance against the legal encroachment of PAS there.

9.7 Conclusion

Viewing PAS from perspectives of social and cultural gender inequality brings awareness of its purpose to restrict women's reproductive freedom in ideological and material ways. The stories examined above contradict the existence of a causative or inevitable link between abortion and mental health. Rather, it appears that women's experiences are shaped to a large extent by the prevailing social and cultural context, as well as their individual (including mental health) histories. Thus, for example, women in Ireland may have a more difficult time mentally processing their experiences of abortion than women in Canada.

I suggest this has less to do with abortion *per se* than with the legal, medical and religious and cultural construction of abortion, and the material obstacles they must overcome to access it in a gender unequal society. Such conditions reinforce a culture of silence, secrecy and shame which prevents them sharing their experience with others (including other post-abortive women) and from receiving the support that is often necessary to counteract the damaging effects of the violent and oppressive language used by anti-choice to punish women and return them to a weak and submissive role. When women are isolated from society and each other in such a manner, they are much easier to control through fear and guilt.

In cultures, particularly North American, where women have fought and used their reproductive freedom to gain control over their lives – publicly exercising their agency in choosing legal abortion – PAS has evolved as the anti-choice weapon to reverse the tide. It is difficult to measure numerically its detrimental effects on the mental health of women there (though this would be a worthwhile 'scientific' study) but, as shown from discursive analysis of the women's stories above, anti-choice language has impacted concretely upon the lives of individual women at different historical periods. It has, worryingly, the potential to exacerbate the already challenging experiences of women, even more so in cultures where pro-choice discourse is not so strong. Feminists in those jurisdictions must take a pro-active stance against PAS discourse before it takes hold, for there it has a greater potential to penetrate the legal arena, setting the agenda even before liberal abortion laws have been achieved.

Cross-culturally, strategies for individual empowerment can be gleaned from stories of women's responses to anti-choice ideology. All women can benefit from access to accounts of how others exercised their agency concretely to overcome discursive and ideological assaults upon their reproductive choice. This type of analysis also holds significance on a wider political level. By injecting these insights into feminist and pro-choice discourse we will have a better tool with which to enter the legal terrain, in resistance to future anti-choice efforts to undermine subtly and indirectly the construction of abortion as a safe, necessary and effective guarantee of women's agency.

Appendix: biographical information

SB   'Sharron', aged 48, unmarried mother of two, continued second unplanned pregnancy, despite fears of foetal abnormality induced by prescribed medication. Her son, now aged 11, was born healthy.

CP   'Catherine', aged 37, married, University Women's Students Counsellor. Terminated first pregnancy aged 26. Subsequently had two children.

ST   'Sue', aged 32, podiatrist, volunteer post-abortion support group leader. Terminated first pregnancy aged 24 – married 'father', tried to get pregnant, suffered miscarriage, divorced, recently re-married, no children.

C   'Christa', aged 27, receptionist, from 'religious' immigrant El Salvador family, raised in rural Interior region of BC. Terminated first pregnancy aged 22.

CD   'Cheryl', aged 35, Abortion Clinic Director. Terminated first pregnancy aged 21, had subsequent 'therapeutic abortions'. Now married, with two children.

JA   'Joyce', aged 41, pro-choice activist. Terminated first pregnancy aged 31 married 'father'. Remains childless.

JC   'Joan', aged 34, government environmental professional. Terminated first pregnancy aged 17. Now married and 'trying for a baby' for several years.

CN   'Carolyn', aged 37, unemployed school teacher, supported by family. Believed infertile. Seven months pregnant.

J   'Jodie', aged 38, 'survivor' of Women's Studies. Widowed aged 19 after one month marriage – terminated previously wanted pregnancy. Now remarried with daughter, aged 13.

JW   'Jandyra', aged 40, unmarried long-term welfare recipient, extensive volunteer work. Believed infertile. Continued pregnancy aged 27, subsequent miscarriage. Son aged 13. Paid interview fee.

SS   'Skye', aged 32, unmarried Social Work University Student. Middle-class background. Three terminations – first aged 19, two further aged 29.

JE   'Judith', aged 36, health care worker. Married, had difficulty getting pregnant, received fertility treatment – 'lost' three pregnancies, had two young children – eight months and three and a half – when decided to terminate sixth unplanned pregnancy.

SR   'Sherrilyn', aged 22, unclassified Master's student, Chinese-Canadian, raised in Singapore. Terminated first pregnancy aged 20. Paid interview fee.

MJ   'Maureen', aged 43, Aboriginal Canadian. Left abusive home aged 15, working as a prostitute on the street. Carried two unplanned pregnancies to term at 15 and 16. Without medical care or state support her second child died days after the birth. The first died of cancer aged 12. Returned to school aged 20, later attended a local business school. Now married, raising three subsequent children – planning to return to employment. Paid interview fee.

DJ   'Donna', aged 52, Creative Writing University Student. Raped in process of securing first illegal abortion aged 16, in 1964. Had second therapeutic abortion aged 29. Now has daughter aged 21. Paid interview fee.

Chapter 10
Defending Battered Women on Charges of Homicide: The Structural and Systemic Versus the Personal and Particular[1]

Julie Stubbs and Julia Tolmie

10.1   Introduction

In this chapter we examine legal responses to battered women who have killed abusers with a special focus on indigenous women in Australia. For many battered women facing charges arising from killing a violent man, the capacity to successfully argue self-defence continues to be limited by the gender bias of the defence and by stereotyped understandings of women, intimate relations, and commonly also of indigeneity, that shape the reception of narratives concerning domestic violence. A well-established literature suggests that the introduction of expert testimony about battered woman syndrome (BWS) in support of defences to homicide has contributed to these stereotypes and to the medicalisation and pathologisation of battered women's behaviour. While compassionate or merciful outcomes are sometimes evident, mercy too often substitutes for an acquittal and distorts women's experiences rendering them as pathetic or irrational.

We agree with that literature, but in this paper our focus is somewhat different. Legal analysis in Australian cases typically pays insufficient attention to the social context of the defendant and the offence. Therefore, in this chapter we examine the consequences of the failure of the criminal law to recognise and respond to structural disadvantage. We argue that what Norrie (2001) has termed the 'psychological individualism' of the criminal law, sometimes in conjunction with psychiatric discourse, typically forecloses the opportunity for social context to be considered other than in a limited and unsatisfactory fashion at sentencing. The individualised focus of the criminal law too often translates structural disadvantage into individual deficit or pathology and obscures the gender inequality of domestic violence. The deficiencies of such a legal analysis are most stark in some cases involving indigenous women. We also argue for greater attention to prosecutorial discretion as an important domain of legal decision-making. Most of the recent cases we have identified of women charged with a homicide offence against a background of domestic violence have resulted in guilty pleas. Few have gone to trial.

This chapter commences with a brief review of the significance of self-defence to feminist interventions on behalf of battered women who kill. It also provides an account of the limitations inherent in the use of battered woman syndrome as a defence strategy including factors that may undermine a claim to self-defence. The

---

1   We would like to acknowledge and thank Renee Lees for her research assistance.

focus then shifts to plea negotiations and sentencing. We draw on Australian cases to argue that many of the features that have been identified as problematic in the use of BWS are reproduced in these contexts and are compounded by the privatised setting of plea negotiations. We conclude with an appeal for a contextualised understanding of battered women's behaviour and point to some legal developments that may offer a way forward.

10.2 Spousal homicides in Australia

Research indicates that some women's spousal relationships can be seriously harmful or life threatening and that society provides inadequate protection from domestic violence for many women. While it is more common for women to be killed by a violent spouse than to kill, some women take matters into their own hands and fight back – sometimes using lethal self-help. In the year 1999–2000 there were 71 spousal homicides in Australia (including current and separated legal and *de facto* spouses, sexual intimates, boyfriend, girlfriend and same-sex relationships), which accounted for approximately 20% of all homicides. Women committed approximately one-quarter of spousal homicides (Mouzos, 2001a, p 3). However, indigenous women in Australia are more than seven times over-represented as victims and offenders in homicide cases and a much higher proportion of indigenous cases involve intimate partners. Over the decade 1989/90–1999/2000 three-quarters of those killed by indigenous women were male intimate partners, as compared with 44% for non-indigenous women (Mouzos, 2001b). We located 15 cases of battered women who appeared in Australian courts charged with a homicide offence between 1999 and 2002 and seven involved indigenous women.[2] This marked over-representation of indigenous women in intimate homicides underscores the need for any analysis of the legal response to these cases to recognise the intersection between gender, race and class (Crenshaw, 1991; Stubbs and Tolmie, 1995).

10.3 Self-defence: validating the structural realities of battered women's lives

For more than two decades, feminist legal activists have worked to make self-defence available on an equal basis to battered women charged with killing an abuser. While they have stressed the connections between some women's resort to homicide, violence against women and gender inequality, legal responses commonly extract domestic violence from its social context (Schneider, 2000). Women charged with offences committed in response to domestic violence have poor prospects that their behaviour will be assessed fairly if the social context of their offending is not recognised and understood (Dutton, 1993, 1997; Stubbs and Tolmie, 1999). The failure to address the context in which the homicide took place is a particular obstacle for self-defence but may have consequences for other defences,

---

2 Indigenous people account for 2.1% of the Australian population (Australian Bureau of Statistics, 2002).

the exercise of pre-trial discretion and sentencing. This focus on social context should not be misunderstood as a denial of women's agency but rather as a means of promoting a better understanding of women's actions as reasonable in the circumstances.

Self-defence has been the focus of feminist work because it offers the potential to acknowledge the structural realities of many battered women's lives, and the circumstances surrounding their killings.[3] It is the only defence that offers a complete vindication of the defendant's actions and results in an acquittal. By contrast, the defences of provocation and diminished responsibility[4] result in a manslaughter conviction rather than an acquittal, based on a concession to human frailty or mental incapacity. Thus, provocation suggests that the accused person's response is an irrational but understandable over-reaction to their circumstances. Diminished responsibility suggests that it is the product of a sick mind, albeit one not ill enough to qualify for insanity. Diminished responsibility is no longer commonly used in Australian homicide cases involving battered women (Bradfield, 2002a) but has been relied on in UK cases (Chan, 1997). Feminist work has stressed that because self-defence is about judging whether the accused woman's response to her circumstances was reasonable, it is imperative that those circumstances be made intelligible to the court. The circumstances that a battered woman faces are not the same as those that men typically face, although men have been the benchmark against which they have been judged. Unfortunately, there is little evidence that self-defence has been interpreted to acknowledge the particular circumstances faced by a battered woman (Chan, 2001). As a consequence, two defence strategies have developed. The first has been to introduce expert evidence on battered woman syndrome in support of self-defence (and possibly provocation in the alternative). The second is pleading guilty to manslaughter in exchange for murder charges being dropped and the chance to argue in mitigation of sentence. Neither strategy emphasises the social context of battered women and both focus on explaining the 'subjective' features of the particular accused.

10.4   Expert evidence on the battered woman syndrome

Early decisions based on women's self-defence work in the US (*State of Washington v Wanrow* (1977)) and Canada (*R v Lavallee* (1990)) offered some prospects that courts were becoming responsive to feminist arguments that challenged the gender bias inherent in self-defence (and other defences). Appellate courts in those cases seemed to appreciate that overcoming gender bias required that the defendant's subjective beliefs and the objective circumstances that she faced needed to be understood. In both countries BWS evidence was accepted, thereby facilitating that understanding (Martinson *et al*, 1991; Schneider, 2000). However, subsequent developments have not borne out this initial optimism. In Australia, notwithstanding some positive outcomes in individual cases, we are yet to see an

---

3   We are not arguing that self-defence should be available to all women homicide defendants who have been battered, but that it would be available to more women if it were interpreted equitably to reflect women's life circumstances.

4   Diminished responsibility (now called substantial impairment in NSW) is not available in all jurisdictions.

appellate court explicitly address the gender bias inherent in self-defence[5] or consider the role that BWS evidence might play in assessing the self-defence claims of battered women (Stubbs and Tolmie, 1999).

10.4.1 The failure to support battered defendants' claims to self-defence

BWS may have contributed to a small number of successful self-defence cases but it has not been successful in shaping the law on self-defence to the circumstances of battered women who kill to protect themselves or their children (Bradfield, 2002a; Shaffer, 1997; Stubbs and Tolmie, 1999). In fact, in some jurisdictions there is evidence that BWS has been used to undermine women's self-defence claims, for instance by contrasting the 'assertiveness, strength, and strategic decision-making expressed by female defendants who had been battered' with the stereotypes associated with the syndrome (Ferraro, 2003, p 110; see also New Zealand cases *R v Oakes* (1995) and *The Queen v Zhou* (1993)). Such results were predicted by some commentators who recognised that fundamental features of battered woman syndrome testimony conflicted with the construct of self-defence.

10.4.2 A focus on the personal versus the structural

Notwithstanding the intentions of feminist litigators, BWS typically has not been understood to explain the social circumstances surrounding the defendant's actions, as would be necessary if self-defence was to be applied fairly (Schneider, 2000). Instead, BWS testimony has been used primarily to describe and justify the defendant's perceptions, often cast as individual pathology, such as her inability to leave the relationship due to personal inadequacy and her distorted understanding of the violent events that occurred (Comack, 1993). Thus, rather than explaining why her behaviour was reasonable in the circumstances, BWS is commonly used in a way that re-inscribes those circumstances as subjective rather than objective. Expert psychiatric or psychological evidence typically used in BWS cases may reinforce individualised understandings of battered women's behaviour in ways that conform to existing narrow stereotypes (Chan, 1997; Stark, 1995). Legal actors, including judges, selectively deploy those aspects of expert evidence that conform to accepted understandings of the facts in question and may substitute one form of common-sense for another. In fact, White-Mair argues that historic forms of 'gender-specific notions of criminal responsibility' have been given new life through battered woman litigation (2000, p 411).

As Barbara Hudson describes, this individualised approach also conflates agency, often conceived of in dichotomous terms as all or nothing, with choice. One consequence is that, '[f]or women, appreciation of their limited range of actual or perceived choices leads to typification of themselves as less rational rather than of their acts as less culpable' (Hudson, 2002, p 43). She argues that a firmer distinction needs to be drawn between the two in recognition that while everyone has agency,

---

5   Other than a passing reference in a provocation case, *R v Chhay*, 1994, p 11.

that is, a capacity to act, choice may be severely restricted (Hudson, 2002, p 37). To the extent that battered women exercise choice, it is a very limited form of choice.

The individualised focus obscures structural patterns and trends – for example, systemic gender and race inequities are rendered invisible.[6] What becomes prominent are the pathology and problems of the particular offender who is standing in front of the court.[7] In the words of Elizabeth Schneider:

> ... the problems that battered women face are viewed in isolation; they are rarely linked to gender socialization, women's subservient position within society and the family structure, sex discrimination in the workplace, economic discrimination, problems of housing and a lack of child care, lack of access to divorce, inadequate child support, problems of single motherhood, or lack of educational and community support. The focus is all on the individual woman and her 'pathology' instead of on the batterer and the social structures that support the oppression of women and that glorify or otherwise condone violence. (Schneider, 2000, pp 72–73)

It is for this reason that we have argued that BWS evidence is particularly inappropriate as a defence strategy for Aboriginal or, indeed, other racialised women (Stubbs and Tolmie, 1995). The reconfiguration of factors such as cultural values and extreme social and economic disadvantage into examples of personal inadequacy on the part of the particular defendant is, besides being inaccurate, deeply offensive.

10.4.3 The construction of the personal as passive and victimised

A number of scholars have argued that women who are dealt with sympathetically in the legal context are those who can be constructed to meet the indices of appropriate femininity (Fox, 2000; Kennedy, 1992; Naffine, 1990; Schneider, 2000, p 141; Worrall, 1990). That is, they are acted upon rather than acting, and they are helpless, hurting, and victimised – preferably whilst simultaneously performing well as wives and mothers (Allen, 1987; Keenan, 2000; Nicolson, 1995). Indeed, it is arguable that BWS has been accepted by courts because it is consistent with such stereotypes. Despite widespread criticism, the concept of 'learned helplessness' continues to be used in some courts as a defining characteristic of BWS. Thus, women who are not passive and helpless or who otherwise do not conform to accepted stereotypes may be judged harshly (Bradfield, 2002b; Chan, 2001). As Shaffer says:

> The more a woman may have displayed anger or aggressive tendencies, have experienced problems with alcohol or drug abuse, have been involved in criminal activities or have demonstrated autonomous behaviour in other spheres of her life, the more risky a defence based on battered woman syndrome may become. (1997, p 25)

Myths about the passivity and victim status of battered women may affect indigenous women in Australia differently and may be destructive on several

---

6 Madame Justice L'Heureux-Dubé's decision in *R v Malott* (1998) is a notable exception.

7 BWS is one significant factor that contributes to this outcome. Another is the tendency of courts to focus on the time immediately surrounding the actual killing and the consequent failure to examine a broader range of circumstances.

levels. Racialised understandings of domestic violence may be doubly distorted where they draw on misconceptions about indigenous peoples. Where entitlement to a particular defence or to mitigation is viewed through stereotyped constructions of the female offender, such constructions typically reflect white (often middle-class) norms. Thus, indigenous women may be judged adversely against such a standard. As Hudson recognizes, '[d]efences and mitigations are differently available, then, to differently situated women' (2002, p 41).

However, ignoring race also may do injustice to indigenous women defendants (Stubbs and Tolmie, 1995). For example, given the over-representation of indigenous women within the criminal justice system, they may be more likely than non-indigenous battered women to have a prior record which may undermine their entitlement to victim status. However, domestic violence and offending behaviour by indigenous women may be linked in at least three ways: they may retaliate against their violent partner; they may resort to alcohol or other drugs as an escape or as self-medication to cope with the violence; or the victimisation they suffer may lead them to abuse or neglect others (Cunneen and Kerley, 1995; NSWLRC, 2000). Cunneen and Kerley note that 'physical force may be the only resistance to domestic violence available given a range of pressures which militate against involvement of the police' (as cited by NSWLRC, 2000, para 6.28).

Although indigenous women experience extremely high levels of domestic violence, including intimate homicides, sexual assaults and other forms of violence (Memmott, 2001), it would be unjust to extract this from the historical and contemporary social context and attribute it to individual circumstances. The historical context includes colonisation, dispossession, and the disruption of indigenous family life through the policies imposed on the stolen generations that is, children forcibly removed from their families. Indigenous women commonly face 'enormous pressures arising from the combined effects of poverty, violence, sole parenthood, alcohol and substance abuse, and gender and race discrimination' (NSWLRC, 2000, para 6.29). Constructing indigenous women as passive victims fails to attest to their considerable resilience within circumstances which commonly involve multiple and severe disadvantages.

10.4.4 Special pleading

Testimony about BWS is often heard as a kind of special pleading for women (Schneider, 1996, 2000, p 113). Because BWS testimony is commonly interpreted as focusing on the pathology of the particular offender, it is easily read as an exercise of compassion for individual tragedy rather than an attempt to highlight systemic inequalities faced by women who are seeking to argue a defence such as self-defence.

10.4.5 Psychological individuality and the exclusion of social context

BWS testimony has been interpreted in ways that are at odds with the requirements for self-defence. However, a more profound obstacle may arise from the underpinnings of the criminal law *per se*. Norrie contends that the criminal law is underpinned by a conception of 'psychological individualism' that:

> is a political and ideological construction which operates to seal off the question of individual culpability from issues concerning the relationship between individual agency and social context. It seeks to exclude a broad view of social relations which would locate individual actions within their determinative context, and to exclude moral and political counter-discourses from the law ... Abstract psychological individualism is presented as an ideal and apolitical representation of human agency, but it stands in opposition to the realities of concrete social individuality, which threatens to undermine the conviction process. (Norrie, 2001, p 224)

According to Norrie, the work of excluding social context is 'ongoing, and determines the evolving shape of legal doctrine' (2001, p 224). Thus, the potential for culpability, responsibility and agency to be re-interpreted in the interests of battered women on trial will be limited by the criminal law's 'psychological individualism' (see also Lacey, 1998).[8]

In a similar way, Schneider has identified profound resistance from some criminal law scholars to the 'affirmative recognition of the significance of social context, and the necessary inter-relationship between individual action, social context and social responsibility' since such recognition 'challenges fundamental assumptions about "free will" in the criminal law' (1996, p 552, 1992; see also Richards, 1996). This continues to represent a major challenge to feminist legal interventions in this area. However, as Lacey argues, law's decontextualisation is in fact the exclusion of 'certain features of context' and an abstraction: 'what matters is what gets abstracted and how' (Lacey, 1998, p 200). Therefore, there may be some space for feminist activism to seek to shape the inclusions and exclusions brought about through legal method.

10.4.6 Re-asserting context

Some legal actors have responded to criticisms of BWS and the failings of self-defence litigation by seeking to re-assert the role of social context. For instance, a major US review affirmed that evidence of social context, also called social framework evidence, and not BWS, had a significant role to play in assisting the courts to assess fairly battered women's self-defence claims (US Department of Justice and US Department of Health and Human Services, 1996). It found that such evidence should be introduced by a broader range of experts than the psychologists and psychiatrists typically used by defence counsel. In a significant Canadian decision (*R v Malott* (1998)), two women judges of the Supreme Court of Canada recognised that *R v Lavallee* (1990) had been narrowly interpreted. They offered a critique of the 'syndromisation' of battered women and also stressed that 'a battered woman's experiences are both individualized, [and] shared with other women, within the context of a society and a legal system which has historically

---

8 He develops this argument in the context of battered women who kill with reference to provocation and diminished responsibility but not self-defence, perhaps because in the UK it is the former defences and not the latter that have been used for battered women.

undervalued women's experiences'.[9] Moreover, in the Canadian Self Defence Review, Ratushny J 'attempted to identify links between abuse and self-defence without focusing on the syndrome issue' (Sheehy, 2000, p 211). It is perhaps too soon to measure the effectiveness of these interventions.

10.5 Plea negotiations and shifting the focus to sentencing

Pleading guilty to manslaughter, typically on the basis of having committed an unlawful and dangerous act, in exchange for the prosecution agreeing to drop murder charges, has emerged as perhaps the most common defence strategy in battered women's homicide cases in Australia.[10] The technical basis on which the murder charges are dropped generally is that the accused lacks the necessary intent to satisfy the *mens rea* for murder. Considerations of the offender's personal circumstances are then used to argue for a reduced sentence for manslaughter. Plea bargaining with an attempt to mitigate sentence is a defence strategy that may be entirely appropriate in any particular case, but it raises many of the same criticisms that arise concerning BWS. In addition to individualising structural problems, it also privatises justice.

10.5.1 Plea negotiations

10.5.1.1 The failure to support battered defendants' claims to self-defence

Battered women who plead guilty to manslaughter necessarily relinquish any claims they might otherwise have to self-defence. We have identified a number of cases in which the defendant pleaded guilty to manslaughter in exchange for murder charges being dropped in circumstances where they arguably had a case for self-defence that should have been put to the jury. This impression is often confirmed by the remarks of the sentencing judge or the nature of the sentences imposed. Two examples will suffice.

In *R v Gutsche* (2002) the defendant's husband was a violent and controlling man. He frequently threatened to kill her and verbally abused the children. He also physically assaulted her, on one occasion beating her until she lost consciousness. He promised that if she ever left him he would hunt her down. He controlled whom she spoke to, monitored her behaviour closely and accused her of having affairs. She became extremely scared of him. His behaviour over the weeks leading up to the night of his death became increasingly bizarre. On that night the defendant and her husband were arguing when he got out of his chair to come towards her. She

---

9 *R v Malott* at 473, *per* L'Heureux-Dubé and McLachlin JJ.

10 Bradfield found that, in Australia over the period 1980 to 2000, 22 women pleaded guilty to manslaughter on the basis of a lack of intention to kill, 10 did so on the basis of provocation, and only one on the basis of diminished responsibility (2002a, p 27). More recent cases collected by the authors confirm Bradfield's findings. Whether this course of action is available to the accused depends on the view of the facts taken by the prosecution and thus is not simply a defence strategy. There is very little Australian literature on plea bargaining and little empirical evidence concerning how it is practised (see Mack and Roach Anleu, 1995; Seifman and Frieberg, 2001; in the UK, see Kennedy, 1992, p 207).

picked up a vegetable knife and stabbed him as he approached her. At her trial, she said:

> I didn't know what was going to come next and I just went into this intense ... it was like fear and just hopelessness ... I didn't mean to kill him. I didn't even think I was going to stab him ... I wasn't thinking, I was just scared. I'm scared to do wrong; I was always really scared of him.

While the facts suggest self-defence may have been available, the accused pleaded guilty to performing a dangerous act causing death. At sentencing, evidence was introduced that she was suffering from BWS and she received a suspended sentence.

In *R v Kennedy* (2000) the defendant, who was Aboriginal, killed her partner with one knife blow to the chest during a drunken fight, after enduring 11 years of severe violence. She'd had three protection orders against him with little apparent effect. The judge accepted that over the years she had done 'all she could to protect herself from the abuse of the deceased' and that it was unrealistic to expect her to remove herself from her community. He said:

> I think that when she realized that she was coming under yet another violent attack she took hold of whatever was close at hand in an attempt in some way to make the deceased modify his behaviour, short of an intention to do him really serious injury. (para 36).

In acknowledging that the accused realistically apprehended serious injury from her attacker on that night and had exhausted all of her legal avenues for self-protection, the sentencing judge arguably characterised the case as one of self-defence. However, the accused had already relinquished any claim to self-defence by pleading guilty to manslaughter on the basis that she had performed an unlawful and dangerous act. The sentencing judge ordered that the accused enter a recognisance to be of good behaviour for four years and deferred sentence.

In *Kennedy* and *Gutsche* the outcomes appear compassionate and suggest that the court found that each offender had a low level of moral culpability for what transpired. However, both women remained under the scrutiny of the criminal justice system, risked incarceration should they breach the conditions of their release and carried the stigma of a serious criminal conviction. Moreover, had they gone to trial they may have been acquitted on the basis of self-defence. Plea bargaining may spare women the trauma of the criminal process but does not necessarily result in a more favourable outcome. It also diminishes opportunities for the legal interpretation and application of self-defence in ways consistent with the life circumstances faced by some battered women who use lethal self-help to protect their lives or physical integrity (or that of their children).

10.5.1.2 The privatisation of justice

The process of plea-negotiation shifts the most important determination, that of guilt, from the judicial to the prosecutorial realm. Thus, police and prosecutorial discretion in determining the original charge and prosecutorial discretion concerning whether to accept a guilty plea and to what offence may assume a heightened significance. The result that is negotiated will have a significant influence on the approach to the facts that can be taken by the sentencing judge. Decisions about guilt are shifted from the public to the private realm and are negotiated between the defendant's counsel and the prosecutorial agencies. There is no longer a judge overseeing the process or 12 members of the community injecting their community values and common-sense into the decision-making process.

The case of *R v Burke* (2000) illustrates the power of the prosecution in plea bargaining negotiations, the problems inherent in having guilt resolved by the prosecution rather than by the judiciary and the degree to which sentencing judges are constrained by the approach taken by the prosecution in plea bargaining. The Aboriginal woman defendant's offer to plead guilty to manslaughter in exchange for murder charges being dropped was rejected by the Crown. After her trial for murder was terminated by a discharge of the jury without fault on her part, the Crown again declined to accept a plea of guilty to manslaughter. Before the re-trial she pleaded guilty to murder. She did so despite total memory failure about what had happened on the night of the homicide. Her extreme intoxication and her bizarre behaviour strongly suggest that she was not capable of forming any kind of intention at the time that she stabbed the deceased. The Crown conceded that this was not the most culpable form of murder and accepted her guilty plea on the basis that she had an intention to cause grievous bodily harm to the deceased, but neither intention nor recklessness as to his death.

This concession was extracted by defence counsel in the hope that it would be seen as mitigation at sentencing. The sentencing judge said that the case raised a level of culpability 'not unlike the culpability which attaches to serious manslaughter occurring in circumstances of intoxication and domestic violence'. He remarked that:

> I am required to sentence the prisoner for murder, not for manslaughter. There are many cases which, although they do not establish any tariff for sentences in such circumstances, for a crime of manslaughter, do give some indications of an appropriate range of sentence. There are few, very few indeed, remotely similar where there has been a plea of guilty to murder. (para 59)

He acknowledged the 'tragic' nature of the case and sentenced the woman to nine years imprisonment with a non parole period of five years. This may seem a lenient sentence for murder but it was the highest sentence of the seven recent Australian cases involving Aboriginal women offenders. We can only speculate what the sentence might have been had she been convicted of manslaughter.

The case raises serious questions about the use of prosecutorial discretion. Should defence counsel be entitled to proffer and the prosecution be entitled to accept a guilty plea in circumstances where there must be serious doubt about the actual guilt of the defendant? Should the judiciary be able to overturn such agreements if it becomes apparent that they were extracted under pressure or wrongly made? Ross has argued strongly that in some battered women's cases the public interest may be consistent with a decision not to prosecute (1998, p 40).

In *R v MacKenzie* (2000), the defendant, who was non-Aboriginal, pleaded guilty to manslaughter on the basis of criminal negligence, and she was sentenced to eight years. She had tripped while carrying a gun, shooting her abusive husband in the back as she tried to get to her car to leave after she had been abused and punched around the head. She appealed the conviction on the basis that accepting the guilty plea amounted to a miscarriage of justice and that she wished to argue self-defence in response to the original murder charge. The appeal court held that there was no miscarriage of justice and refused to allow her to withdraw her guilty plea, but allowed her appeal on sentence and reduced her sentence to five years, with a non parole period of 12 months. The court held that the advice she had received to plead guilty to manslaughter rather than defending the charges that she faced on the basis of self-defence was competent because by pleading guilty to manslaughter as recommended by her lawyers she avoided the possibility of being convicted of the more serious charge of murder. The court suggested that there was in fact a risk that she could be convicted of murder, although none of the judges explored this in detail and it would appear to have been a slim risk.

The appeal court was also unanimous that no rational jury could have found self-defence on the facts because her belief that the gun was unloaded meant that she could not have been intending to use it to defend herself. Thus, it found that there was no possibility that if she had gone to trial she would have received a complete acquittal. McPherson JA was the only judge to raise the possibility that the accused may have been intending to try and escape the deceased by threatening him with a gun that she did not intend to fire but hoped he would wrongly think was loaded. He dismissed this as an argument for self-defence on the basis of her handling of a gun in this fashion, given her lack of skill with them, was grossly negligent and thus amounted to manslaughter. In other words, he appeared to erroneously suggest that actions which carry a risk of death or serious harm to the perpetrator cannot be characterised as self-defence in respect of the offence of manslaughter.

The court also rejected the argument that she had not made the decision to plead guilty as a true exercise of free will. The court characterised this as an argument that she was essentially a submissive individual who, in the presence of men, would 'do what she was told'. McPherson JA rejected this argument on the basis that she had attended teacher training college at a time when that was 'no small achievement' for a woman from rural Australia, she had a good command of English, she appeared intelligent and strong and they didn't think she would have any difficulties in making up her mind for herself. Accordingly, the court did not believe that she had deferred to her lawyer's judgment or felt bullied. This approach is problematic because it focuses on what kind of person the accused was, rather than on the pressures that she may have been under when she was initially required to make decisions about the homicide charges she faced – which included the trauma and confusion that might follow the recent participation in a homicide and survival of an extremely violent long-term relationship.

The fact that plea bargaining has become standard practice in this area highlights the considerable pressures that battered women are under not to go to trial – a fact that compounds the power of the prosecution during plea negotiations and emphasises the public importance of the prosecutor's role in the justice system (Margulies, 2001; Sheehy, 2001). The pressures on women not to go to trial include the problematic nature of BWS evidence that can undermine a self-defence case, the uncertainty of the law on self-defence applied to these situations, the lack of appellate decisions giving clear guidance in this respect, the trauma involved for the accused in testifying about the abuse publicly and in front of the deceased's family and any children, and the potential trauma to her children if they are needed to testify. Another pressure is remorse about what occurred and the fact that there are typically no independent witnesses to verify the accused's claim that she was responding to abusive conduct which means that the success of her defence will rest heavily on her own credibility (Bradfield, 2002a). As the Canadian Association of Elizabeth Fry Societies (CAEFS) notes:

> Women who allege that they killed violent mates face widespread disbelief and misogynist denial, an enormous lack of legal, social and economic support for their defence, and the prospect of the loss of their children for decades. Added to this is the loss of self-worth, confidence, and clarity engendered by male control and violence. (CAEFS, 1998, p 13)

In some jurisdictions there are mandatory minimum sentences for murder, including life sentences. These sentences provide a strong incentive for plea bargaining as they make the stakes for a murder conviction unbearably high for many battered defendants (Bradfield, 2002a; Margulies, 2001; Sheehy, 2001). A further incentive to plea bargaining is that significant sentencing discounts may attach to early guilty pleas. In New South Wales this discount may be in the range of 10–25% (*R v Thomson* (2000)). Bradfield found 'reason for concern that the existence of the sentencing discount encourages innocent women to plead guilty to manslaughter' (2002a, p 330).

There may be additional pressures on indigenous women to plea bargain. Those residing in rural or remote areas may find it hard to access good legal advice. They may face greater levels of trauma, risk and difficulty in going to trial (Stubbs and Tolmie, 1995). Many indigenous communities express fear and distrust of the justice system. In some indigenous communities strong cultural traditions make it inappropriate to speak about a deceased person, and dictate some things as men's or women's business not to be spoken of publicly. Kinship ties may dictate who can speak to whom. There may be difficulties in communication due to the absence of interpreters in indigenous languages and because standard English terms do not necessarily have the same meaning in Aboriginal English. As well, standard cross-examination practices are at odds with the form of information exchange accepted in indigenous language practices (Criminal Justice Commission, 1996). As noted above, stereotypes about battered women may also undermine indigenous women's claims to a defence or mitigation of sentence. We were unable to find any recent cases involving Aboriginal women that were determined at trial,[11] even though there were cases in which it appeared that self-defence might have had some chance of success on the facts.

It needs to be acknowledged that there are pressures on the lawyers conducting these cases to plea bargain and these pressures may have a considerable influence, whether consciously or unconsciously, on the advice they give to their clients (Margulies, 2001). For example, there are budgetary/managerial pressures on the prosecution, such as the need to reduce the costs of going to trial and the desire to reduce court delays. Defence counsel may be influenced by matters like the poor

---

11 *R v Burke* (2000), noted above and *R v Churchill* (2000) commenced by trial but resulted in guilty pleas.

fees paid by legal aid in deciding to accept a guilty plea on behalf of their client instead of going to trial.

The private and discretionary nature of the plea bargaining process has a number of troubling consequences. First, there is little or no public scrutiny of the decision-making process and little chance for the public to learn how the decision was reached, with the risk that the outcome might be seen as inexplicable or unfair. Secondly, the results are not treated as exercises of judicial power by the prosecution but free choices by the accused women in their own best interests. Thus, there may be little prospect for having the plea overturned other than by the difficult route of proving that they had incompetent legal advice or that they lacked capacity to take that advice. Conservative opinions proffered by their lawyers with all the weight of legal authority in circumstances where the women concerned are extremely vulnerable will be unlikely to satisfy the test (Sheehy, 2001). Thirdly, there is no way of identifying or challenging misconceptions about domestic violence that shape the decisions reached. Finally, as Bradfield (2002a, p 330) has argued, innocent women may be pressured to plead guilty.

10.5.2   Sentencing

Given the focus of feminist activism on self-defence as the preferred strategy for battered women charged with killing an abusive spouse, it is perhaps not surprising that relatively little attention has been paid to the sentencing of battered women (but see Bradfield, 2002a; Warner, 1996). Sentencing discretion requires weighing and applying competing principles to the facts and circumstances of the individual case. It is sometimes argued that sentencing allows the context of the offending to be given due recognition, especially in determining the objective seriousness of the offence and the extent of the offender's culpability. However, we found that where social context was considered it was commonly transformed to individual deficit or pathology. Moreover, we remain concerned that the sentencing process offers little prospect for gendered and/or raced inequalities that provide the context for offending to be recognised as such.[12]

It must be acknowledged that sentencing judges are constrained from taking into account facts that are inconsistent with the verdict or plea. Where the basis of a jury verdict or plea is unclear, judges must infer the foundation of that plea or verdict on their own interpretation of the facts (Bradfield, 2002a, pp 326–27). This latter point highlights the risk that myths and stereotypes about domestic violence may significantly shape sentencing outcomes in these cases (Nicolson, 2000). We cannot assume that a judge's attempts to place the behaviour of a battered woman in context for the purposes of sentencing will necessarily challenge rather than reinforce stereotypes about sex/gender and violence against women and/or

---

12 Our focus on the need to examine the social context in sentencing battered women is not an argument based on 'rotten social background' (see Hudson, 2000), although it may be consistent with that argument, but is based on the fact that women's resort to lethal self-help must be judged in light of the systemic nature of violence against women and the absence of other realistic means of self-preservation.

indigenous peoples. The sentencing process may reproduce such stereotypes in a setting where there is little prospect for challenge, and unless there is a legal error or a manifestly excessive sentence, there will be little room for appeal. Here Nicola Lacey's work is particularly apt. She has warned that the call for the contextualisation of criminal offending may be an important deconstructive device that exposes the ideological operation of criminal law doctrine but, at the same time, it is a naïve feminist strategy (1998, pp 197–205). That is, 'we need to think about the broader assumptions which will inform the ensuing judgements about who we are and how we live' (p 203). Thus, the call to contextualise the offender's conduct is not in and of itself enough. The range and type of information drawn on in assessing the broader context will be a crucial determinant of the outcome (see Dutton's detailed work on this issue, 1996, 1997).

10.5.2.1   A focus on the personal versus the structural

At sentencing, the link between the defendant's criminal actions and the deceased's violence is rarely properly credited. In some cases this is because, unlike the formal defences of self-defence and provocation, the nature of the manslaughter does not require a link between the behaviour of the deceased and that of the accused. This point is illustrated in *R v MacKenzie* (2000) described above. The accused pleaded guilty to manslaughter on the basis of criminal negligence. She had tripped while carrying a loaded gun and shot the deceased in the back. On appeal McPherson JA remarked:

> In a case of killing by criminal negligence like this, it seems difficult to find a completely logical rationale for taking account of the applicant's earlier brutal treatment by her deceased husband. The very nature of the offence of manslaughter on the basis of criminal negligence to which she pleaded guilty might be thought to exclude consideration of that factor if she caused his death through the reckless handling of the gun, rather than because of some degree of provocation or self-defence. Still it might serve to explain why she went and got the gun in the first place. (para 56)

The disconnection between the violence of the deceased and the response of the defendant is most evident in the remarks that sentencing judges commonly make about the need for general deterrence as a sentencing consideration. For example, in *R v MacKenzie*, McMurdo P remarked that a substantial period of imprisonment needed to be imposed for two reasons:

> first, to deter those who would handle dangerous guns in this criminally negligent manner, especially in the context of domestic arguments fuelled by the consumption of alcohol and second, to recognize the applicant's criminal responsibility for the death of another. Such conduct is unacceptable in a civilized society; even the grim history of domestic violence present in this case cannot neutralize such criminally negligent conduct. (2000, para 24)

The remarks fail to acknowledge that the deceased's extreme violence constituted the circumstances in which the defendant acted. Instead, those circumstances are re-presented as something muted and historical; that is, domestic arguments fuelled by alcohol.

In *R v Denney* the court remarked that:

> Of course provocation manslaughter is a serious offence and the court must be seen to uphold the sanctity of human life, moreover the court should endeavour to deter

violence as a problem solving technique. There is no right to take the life of a person because their behaviour may be regarded as despicable and the court must not appear to condone such action. (2000, para 36)

This account fails to acknowledge the accused women's fear that her husband was going to kill or seriously harm her. Her terror was induced by the intensity of his anger towards her on that night, including his assault, threats to kill and 'vicious' rape.

Domestic violence is frequently presented in sentencing remarks as mutual – a dysfunction of two individuals – or simply as a human tragedy. In *R v Churchill* (2000) the Aboriginal woman was tried for murder resulting in a hung jury. She then pleaded guilty to manslaughter despite the fact that self-defence or automatism may have been available defences on the facts. The deceased had beaten her on numerous occasions, including to the point of unconsciousness. She said that after an evening of drinking, they argued because she didn't want to sleep with him and he accused her of having another man. The argument 'became heated' then 'everything went blank' and she found the deceased on the floor with blood pouring from his neck and a knife in her hand. She denied any recollection of stabbing him.

The judge quoted extensively from a psychologist who summarised the position as follows:

[she] is a young woman who does not show clinical signs of any mental disorder but who has grown up amongst chaotic and violent people. In many respects her life has been typical of the extreme of the heavy drinking sub-culture, which is characterized by sordid and violent relationships and lack of parental responsibility. Her offence is the seemingly inevitable yet almost chance outcome of an abusive and violent relationship with the deceased, in which Ms Churchill might as easily have been the victim as the perpetrator. Although she has many positive qualities and would like to be a good mother, her lifestyle will not change for the better unless she finds some way of overcoming her addiction to alcohol. I know from long experience of people from similar backgrounds how unlikely that is, but a sentence requiring a period of supervision in the community would give Ms Churchill an opportunity to consider making such an effort. (para 17)

This characterisation of the facts in *Churchill* arguably suggests that the violence is a mutual phenomenon and a feature of the accused's 'lifestyle', along with her bad parenting skills. In turn, her lifestyle appeared to be seen as a product of her alcoholism and therefore something that she had to make the decision to overcome. Her indigenous community is rendered as chaotic and characterised by sordid and violent relationships.

New South Wales courts have attempted to give recognition to relevant circumstances in sentencing Aboriginal offenders while at the same time not offending the principle of equality before the law. *R v Fernando* (1992) set out principles to be applied in sentencing Aboriginal offenders and stressed that:

the same sentencing principles are to be applied in every case irrespective of the identity of the particular offender or his membership of an ethnic or other group but that does not mean the sentencing court should ignore those facts which exist only by reason of the offenders' membership of such a group. (p 62)

The decision acknowledges that alcohol abuse and violence are rife in Aboriginal communities. It also stresses that 'the court must avoid any hint of racism, paternalism or collective guilt', but must also 'assess realistically the objective seriousness of the crime within its local setting and by reference to the particular subjective circumstances of the offender' (see NSWLRC, 2000, para 2.18).

There is little available commentary on how these principles have affected sentencing in practice and little guidance in the case law. We are not aware of any analysis of application of the principles to indigenous women. Our analysis of cases suggests that courts rarely make specific connections between the extreme circumstances of dispossession faced by Aboriginal defendants and the immediate course of action that a particular defendant took in relation to the violence that they faced. Instead, the broader social and structural context tends to be presented through the personal lens of the accused as an example of individual tragedy or of a deprived lifestyle (Stubbs and Tolmie, 1995). While such circumstances may be seen to lessen the defendant's moral culpability, this inference relies on a deficit discourse that suggests that less can be expected of the accused because of her personal characteristics.

In *R v Burke* (2000) the judge alluded to the violence that the defendant had experienced as being a component of her 'deprived lifestyle'. He remarked that:

> the prisoner's personal history reveals a history of unrelenting tribulation and harshness which is most difficult for most people to comprehend. She is a person who has existed in socially deprived circumstances, as was submitted, consigned to a lifestyle of poverty, deprivation and entrenched alcohol abuse in an atmosphere where she is the subject of violence and conditioned to violence as a social response. (para 43)

> It is not necessary to go so far as to exemplify her life as a direct result of the problems faced by members of the Aboriginal community in the remoter locations of Australia, nor does the evidence on this plea deal with the more general phenomenon of deprivation and dispossession suffered by the Aboriginal community, but it is enough, and the evidence persuades me, that the conditions personal to her of alcoholism, emotional disturbance and intellectual impairment and the deprived lifestyle in which she has been involved are such as to set a context for conditioning her to react in the way in which she did under whatever the emotional stimulus she suffered that night. (para 44)

This reasoning suggests that the accused woman's incredibly difficult circumstances – which the judge says that he doesn't need to link to the general dispossession of her people – produced various *personal* attributes including a deprived lifestyle and a violent relationship. These personal attributes meant that she was conditioned to react violently to an unspecified 'emotional stimulus'. The judge's analysis demonstrates all of the problems highlighted above. The structural is mediated through the personal in that the violence and the circumstances of social constraint the accused faced are acknowledged only to the extent that they have rendered her a person who is prone to use violence. Linkages between her circumstances and her response to those circumstances are not adequately described and systemic issues are muted or erased.

10.5.2.2 Psychological and psychiatric evidence in sentencing

Psychological and psychiatric evidence commonly facilitate the reinterpretation of structural factors as personal characteristics. As *R v Churchill* (2000) illustrates, it is not uncommon in sentencing for psychological and/or psychiatric reports outlining the accused's personal history and assessing both her personality and personal culpability to be accorded great significance (see also Henning, 1995). Frequently, but not invariably, if the defendant is battered, this evidence might take the form of testimony that she suffered from BWS (for example, see *R v Denney* (2000)). Expert psychological or psychiatric evidence need not be narrowly circumscribed but may be a useful vehicle for introducing an explanation of the objective circumstances of women's lives. However, as observed in relation to the operation of BWS, such evidence has a focus on interpreting the offence with reference to the defendant's individual psychology. Moreover, the psychological individualism of the criminal law is consistent with deploying this evidence in a narrow and individualising manner even where the expert testimony might set out a broader account.

In *R v Melrose* (2001), the Aboriginal woman defendant pleaded guilty to manslaughter on the basis of an unlawful and dangerous act despite what appeared to be a reasonably strong case of self-defence on the facts. The Crown agreed to drop murder charges because of difficulty in proving the *mens rea* for murder. The deceased had physically abused the defendant frequently during their 14 years together. She had scarring and had received regular lacerations from being hit in the mouth, kicked in the head, and beaten with a vacuum cleaner handle. Her two older daughters were so fearful of him that they had gone to live with their aunt. She became more isolated after they had moved to an area where the deceased had more family support than she did and the beatings became more frequent. On the night in question he assaulted her at a local dance. She went to the police station which was unattended and then tried unsuccessfully to contact police in an adjoining town asking for assistance to go into a refuge. She went home, smashed some things, put a knife up her sleeve to protect herself, and returned to the dance where she was again verbally and physically assaulted by the deceased. During this confrontation the knife fell out of her sleeve, she picked it up and stabbed the deceased in the shoulder. She did not realise that the wound was serious or, indeed, fatal.

The judge characterised the marriage as an 'unhappy relationship' and remarked that the psychiatrist had 'posed the question which many would ask in these circumstances' as to why she did not leave it. The psychiatrist stressed the obstacles that the women faced and said:

> I think it would have been almost impossible for her to make such a change. She reports that she did pack her bags and attempt to leave on a number of occasions. She took out apprehended violence orders. She went to live with her mother or other relatives, but he found her and forced her to return. She went to a refuge in Walgett, but that arrangement could only be temporary. From her description ... (the deceased) had pathological jealousy and believed that she was interested in another man, and would have followed her if she had tried to move out of the area. She felt powerless because of the fact that he was physically violent towards her and the children. (para 24)

However, no link was made by the court between this evidence and the defendant's actions in arming herself and stabbing the deceased during a violent confrontation. Instead, the court emphasised the psychiatrist's finding that the defendant had developed a depressive illness at the time of the killing and possessed a 'dependant personality'. The desperation of her situation was acknowledged only as it manifested in the form of a depressive illness.

This bias towards explaining the accused and her circumstances in terms of her individual pathology was also evident in the psychological evidence that was received in sentencing in *R v MacKenzie* (2000). In that case, one of the appellate judges considered the mitigating effect that the history of abuse had on the defendant's sentence for manslaughter by criminal negligence. He used the psychological evidence to suggest that the narrowing of the accused's options for dealing with the violence that she faced was an irrational but understandable impression that she had, as opposed to an objective reality:

> [the psychologist] noted that one of the impacts on the applicant of the long term abuse and violence in the relationship was that it contributed 'to ineffective problem solving behaviour and a perception by [the applicant] of the narrowing of her options over time. A perception of narrowed options can often result in decisions made by the abused woman that from the outside look like poor judgment ...' (para 21)

10.5.2.3 The construction of the personal as passive and victimised

Sentencing decisions involving battered women who have pleaded guilty to manslaughter are consistent with the broader research on the sentencing of women. That is, women who can be constructed to meet the appropriate indices of femininity – those who can present themselves as victimised and deserving of compassion, as well as being good mothers and wives – may benefit from compassionate outcomes.

R v Kirkwood (2000) involved an Aboriginal woman who pleaded guilty to manslaughter in exchange for murder charges being dropped.[13] She received a minimum sentence of 12 months imprisonment with an additional term of 18 months in recognition of the 'strong subjective circumstances of the case' as well as the fact that the she had 'acted impulsively in response to a stressful situation created by the deceased'. The court detailed a series of life tragedies and difficulties the accused had experienced. The judge relied heavily on the report of a psychologist. In summarising the personal factors that mitigated her sentence, the judge noted that:

> ... she is described as having been a good mother and caring person. [The psychologist's] report reinforces that view. I accept it. Despite her intellectual limitations and long-standing addiction to alcohol, she has managed to raise her children well and to provide ongoing support for Gary [her brain injured son]. (para 28).

---

13 Another example is provided by *R v Denney* (2000) in which the judge outlined the physical, sexual and emotional violence that occurred in the relationship before going on to comment that:

> In front of your family and in public social settings, you endeavoured to play the dutiful wife and John Denney played the devoted husband. However, the real situation was one of marital conflict, which you endeavoured to keep hidden from your children. (para 15)

After outlining the facts of the killing the court weighed up mitigating and aggravating factors for sentencing purposes, including the fact that:

> ... you are blessed with the support of your children, who not only acknowledge your role as their mother, but also as grandmother to their children, of which there are currently three. (para 35)

As Rebecca Bradfield has argued, judges tend to express these apparently lenient sentences as exercises of mercy and compassion rather than of principled justice (2002a, p 340).

10.6   Conclusion

In this chapter we have attempted to shift the analysis of battered women's homicide cases from a singular focus on the failings of BWS to a broader consideration of the criminal justice process. The psychological individualism of the criminal law shapes the manner in which evidence of domestic violence is received and deployed at each stage of criminal justice decision-making. It is also consistent with the substantial weight typically attached to psychiatric evidence during trials and at sentencing. However, despite the individualism and the apparent resistance of the criminal law to contextual information, legal decision-making is not devoid of context as it draws on common myths and understandings to assist in the interpretation of behaviour. Thus, women are measured against indices of appropriate femininity rendering them as deserving of compassion, or not. Indigenous women may also 'benefit' from the exercise of compassion but too often this seems to be derived from seeing them as tragic or damaged, rather than in more complex ways as acting within desperate circumstances reflecting structural and systemic forms of raced and gendered inequalities.

The enduring influence of those myths and stereotypes demonstrates that changing legal and broader cultural understandings of domestic violence remains an urgent task. For battered women charged with a homicide offence the stakes are very high. Lacey (1998, p 202) is no doubt right to warn that the simple resort to contextualise the behaviour of women accused of criminal behaviour as a feminist strategy is naïve, although she notes 'that local instances [may] afford opportunities of progressive recontextualisation'. However, where spaces exist in the criminal justice process to contextualise women's offending by inserting feminist understandings of domestic violence, this remains a strategy worth pursuing. The endorsement of social framework evidence by the US Department of Justice and US Department of Health and Human Services (1996) as valuable at all stages of criminal justice decision-making, together with a small number of pro-feminist judgments, offer some tools to aid a meaningful, pro-feminist contextualisation of women's offending. Mary Ann Dutton's (1996) work specifies in detail how such material could be used to assist the courts and replace discredited BWS evidence. The challenge remains one of ensuring that the context that courts rely on, implicitly or explicitly, is informed by a feminist understanding. While there is good reason to be modest in our expectations of feminist engagement with the law, social framework evidence offers a strategy that is preferable to BWS evidence and has the explicit purpose of moving beyond narrow, individualistic conceptions of women's offending.

Chapter 11
At the Centre of the New Professional Gaze: Women, Medicine and Confinement
Joe Sim

> Criminal women have been a central concern for prison managers and medical and psychiatric professionals since the emergence of the modern prison system at the end of the eighteenth century. They have been studied, probed and tested not only because of their supposed uniqueness but also because of the threat they posed to the social order of stable family relationships ... And at the centre of this iron therapy stood the figure of the medical man. (Sim, 1990, p 129)

The quotation above is taken from my book, *Medical Power in Prisons*. The book was concerned with the history of prison medicine in England and Wales and took issue with the liberal orientated, pluralist paradigm of progress underpinning the few historical narratives that had been published up to 1990. In particular, it challenged the politically disembodied, value-free views of science that legitimated these narratives. Instead, it pointed to the potent exercise of medical power utilised by medical experts over and against prisoners and the dialectical relationship between these experts and the state's apparatus of punishment behind the prison's walls. Central to the book's critical argument was an analysis of the gendered nature of medical and psychiatric power. Chapter Five – 'At the centre of the professional gaze: women, medicine and confinement' – built on the work of feminist and other radical scholars who were critical of the lack of a gendered analysis not only within liberal histories but also within the self-styled revisionist histories of the prison that had appeared since the mid-1970s. The differential and distinct experience of confined women with respect to the 'iron therapy' of medical power was thus central to the book's argument.

What has happened since the book's publication? This chapter focuses on a number of developments that have occurred since 1990 with respect to medical power and women in prison in England and Wales. Over the last 14 years there has been a significant increase in the number of women in prison, particularly ethnic minority women, a phenomenon that has been repeated internationally in other prison jurisdictions (Sudbury, 2002).[1] A range of official and unofficial reports detailing the state of women's prisons have also been published and, crucially, for the purposes of this chapter, it is a period that has seen the introduction of a number of state-inspired reforms. In theory, these reforms are supposed to confront and

---

1 At the end of June 2001, 26% of the female population were ethnic minority women. Furthermore, the incarceration rate for white people was 170 per 100,000 of the population; for black people it was 1,140; for South Asians it was 166; and for Chinese and other groups it was 536 per 100,000 (Home Office, 2003, pp 106 and 113).

challenge the 'criminal tendencies' of confined women and banish the pains of imprisonment experienced by many of them. In practice, as this chapter will argue, the iron therapy of medicine is being reinforced by the iron cage of responsibilised behaviourism which 'governs through the individualisation of social problems, victim blaming and self-regulation' (Kendall, 2002, p 197).

The chapter is organised into four parts. First, it considers the relationship between the construction of women as less eligible subjects and more recent developments with respect to health promotion in prison. Secondly, it considers the emergence of new reform programmes inside. In particular, it points to the consolidation of the new accredited experts operating within prisons and the relationship between these experts, the classicist/positivist paradigm that underpins their explanations of female criminality and the policies of individual adjustment which flow from these explanations. Thirdly, the chapter situates these reforms within the context of New Labour's authoritarian modernisation of the criminal justice system and the discourse of the respectable, married family that underpins this modernisation with respect to 'deviant' women. Finally, the chapter concludes by briefly considering the future of women's prisons.

11.1 Less eligibility, health promotion and self-governance: accentuating the politics of pain

11.1.1 Less eligible women

One of the central arguments in *Medical Power in Prisons* was that confined women (and prisoners in general) were confronted historically by a health care system that conceptualised and labelled them as less eligible subjects. This process had two profoundly detrimental consequences. First, the medical and psychological care and attention the women received, and the conditions in which they received this attention, were set at a level lower than that experienced by the non-prisoner subject beyond the prison gates. Secondly, this corrosive process exacerbated and intensified the psychic dislocation that many prisoners had already experienced outside before they came through these same gates. For the purposes of this chapter, it is important to note that this process has not diminished since the book's publication. Despite (or indeed, because of) the reforms instituted since 1990 (in particular by the New Labour government which are discussed in greater detail below), the conditions in which women prisoners live, work and receive treatment continue to exert a deleterious influence on their everyday lives inside. Consider three excoriating reports from inspections conducted by Her Majesty's Chief Inspector of Prisons which were published in 2002. At Eastwood Park prison, the environment in the health care centre:

> was described as very bleak by the acting governor who said, 'After five minutes you would need to get out'. At the time of the inspection the health care centre held extremely agitated women who had varying degrees of mental health problems. Women were crying, screaming and shouting and were continually requesting medical staff attention. (Her Majesty's Chief Inspector of Prisons for England and Wales, 2002a, p 56)

Outside of the health care centre, conditions were equally detrimental. The visiting arrangements were 'degrading and demeaning' to the point where 'there was nowhere for visitors to wait except a shelter, with no seats or toilet facilities, so that visitors, some with babies and children, sometimes had to use a nearby bush' (Her Majesty's Inspectorate of Prisons for England and Wales, 2002, p 28).

At Styal, inspected in February 2002, a mental health, in-patient unit, The Reeman Unit, had been opened three years previously. According to the Inspectorate, its planning had taken place without 'knowledge of modern clinical, particularly nursing needs' (Her Majesty's Chief Inspector of Prisons for England and Wales, 2002b, p 88). There was a shortage of space for staff, there was no privacy for clinical discussions about the condition of the patients, psychiatric input 'seemed poorly organised' and those women who were most disturbed and who could not be managed in the Unit were being held in segregation where 'despite the efforts of staff ... the care [was] not equivalent to that in the National Health Service (NHS). Health Care in the Segregation Unit was, by its nature, minimal' (Her Majesty's Chief Inspector of Prisons for England and Wales, 2002b, p 89). Crucially, the Inspectors expressed 'great concerns about the wider impact' the Reeman Unit was having in that it seen by some courts as a place where women could receive specialist treatment equivalent to that delivered in the NHS. This meant that the judiciary 'were sending mentally ill women to prison rather than arranging a more suitable disposal to the National Health Service' (Her Majesty's Chief Inspector of Prisons for England and Wales, 2002b, pp 89–90).

The Chief Inspector visited Holloway in July 2002. The inspection team found that primary care clinic areas were 'generally dirty and poorly maintained' while treatment rooms on the wings were 'poorly equipped and dirty', in contrast to the 'clean and well maintained clinical areas in women's health and the detoxification unit' (Her Majesty's Chief Inspector of Prisons for England and Wales, 2002c, p 92). The floor of the dental surgery was 'dirty' while the units and work surfaces were 'unsatisfactory'. Dental equipment was 'over 17 years old and had reached the end of its natural life. It did not meet current guidelines on health and safety requirements' (Her Majesty's Chief Inspector of Prisons for England and Wales, 2002c, p 93). In-patients, that is those who had mental health problems or who self-harmed, had 'very little by way of a therapeutic regime, being locked up much of the day' (Her Majesty's Chief Inspector of Prisons for England and Wales, 2002c, p 104). Furthermore:

> The generally poor quality of primary care and a tendency to 'medicalise' behaviour, as was evidenced by the high number of women on open F2052Hs, [suicide watch reports] further increased the pressure on in-patient care. There was no system of a 'named' nurse or health care worker for each patient. We were told that staffing levels would not permit this. This was also the reason given for the lack of properly completed care plans. We were deeply concerned for one lifer in-patient who had been on 24-hour watch for 15 months at the time of the inspection ... We were very concerned about the lack of the presence of doctors, either undertaking routine ward rounds in C1 or on normal location. This coupled with poor record keeping in the individual medical records and incomplete care planning, led to uncertainty about patient management. (Her Majesty's Chief Inspector of Prisons for England and Wales, 2002c, pp 105–06)

The discourse of less eligibility is therefore still a pivotal element for inducing pain in the contemporary prison. Furthermore, even on its own financial terms, the commitment of the prison service to providing medical facilities that are the equivalent to those on the outside is debatable as prison health care remains low on the ladder of state expenditure. The prison system accounts for 16% of the total expenditure on the criminal justice system in England and Wales. In November 2002, it was announced that expenditure was to rise by 11% to £2.8 billion in 2003/04 (Prison Reform Trust, 2003, p 4). In contrast, the government was committed to spending an extra £62.9 million in the *three* years from 2001 to improve prison health care (*Hansard*, 10 June 2002, col 798). This was designed to augment the already existing budget. In 1997/8 (the last year for which figures are available) this was estimated to be £85 million (*Hansard*, 26 June 2002, cols 969–70).[2]

Clearly, there is a danger that in calling for more resources to be utilised for prison health care, as in the case of the Reeman Unit discussed above, the state can employ more medical experts who in conjunction with the courts could simply use the increased expenditure to justify detaining women in ever-greater numbers. Resourcing and reproducing an expanding medical state therefore presents as great a danger as resourcing an expanding punitive state. It is worth noting that out of the 4,337 staff recruited during 2001–02, over 10% (494) were recruited as psychologists (57), psychologist assistants (144), medical officers (7), nurses (276) and pharmacists and pharmacist technicians (10) (Her Majesty's Prison Service, 2002, Appendix 3). It is also worth noting that 81% of these new recruits were women. This in itself raises some very important questions concerning what Karen Corteen has called the 'new philanthropy' that is materialising inside prisons.[3] Like its 19th century predecessor, this contemporary philanthropy is heavily gendered. This development provides an interesting and important parallel with Kelly Hannah-Moffat's analysis of Canadian prisons in the two decades between 1950 and 1970. These institutions, while built on the infliction of punishment, were also socially and ideologically constructed as 'caring' places due to their reliance on 'expert and professionalised maternal knowledges' (Hannah-Moffat, 2001, p 126).

It is therefore important to debate *how* the prison system (and indeed the criminal justice system in general) is financed and *where* resources go once budgets have been established, particularly in a culture dominated by a law and order ethos (Crow, 2001, p 212). The emphasis on, and cost of, security and control measures (many of which are unnecessary in women's prisons), coupled with expenditure on salaries and administration, means that resources for other initiatives around rehabilitation for prisoners and the widest possible training for prison staff have been and remain subordinate to these other demands. At the same time, the operation of stricter regimes in women's prisons, the aimless suffocation engendered in many institutions and the patriarchal nature of the wider sentencing culture which continues to send women to prison who should not be there (as well

---

2   In July 2003, the government indicated that it was investing £100 million 'over the next three years to improve' health care services (www.doh.gov.uk). It is unclear what the relationship is between this figure and the figure quoted earlier but the general point still stands, namely that less eligibility is still a key underpinning discourse in the delivery of health care to prisoners. The same announcement also indicated that the government aimed to have 300 additional mental health staff recruited by 2004.

3   Personal communication from Karen Corteen.

as the expenditure patterns described above) in combination have a seriously detrimental impact on the lives of many inside who experience the institution as a less eligible place of power, punishment and pain.

The issue of suicides illustrates this point. Between January 1999 and January 2004, 44 women died of self-inflicted injuries (Inquest, 2004). In 2003 alone, a record number of women – 14 – killed themselves. Amongst the dead was 18 year old Leanne Gidney, a single parent who was found hanging in her cell after being jailed for stealing £1 (*Private Eye*, 24 January–6 February 2003). As Deborah Coles of the pressure group Inquest pointed out in response to the suicides:

> Women in prison are an invisible issue. Many suffer terribly; the regimes are more restrictive than in men's prisons and staff are not trained to cope with such damaged people. Yet more and more women are being sent to prison when clearly they should be being treated for mental illness. (*The Times*, 25 April 2003)

11.1.2   *Promoting health promotion*

The 1990s also saw the emergence of the discourse of health promotion which officially has come to be designated as 'particularly important' for women prisoners with respect to minimising the risk of ill health and empowering them to take individualised and responsibilised control of their lives (Her Majesty's Inspectorate of Prisons for England and Wales, 1997, p 104). Central to this exercise in soul governance have been the professional and clinical discourses of a conclave of health promotion, actuarial experts whose cleansing physiological and psychic interventions are designed to create the born-again, nurturing, female subject. According to these experts, such interventions have a double benefit: 'in the short term in prison for the individual woman and *in the longer term for the woman's current and future children, and partners*' (Willmott, cited in Kenney-Herbert, 1999, p 64, emphasis added).

In some respects, there is a contradictory process at work here in that the individual commitment to a notion of social justice with regard to the delivery of health care shown by some health care professionals is the diametric opposite of, and may generate a challenge to, the punitive disciplinarians who dominate the everyday, informal culture of the modern prison. At the same time, many of these professionals could also be classified in Pat Carlen's phrase as 'prison-illiterate therapeutic experts who have failed to remember (or who have never realised) that prison is for punishment by incarceration' (Carlen, 2002a, p 156). As Catrin Smith has also noted, the appearance of health promotion experts:

> has the potential to create or exacerbate several undesirable outcomes including the (re)allocation of scarce resources to a relentless search for 'risk Factors'... Illness becomes *symptomatic* of an unhealthy 'lifestyle' and is, therefore, the fault of the individual: the 'wages of sin' described in the statistical language of 'risk Factors'. (Smith, 1996, p 255, original emphasis)

Furthermore, experts working in the new multi-disciplinary mental health in-reach teams may simply be encouraging a process of prisoner ossification in that the services they offer may be 'doing nothing more than maintaining prisoners on their medication while making no real progress towards rehabilitation' (Mills, 2002, p 116).

The majority of these new professional penologists, embedded experts in the command and control network of modern penality, are therefore unlikely to confront the differentials in power that remain central to the design and direction of modern penal regimes and, in particular, the immense discretion given to prison officers which reinforces and reproduces the subordination of the confined. Take the issue of exercise. Those in the health promotion lobby would argue that this is fundamental for physical health and psychological equanimity yet, in the case of the confined, being *allowed* to exercise will often depend on which staff are on duty and the discretion they utilise. Conversely, denying exercise can be particularly painful and psychologically debilitating. At Eastwood Park, the Chief Inspector of Prisons noted that the regime was:

> ... impoverished and constantly disrupted. Exercise was frequently cancelled (and those cancellations not accurately recorded) ... Women prisoners in the Health Care Centre complained they could not gain access to fresh air and although criticising the regime, said that the nursing staff tried to put on this activity. Generally no supporting staff were made available to the Health Care Unit ... No exercise period outside in the fresh air took place during the inspection and we were told that it had been two weeks since they last went out. (Her Majesty's Chief Inspector of Prisons for England and Wales, 2002a, pp 4 and 56–57)

There is, therefore, now a double process of disempowerment at work with respect to women in prison. On the one hand, they are still being confronted by regimes which, despite the official rhetoric of equivalence in care, philosophically and practically constructs them as less eligible subjects existing like shadows in the bleak landscape of many health care centres, where standards of physical and psychological support remain subservient to the coruscating discourses of paramilitary discipline and neo-liberal, financial managerialism that dominate contemporary penal arrangements. In many ways this should not be surprising. In a cultural and populist climate dominated by a political consensus built on the demand for an authoritarian response to the problems of law and order, the incarcerated will inevitably fail to generate empathy and sympathy. As noted below, for women prisoners, this is exacerbated by their apparent rejection of the role of subservient, tranquillised homemakers for a life of transgression and deviance.

On the other hand, the appearance of the prison-embedded health care professional, legitimated by New Labour's commitment to the creation of networks of partnerships, has failed to dent the prison's disciplinary armoury, is unlikely to alleviate the gendered nature of the pains of imprisonment and, crucially, will not challenge the structured inequalities and divisions that demonstrably confront the women beyond the prison gates. This point is particularly evident with respect to the interpretation of the needs of women prisoners and their determination. As with the issue of risk discussed below, this has become an unproblematic, taken-for-granted assumption within the *habitus* of the new prison professionals. Officially, women prisoners have been identified as one of a number of 'groups who have special needs ... which need to be identified and addressed' (Department of Health/HM Prison Service, 2001, p 23). However, needs in this context are likely to be defined in narrow, epidemiological terms, thus marginalising a range of other prisoner-defined demands, desires and expectations which are also crucial for the psychological well-being of the confined.

The discussion above on the issue of prison exercise is an important example of this point. Other demands include the desire for autonomy and for an environment that transcends the alienating scarring engendered by contemporary penal arrangements. As Francis Crook, the Chair of the Howard League for Penal Reform, pointed out in a radio interview in the wake of the escalation in women's suicides discussed above:

> there are things that prisons could do which would make things easier for women who are suffering particular strains ... whether it's drug addiction, mental health issues or whatever. There are two things I'd like to see and they both arise from women telling us what they wanted ... One is women should be given more control over their own lives and allowed to make decisions, sometimes small decisions, about when they see their children, when they eat, what they do during the day and secondly women told us that they wanted to do more creative work, they liked doing art and music and drama. They found that that form of self-expression alleviated some of the pain and tension ... (Woman's Hour, BBC Radio Four, 7 March 2003)

There are three issues that arise out of prisoner generated demands from below. First, these demands will often challenge the power of prison managers or conflict with the everyday pragmatics in the running of the institution. Because of this, they will be subordinated to the narrow epidemiological definition of needs generated by the audits, surveys and positivist hypotheses of the health care professionals which fit more easily with the needs of the institution (Sim, 2002). Or as Gillian Balfour has put it: 'women's "subversive stories" have been redefined as a "needs" discourse that conform to the hegemony of correctionalism' (Balfour, 2000, p 102). Secondly, the discourse of needs is itself imbued with a psychological resonance which translates and transforms the more politicised and collectivised discourse of demands into a concern with the individualised, atomised self who is failing to cope with the power of the institution. In addition, as Nancy Fraser has argued, basing social change on a discourse of needs opens up a space for experts – social scientific, legal and therapeutic – to reposition the groups at the centre of their gaze: 'they become "cases" rather than members of social groups or participants in social movements ... they are rendered passive' (Fraser, 1989, p 174).

Finally, the programmes which have been developed as a result of the interventions of state servants and accredited experts acting in ideological unison reinforce the place of the prison as *the* institution for dealing with criminal women:

> The move towards 'programming' could ... claim to meet another objection to women's imprisonment: that the women most vulnerable to imprisonment were also those with multiple social problems and deprivations. 'Agreed', said Prison Speak, 'Therefore we must develop programmes to address those needs and this can be done better in prison than in the community where the resources are just not available'. But the needs addressed turned out to be only those which could be represented as related to 'criminogenic' behaviour ie needs rooted in the women, rather than in their social circumstances. (Carlen, 2002a, p 165)

Kelly Hannah-Moffat has reinforced this point:

> ... the emergent 'needs-talk' which informs women's correctional management does not rely on feminist interpretations of women's needs or their claims to entitlement; rather it depends on correctional interpretations of women's needs as potential or modified risk factors that are central to the efficient management of incarcerated women. (Hannah-Moffat, 2000, p 38)

11.2 'Judges of normality'[4] and adjusting the female mind

Barbara Hudson has argued that there has been a shift in the nature of the professional expertise working in the criminal justice system and in the application of that expertise within the system. These new experts include geographers and psychologists whose expertise 'instead of prescribing treatment ... is now being used to calculate risk' (Hudson, 1996, p 154).[5] Preventing the risk of reoffending has increasingly become the template against which the activities of criminal justice professionals are being judged *and against which they are judging themselves*. With respect to the criminality of women, this development has been underpinned by the consolidation of an explanatory paradigm which combines fragmented elements of classicism and positivism. Within this discourse, criminal women are pathologically different from 'ordinary' women as forces beyond their control have determined their criminality. At the same time, these women have made a choice, albeit the *wrong* choice to commit crime.

This 'New Official Criminology for Women in Prison' (Carlen, 2002a, p 169) is definitively represented in an official document, *The Government's Strategy for Women Offenders*, published by the Home Office in 2000. This document brings together the elements in the classicist/positivist dyad referred to above and builds them into an official melange with respect to the causes of crime and deviance. It points out that women and men share similar characteristics with respect to reoffending. These characteristics include: 'poor thinking skills, including a lack of decision-making ability, impulsiveness, and an inability to learn from past experience; relationships supportive of anti-social behaviour, such as a partner who is an offender and who may coerce a woman to offend; criminal history; unemployment; low educational attainment; substance abuse; a disrupted family background; and financial difficulties' (Home Office, 2000, p 6). Crucially, there are also other factors:

> that make re-offending *more* likely for women, factors which do not seem to be risk factors for men. These include failed relationships with other women (mother, best friend, partner etc), and *difficulties developing intimate relationships with men*. (Home Office, 2000, emphasis added)

The problem of failing to develop 'intimate relationships' with men has also been cited in the case of the 72 year old poet Janet Cresswell, who in May 2003 was denied release from Broadmoor Special Hospital where she had spent 25 years for attacking her psychiatrist with a vegetable knife. Although admitting that she no

---

4 The phrase 'judges of normality' is taken from Foucault (1979, p 304).

5 It is debatable if rehabilitation was ever actually put into practice between 1945 and the mid-1970s, the so-called high point of reforming liberalism. This, in turn, raises significant theoretical and political questions concerning the current 'turn' in criminology towards those analyses built around the 'new penology' (Feeley and Simon, 1992) or variations on it (Garland, 2001). These scholars have constructed an ideal typical model of social structures and action in order to explain the change from a welfare model of penality which, it is argued, prevailed until the 1970s to the neo-conservative model of penality which has been dominant since that time. Arguably, such contrasts are too stark and in Feeley and Simon's case lack historical specificity (Brown, 2001). It is also worth pointing out that these analyses are sorely lacking a gendered analysis with respect to these changes.

longer required to be kept in conditions of maximum security, a special tribunal panel reasoned that *as she had been isolated from men* she would not be able to cope with the world outside of the institution (*The Independent on Sunday*, 4 May 2003, emphasis added).

What are the implications of Carlen's 'new official criminology for women prisoners'?

First, there has been 'an inexorable widening of the risk net' (Kemshall, cited in Horlick-Jones, 2002, p 166) to the point where a Prison Service spokesperson could use '"risk assessment" as justification for chaining a woman prisoner with multiple sclerosis to a hospital bed after she suffered a stroke' (*The Guardian*, 10 July 1998, cited in Horlick-Jones, 2002).

Secondly, Jennie Williams has argued that social inequalities based around class, 'race', gender, age and sexuality 'are a root cause of the despair, distress and confusion that is named "mental illness"'. Furthermore, she maintains that, given psychiatry's difficult relationship with women, 'being female is a risk factor for being labelled mad' (Williams, 1999, p 36). In other words, the increasingly widespread and indeed uncritical use of the discourse of risk across state institutions, and between state and non-state personnel who staff these institutions, is likely to reinforce the official (and common-sense) view that defines 'madness as synonymous with femininity' (Ussher, 1991, p 70).[6] This discourse also legitimates the disproportionate use of psychotropic drugs to regulate and control the behaviour of women in prison. This was identified as far back as 1984 (Owen and Sim, 1984) and continued right into the 1990s. Angela Devlin 'heard repeatedly of high levels of medication' in the 12 women's prisons she studied. This included the overuse of the anti-psychotic drug Largactil which induced side effects such as a shuffling walk known as the 'Largactil shuffle' and 'the kind of lethargy ... [which] was quite unlike anything I had seen in any of the six men's prisons I visited during earlier research' (Devlin, 1998, p 264). The Office of National Statistics also noted in 1997 that 50% of women in prison were being prescribed psychotropic drugs. Prior to their imprisonment only 17% of the women were on similar prescriptions (cited in Kesteven, 2002, p 25).[7]

---

6   This issue, however, is also complicated by the fact that when women kill their partners, the courts often ignore the humiliating and often violent experiences that many of them have endured, to the detriment of their mental health. At the same time, judges tend to show 'an over indulgence towards male behaviour' with respect to men who kill their partners (Roberts, 2003, p 29).

7   It is important to note that the process of medicalisation is also differentiated by 'race'. Within psychiatric diagnoses, 'black and minority ethnic people are more often diagnosed as "schizophrenic"; more often compulsorily detained under the Mental Health Act; more often admitted as "offender patients"; more often held by the police under section 136 of the Mental Health Act; more often transferred to locked wards; more often given high doses of medication; more often sent to psychiatrists by courts and more often not referred for psychological therapies' (Patel and Fatimilehin, 1999, p 65). Black women, in particular, are 'more likely to receive psychotropic medication' compared with white women and are more likely to be 'referred by the police to mental hospitals under section 136 [of the Mental Health Act]' (Chigwada-Bailey, 1997, p 45). Much more research needs to be done with respect to the relationship between medical power and black women in prison in order to uncover the processes behind their medicalisation.

Thirdly, the discourse of risk has legitimated the development of accredited offender behaviour programmes usually built on the acquisition of cognitive skills. This is underpinned by the official demand to 'evaluate' these programmes and therefore to identify 'what works' for women in prison. This demand is increasingly cutting through the research being conducted (*and that is allowed to be conducted*) in prisons and other criminal justice institutions in England and Wales. Disciplines such as criminology, many of whose practitioners work in universities and who have become caught up in a regressive spiral of declining resources and limited research time, have legitimated this drive towards short-term, micro evaluations to the detriment of long-term, macro analyses of the problem under study (Hillyard *et al*, 2004). This development reflects (and indeed reinforces) New Labour's 'third way' commitment to tackling offending behaviour through inter-agency co-operation and integrated services.

Fourthly, the prison service is increasingly working with other state institutions such as the probation service and with voluntary agencies, to develop a web of professional partnerships in order to implement the programmes referred to above. By 2000/2001 these programmes were being delivered in over 100 sites across the prison estate by over 1,700 staff, including psychologists, prison officers, education workers and probation officers. At the end of March 2000, over 1,300 tutors had delivered at least one of these programmes, 41% of whom were basic grade prison officers (Blud *et al*, 2003). This process, the development of a medico-punitive state form, in itself raises some interesting questions. For example, what kind of training do the tutors receive? How long does the training last? And perhaps most crucially, given the training they receive, what influence do tutors have in deciding the future direction of a prisoner's institutional career, particularly with respect to those prisoners who refuse to participate in the new prison programmes and who are then subsequently 'denounced as being "in denial"' (Faluyi-Smythe, 2003, p 14)?

In 2000, the programmes included Reasoning and Rehabilitation, Enhanced Thinking Skills, Problem Solving, CALM (Controlling Anger and Learning to Manage It) as well as a programme for 'acquisitive offenders'. The majority of women's prisons were involved in running them (Stewart, 2000).[8] Importantly, those responsible for the programmes mobilise the discourse of 'needs' and 'deficit' in order to justify even greater levels of intervention into the psyches of women prisoners. Thus, in a study of the impact of the Reasoning and Rehabilitation and the Thinking Skills Programme on a sample of 5,255 prisoners including 264 women, Blud and her three colleagues (two of whom worked for the Home Office, one for LMB Consultancy UK, while the fourth worked for Sand Ridge Secure Treatment Centre in Wisconsin) argued that:

> There was some evidence that the impact was greater on some measures for women prisoners. These differences warrant further investigation to ascertain whether they reflect issues around the test materials themselves, programme content, quality of delivery or responsivity. *They may perhaps be simply reflecting greater deficits at the pre-test stage, indicating that women offenders are likely to have a higher need for this kind of intervention.* (Blud *et al*, 2003, p 78, emphasis added)

---

8 However, only 5% of completed programmes actually took place in women's prisons in the financial year 2001–02 (Home Office, 2003, p 189).

As Pat Carlen has noted, 'what works' is the official discourse which underpins and legitimates these programmes. This discourse marginalises other, unofficial, more structural explanations regarding deviant women. Furthermore, the programmes are based on a reductionist presupposition, namely that it is their mangled perspective and understanding about the world that need to be altered. Thus, adjusting their minds to suit reality becomes the key to success, or as Carlen puts it: 'Change their *beliefs* about the world; the problem is in their heads, not their social circumstances' (Carlen, 2002a, p 169, original emphasis). A good illustration of this point is contained in *The Government's Strategy for Women Offenders*. The anonymous authors of the document point to a programme piloted in one probation area for 'acquisitive women offenders'. The programme is underpinned by the 'idea of "bounded rationality" – *that women perceive their actions in committing acquisitive offences to be rational'* (Home Office, 2000, pp 18-19, emphasis added). Furthermore, as Kathy Kendall has pointed out, the 'what works' debate is based on a set of presuppositions and assumptions which are epistemologically flawed. It is an epistemology 'rooted in traditional notions of the scientific method which devalues subjectivity, assumes a linear causality and emphasises universality' (Kendall, 2002, p 191). As significantly, 'by insisting that the problem of crime inheres in cognitive deficits, the focus of intervention remains at the level of the individual. Thus social inequalities and oppressions need not be addressed' (Kendall, 2002, p 197; see also Gorman, 2001).[9]

11.3   Gender and the prison in the age of modernisation

One of the central characteristics of neo-liberal governance involves a process of perpetual change legitimated by the seemingly neutral discourse of 'modernisation'. In mobilising this discourse, the Conservative governments of both Margaret Thatcher and John Major ferociously attacked the institutional framework of the UK's post-war settlement in their attempt to construct a society built on the sanctified triad of the capitalist free market, minimal state intervention and the construction of the traditional, entrepreneurial, responsible Queen's subject. The institutions of the criminal justice system have not been immune to this process of modernisation which was, and continues to be, legitimated by the three 'E's' of monetarist managerialism: economy, efficiency and effectiveness (McLaughlin and Muncie, 1993).

Since New Labour came to power in 1997 the rhetoric of reform and the discourse of modernisation have been pivotal to Tony Blair's messianic 'third way' project for propelling the UK forward in order to ensure that the Queen's subjects maximise the alleged benefits of globalisation while the presence of a coercive state minimises the potential for dissent and discontent (Sim, 2000). So while Blair can refer to 'modern', 'modernise' and 'modernisation' over 170 times in only 53 speeches (cited in Finlayson, 2003, p 66), Labour Home Secretaries have helped to create over 600 new crimes and have been instrumental in the passing of 45 law and

---

9   As with the issue of medicalisation discussed above, much more research is needed with respect to the impact of the programmes on black women prisoners.

order and immigration acts since 1997 (Cohen, 2003, p 18).[10] The government also plans to introduce a raft of further street-cleaning legislation including three month prison sentences for groups of youths (defined as two or more) who gather on street corners in an 'intimidating' manner and who fail to disperse on the orders of the state's own street-cleaners in the shape of the police (*The Observer*, 13 April 2003).

For the Conservatives, the family and particularly the 'married family' was central to their modernising project. As Margaret Thatcher told the *Sunday Express* in 1975: 'What is right for the family is right for Britain' (cited in McFadyean and Renn, 1984, p 119). This dogmatic belief in the married family has continued under New Labour. In a consultation document published in November 1998, the government, while recognising that the structure of the family had changed, nonetheless argued that 'we ... share the belief of the majority of people that marriage provides the most reliable framework for raising children' (Ministerial Group on the Family, 1998, p 55). Crucially, it is an image of the family that is also directly linked to an imagined, idealised, sepia-tinted vision of 'community' in which 'large factories and pit villages provided their own stable social conditions. In particular, they helped to foster the transition from adolescence to adulthood' (Labour Party, 1998, p 6).

Leaving aside the different feminist critiques of such communities with respect to the prevalence of domestic violence and incest within them (crimes which are, of course, not restricted to working-class areas), this discourse is important in that it maintains and reproduces the crucial binary divide between those who are inside the married family and the protective shield of the community and those who are outside of this shield: in the language of New Labour, the socially excluded. For New Labour, the prison system, discursively and materially, has become a key (albeit a crisis-ridden) player in dealing with the socially excluded within a criminal justice system that emphasises partnerships built on expertise and a political system that emphasises 'joined-up' government, social inclusion and reintegration. This emphasis allows the government to marginalise and stifle any reference to the social inequalities and divisions generated by the globalisation of capitalist social arrangements and the role of 'the superclass associated with that globalizing capital' (Byrne, 1999, p 137).

Thus, for New Labour, the prison can be made to work for the incarcerated through a combination of joined-up policies, partnerships and programmes. In official and expert discourses, the confined are constructed as socially excluded subjects whose reintegration will allow them to participate in the globalised marketplace, as opposed to individuals whose identities have been forged, and social subordination maintained, through the dialectics of class, gender, 'race', age and sexual divisions. These programmes are being built into an expanding system through the construction of new institutions and in the 're-roling' of former male prisons which are being transformed into female prisons. Thus, the 21st century

---

10 Some of these developments have not been totally negative in that they have been concerned with the criminalisation of racial and domestic violence, but others are very clearly orientated towards reinforcing social authoritarianism and intensifying state control. For example, at the time of writing, the Sexual Offences Bill which was currently before Parliament would make it a criminal offence for two 15 year olds to kiss in public (*The Guardian*, 11 July 2003).

working prison has arrived. Within these places, programmes will be implemented which will encourage disreputable slatterns to jettison their criminalistic attitudes and behaviour in favour of a family orientated, community imbued subjectivity that shuns deviant transgression in favour of respectable and compliant feminine conformity. This official discourse has been perfectly summed-up by Caroline Stewart of the Prison Service's Women's Policy Group. Writing in the in-house *Prison Service Journal*, Stewart has argued that:

> Prison can, and will *increasingly*, play its part in addressing educational level, providing opportunities to develop transferable vocational skills, facilitating better links with the community to which a woman is returning, supporting and strengthening family ties. (Stewart, 2000, p 43, emphasis added)

11.4 Conclusion

Pat Carlen has made the point that the modern prison operates through a form of 'carceral clawback' in which reforms are consistently worked and reworked, incorporated and reincorporated into a system where 'there has been no serious attempt to develop strategies for a reduction in the use of imprisonment' (Carlen, 2002b, p 120). For Carlen, and a number of other authors (Hannah-Moffat, 2001; Hannah-Moffat and Shaw, 2000), reform programmes in women's prisons, even those built around a feminist praxis, have consistently been subverted and incorporated into the regimented power structure of the modern prison. In Kelly Hannah-Moffat's words: 'Although correctional practices and logic may *appear* to incorporate feminist logics, pre-existing relations of power have not been displaced by them' (Hannah-Moffat, 2001, p 199, original emphasis).

Thus, despite some powerful critiques both from researchers and from the confined themselves, the women's prison remains on an expansionist course. One of the principal causes of this expansion has been the sentencing policies pursued by a judiciary who, as a body, have been enmeshed in the wider crisis of hegemony that has ideologically gripped the powerful since the mid-1970s to the point where a retributive law and order response to this crisis remains central to their collective culture and individual world view (Box, 1981).

For women, the impact of this retributive sentencing culture has been profound. In the decade up to 2001, adult female receptions rose by 223% compared with 74% for adult male receptions (Home Office, 2003, p 75). Importantly, the Home Office has concluded that the greater use of custody is not due to an increase in serious offences committed by women. Rather, it is 'being driven by a *more severe response to less serious offences*' (Home Office, 2002, p 21, original emphasis).

As insidiously, community penalties have been caught up in this punitive and retributive noise. A combination of net widening, under-resourcing and lack of consistency (Edgar, 2003), coupled with an intensification in the contracting out and privatisation of these penalties (*Private Eye*, 7–20 March 2003) has meant that the old critical criminological adage that community penalties have in fact become additions to an expanding prison system still retains its potency and provides a cogent reminder of the difficulties that remain in tearing down the walls of the prison. Community penalties for women prisoners have not deconstructed the prison as a source of punishment (Barton, 2000; Maidment, 2002). Rather, the institution and its alternatives remain linked across a punitive continuum by a set of discourses built around domesticity, motherhood and sexual respectability which insidiously continue to govern the behaviour of the women detained within them.[11]

Community punishments for women have, therefore, decidedly *not* been alternatives but instead have fulfilled the role of 'semi-penal institutions' (Barton, forthcoming) which continue to be guided by a set of religious (as well as medical) discourses which are orientated towards the genesis of the self-disciplined, non-deviant, law-abiding, female subject. At the same time, the programmes discussed in this chapter, which have been developed in women's prisons and which encourage the adaptation of the confined to the regime, have themselves contributed to the marginalisation of radical alternatives to custody for them (Kendall, 2000). More generally, even when those classified as 'mentally ill' are discharged into the community, they are still confronted by a system of power which is 'imbued with notions of femininity, masculinity and gendered roles within society' (Orme, 2001, p 124). Finally, women who attend community programmes which are built on a cognitive behavioural therapy approach to crime may experience 'an increased chance of failure' for a range of reasons including the male orientated design of the programmes, their family commitments which impact on their attendance and the fact that 'women have to wait much longer in order to commence a programme' (Deakin and Spencer, 2003, p 132). Therefore, even on the state's own terms, these programmes are immensely problematic. As with many state practices, the difference between liberal rhetoric and grim reality is profound.

In conclusion, the potential for radically altering the future punitive trajectory of women's (and men's) prisons looks bleak. At the beginning of the 21st century, not only has England and Wales become the prison capital of western Europe, but it is a society whose politics and culture have increasingly become bound up with a 'synoptic' obsession with events and personalities (Mathiesen, 1997) which 'stand in implacable opposition to policies' (Bauman, 2002, p 176). This, in turn, precludes serious sociological reflection with regard to social problems to the point where the political impetus is towards '"turning outside inside" ... [thus] shifting the task of resolving [these] problems to individual biographies' (Bauman, 2002, pp 169, 174). Therefore, in such a cultural and political climate, taking a critical position around prisons, for example, advocating their abolition or neo-abolition, is likely to be derided by those in power, particularly politicians.

In attempting to construct a hegemonic consensus across the society with respect to law and order, the worldview of this governing class is dominated by populist banalities posing as solutions to this most complex of social issues, a process which is reinforced by an overwhelmingly quiescent mass media whose news coverage is also based on a toxic combination of banality and retribution. The unswerving belief in the prison as an incapacitating panacea in the everyday struggle against crime comes as naturally to the different fractions of this class as breathing. The institution is a taken-for-granted, symbolic and material presence in this struggle. At the same time, the volubility of support for the prison has reduced to a whisper but,

---

11 See Ballinger (2000) for the impact of these discourses on women charged with murder.

importantly, has not silenced those different voices articulating alternative visions with respect to crime and punishment. Given the crisis-ridden nature of the institution and its inability to deliver a social order free from conventional crime, never mind crimes committed by the powerful, these voices remain able to exploit the contradictions and contingencies surrounding prisons in order to highlight the devastating impact of penal power on the confined, as the suicide statistics in this chapter have shown. However, whether the society can transcend the retributive discourses that are in the ascendant at this historical moment, embrace more fundamentally these alternative visions and recognise the suffering inflicted by the prison remains to be seen. What is undeniable is that these *are* places of pain and that the majority of women prisoners remain locked in a suffocating world that delivers very little beyond this pain which the programmes of reform discussed in this chapter, like the liberal reforms of the past, will do little to alleviate.[12] Indeed, in denying the often brutal reality of the prison, these programmes may well be prolonging the very suffering they claim they are helping to diminish. That is the ultimate and desperate irony confronting the newly embedded penal expert in the new millennium.

Acknowledgments

Thanks to Anette Ballinger, Mary Corcoran, Karen Corteen and Gillian Hall for discussing different aspects of this chapter with me. Thanks also to the editors of this text for their sterling editorial work and their supportive comments.

---

12 There are some honourable and exceptional individuals working on these programmes and in prisons more generally whose belief systems are categorically opposed to the pain-delivering punitiveness that pervades the landing culture of the prison service (Sim, 2002). Many of these individuals often leave the service not because of the attitudes of prisoners but because of the impact of this culture on their ability to deliver a humanised and humane regime and the consequent lack of support they receive. For radical critics of the system, this issue raises some very important questions. For example, how can radicals make alliances with progressive forces in the system? How can these individuals and the spaces that they open up not only be defended but also expanded so that the punitive regimes can be subverted and eventually abolished? These questions, which inevitably concern the contingent nature of state power, have remained outside of the theoretical and political concerns of radical prisoners' rights groups in particular and the left in general.

Chapter 12
The Treatment of Women Patients in Secure Hospitals
Ann Lloyd

12.1   Introduction

Looking back at Rampton, there were some hard times. I don't think things could ever be as terrible. They say if you can survive Rampton, you can survive anything. It wasn't all bad: there were some good things. In some ways it did me good. I was sentenced to eight years but was transferred to a Special Hospital and ended up doing ten years. Two in Ashworth and eight in Rampton.

My problem was drugs but I never got any help for that in Rampton and it was only when WISH[1] published an article in Open Mind about my not being able to leave Rampton until I had seen a psychologist and my having to wait over a year to see one that I got to talk with anyone, properly, about my offence.

The bad ones [staff] dominated my life there. If anyone stepped out of line they didn't do it again. I've seen acts of brutality; there was no need for it ... My RMO [Responsible Medical Officer] was a lovely man; he wanted me to go sooner but he left and then I had various RMOs. Each one has to get to know you, which puts you back.

My daily life was better than most because I worked in the print shop; very few women get to work there. The man who ran it was brilliant. In there you weren't a patient, you were a person, a friend. I don't think I would have survived without the print shop ... My salvation was going to work, otherwise you'd be stuck in the yard, you couldn't go to your rooms, the cigarette lighter was turned off at nine o'clock so you couldn't smoke again until dinner time. At weekends your rooms were closed, apart from an hour on Saturday morning whilst you cleaned them just before dinner and tea time. If you wanted anything you had to wait until then. Everything fitted round the needs of the staff, what was convenient for them.

Nothing ever seems to happen to the staff: they can humiliate you, make your life a misery but nothing ever happens to them. You can complain to the Mental Health Act Commission but after they'd talked to you they'd go into the office and as soon as they'd gone the staff would really go to town on you.

I think the Specials should close. I saw and mixed with a lot of different patients from all the wards. There was one patient I would have been afraid to be in a room with. I think people need smaller units where you can gradually go out into the community. People need help, but they don't need that [the Specials], they don't need locking up 24 hours a day and the key thrown away. You don't get the help you need. (Lloyd, 1995, pp 158–59)

That account of life in 'the Specials' was written by a woman who left Rampton Special Hospital in 1993.

In August 1992 the Committee of Inquiry into Complaints about Ashworth Hospital, another Special Hospital, published its report. It emerged during the

---

1   Women in Secure Hospitals is a charity that campaigns for women in the secure system.

inquiry that, of 600 complaints made by patients over the previous 10 years, none had been upheld. Moira Potier, a team psychologist who worked on three of the four all-female wards at Ashworth from 1987 to 1993, gave evidence to the inquiry. According to Potier:

> women in Ashworth ... are controlled, suppressed ... their overwhelming experience is that they are treated like children. They are almost constantly emotionally abused and at times physically abused. It is my observation that they feel chronically frightened and overwhelmingly powerless, and that they are unable to do anything substantially to alter their lot. (Lloyd, 1995, pp 138–39)

> There is a common existential experience shared by the women of not being heard and rarely believed ... (Lloyd, 1995, p 142)

Jennifer McCabe of WISH agreed with Moira Potier that the experience of life in the Specials re-created and reconfirmed:

> all the bad early experiences which so many of the women have suffered. So, far from being a therapeutic environment, it's going to make things worse.

> It's impossible to treat women in the environment of the Specials.

> How can you even begin to treat them when they are living in what you might call a state of shock, a state of fear? And they do live with fear every minute of the day. Fear of being abused or attacked, either by a member of staff or another patient; fear of putting a foot wrong. Most of this fear is managed by unconscious denial on the part of both the staff and the women so that 'happy families' can be played out, masking the underlying reality.

> They walk on eggshells all the time. They feel unsafe. I don't think the women in Specials ever experience a moment's peace. Not really. They live with a deep lack of security. And I think the staff live with that as well; and they cope with that by keeping a big barrier between them and the patients. This is not necessarily an obvious physical distance but rather an emotional barrier that is unconsciously maintained, whereby power remains with the staff and the women are thereby unequal, dependent, infantilized. What they need is some healthy loving care, some good experiences for a change, in a supportive environment where they feel safe. In the Specials they get the opposite. (Lloyd, 1995, p 143)

The report of the committee of inquiry, which was chaired by Louis Blom-Cooper, concluded that:

> The current regime for women in Ashworth is infantilizing, demeaning and anti-therapeutic. Mr Pleming for the MHAC [Mental Health Act Commission] could have been speaking for us when he stated: '... the Commission's position, I hope is clear, that radical changes ... are necessary if *women in high secure hospitals* are to receive the type of care which will improve their situation. (Lloyd, 1995, pp 139–40, emphasis added)

The quote from Mr Pleming makes it clear that he is referring not only to Ashworth but also to the situation of women in high secure hospitals in general.

So, what has changed for the women in the Specials? Are they now heard and listened to? Are they still afraid? Do they now have healthy loving care in an environment where they feel safe? What has happened to improve the situation of women in the Specials over the past 10 years?

Have there been 'radical changes' that were called for? The short answer is: Yes. And, er, No.

12.2 What the women and the campaigners wanted 10 years ago

Back in the early to mid-1990s, what WISH and other campaigners were telling the authorities who ran the Specials, and the government, was that the vast majority of the women in the Specials shouldn't be there: they simply did not require that high level of security. They also pointed out that detaining women in levels of security higher than they needed was in fact an offence against their human rights; and on top of that, they said, what most of the women experienced in the Specials, far from helping them to get better, was actually making things worse. The system was in effect deepening the psychological and emotional wounds they already carried and, quite possibly, creating new ones.

What the women themselves and the campaigners wanted therefore was:

- most of the women to be out of the Specials;
- women's services to be seen and provided as a separate and distinct service, designed specifically to meet women's needs and requirements and not simply be an 'add on, afterthought' service to the men's services;
- specially recruited staff, trained to understand the powerful role that social issues and gender issues played in creating women's problems, difficulties and their very real distress;
- women only units, with a good choice of women only activities and courses;
- women to be treated – appropriately – in smaller, supportive units as near as possible to their families and friends; and
- more small units providing different levels of care so that women could be supported appropriately and prepared at each step of their way from higher security to living back in the community: a clear pathway back to living their own lives.

12.3 Some background

What used to be called Special Hospitals are now known as High Secure Hospitals, perhaps unintentionally reflecting a higher emphasis on security over the last decade or so. There are three High Secure Hospitals in the UK: Ashworth in Liverpool, Rampton in Nottinghamshire and Broadmoor in Berkshire. The most recent figures show there are 35 women and 302 men in Ashworth, 43 women and 322 men in Rampton, and 48 women and 276 men in Broadmoor, for a total of 126 women and 900 men. In late 1993 the comparable figures were 259 women and 1,337 men.[2]

---

2 There is a strong temptation to put the figures for the men first, presumably because they are larger. I note this because it is a tiny pointer to the tendency, albeit unconscious, to put the men first in many other ways, which has had serious implications for how women were/are treated in the system.

Men are more likely to have committed serious offences: in 1999 only 38% of women detained in high security had index offences involving violence against the person, compared to 78% of men in High Security Hospitals. Over a quarter of the women had an index offence of arson, compared with just 5.4% of men. When an index offence is recorded as arson, no harm was intended or inflicted on another person(s) (WISH, 2002, p 17).

I asked Laila Namdarkhan, WISH's regional manager for London and the South, whether the characteristics of the women in the secure hospitals had changed. She didn't need to look up any research, saying she could describe the pattern off the top of her head:

They are young women who have experienced high and consistent levels of sexual and violent abuse in childhood; they have experienced chaotic childhoods; they have been in multiple care homes and statistically they go in and out of more homes than boys do because they seem much harder to deal with; some left education around the age of eleven, some haven't completed their education; they've never had employment; there are high levels of self harming behaviour; incidences of fire setting; levels of alcohol, drugs and substance abuse are quite high from an early age; there is delinquent behaviour – petty crime; they attach themselves to older men or men who are already involved in crime; they are likely to have come to the attention of the psychiatric services early in their lives, and it is unlikely that they will have been asked if they have experienced abuse.

We have a lot of information about these young women: we should be able to spot them easily. People are still fixed on this gender notion; if a girl is acting out, behaving too badly, if she is not conforming enough then there's a problem, and she's more likely to be labelled as borderline personality disorder or severe personality disorder because she doesn't conform to society's continuingly rigid view of what it is to be female.

And when they try to tell people what happened to them, about the abuse, they are less likely to be believed than other young women. And this continues through their whole lives. I talk to women of 35 in the secure hospitals and medium secure units who say to me: 'It doesn't matter what I say to them, they never believe me. I'm down on paper as a liar. I am told I am a known liar.'

The profile Ms Namdarkhan outlined is the same as 10 years earlier; the comments about not being believed are also the same. And women continue to rush up the security ladder faster than men partly because there is so little interim provision for them and partly because of this perception of them being 'badder and madder' if they don't conform to how society says women should be.

12.4 So what's changed?

Moira Potier is one of the women who spoke up for the women patients at the 1992 Blom-Cooper inquiry into Ashworth Hospital; at the time she had been afraid because of threatening phone calls and such incidents as her car tyres being punctured in the drive of her home. She had felt at work that she was kept at arm's length, that she was someone whom people were cautious around. Although she received an MBE for her services to the National Health Service in 1993, she resigned from Ashworth before she received it.

Now she is back there again, after a spell in academia, as head of psychological services. When I ask why she went back she says a colleague who was working there urged her to come back. 'It had changed, he said. And when he left there was no one else willing to take over as head of psychological services,' she says:

> and anyway, it's been the heart of my professional life, hasn't it, Ashworth, the men and women at Ashworth … Two important things that have happened – you could say WISH and all the campaigners have won the argument – that there is now a government sponsored mental health strategy for women, and it has been acknowledged by government that there are far too many people, both men and women, in the high secure system. Years ago WISH and some of us were way out on the margins trying to get people to realise that women in the Specials needed their own women's services and saying that almost all of them should not be there. So that message has now come in from the margins, the official thinking has changed, and these views are now mainstream.

In fact, the Department of Health document outlining plans for women's mental health services is entitled *Women's Mental Health: Into the Mainstream: Strategic Development of Mental Health Care for Women* (DoH, 2002). Eight of the 12 chapters in the document contain the words 'gender sensitivity' and there are special sections on secure forensic services; services for women with experience of violence and abuse, and services for women who self-harm.

There is also acknowledgment that women's 'therapeutic and safety needs are unlikely to be met in mixed-sex wards. Women's secure services should be provided in single-sex units, alongside the development of women specific programmes of care' (DoH, 2002, p 66).

Under the heading 'Current provision' in the section on 'Secure/forensic services' it is acknowledged that 'There has been regular criticism of current secure care provision for women, including by the Mental Health Act Commission, the Health Select Committee, WISH and NACRO [National Association for the Care and Rehabilitation of Offenders]'. And the document quotes women in secure care:

> *No-one has ever discussed why I did my crime, to try and understand why I did it. I'd like someone to talk to.*
>
> *Men get away with it. If women do something they get a harder time.*
>
> *I was severely abused as a child so I do not want to go and talk to a sixty year old man.* (DoH, 2002, p 63)

The document quotes the conclusions of an indepth patient consultation exercise with women, predominantly in high security cases, commissioned by WISH:

> Their stories revealed a shared belief that the dream of discharge could best be achieved by toeing the line rather than fully addressing the causes of their distress. With little responsibility or choice over their daily lives or futures: 'We're expected to behave like adults but we get treated like children. (DoH, 2002, p 63)

So, I say, a women only strategy, which clearly recognises the importance of gender and social issues, and which actually quotes the women themselves – clearly the message has been received and understood? Yes?

Potier says, yes, these are major steps, a big improvement. The issues that were not given any credence a decade ago are now clearly at the centre of the agenda. 'And there's a big modernisation programme going on across the high secure hospitals,' she says, 'which is in effect downsizing. The numbers are shrinking. There is going to be only one high secure unit for women in the future and that will be at Rampton. Broadmoor's women's services are closing down gradually and Ashworth's women's unit will close by April 2004 at the latest.' She pauses for a second and smiles. 'It will be a very significant day. But ...' And there is more than one but.

'Things are not nearly so crude as they were.' She frowns, concentrating on finding the right words to describe how things in a sense haven't changed, when it appears that everything is going in the right direction:

> For instance, if you ask staff about the use of seclusion they will say they don't use seclusion anymore. But what they do now is give the women something called 'special observation,' which means you give them lots of nurses to look after them so they are surrounded by nursing staff. And this creates enormous dependency in women. It's infantilising: it is still not empowering them. The attitude is still, 'women need all this, they can't think for themselves' when what they really need is a safe, supportive atmosphere, especially when they are going through a bad patch, until they get to where they can take back their own autonomy completely. But how do you do that in somewhere that has an atmosphere like an institution and which is still focused on containment?

But obviously, she goes on, this has been recognised and it's been decided that only one high secure unit for women is needed and that's going to be at Rampton. 'But what will that be like? And how many women will be there?'

Other campaigners share her concern about this. Liz Mayne, Director of WISH from 1996 to 2001, stands by the view that probably only between five and 10 women currently detained in secure mental health services across the country require the high *physical* security that the Rampton women's unit will provide. 'But what if it has a large number of beds?', she asks. 'Chances are, given the lack of appropriate therapeutic provision for women, they will be filled and once again we'll have lots more women in high security who don't require it and who should not be there. And a lot will depend on who is in charge and what the ethos of the unit is.' Speaking of proposed changes in general, Moira Potier believes that:

> if there is an emphasis on things running smoothly, for instance the staff don't want the psychologists 'stirring up' the women, perhaps by talking with them about their experience of abuse, then it just won't work. If treatment is organised on the lines of the medical model, with individual women being diagnosed as suffering from this or that, and drugs being prescribed as the cure or control, with no awareness of social and gender issues, then it just won't work. Any medical approach to these women is purely about power and containment, whatever language you use.

> There are a lot of questions to be answered. About Rampton; about the way the women's services will develop, and about where the women now in the secure hospitals will go. And, yes, there is a women only strategy now, but what is to say that it will be implemented, actually put into place.

While the first official steps along the way towards providing the sort of services women in secure services (and all women with mental health problems) have been taken, it remains to be seen whether there is the political will to make it happen. The campaigners, and the women, will believe things have changed for the better when the women's experiences of secure hospitals change for the better. So far, it seems that while the message has been received and the official thinking has changed – a prerequisite for change in the system – the changes have not had a significant impact on the women's daily lives. I heard of improvements in secure settings such as Broadmoor, where the change in policy has begun to take effect, but women in medium secure units seem to be stuck further back in history, if the testimony of one women currently in a medium secure unit is any guide.

12.5   Diane's story

Diane Cushor (a pseudonym), now aged 37, was born and brought up in Bedfordshire. Her mother was a secretary and her father worked for a building society. She has an elder sister. She went to a private Catholic convent primary school until the age of 11. Around that time, when she was 11, her parents divorced and Diane began at a comprehensive school. After the divorce there was no longer any money for a private school:

> I hated the comprehensive. I didn't get on very well there. I was teased a lot, you know, I was an ex-convent girl and had a posh voice; I was different. It was really a bit rocky for the first year especially. I had to work really hard to keep up; I was very poor at maths. I wasn't very happy at school.
>
> Because of my disruptive behaviour and stories to other students I was moved to another comprehensive for the last year and my CSEs and O levels. It was awful moving and not knowing anyone. I find it hard to make friends and open up. I was very much a loner at that age. I think it was for fear of people getting to know me and rejecting me. I was seen as the school weirdo ... My sister's really brainy. She can do exams just like that; she sailed through everything. Went to university.

When she was 16 her mother remarried:

> By the time I was sixteen I was truanting, running around, dropping out. I began to steal. I found it all very difficult. I was fairly wild as a teenager. I was scared of my stepfather. Not because of the man he is but because he was a man. I was frightened there would be a repeat of the relationship with my real Dad. My Dad sexually abused me from an early age until I was 17. At that age I decided what he was doing was wrong and that I had to stop him. Even though deep down I knew I had that right I felt tremendously guilty and as though I was betraying the special relationship we had. I felt if I stopped it, it would be the end of him loving me and feeling special. It is hard because you know it isn't the right kind of special but you still crave it and feel if it wasn't right your Dad, who loves you, wouldn't do it. Then there is the feeling of needing to be needed.
>
> After Mum remarried she and I moved into my step-dad's house. His three children were still living at home so I had the main bedroom and Mum and my step-dad slept downstairs in what used to be the dining room. I felt very jealous and pushed out suddenly, having to share my Mum with four other people. Instead of talking I let it build up to a point where I wanted them all to hate me. If they hated me, especially my step-dad, he would leave me alone. There were massive rows as I started stealing from the others. It got so bad that my sister took me in for a while until things had calmed down.

I decided I couldn't go back to live at home. Things were so bad. My sister helped me to find a flat, which I shared with two other women. It was a nice flat but the women were young and wild. I was working in a bakery; it was the highlight of my day to go to work. I made some loose friends that were older than me and sort've kept an eye on me.

I started feeling out of control and had trouble sleeping as I had vivid nightmares. I had thoughts of seriously hurting myself and I knew I had to stop things getting out of hand. I didn't know how to find the words so I started stealing at work. I was found out and my Dad came to the rescue and moved me back to Wales with him and his new wife. They had been married since 1976 and my new step-mum was OK. But I started feeling controlled by him and so scared he would start abusing me again. He was drinking even more heavily ... The thoughts of suicide were beginning to return. I was doing things that were just so unlike me and I was scared of myself. And I was using prescribed drugs to blot the crap out.

I left Wales and moved back to be near my Mum and found a room in a house. I got a job as a nanny. It was good but things started to go wrong and I left before they sacked me. I started to go in 'strugg' – I stopped looking after myself, stopped eating, wasn't sleeping. I started using drugs and drinking. The drugs and the drinking were not for fun but just to cut the crap, to dull the pain. I really got quite poorly.

It is hard to describe the pain but it is like knowing that you want to end your life to stop the crap and before you really hurt someone other than yourself, but not having the strength to carry it out. All the crap you learn at a Catholic convent about suicide being a sin and selfish. That you would rot and not have eternal life. I have a deep inner belief that I am evil for the thoughts I have and the life I lead. I need to be punished and continuously make people hate and judge me. I can't handle a good day as I don't deserve them.

Then I met somebody who was very nice. I thought he was very nice. I moved in with him. But he abused me and the whole thing got out of hand. The sexual abuse was violent and demeaning and left me totally powerless and controlled. Why did I put up with him? Because I was besotted and felt I deserved his behaviour and he was so loving and thoughtful at times. Also his threats of having no drugs or work (I was sleeping with his 'mates' to earn what he provided me) if I left and therefore no money. Eventually he got tired of me and I found my own blokes. And heroin.

Then I got involved with a religious group led by a very powerful and charismatic man. I lived outside; meetings were held in his or other leaders' houses. There were often sacrifices at the beginning to show our commitment to this man, the Father. These were large animals that were tortured and killed. I am not sure how I was party to it. The whole experience of these meetings was of not being there, of not being in control. This was down, I think, to the continuous use of drugs and no food or nourishment ... The Father knew when and what you needed to live a good and enlightened service. You didn't exist to live for you or others, just for the Father. Sexual activity was wild and free but only the truly chosen and pure got to sleep with the Father.

It was after one spectacular meeting that everything changed. The Father stood and set light to himself. There were no burns or marks on him. He said this is how we know when we are truly pure and succeed in our role of service. I felt I really needed to be pure. It had been a word used all through my life that was said to be good.

The next few weeks this really played in my head. I saw images of me burning and the feeling of being cleansed afterwards was just so overpowering. I spoke to my counsellor, I was on counselling for drugs, and to the Samaritans. I told them of the nightmares and how I woke feeling things were climbing on me. How I had been hurting animals and even killed one of my landlady's cats. How I felt out of control and shit scared of what was happening to me.

I began to get really ill at this time. I set light to a loo roll in a public building. I stayed there, when I had done it, I couldn't leave. I somehow had to stop all these crazy and so powerful thoughts. The police knew me well from the fires I'd been setting and drugs. I was registered as an addict and on Methadone.

Before setting light to the loo roll I had soaked myself in meths, but I had lost the courage to light it, so lit the loo roll instead, hoping I would be stopped. I thought I would be on watch at the police station, due to being a risk to myself but they left me alone. I had a lighter in a pocket of my dungarees. I tried to shut out the thoughts that were so strong and overpowering of the peace this [death by immolation] would bring. A truly pure way to die. I would be cleansed of all the wrong I had done to others and allowed others to do to me.

I don't remember actually lighting my clothing. I remember the feeling and the involuntary scream. The policewoman pressing the alarm, the horrendous noise of bells and keys and locks and men shouting, being dragged out and taken to a hosepipe they used to wash panda cars. Then I don't remember much until being in the ambulance and the paramedic saying 'She can't even do this properly. She'll be out in a couple of hours to try again'. I can remember the feeling of panic but most of all failure that I hadn't succeeded. That was the most scariest and lonely moment. It was then I vowed to myself I would succeed if only in my own head.

I was in hospital quite a while and while I was there someone came from the local regional secure unit and I was then sent to my first regional secure unit and then to Broadmoor. I was 23 when it happened and I'm 37 now so I've been in the secure system now for 14 years. My RMO, that's my Responsible Medical Officer, says I'll never get out; she told me that. She said I'll never get out of the secure system.

So, what does Diane think of the way the system has treated and is treating her, and how it could be improved?:

I've been in Broadmoor, which is a High Security Hospital, and I would say generally speaking, that a lot of money has been put into those hospitals; I think they are changing. There are some good women's services. But the system of going from them down into medium security, like where I am now, that's just crap. It's just awful. Suddenly everything is stopped; all the help, the services, they just stop when you go down to medium secure. But you're not really able to cope, you still need help and support but there is no help, no support. What's needed is somewhere safe for women to go. We don't need all these codes and controls, we need a safe place where we can get the help we still need.

In Broadmoor there was more understanding. I was very lucky, I had a good primary nurse, that's the nurse designated to look after you. But I understand that Broadmoor has deteriorated now from how it was five years ago, that it's become more secure, that there's more emphasis on security now than then, and less on helping the patients. After the Tilt Report[3] the emphasis was on security, very much on tight security. That was because they were thinking about the men. But the tighter security affected the women so badly that people then began finally to realise that 99.9% of the women were getting this absolutely top grade security when most of them needed not to be in secure conditions at all. So the gap between the men and the women, when security was so high, and the effect this had on the women made them, finally, look at the need for secure women's services.

What needs looking at now are the regional secure units like the one I am in. The way it is organised is through a multidisciplinary team. You have a key worker and everything is meant to go through them and there are co-workers who will support the key worker and who will support you when your key worker is away.

---

3   This 2000 report by Sir Richard Tilt, on security at the High Secure Hospitals, recommended even greater emphasis on a security driven rather than a clinically driven ethos.

I ask about treatment:

> I see a psychologist once a week but it's not gelling; there's no trust. I might tell her something and then as a result [when she reports back to the team] my leave is cancelled. Just recently I gave up some self harm stuff I owned up, gave the stuff in, which was very hard for me, I have been self harming for 25 years, and what was the result? Leave cancelled.

> So what you have is conflicting rules and regulations; there's no consistency, it all depends who's 'on'; if it's somebody who's 'old school'.

She shrugs: that's that:

> You are at the whim of the person or of the personality 'on' at the time, so you are on your guard all the time, not knowing which way they'll go. Also, many of the staff will not stand up to a medical person. It's supposed to be multidisciplinary but it's not, it's hierarchical.

I say it sounds like some things have got better but others are just as bad as they were before, when I wrote the book which was published in 1995:

> In the high security there is more understanding but in medium secure they are very set in their ways. To be fair, it may be just here that's like this. I don't know about the other medium secure units. But here needs to change; and if the others are like this, they need to change. There's such different treatment between the men and the women. For instance we're supposed to do OT, occupational therapy – we call it going to group. You might be down for classes in enhanced thinking skills or problem solving skills but if the men duck out of classes and go on community leave nothing's done. But women aren't allowed to do that.

Why is there a distinction, I ask. Diane replies:

> There isn't a 'why'. There is no reason. It just seems like there's one rule for the men and another for the women. Leave is handed out to the men really easily even if they are supposed to be going to groups, but it's a different matter when it's a woman. I know of a case of a man who has absconded while on leave six or seven times who had his permission to go out again restored the day after he got back. Whereas there was a woman who absconded once and her punishment was that she had to wait four months just to get permission to go out of the building into the grounds of the hospital. It was the same doctor and the same team, in both cases. There are just different rules for men and women.

Talking again, about the RMO who told her she'd never get out, she says that the RMO tells her how she, Diane, feels:

> She says to me: 'Oh, you don't get depressed.' Last year she took me off my medication and I got quite ill; she said I was doing that just to get attention.

I recall that when I was writing my book women kept saying to me that they had to be careful what they said to whom because it might go on their report and be used against them to delay their release. One woman only finally was able to get help when she decided to trust a priest who visited the ward regularly. She felt she could talk to him because she could trust him, as a priest, not to repeat what she had said. She wanted somebody whom she could trust to listen to her, but only felt able to trust a non-member of staff:

> You never know what any member of the team is going to say about you in the team meeting, you just don't know. In the clinical team meetings, CTMs, the whole team meet to discuss you; you are allowed in for the last five minutes. You don't know what they have been saying about you.

They say they want you to talk to them but how can you? If you have a different opinion from them, they say that's because you're ill. You can't win. Yes, we do want them to listen to us but at the same time we are a bit frightened of speaking to them because if you open up and say something they don't like, they might write it down and use it against you. And you'll not get out. Or they might twist it. So how can you trust them? I saw some notes about me one day; they reported that I'd said something which I never said. What I had said was something totally different. But when I challenged the nurse she said that because of my illness I had misremembered. But I hadn't. Isn't it possible that she could have misremembered? No, because she's staff and I'm a patient.

So, I say, really you are living in a world where others are in control and you do something one day and that's good and you do the same thing the next day, and that's bad:

Yes, it's scary isn't it?

I reply that it's quite Kafkaesque and enough to drive anybody mad. She agrees:

Luckily I have two good friends who help me to keep calm. They're always telling me to stay calm and take deep breaths. I don't know what I'd do without them.[4]

12.6   Gender awareness training: a clear step forward

Over the years it had become obvious that the help the women needed was not being delivered. That is, it had been known, anecdotally, but where was the solid evidence? Aware of the need to remedy this problem, Liz Mayne commissioned the first gendered analysis of the social and offending profiles of women and men patients held in high security. The resulting report, entitled *Defining Gender Issues ... Redefining Women's Services* (Stafford, 1999), provided solid evidence, based on the hospitals' own data, of what WISH and others had been saying all along.

Mayne then went on to set up, in association with the University of Liverpool, a gender training initiative. The purpose of the initiative was to analyse staff training needs in the area of social and gender issues, and to develop a gender and social issues training programme.

As part of the Gender Training Initiative, Scott and Parry-Crooke (2001) produced an analysis of workers in secure settings which reported that:

only a minority had received any training that had alerted them to the mental health implications of gender inequality. Only 10 (15%) reported that their initial training had addressed these issues. Very few respondents had received any training about the effects of domestic and sexual violence on the lives of women and girls (n=13; 20.6%) or about working with survivors of early trauma and abuse (n=17; 26.9%). In the main, this training had been optional and had taken place in the context of conferences and workshops. (in Williams, Scott and Waterhouse, 2001, p 96)

Similarly, Liebling, Chipchase and Velangi (1997) found in a study of nursing staff working in a secure hospital that 86% of staff had not received any training to deal with self-harm (Williams, Scott and Waterhouse, 2001, pp 89–104). 'It is not therefore

---

4   Identifying details were changed by Diane, at my suggestion, but without my knowing which these were.

surprising,' continues the paper by Williams, Scott and Waterhouse, 'that while the majority of staff in the study by Scott and Parry-Crooke ... recognised that various forms of abuse had impacted on their patients' mental health they were unclear precisely what the effects might be, what might be aggravating or mitigating factors or how the "problems in living" they observed had their origins in childhood relationships and traumas.' These authors note the 'puzzlement' expressed by an interviewed staff nurse as being 'typical of many responses to questions about the origins of patients' difficulties':

> I reckon a lot of the patients on our ward have been sexually abused when they were children [... and] that probably, to a certain extent, has contributed to the problems that they are having now. [... But] who knows? There are quite a lot of people out there that have been sexually and physically abused but got on with their lives and are living quite normal, happy family lives or careers or whatever. (Staff nurse quoted in Scott, 2000, pp 96–97)

Writing about sexism and gender awareness, Williams, Scott and Waterhouse say that both:

> ... individual members of staff and the staff cultures of secure settings are marked by the sediment of exclusion, oppression, hierarchy and gender prejudice. Anti-social behaviour is still widely regarded as 'doubly deviant' in women. Working with disturbed or violent men has a certain 'macho' status in some organisations; caring for 'mad women' has no such prestige. In interview with one of the authors, staff from a range of disciplines and secure settings contrasted male and female patients on the following dimensions:

Women	Men
Difficult	Self contained
Demanding	
Emotional	Straightforward
Lack motivation	
Interact	
Needy	Uncommunicative
Manipulative	
Aggressive	
Attention seeking	Accept the rules
Hormonal (unpredictable)	

Another staff nurse described her experience thus:

> Nursing men is much easier – they don't want much from you. They seem to be able to accept where they are and get on with it. If they don't get on with another patient they'll just keep out of their way. They'll get their meds and meals and go back to their rooms mostly. With women it's completely different – they're always in your face ... and the ward is never quiet.

'What emerged from the three year training initiative,' says Liz Mayne, 'was basically a three-day flexible training module designed ideally for members of a team who actually work with each other. An independent evaluation was done of the module and the results were incredibly positive. Whether the respondents were health care assistants, psychiatrists or psychologists, whatever, they all said it was hugely beneficial, that it really changed their attitudes.' Alongside the training module a training course for trainers was also developed.

Jennie Williams and Sara Scott, both mentioned above, were responsible for piloting the Gender Training Initiative. Jennie Williams, now director of Inequality Agenda, which provides training for mental health staff, has been involved with mental health training for nearly 30 years. She stresses heavily the importance of staff's relationship with patients and their attitudes towards them. 'What is really important, rather than the form of the therapy, whatever it is, is how you share yourself with another person; it's *how* you do it that's so important. The attitude is all important … You must speak to people as adults and with respect, and you must listen.'

There are a few more opportunities at the moment than in the past, she says, and the Department of Health are being more constructive:

> Overall what needs to change is the whole way of working, the whole ethos, of how the staff work. It can be a big challenge for staff, listening to women and not being defensive but in the main staff coming on the courses are more receptive than they were ten years ago. They tell me they know they can't do the job properly, that they haven't been trained for it. They know they are not doing what is needed. They need creativity to be brought back into what they do, they need to have a sense of job satisfaction, and also they need to be supported.

However, as Williams and Scott state in their paper (2001), evidence suggests that supervision and support is a scarce resource across statutory and mental health settings. Williams asked mental health professionals and practitioners with a declared interest in women's mental health to complete a short questionnaire:

> Nearly three quarters of the sample (72% n=75) reported that they always, or sometimes, brought this perspective to their work with women. However, only just over a third of the sample (36% n=37) reported that an inequalities perspective was an accepted approach to working with women in their services. This suggests that many mental health workers who are trying to meet women's mental health needs from an inequalities perspective, are doing so without organisational support. (Williams, Scott and Waterhouse, 2001, p 98)

While agreeing completely with the urgent need for training in gender and social issues, for which WISH has, of course, campaigned for years, Laila Namdarkhan stresses also the need for staff to be recruited who are 'positively for women. You need staff who don't see women as problematic, difficult, a nuisance, or "in your face" – all of those awful labels. If that's your attitude, then it doesn't matter what kind of therapy you are providing, you might as well give up. What is needed is staff who actually care.' She adds that it is very important to point out that there are some great staff:

> who do go the extra mile, who do stay late, who do follow things up properly, and who do get back to the woman about a particular issue and don't leave her dangling. I've had women say to me that when they have looked back over the last two or three years, say

at Broadmoor, that they had a good staff team who were helpful to them, and a good primary nurse who made all the difference to them leaving and moving on. When they get that genuine support they certainly know it and they really appreciate it.

Liz Mayne: 'When women are cared for in a totally appropriate therapeutic environment with everything in place that they need, in a surprisingly short space of time, the so called "bad presentations", which are often outbursts of justified anger, all of that, and the self harming goes down dramatically. It is difficult to convince people of that but I have seen it happen, it works.'

12.7 The way forward

Laila Namdarkhan, Liz Mayne, and indeed all the other campaigners I spoke to, and Diane, agree that small community units with levels of support appropriate to a particular woman's needs at that time is what should be provided, based on an awareness of the fundamental importance of gender and social inequalities, and staffed primarily by women who care for the patients in their charge and whose attitudes are aimed at empowering, not infantilising, them.

No one, however, is expecting miracles tomorrow, or even the next day. 'Some people like us [WISH] being involved and are actively seeking our support and advice in terms of consultation work about the development of these new services,' says Laila Namdarkhan, 'but some don't want to know us at all and think, or believe, they know enough to go it alone, even though history tells us they are the same people who were reluctant to change their practices before.' Moreover, adds Namdarkhan:

> now women's services have become flavour of the month and there's money around for new building and the development of new services. The point is, though, like I said earlier, if all they are going to do is replicate what we have had before in new buildings with nice new furniture and curtains but the attitudes remain the same then it's not going to make one jot of difference because at the end of the day the process should be that women come into the system for a specific reason, for a specific period of time, and move through clear pathways out of the system. All the pathways should be clearly defined. But they are not.

Liz Mayne agrees and adds that:

> one of the most urgent gaps is the need for high support community residential facilities. Women could come out of the secure system a lot quicker if they could continue to get the social and therapeutic support they need in the community, the opportunity to heal and recover and move at their own pace towards eventual independence. It needs to be acknowledged that, especially when women have been incarcerated for years, helping them to move back into the community will take time. You need to do everything you can to make sure that once out in the community they are not going to fail.

And at the other end of 'the system' there is a real need for prevention: services that spot women at risk of entering the secure system and prevent that from happening. As Laila Namdarkhan said earlier, there's a lot of information about the characteristics of women at such risk: it should be easy to identify them before things go too far and they become enmeshed in the secure system.

'If you had community based mental health staff who were able to work sensitively with severely abused women when they were younger,' points out Liz Mayne, 'they could help them with their problems before things got worse and before they spiralled up into the secure system.' 'What we are finding,' says Laila Namdarkhan:

> is that women who are at risk of coming into the system are being very ill served. There's very little emphasis at the moment on prevention, that is, providing at risk women with support so they don't get into the system in the first place. There's very little emphasis on identifying who is at risk and on stopping them coming into the system. Of course we want the best service possible for women already in the system but the best thing of all would be if women never got into the system at all.

> If the services were there for young women, teenage women, women just coming into adolescence, if you started to work then, building bridges between child protection and adolescent and adult services, if there was a proper seamless service, which identified and helped these at risk young women then they needn't get into the secure system. That's something that is needed urgently, but where little seems to be being done.

> And there is still a lot to do. We have won the argument about policy over the last ten years, yes, but that thinking doesn't seem to have much effect on the day to day lives of a lot of women in the secure system. It's still got to filter down, especially to the medium secure units. Where we are now is not anywhere near the end; it's only the beginning.[5]

And I have to say that, nearly 10 years on, that is how it feels to me too.

While it is useful to have, in a book like this, a chapter which focuses on women in secure hospitals (they need all the publicity they can get), there is also a danger that, because of that tight focus, the big picture will be lost and these women will emerge as freakish: women who are in secure hospitals because we need to be protected from them. In spite of everything they, the campaigners and I have said so far, the common-sense, everyday view of most people will still be that these women are locked away for our protection and theirs, and because they did wrong; and, the common-sense view continues, any *woman* who is locked away must be a thoroughly bad lot – otherwise why would she be locked away? 'Smoke,' 'fire,' 'bleeding heart liberals' and 'feminist troublemakers' are likely to be mentioned next, the first two self-righteously and the third and fourth epithets, at best, dismissively.

And it is here that the roots of these women's problems lie: not in a secure hospital or in a medium secure unit set up, not in the government organised system of care, but in the society of which they are a part. And although the position of women in our society is better than it was 50 years ago – when anything that

---

5   In a subsequent email on 14 July 2003, Laila Nandarkhan reinforced her earlier point that changes which further institutional goals and practices may not benefit those who are institutionalised:

> Ashworth Women's Services are due to close in Oct 03 6 months ahead of target date April 04 because the new dedicated services are either NOT ready or not going to be built so that from 12 to 24 women will be transferred to Rampton, against everything 'they' were told at the time closure was announced. 6 to 8 women with WISH's support have taken this matter up as in breach of their human rights, placing them in conditions of security higher than they have been clinically assessed to require. They are not being moved for 'clinical' reasons but for operational service reasons ... with a risk that this act could harm them ...

affected women badly, as women, didn't even have a name – women are still predominantly seen as women first and individuals second.

Certainly we can be called 'Ms' now if we choose – that is a step forward – but how many men, or women for that matter, understand why it is an important step forward? How many of us are aware of how deeply and how pervasively stereotypical thinking about women still goes, outside of the professions, outside of academia, beyond the educated elite?

The extent of my own prejudices was revealed to me when a leaflet about a conference on women and violence landed on my desk. 'Oh no, not another conference on battered women,' I cynically groaned. Not knowing whether it would make 'a story' for *The Guardian,* for which I wrote fairly regularly at the time, I sent it off with a brief note to the editor of the women's page. It was only when she rang to talk about my covering the conference that I realised the conference was about women who were violent. It was clearly stated on the front of the leaflet. How had I missed it? My own 'deep knowledge', for which read 'prejudice', had been that women only had violence done to them; they couldn't be violent themselves. That idea was positively counterintuitive. What on earth would, could, a violent woman be like? And as I began the research for the book I wondered further, with some apprehension, what the women who ended up in the then special hospitals would be like.

What I found, as I have described above, were women who had been so hurt emotionally, psychologically, and physically, almost from the beginning of their lives that they were in great need of help to even begin to sort out their problems. Women who were angry and frustrated that their voices weren't heard, that they weren't listened to. Women who, it seemed to me, were still being treated as doubly deviant women in that they were not passive, accepting, trying to be pleasing but were angry and frustrated on top of being deeply hurt. Women who did not conform to the pattern of how a proper woman should be in our society. Women who were where they were primarily because they were women. In their violence they were perceived as frightening and repellent – more frightening than men in that their violence was so unusual, so somehow 'out of control'; and repellent because, in their anger and aggression, they fell such a long way short of being either attractive young women or caring and eager to please *older* women.

Look again at the above list contrasting male and female patients. There is one mild pejorative applied to the men: 'uncommunicative.' Otherwise staff found them self-contained, straightforward and accepting of the rules. They sound rather like model patients, are at the very least approved as someone you could do business with. But the words used to describe the women tell a very different tale. The real story here is that, whilst 'male' characteristics are seen as virtues, when women are not acting to an approved stereotypical pattern of conforming passivity and docility they are perceived as difficult, demanding, emotional, and so on.

My fundamental point here is that many of the women's problems arise because they are women in our society. They have been a great deal unluckier than most and have grown up not only badly hurt but not conforming to the bedrock stereotypes that still dominate much of our thinking whether or not we are aware of it, and especially if we are not.

This at root is what the campaigners are trying to change, and this is why it is taking so long. The women of the secure hospitals are those who conform the least, who are most off centre, and who throw into sharp relief the prejudices about women that still flourish in society today. Until that society itself changes – not at the level of words, or gestures, or government initiatives but in itself, by turning against such prejudices – any efforts to improve the lot of women in the secure hospitals run the risk of being superficial rather than fundamental. However, in trying to bring about any change the campaigners are not only helping the women to some degree, they are also contributing to the long slow struggle to change the society in which the secure hospitals are embedded. We are indeed only at the beginning, but at least a start has been made.

Postscript: author's note about the interview with Diane

If readers find the report of the interview with Diane somewhat disjointed, with gaps and questions left unanswered, I will not be surprised. This is because of the circumstances of the interview.

I originally asked several campaigners if they knew of any woman or women who were at present in the secure system, or who had just recently left, who might be willing to talk to me. One campaigner spoke later to a group of women in a medium secure unit and mentioned my request, adding that if anyone decided they wanted to speak to me they should approach her for my phone number. That way I need never know the name of the woman; she could be assured of her privacy being protected.

One woman rang me and we chatted for perhaps half to three-quarters of an hour about the project and things in general. 'Diane' said she would like to talk to me, for the book, to do a face to face interview. It was arranged, through a member of staff, that I would go along to visit her in a few days' time to have an hour long interview.

A couple of days later I had a call from a doctor, whose name I don't recall, saying that 'Diane' had asked her to ring and say she did not want to see me; she was upset. I said I was sorry to hear that, asked her to give my best wishes to Diane, and thanked her for phoning.

Then came a phone call from the campaigner who had first been in touch with Diane: the reason the proposed interview had been cancelled was because her RMO had insisted that it be a supervised meeting, that is, that a member of staff sat in on the interview. Diane did not want that. The campaigner asked me to phone Diane, as she was prepared to do the interview on the telephone. When I spoke to Diane on the phone I said I was surprised to hear she was willing to speak on the phone because she had told me earlier that the phone was a public phone, in the day room, and so she could not speak personally. Yes, she said, that was true but she did not want a face to face visit with a member of staff present. We arranged that she would say only what she felt comfortable saying on the phone and that I would send her the notes of the conversation so she could expand on them, in writing, and return the amended version to me.

But by the time I had done that she had attempted suicide and was, the contact campaigner told me, in the crisis intervention unit. What mattered most now, she said, was for Diane to get through this very bad patch. I agreed and said if no more could be done, I would simply use the notes of the telephone conversation that I had sent to Diane, with all my further questions deleted. Not having heard back from Diane, this is what I did.

However, a week after the chapter had been written, answers to my questions arrived by post and also by email, sent on by the campaigner. I then added details from the new information to what Diane had originally told me.

I mention this here for two reasons: first, because had Diane and I been allowed to meet and talk properly the interview and the report of the interview would have been better: there is no substitute for talking one to one in circumstances in which both of you feel comfortable; and secondly, and more important, because the difficulties we encountered in trying to meet strike me as significant and ironic.

When I interviewed a woman patient in Ashworth Special Hospital in 1993 it was during the lunch break of a conference held at Ashworth which both the woman and I were attending. That was 'in the bad old days' of a closed system. Now we are 'into the mainstream' and there is much talk of listening to the women, yet it proved impossible to talk face to face with a woman in medium secure, without supervision, which she didn't want.

It certainly seems, as Diane says, that 'in medium secure they are very set in their ways'. She does go on to add that 'to be fair, it may just be here that's like this. I don't know about the other medium secure units. But here needs to change; and if the others are like this, they need to change'.

And once again, as 10 years ago, I am struck by the strength and endurance of yet another woman who has suffered greatly, and is still suffering, but who has the courage to speak out, and remains sufficiently fair-minded to give the benefit of the doubt to a system which, as far as I can see, continues at least to fail her, if not to add to her suffering.

Chapter 13
Feminist Antipsychiatry Praxis – Women and the Movement(s): A Canadian Perspective

Bonnie Burstow

This chapter is about movements and feminism – more specifically about feminist initiatives in challenging psychiatric oppression. An operant assumption is that liberation is always contingent on the social movements of the oppressed. As Freire (1970) suggests, emancipation requires that people co-reflect on their experience, name their oppression, and take up tasks to alter the oppressive situation. Coming together on the basis of identity and co-naming experience are crucial, for oppression depends on isolation, and one of the most insidious aspects of oppression is having other people's names and worlds imposed upon one. At the same time, social change is more complex than this articulation suggests. For one thing, oppressed people need allies – a need which brings with it real possibilities and real dangers. For another, while we cannot play the same roles, simply by virtue of being human beings, we all have a responsibility to alter the social structures by which some people are oppressed, some are privileged, and all are dehumanised. What further complicates praxis is that, given the complexity of location, it is never the case that only one movement has bearing on people's situations. All this being so, it is no simple matter to write about feminist initiatives in 'the movement' against psychiatry.

When women psychiatric survivors and their allies combat psychiatry, two highly inter-related movements have been particularly focal – the psychiatric survivor movement and the antipsychiatry movement. Both are headed by both men and women, and both are based on the recognition that, despite the differences, male and female psychiatric inmates have common cause. The women's movement(s) has also been important, although it has not been a major player in this arena for some time, and it centres very different common causes. Other significant movements include the disability rights movement, the anti-poverty movement, and the gay rights movement.

In this chapter, I am exploring feminist initiatives within the antipsychiatry movement (particularly the psychiatric survivor part) and the psychiatric survivor movement (particularly the antipsychiatry part) while bearing in mind the women's movement(s) – and making some links. The Canadian experience is particularly focal, as I am grounded in it, though I am theorising broadly. Questions which I am asking include: What are these movements? What types of feminist praxis has happened within them? What are some of the obstacles? And what sort of feminist praxis might be taken up in the future?

13.1   Who am I?

Whenever we talk about movements and identities, it is important to locate oneself. To highlight some aspects of my identity that I see as most relevant, I am a long-term Canadian antipsychiatry activist. For over 25 years, I have fought psychiatry in ways that include writing, speaking, co-organising demonstrations, making deputations to governing bodies, being part of sit-ins, getting hauled away by police, making videos, sitting on boards, attending countless meetings – essentially, being an active member of antipsychiatry collectives and organisations, whether it be of the antipsychiatry magazine *Phoenix Rising* or groups like the Ontario Coalition to Stop Electroshock.

Two other truths about my identity are equally important. The first is that I am not a psychiatric survivor. That is, as Kate Millett (1990) would put it, I have not been on 'the loony bin trip' and, accordingly, there are many, many aspects of being a psychiatric survivor which I cannot pretend to understand the way a survivor understands them. The other is that I have the identity of being someone negatively affected by and threatened by psychiatry. Three of my relatives were institutionalised, including my father, who was subjected to hundreds of electroshocks. I was forced to see a psychiatrist when I was a child. And significantly, in my early life, I was considered 'normal' by almost no one and was threatened with institutionalisation on a number of occasions. Indeed, twice I was dragged to an institution against my will, and while I was fortunate and, indeed, privileged enough to talk my way out on both occasions, you cannot have experiences like that without being shaken and without taking in something of the horrendous power of this institution.

Other identities, some of them conflicting, which have a bearing are: I am a lesbian who is well aware of psychiatric homophobia: I am a Jew; I come from the welfare class; I am a white academic with privilege; I am a feminist therapist with privilege and credibility; I am someone who has devoted decades to consciousness-raising about psychiatry within feminist therapist circles and challenging feminist therapists and psychology students on their practice; and I am a feminist anarchist who opposes professionalisation and is committed to co-building a world in which caring and helping are not commodified.

13.2   Background information: names, definitions, history and relationships

To understand the feminist initiatives in question, it is important to have some sense of the antipsychiatry and the survivor movements. To begin with the latter, the psychiatric survivor movement goes by many names, all of them somewhat interchangeable. Examples include the 'mad movement', the 'inmate liberation movement', and the 'ex-patients' movement'. Survivors likewise self-identify differently. 'Psychiatric survivors' connotes that psychiatry is an ordeal which has been survived. 'Psychiatric inmates' suggests that psychiatric institutions are essentially psycho-prisons. While there is no hard and fast rule, the most common criterion for use of any of these terms is that the person has spent 24 hours or more in a psychiatric facility.

The movement is based on an understanding of the common cause of those who have been incarcerated in psycho-prisons. There are enormous differences between different survivor organisations. As explained by Chamberlin (1990), Lapon (1986) and Reaume (2002), some reject psychiatry completely. Some see it as legitimate. Some allow allies to join. Some reject non-survivors. What almost all have in common is a commitment to the centrality of psychiatric survivors, a commitment to appreciate difference, an ethic of common support, and, what is fundamental, an appreciation that psychiatry is or can be oppressive. For the most part, they also make some demands on psychiatry. While the differences here are particularly important and while there are exceptions, demands that are fairly standard include the right to be treated with respect, the right to have input into one's own care, and the right to accurate information.

It is hard to say when the survivor movement began. Some, such as Chamberlin (1990), use the late 19th century as a date, when Elizabeth Packard of Jackson, Illinois organised fellow inmates to resist and brought a writ of habeas corpus to get out of the institution in which her husband had imprisoned her. Whatever date is used, it is clear that the survivor movement has been around a long time, that American psychiatric survivors have been pivotal in congealing a full fledged survivor movement, and that one moment in the antipsychiatry movement is critical – the 3rd Annual International Conference on Human Rights and Psychiatric Oppression in 1975. This brings me to the antipsychiatry movement.

A case could be made that antipsychiatry also began with individual inmates who resisted. This notwithstanding, antipsychiatry is generally thought of as originating with professionals – with Laing in England, who brought a left-wing reading to madness and created healing communities and with the radical therapy movement in the United States, which introduced politically aware approaches.[1] However the beginning is theorised, it was in America that the movement began to get organised; and it is the American writer and professional, Thomas Szasz, whose philosophic stamp it eventually took. The pivotal book was *The Myth of Mental Illness*, in which Szasz (1961) argued that the concept 'mental illness' was pure metaphor and that institutional psychiatry was antithetical to human freedom. Herein lies the foundation of modern antipsychiatry praxis.

The 3rd Annual International Conference on Human Rights and Psychiatric Oppression, held in 1975, was pivotal in both the psychiatric survivor movement and the antipsychiatry movements. The professionals dominated, ignoring survivors' needs and issues. As outlined in Lapon (1986), survivors responded by boycotting the professionals' sessions, hearing each others' stories, and declaring their independence. From this extremely important reclaiming came the flowering of the survivor movement. Likewise, came a repositioning of antipsychiatry. While Szasz remained important and while academics and professionals continued to play a role, from this moment onward, antipsychiatry centred primarily around psychiatric survivors, and its agenda was set largely by survivors. Significantly, all subsequent conferences were organised and controlled by survivor groups.

---

1   In this regard, see Angel, 1971.

The survivor movement and the antipsychiatry movement remain overlapping movements that are commonly not distinguished from each other. Those parts of the survivor movement which are antipsychiatry form both the overwhelming majority within and the activist centre of the antipsychiatry movement, with the rest of the survivor movement variously placed and with other activists and theorists included. On top of some differences in membership and in degree of theorising, what distinguishes the antipsychiatry movement from the survivor movement is the philosophy and the agenda. Antipsychiatry utterly rejects and is committed to dismantling institutional psychiatry. A further difference lies in the emphasis of the activists themselves. While different parts of the survivor movement vary, the emphasis within antipsychiatry groups – Canada's Resistance Against Psychiatry, for example – is almost invariably on political actions. Another difference is that people who are not survivors have a greater role within the antipsychiatry movement, though in both cases there is a general understanding that survivors take the lead, as regards action at least. That said, in both movements there are non-survivors who know what it means to be allies and so who are an asset, and there are non-survivors who try to take over, and as such, constitute a problem.

13.3   An additional context: antipsychiatry and the women's movement(s)

One clear relationship between antipsychiatry and the women's movement(s) arises from a mutual dissatisfaction with psychiatry. Feminists within the larger women's movement(s) also critique psychiatry and, indeed, have created knowledge which people in the antipsychiatry movement and the survivor movement draw on. Note, in this regard, Chesler's (1972) *Women and Madness*, which explores how women drive women crazy and how women's various responses to the patriarchy are pathologised. Noteworthy likewise is Smith (1990), which illustrates how psychiatric hegemony operates. Feminist therapy, which arose out of the women's movement(s), also has a relationship to antipsychiatry, for it theorises psychiatry as problematic.[2] Other relationships arise from joint actions between certain feminists within the women's movement(s) and feminist psychiatric survivors, and from the use of feminist critiques of psychiatry by survivors and other theorists.

The significance of these relationships notwithstanding, although there is a potential, it would be a mistake to see the women's movement(s) overall or feminist therapists overall as part of antipsychiatry. As survivors have justifiably protested, some 'feminist therapists' have not only used psychiatry as a resource but have dragged clients to institutions against their will. Aside from a number of my own works (such as Burstow, 1992), I know of no writing by feminist therapists that calls for a total break with the psychiatric system.[3] While there are exceptions, most theorists have largely ignored the reality of male survivors. Few of the feminist critics are activists in the struggle against psychiatry, and few have called for the

---

2   See, for example, Greenspan, 1983; and Burstow, 1992.

3   For discussion of this problem, see Bolt and Nihera, 1985. For a thorough antipsychiatry articulation of feminist therapy principles, see Burstow, 1992, pp 1–39 and pp 235–66.

dismantling of any part of the psychiatric system. As such, to date, the women's movement as a whole could not be considered antipsychiatry, and few of the feminist critics who problematise psychiatry could be considered part of the antipsychiatry movement, despite their contributions.

13.4 The women and feminist initiatives in the antipsychiatry/survivor movements

As long as the psychiatric survivor and antipsychiatry movements have existed, women psychiatric survivors have been a critical part of them. From Packard onward, women have resisted and have brought women's consciousness to the movement(s). Highly significant women leaders whom I would particularly like to acknowledge and honour include: Judi Chamberlin, whose book *On Our Own* (1979) inspired the creation of many groups; Persimmon Blackbridge and Sheila Gilhooly, who brought a lesbian feminist analysis into antipsychiatry; Rea Maglajlik, for her work initiating survivor groups in Eastern Europe; Kate Millett, for writing *The Loony Bin Trip* (1990); Jean Grobe, for editing one of the few books by women psychiatric survivors (Grobe, 1995); and Jennifer Reid and Judy Johnny, for always insisting that psychiatric racism, sexism, classism, ableism and homophobia all be addressed (Burstow, 1994).

All-women psychiatric survivor groups constitute a particularly important avenue for feminist praxis. Activities by all-women groups have included acting as a support group, writing, demonstrating, lobbying for the creation of safe houses for women, helping create decent services for women, and mounting educationals. Traditionally, all-women groups have looked at how women inmates are oppressed in the psychiatric system and in society at large, including within the survivor movement. While some have participated in events in the larger feminist community, groups traditionally have a primary allegiance to the psychiatric survivor/antipsychiatry movements.

Women Against Psychiatric Assault (WAPA) appears to be the first American all-women group and perhaps the first women's group in the movement. Begun in 1975 in San Francisco, its activities included creating a leaderless support group for women survivors, presenting workshops on psychiatric assault at a violence against women conference, demonstrating outside a psycho-prison that was electroshocking a young woman, and putting out a women's issue of the magazine *Madness Network News*.[4] A later American feminist group was the Women Psychiatric Inmates Liberation Front. Founded in the early 1980s, the Front hosted the 12th Annual International Conference on Human Rights and Psychiatric Oppression in Colorado in 1984. In this conference, parallels were drawn between the prison and psychiatric systems, and the specificity of women's oppression in the system was explored.[5]

---

4 For these and other details on WAPA, see Arrow, 1981.
5 For details about the Front as well as other organisations in the international mad movement, see Bolt and Nihera, 1985; and Dubay, 1985.

While most women's survivor groups have been oriented to education, support, and demonstrations, some have taken a more artistic bent. A particularly creative albeit very short-lived group was Psycho Femmes – a Toronto group in the mid-1990s. Sue Goodwin – the primary organiser – realised that all-women groups were important because women do not talk freely in mixed groups. Accordingly, she formed Psycho Femmes, which brought together theatre, music, and clowning. Psycho Femmes put on 12 performances about women in the psychiatric system.[6]

Advantages of the women's groups are many. They are places where both male chauvinism and sane chauvinism can be left behind and mad women's identities celebrated. They help women survivors abandon the shackles in which patriarchy has confined them. They help women reclaim and theorise those aspects of being a woman that the patriarchy labels 'crazy'. They can be safe spaces in which to give and get support. They facilitate exploration of the particularity of women's psychiatric experiences and their relationship to other oppression against women. Correspondingly, they are a locus for education and more militant action. Additionally, they are sometimes an avenue for linking up with the larger feminist movement.

This last potential notwithstanding, it is important to note that in North America linkups have not happened often and, when they have, women inmates have often found them damaging, and understandably so. The dissatisfaction with and separation from the women's movement are far more pronounced in the United States than in Canada, and the anger is particularly focused on feminist professionals in the 'mental health system'. Instructive in this regard is the WAPA experience, in which ex-professionals who were not survivors ended up dominating the group and engaging in problematic discourse predicated on the overall 'acceptability' of involuntary incarceration – something in clear violation of antipsychiatry principles (Arrow, 1981, p 20). American activists largely responded by denouncing and withdrawing. By contrast, as is evident in Sartori (1997), while Canadians have also had bad experiences and have theorised on the basis of them, the movement has also been able to nurture and enjoy good relations with various feminist service organisations. Moreover, in a number of other countries – especially Holland and Denmark – women ex-inmate groups (Holland's Der Helse Hex, for example) interact considerably more with other feminists and appear to have a more benign relationship.[7] Unfortunately, given the size of the American movement and the extent of American hegemony within the movement, most of us know little about these other experiences and vantage points.

There have never been many all-women groups. Accordingly, the average woman wanting to join a survivor group is generally faced with joining a mixed group or joining no group at all. An accompanying problem is that women's groups do not last long. I know of no North American women's survivor group which has lasted longer than a few years. Fortunately, for the most part, the individual women involved do not stop being active when these all-women groups dissolve. However, their praxis ends up primarily within mixed groups (male and female) and,

---

6   For details on Psycho Femmes, see Goodwin, 1997.
7   For a discussion of the different experiences, see Bolt and Nihera, 1985, p 9.

expectably, in these groups, feminist content is lower, and some sexism is to be expected.

I do not wish to overemphasise sexism within the mixed groups, for, as the world goes, these movement groups are places where difference is accepted and celebrated. This notwithstanding, men in these groups and group dynamics can present problems for women members. While some problems have not been tackled or even named – for example, the prioritising of traditionally male approaches and solutions – feminist ex-inmates have challenged overt sexism.[8] They have also issued statements like Raymond *et al* (1985, p 6), who write: 'We join the ex-inmate movement and expect to find sexism, but we do not accept the failure of members to recognize and be held accountable for it.'

The most common avenues for feminist initiatives are general antipsychiatry groups and general psychiatric survivor groups, with those initiatives largely organised by women and, in many cases, actively supported by the men. Some of the actions in question are done in collaboration with all-women's groups, though most occur independently. One example of a collaborative effort occurred when Psycho Femmes performed at Psychiatric Survivor Pride Day in Toronto 10 years ago.

Examples of feminist praxis in antipsychiatry/psychiatric survivor groups include creating special feminist educationals, helping create woman and woman-positive services, having women-only workshops in survivor conferences, writing explicitly feminist literature, and making feminism integral to the analyses in manifestos, position papers, presentations, and briefs. Feminist praxis also occurs within antipsychiatry/survivor magazines. Significantly, the Canadian antipsychiatry magazine *Phoenix Rising* produced two special women's issues (1981 and 1985), as did the American magazine *Madness Network News* (1976 and 1977). All four issues contain numerous articles exploring the situation(s) of women survivors. Particularly noteworthy is Raymond *et al* (1985) – a replication of a position paper presented at the 10th Annual International Conference on Human Rights and Psychiatric Oppression. In it, the authors analyse the relationship between psychiatric violence against women and other forms of violence against women, point out the greater vulnerability of women who are not white and middle-class, highlight betrayals by feminist therapists and women's centres, and respond to sexism within the survivor movement. Additionally, many antipsychiatry magazines have maintained fairly high feminist content throughout, albeit a feminism that generally pays insufficient attention to issues of class, race, and ethnicity. Correspondingly, given the high profile of lesbians within the movement, movement magazines have highlighted homophobia. The *Phoenix Rising* collective, for example, printed numerous pieces on psychiatric homophobia during its 10 years, and we ended our publication history with a special lesbian and gay issue (*Phoenix Rising*, 1990).

Some antipsychiatry groups have had a particularly strong feminist bent, with the feminism in question being one that integrates multiple oppressions. Resistance

---

8   Examples of male approaches and solutions are heavy confrontation and treating being left alone as an adequate solution to the problems that psychiatric survivors face.

Against Psychiatry (RAP) – an Ontario group of survivors and other activists – is a case in point. Examples of feminist actions pursued in RAP include: producing a pamphlet on psychiatric sexism, racism, classism, and heterosexism; creating a pamphlet on electroshock as a feminist issue; and creating numerous feminist educationals, sometimes in collaboration with specific parts of the women's movement(s), sometimes not. One example of an educational was Feminist Antipsychiatry Perspectives. At this event, Kate Millett and I critiqued psychiatry as a patriarchal, ableist, racist, and classist institution; Helen Levine and Kate Millett spoke of their personal struggles with psychiatry; Aboriginal activist Carmen Pratt spoke of the psychiatrisation of Aboriginal women; and numerous survivors came to the mic and gave personal testimony.

Another group which has historically undertaken major feminist initiatives is Second Opinion Society (SOS) in the Yukon. SOS has demonstrated that it is sometimes possible to work through issues with outside women's organisations that have put survivors in jeopardy. To quote director Giseila Sartori in this regard:

> We worked really hard at changing the view of some of the people at the Women's Centre ... One of our members was badly screwed around by them. They didn't respect her confidentiality and she ended up being locked up ... They've attended some of our events and we've seen a big difference in how they operate. They've realized that psychiatry is a women's issue. (Sartori, 1997, p 130)

A consequence of such persevering is that meaningful joint projects became possible.[9]

Some antipsychiatry groups have consistently highlighted sexist facts and featured women survivors telling their story. Besides RAP, a historical case in point is the Ontario Coalition to Stop Electroshock. A feminist analysis of electroshock was integral to the Coalition's deputations to the Toronto Board of Health (see Weitz *et al*, 1984). And our submission to Ontario's ECT Review Committee (Ontario Coalition to Stop Electroshock, 1984) systemically exposed sexist doubletalk, including the sexism inherent in standard medical excuses for shocking women two to three times as often as men. Correspondingly, under the auspices of the Coalition, shock survivors such as Shirley Johnson told personal stories that drew attention to the danger which electroshock poses to overworked housewives and women who have just given birth.[10]

While organisations have been extremely important sites for feminist praxis, feminist praxis has also happened individually and in very small ad hoc groupings. Important individual and ad hoc initiatives have included mounting conferences on the psychiatrisation of women, talking to other feminists, drawing, making feminist points on survivor listservs, making feminist statements at demonstrations, editing anthologies of writings by women survivors (eg, Grobe, 1995), contributing to anthologies produced within the women's movement (eg, Chamberlin, 1975), and writing a woman-identified book on one's psychiatric ordeal (eg, Funk, 1998).

---

9 For further details, see Second Opinion Society, 1994, p 16.
10 As discussed in Burstow (1994), many women get electroshock for post-partum depression. For Shirley's story, see Weitz *et al*, 1984, p 16A ff.

The arts have been a particularly important venue for feminist initiatives. Indeed, they are a valuable venue for survivors and their allies in general, for they facilitate the expression of people whose words have been invalidated, forge connection between survivors, create multiple witnesses to psychiatric traumatisation, and move people in ways that can lead to action. Theatre groups have been especially liberating, for theatre is immediate, and it has the capacity to foster celebration and community. In this regard, I would especially like to call attention to the ongoing work of Friendly Spike Theatre.

Friendly Spike is a remarkable theatre company which has embraced and been embraced by the Toronto survivor community. It has created numerous evenings for psychiatric survivors; it has brought together psychiatric survivors, battered women, and women prison inmates; and it has produced many plays which highlight the reality of caged women. Particularly noteworthy in this last regard is the play, *The Girls of Grandview*, which dramatises the rape, solitary confinement, and other abuse inflicted on hundreds of young girls at the Ontario Training School for Girls.[11]

Feminist documentaries have likewise constituted important initiatives. An example is *When Women End Up in Those Horrible Places* (Burstow, 1994) – a video which weaves together multiple oppressions. The documentary combines feminist commentary with interviews with 19 women who have been locked up in psychiatric institutions throughout Canada, including lesbians, Jews, African Canadians, Aboriginal women, refugees, and women who use wheelchairs. The stories highlight the central role of childhood sexual abuse and wife abuse in the psychiatrisation of women; the damaging nature of the 'treatments'; the inherent sexism, racism, ageism, ableism, and lesbophobia; and women's efforts at liberation.

Some feminist projects have taken multiple forms. One that is exceptional and which gives us critical lessons in how to bring together oppressions, multiply witnessing, and work collaboratively is 'Still Sane'. The Still Sane project began with two Vancouver lesbians, Persimmon Blackbridge and Sheila Gilhooly. Sheila was a survivor who had spent three years in a psycho-prison. Persimmon was an artist who had been labelled 'learning disabled'. Together, they decided to make body sculptures of the oppression which Sheila had undergone.

Unlike patriarchal art creation, where there is a sharp division between 'artist' and 'model', the work was done collaboratively. Together, Sheila and Persimmon cried about Sheila's experiences, laughed, read antipsychiatry literature, crafted. Persimmon made body casts of Sheila, as Sheila held poses symbolising her ordeals and embodying the psychological states in which she had found herself. Both worked on fitting clay into the plaster moulds. Together, they made decisions about the art. Additionally, Sheila wrote about her experiences; Persimmon and Sheila jointly edited down the written pieces so that the writing could be included on the sculptures themselves. An example of a statement written on one of the body sculptures is '19 shock treatments and I still didn't want to be cured of being a lesbian' (Blackbridge and Gilhooly, 1985).

---

11 See Friendly Spike Theatre, 2002.

In the fall of 1984, the sculptures were exhibited at the Women in Focus Gallery in Vancouver. In the guest book which was put out, woman after woman said that she could relate and shared something of her own experience. Subsequently, Persimmon and Sheila made slides of the sculptures and travelled across North American doing slide shows. Later came the book and the video – both of them extensively distributed. Edited by Blackbridge and Gilhooly (1985) in co-operation with others, the book includes articles by other women survivors. Produced by Ingratta and Patriasz (1984), the video features sculptures as well as interviews with Persimmon and Sheila. And it folds in other lesbians who have been psychiatrised and who resisted.[12]

This project was exceptional and is important for a number of reasons. The co-investigation and embodied representation of the psychiatric oppression of lesbians brought antipsychiatry in North America to a new level of complexity. The mutuality of the art-making and the progressive 'folding in' of other women exemplified a feminist way to do art and to 'do antipsychiatry'. Correspondingly, the women's use of one art form after another illustrates the type of creativity which is possible.

I am unsure what Sheila is doing at this juncture. Persimmon is still thrilling audiences of survivors and other activists with antipsychiatry lesbian feminist art. Two of her most recent initiatives are antipsychiatry lesbian feminist novels – *Sunnybrook* (Blackbridge, 1996) and *Prozac Highway* (Blackbridge, 2002).

As can be seen from the foregoing, to date, feminist initiatives have been diverse. Individually and collectively, with male comrades and independently, in art, in print, in cyberspace, and on the streets, feminist projects and agendas have been put forward. There is much to celebrate. At the same time, it is important to look toward the future – to ask what else might be done and what might be done differently.

13.5 Directions for the future

One obvious and necessary direction is doing more of those actions which many of us in the movement already recognise as sound, and, indeed, pushing them further and making them more strategic. One way to do so is through cutting-edge feminist art. Optimal is feminist art with the depth and integrity of the Still Sane project, with its mutuality, attention to multiple oppression, and progressive folding in of others. With at-the-bone feminist art, women could body forth their multiple realities as women psychiatric survivors. Story telling, painting, sculpture, theatre, and music could take the tradition of women survivors 'speaking out' to a new level so that it becomes witness art. And with sufficient work done to ensure that the art is widely seen, heard, and discussed, the multiple witnessing could raise awareness and build support on a broad scale. Moreover, such art could be used strategically by embedding it within campaigns – against electroshock, against the multinational pharmaceuticals, against childhood sexual abuse, against involuntary confinement.

---

12 For further details on this project, see Blackbridge and Gilhooly, 1985.

Additionally, it would be good to go beyond the special feminist issues of movement papers. All-women antipsychiatry magazines might be created, with specific issues used as catalysts within campaigns. By the same token, there could be conferences on the psychiatrisation of women complete with art exhibits, demonstrations, and other feminist initiatives so that a kind of feminist antipsychiatry synergy happens.

On a different but related level, it would be good to see more all-women groups, and clearly such groups could spearhead or contribute substantially to the efforts just described. Ensuring the success of all-women groups would entail exploring and coming to terms with the various dynamics which have historically led to the early demise of such groups. Examples of questions that might be asked in this regard are: Is there more infighting in these groups? And if so, why, and what can be done about it? Is assistance needed from other groups? And if so, what type?

On a more care-taking level, it would be important to create more anti-sexist safe houses for women – places where women survivors can live, eat well, work through crises, and get nonjudgmental support. For places to be truly safe, of course, their policies and actions would have to be such that they do not promote psychiatric drugs, or use diagnoses, or endanger people through problematic referrals, or force incarceration on people, or push people to 'go to hospital', or impose unrealistic rules such as 'no self-injury'. Correspondingly, it is vital that there be *women-only* safe houses. By the same token, it is critical that more safe houses for women survivors be *run by women survivors* themselves. The last thing that most survivors want or need is more professionals regulating their lives. I see the creation of such safe houses as critical feminist initiatives.

Another direction that I would also like to see pursued is increasing the venues in which feminist antipsychiatry initiatives are taken up and psychiatric assaults on women combated. Venues rarely used for explicitly feminist initiatives but which are promising include radio, the internet, and the courtroom. I would particularly emphasise the courtroom. Many countries – Canada and the United States included – have laws prohibiting discrimination on the basis of gender. However, although institutional psychiatry treats both sexes abysmally, the treatment of male and female psychiatric inmates is demonstrably unequal. As shown in Burstow (1994), women, for example, are disproportionately subjected to psychiatric drugs that, significantly, are neurotoxic; and women receive electroshock – a brain damaging treatment – two to three times as often as men. It is worth contesting the constitutionality of such differences. Even lost cases are beneficial, for legal actions bring publicity. As such, they are an opportunity to educate the public about the horror of psychiatry generally and the treatment of women in particular.[13]

More substantial shifts, which I would also welcome, would necessitate taking a far harder look at mistakes and shortcomings. One shortcoming that is particularly important to address is the limited scope of feminism within the survivor/antipsychiatry movements. While there are exceptions to be sure, the feminism in question is largely white North American feminism. It is critical that

---

13 Of course, it would be important to explore the likelihood of a win backfiring and 'equality' being achieved via an increase in shocks and drugs administered to men.

more women of colour take leadership roles, that work on other continents be acknowledged, and that the jeopardy and psychiatrisation of Black women, Asian women, and Aboriginal women be front and centre in analyses and actions.

Along the same vein, it is important to move more and more toward a feminism which is transformative – that is, a feminism aimed at a fundamental transformation of the world. There is something profoundly wrong with how most of human society arranges itself. There is something wrong when patriarchal, capitalist, and racist elites create systems which cause widespread misery and subject people with trouble coping to incarceration and damaging 'treatments'. A huge challenge facing the survivor/antipsychiatry movement is addressing that larger picture while focusing on psychiatry. To do so means moving to another stage of both analysis and action.

In this regard, all social movements go through stages. As stated earlier, the 1975 action of locking out the professionals was necessary and critical. It similarly has been and remains important to have distinct survivor-based communities, for oppressed people need community and need to take the lead in naming and altering critical aspects of the oppressive situation in which they find themselves. This notwithstanding, once separation is achieved and consolidated, while continuing to build the community and to take the lead, it is important to move toward connection for, ultimately, a better world for psychiatric survivors cannot be achieved without creating a better world for everyone. Correspondingly, as Rosenthal (1996) suggests, there is a limit to what any comparatively small disenfranchised community can achieve without the active collaboration of others, whether that community be psychiatric survivors, people who are homeless, prison inmates, or undocumented persons.

There are many related movements with which greater connection is needed – for example, disabilities rights, antiglobalisation, antipoverty, anti-racism, and penal abolition. The women's movement(s) is particularly important to cultivate and work with, for it incorporates transformative feminism; it has a history of addressing psychiatry as an oppressive institution; and women are particularly vulnerable to psychiatric intrusion. As such, the women's movement(s) is a natural ally, despite the very real problems and betrayals documented by writers like Bolt and Nihera (1985). What is likewise important, it has the capacity to significantly advance the antipsychiatry agenda.

In this regard, I ask people to consider what might be possible if the women's movement genuinely took up the antipsychiatry cause. Imagine what could be possible if it took up the fight against electroshock. The women's movement is a huge and powerful international movement. It has the resources and the power necessary to exert considerable pressure on governments to withdraw support for shock or ban it outright. Correspondingly, if, as a result, electroshock were banned, it would be banned for everybody. The same principle holds for other psychiatric injury, though electroshock is a strategic place to begin, for people intuitively recognise it as horrific.

A widespread feminist commitment to antipsychiatry principles is possible and has the potential to make a huge difference, but it will not happen unless women survivors make it a priority and connect with the women's movement. Janet

Foner's (1995, p 143) words are significant in this regard: 'The most basic thing we women psychiatric survivors need to do is make friends and alliances with other women, particularly those who are active in the women's movement ... Our issues are important for all women because mentalism acts as a threat to all women.' Survivors' issues are likewise important to all women because mentalism threatens women's families and children. And these realities, if fully appreciated, would bring the women's movement on-side. What is involved is strategising, reaching out, and educating so that more and more feminists become aware that psychiatry is an issue of relevance to women as a whole, to women's children, to the world. On a more intricate level, what is needed is devoting time and energy to identifying and nurturing potential allies, distinguishing which individuals will go the distance, systematically turning up at women's conferences, making presentations, enlisting and building support for specific actions – in other words, rigorously doing the ongoing work necessary to place antipsychiatry squarely on the feminist agenda. As feminist professionals are among the most likely allies, correspondingly, enlisting and educating feminist professionals is part and parcel of the job at hand.

To do all of this, of course, means moving beyond isolationism. It means seeing the relevance of and endorsing the women's movement overall. On a more personal level, as Foner (1995) suggests, it means moving beyond fury at the women's movement and at women professionals. Significantly, while feminists and feminist therapists have unquestionably let women survivors down, the work that needs to be done is obstructed by blaming feminist therapists for earning an income, as many women survivors have, and by trashing women in the women's movement(s) for not understanding.[14] I agree, of course, that people who are complicit in the oppression of psychiatric survivors must be held accountable – feminists included – and that it is important not to trust individuals in those areas where they do not act trustworthy. This notwithstanding, it is essential that allies and potential allies be treated fairly; that women work against the default mode of blaming other women for their pain; that individuals be judged in accordance with how they act – not how others who are similarly situated act; that serious thought be given to how to create alliances; and that mistakes and shortcomings be expected.

By the same token, it is critical to mend internal divisions. By way of example, it is important to stop dismissing those who identify as 'antipsychiatry' as academics who do nothing, as some survivors have.[15] What is telling in this regard is that most of the pro-feminist survivor/activist groups discussed in the chapter have always identified as antipsychiatry – Phoenix Rising, Ontario Coalition to Stop Electroshock, and Resistance Against Psychiatry, for example. And they are not academic. What is likewise important, the movement(s) needs scholars. Indeed, we need the contributions of everyone who is willing to lend a hand and who respects the rights and centrality of survivors. My hope is that we embrace them and build.

In ending, I would reiterate that there are challenges ahead – challenges involving connection, creativity, and broader vision. And women survivors have an

---

14 For instances of the kind of mistakes in question, see Raymond *et al*, 1985; and Bolt and Nihera, 1985.

15 See, in this regard, Chamberlin, 1990.

absolutely critical role to play if those challenges are to be met, for women are more oppressed by psychiatry, and the broader support of the women's movement is needed and is possible. Moreover, the masculinist principles which have largely governed the world have not stood us in good stead.

I look to the day when there are no hierarchies and care is not commodified. I look to the day when no one is caged, when no one is zapped with electricity, when everyone has a home, and when difference is celebrated. I look to the day when no one will be put down because of skin colour, and no one can even remember the last time when anyone was jabbed with a needle which he or she did not want. Indeed, like so many around me, I look to the day when we all care for ourselves, each other, other species, and the environment and live at peace on the planet. Herein lies a transformation worth fighting for. I see women and especially women from disenfranchised groups as pivotal players in the transformational work ahead.

Books and articles

Adler, DA, Drake, RE and Teague, GB, 'Clinicians' practices in personality assessment: does gender influence the use of DSM-III Axis II?' (1990) 31 Comprehensive Psychiatry 125

Adler, F, *Sisters in Crime*, 1975, New York: McGraw-Hill

Ainsley, JN, '"Some mysterious agency": women, violent crime, and the insanity acquittal in the Victorian courtroom' (2000) 45 Canadian Journal of History 37

Alcoff, L and Gray, L, 'Survivor discourse: transgression or recuperation?' (1993) 18 Signs 260

Allen, H, *Justice Unbalanced: Gender, Psychiatry and Judicial Decisions*, 1987, Milton Keynes: Open University Press

Allison, DB and Roberts, MS, *Disordered Mother or Disordered Diagnosis? Munchausen by Proxy Syndrome*, 1998, Hillsdale, NJ: The Analytic Press

American Psychiatric Association, *Diagnostic and Statistical Manual of Mental Disorders*, 1952, Washington, DC: APA

American Psychiatric Association, *Diagnostic and Statistical Manual of Mental Disorders*, 3rd edn (revised 1987), 1980, Washington, DC: APA

American Psychiatric Association, *Diagnostic and Statistical Manual of Mental Disorders*, 4th edn (revised 2000), 1994, Washington, DC: APA

Anderson, E, *Hard Place to Do Time: The Story of Oakalla Prison, 1912–1991*, 1993, New Westminster, BC: Hillpointe

Anderson, FW, *Hanging in Canada: A Concise History of a Controversial Topic*, 1982, Surrey, BC: Heritage House

Anderson, KJ, *Vancouver's Chinatown: Racial Discourse in Canada, 1875–1980*, 1991, Montreal, QC and Kingston, ON: McGill-Queen's University Press

Anderson, R, '"The hardened frail ones": women and crime in Auckland, 1845–1870', unpublished MA thesis, 1981, University of Auckland

Angel, A (ed), *The Radical Therapist*, 1971, New York: Ballantine

Armstrong, L, *Kiss Daddy Goodnight*, 1982, New York: Simon & Schuster

Armstrong, L, 'Surviving the incest industry' (1991) 21 Trouble and Strife 29

Armstrong, L, *Rocking the Cradle of Sexual Politics: What Happened When Women Said Incest*, 1994, Reading, MA: Addison-Wesley

Armstrong, L, *Rocking The Cradle of Sexual Politics: What Happened When Women Said Incest*, 1996, London: The Women's Press

Arrigo, BA, *Punishing the Mentally Ill: A Critical Analysis of Law and Psychiatry*, 2002, Albany, NY: State University of New York Press

Arrow, 'Woman against psychiatric assault' (1981) 1 Phoenix Rising 19

Astbury, J, *Crazy For You: The Making of Women's Madness*, 1996, Oxford: Oxford University Press

Atwood, M, *Alias Grace*, 1996, Toronto: McClelland and Stewart

Atwood, M, *Alias Grace*, 1997, London, Virago

Australian Bureau of Statistics, 'Aboriginal and Torres Strait Islander Australians: a statistical profile from the 1996 Census' *Year Book Australia*, 2002, www.abs.gov.au

Backhouse, C, 'Desperate women and compassionate courts: infanticide in 19th century Canada' (1984) 34 University of Toronto Law Journal 416

Backhouse, C, 'White female help and Chinese-Canadian employers: race, class, gender, and law in the case of Yee Clun, 1924' (1994) 26 Canadian Ethnic Studies/Etudes Ethniques au Canada 34

Backhouse, C, 'The shining sixpence: women's worth in Canadian law at the end of the Victorian era' (1996) 23 Manitoba Law Journal 556

Bacon, W and Lansdowne, R, 'Women who kill husbands: the battered wife on trial', in O'Donnell, C and Craney, J (eds), Family Violence in Australia, 1982, Melbourne: Longman Cheshire, pp 67–94

Badger, D, Waughan, P, Woodward, M and Williams, P, 'Planning to meet the needs of offenders with mental disorders in the United Kingdom' (1999) 50 Psychiatric Services 1624

Baker, J, 'Female criminal lunatics: a sketch' (1902) 38 The Journal of Mental Science 13

Bala, N and Schuman, J, 'Allegations of sexual abuse when parents have separated' (2000) 17 Canadian Family Law Quarterly 191

Balfour, G, 'Feminist therapy with women in prison: working under the hegemony of correctionalism', in Hannah-Moffat, K and Shaw, M (eds), An Ideal Prison? Critical Essays on Women's Imprisonment in Canada, 2000, Halifax, NS: Fernwood, pp 94–102

Ballinger, A, Dead Woman Walking: Executed Women in England and Wales 1900–1955, 2000, Aldershot: Ashgate

Ballou, M, 'Threats and challenges to feminist therapy', in Ballou, M (ed), Foundations and Future of Feminist Therapy, in press, Binghamton, NY: Haworth

Ballou, M and Brown, LS (eds), Rethinking Mental Health and Disorder: Feminist Perspectives, 2002, New York: Guilford

Ballou, M, Matsumoto, A and Wagner, M, 'Towards a feminist ecological theory of human nature: theory building in response to real world dynamics', in Ballou, M and Brown, LS (eds), Rethinking Mental Health and Disorder: Feminist Perspectives, 2002, New York: Guilford, pp 99–141

Bancroft, J, 'The premenstrual syndrome – a reappraisal of the concept and the evidence', Psychological Medicine, Monograph Supplement 24, 1993, Cambridge: Cambridge University Press

Barreau du Québec, Développements récents en droit de la santé mentale, 1998, Cowansville, QC: Les Éditions Yvon Blais Inc

Barrett, M, Women's Oppression Today: The Marxist-Feminist Encounter, 1988, London: Verso

Barrett, M and McIntosh, M, The Anti-Social Family, 1982, London: Verso

Barrett, M and Roberts, H, 'Doctors and their patients: the social control of women in general practice', in Smart, C and Smart, B (eds), Women, Sexuality and Social Control, 1978, London: Routledge and Kegan Paul

Barton, A, '"Wayward girls and wicked women": two centuries of semi-penal control' (2000) 22 Liverpool Law Review 157

Barton, A, Fragile Moralities and Dangerous Sexualities: Women and Community Punishment, 1823–2003, forthcoming, Aldershot: Ashgate

Batacharya, S, 'Racism, "girl violence" and the murder of Reena Virk', 2000, unpublished MA thesis, Department of Sociology and Equity Studies in Education, Ontario Institute for Studies in Education of the University of Toronto

Bauman, Z, Society Under Siege, 2002, Cambridge: Polity

Bebbington, P, 'The origins of sex differences in depression: bridging the gap' (1996) 8 International Review of Psychiatry 295

Becker, D, *Through the Looking Glass: Women and Borderline Personality Disorder*, 1997, Boulder, CO: Westview

Becker, D, 'When she was bad: borderline personality disorder in a posttraumatic age' (2000) 70 American Journal of Orthopsychiatry 422

Becker, D, '"Posttraumatic stress disorder": panacea or problem?', in Caplan, PJ and Cosgrove, L (eds), *Bias in Psychiatric Diagnosis*, 2004, Lanham, MD: Jason Aronson/Rowman & Littlefield, pp 207–13

Becker, D and Lamb, S, 'Sex bias in the diagnosis of borderline personality disorder and posttraumatic stress disorder' (1994) 25 Professional Psychology: Research and Practice 55

Belich, J, *Paradise Reforged: A History of the New Zealanders from the 1880s to the Year 2000*, 2001, Auckland: Penguin

Benjamin, LS, 'Structural analysis of social behavior' (1974) 81 Psychological Review 392

Benjamin, LS and Wunderlich, SA, 'Social perceptions and borderline personality disorder: the relation to mood disorders' (1994) 103 Journal of Abnormal Psychology 610

Bernier, J and Cellard, A, 'Le syndrome de la femme fatale: "maricide" et représentation féminine au Québec, 1898–1940' (1996) 29 Criminologie 29

Bertrand, M-A, *Les femmes et la criminalité*, 2003, Montréal, QC: Athéna Éditions

Bhaskar, R, *Reclaiming Reality: A Critical Introduction to Contemporary Philosophy*, 1989, London: Verso

Billig, M, *Ideologies and Beliefs*, 1991, London: Sage

Birch, H, *Moving Targets: Women, Murder and Representation*, 1993, London: Virago

Bjorklund, DF (ed), *False-Memory Creation in Children and Adults: Theory, Research, and Implications*, 2000, New York: Lawrence Erlbaum Associates

Blackbridge, P, *Sunnybrook*, 1996, Vancouver, BC: Press Gang

Blackbridge, P, *Prozac Highway*, 2002, Vancouver, BC: Press Gang

Blackbridge, P and Gilhooly, S, *Still Sane*, 1985, Vancouver, BC: Press Gang

Blashfield, RK and Draguns, JG, 'Toward a taxonomy of psychopathology: the purpose of psychiatric classification' (1976) 129 British Journal of Psychiatry 574

Bloom, B (ed), *Gendered Justice: Addressing Female Offenders*, 2003, Durham, NC: Carolina Academic Press

Blud, L, Travers, R, Nugent, F and Thornton, D, 'Accreditation of offending behaviour programmes in HM Prison Service: "What Works" in practice' (2003) 8 Legal and Criminological Psychology 69

Bolt, A and Nihera, D, 'The international mad movement' (1985) 5 Phoenix Rising 48

Bordo, S, 'Anorexia nervosa: psychopathology and the crystallization of culture', in Diamond, I and Quinby, L (eds), *Feminism and Foucault: Reflections on Resistance*, 1988, Boston, MA: Northeastern University Press, pp 87–117

Boritch, H and Hagan, J, 'A century of crime in Toronto: gender, class and patterns of social control, 1859 to 1955' (1990) 28 Criminology 567

Borum, R, Deane, MW, Steadman, HJ and Morrissey, J, 'Police perspectives on responding to mentally ill in crisis: perceptions of program effectiveness' (1998) 16 Behavioural Sciences and the Law 393

Box, S, *Power, Crime and Mystification*, 1981, London: Tavistock

Boyd, SB, *Child Custody, Law, and Women's Work*, 2003, Oxford: Oxford University Press

Bradfield, R, 'The treatment of women who kill their violent male partners within the Australian criminal justice system', unpublished PhD thesis, 2002a, University of Tasmania

Bradfield, R, 'Understanding the battered woman who kills her violent partner – the admissibility of expert evidence of domestic violence in Australia' (2002b) 9 Psychiatry, Psychology and Law 177

Brandon, D, *Innovation Without Change? Consumer Power in Psychiatric Services*, 1991, Basingstoke: Macmillan

Breggin, P, *Toxic Psychiatry. Toxic Psychiatric: Why Therapy, Empathy and Love Must Replace the Drugs, Electroshock and Biochemical Theories of the New Psychiatry*, 1993, London: HarperCollins

Bridgeman, J and Millns, S, *Feminist Perspectives on Law*, 1998, London: Sweet & Maxwell

Brinded, P, Malcolm, F, Fairley, N and Doyle, B, 'Diversion versus liaison: psychiatric services to the courts, Wellington, New Zealand' (1996) 6 Criminal Behaviour and Mental Health 167

Briscoe, M, 'Sex differences in psychological wellbeing' (1982) Psychological Medicine, Monographs, Supplement 1

Brookes, B, 'Women and madness: a case-study of the Seacliff Asylum, 1890–1920', in Brookes, B, Macdonald, C and Tennant, M (eds), *Women in History 2*, 1992, Wellington: Bridget Williams Books, pp 129–47

Brookes, B, 'Women and mental health: an historical introduction', in Romans, S (ed), *Folding Back the Shadows*, 1998, Dunedin: University of Otago Press, pp 15–22

Brookes, B and Thomson, J (eds), *'Unfortunate Folk': Essays on Mental Health Treatment*, 2001, Dunedin: University of Otago Press

Broverman, IK, Vogel, SR, Broverman, DM, Clarkson, FE and Rosenkrantz, PS, 'Sex role stereotypes and clinical judgements of mental health' (1970) 34 Journal of Consulting and Clinical Psychology 1

Broverman, IK, Vogel, SR, Broverman, DM, Clarkson, FE and Rosenkrantz, PS, 'Sex-role stereotypes: a current appraisal' (1972) 28 Journal of Social Issues 59

Brown, LS, 'Toward a new conceptual paradigm for the Axis II diagnoses', paper presented at the Convention of the American Psychological Association, 1987, New York

Brown, LS, *Subversive Dialogues: Theory in Feminist Therapy*, 1994, New York: Basic Books

Brown, M, 'Race, science and the construction of native criminality in colonial India' (2001) 5 Theoretical Criminology 345

Brown, P, *The Transfer of Care: Psychiatric Deinstitutionalization and its Aftermath*, 1985, London: Routledge and Kegan Paul

Brown, S, 'The Mental Health Tribunal of Queensland: a useful model for UK forensic psychiatry?' (1999) 10 Journal of Forensic Psychiatry 325

Bruch, CS, 'Parental alienation syndrome and parental alienation: getting it wrong in child custody cases' (2001) 35 Family Law Quarterly 527

Brunton, W, 'Institutionalisation: a romance for all seasons', in Haines, H and Abbott, M (eds), *The Future of Mental Health Services in New Zealand*, 1986, Auckland: The Mental Health Foundation, pp 44–63

Burman, E (ed), *Feminists and Psychological Practice*, 1990, London: Sage

Burman, E (ed), *Challenging Women: Psychology's Exclusions, Feminist Possibilities*, 1996, Buckingham: Open University Press

Burman, M, 'Breaking the mould: patterns of female offending', in McIvor, G (ed), *Women Who Offend*, 2004, London: Jessica Kingsley, pp 38–65

Burns, J, 'Mad or just plain bad? Gender and the work of forensic clinical psychologists', in Ussher, J and Nicolson, M (eds), *Gender Issues in Clinical Psychology*, 1992, London: Routledge, pp 106–28

Burr, V, *An Introduction to Social Constructionism*, 1995, London: Routledge

Burstow, B, *Radical Feminist Therapy: Working in the Context of Violence*, 1992, Newbury Park, CA: Sage

Burstow, B, *When Women End Up in Those Horrible Places*, 1994, video, Toronto

Burstow, B and Weitz, D (eds), *Shrink Resistant: The Struggle Against Psychiatry in Canada*, 1988, Vancouver, BC: New Star

Busfield, J, 'Gender, mental illness and psychiatry', in Evans, M and Ungerson, C (eds), *Sexual Divisions: Patterns and Processes*, 1983, London: Tavistock Publications, pp 106–35

Busfield, J, *Managing Madness: Changing Ideas and Practice*, 1986, London: Unwin Hyman

Busfield, J, 'Sexism and psychiatry' (1989) 23 Sociology 343

Busfield, J, 'The female malady? Men, women and madness in nineteenth century Britain' (1994) 28 Sociology 259

Busfield, J, *Men, Women and Madness: Understanding Gender and Mental Disorder*, 1996, New York: New York University Press

Butler, JP, *Gender Trouble: Feminism and the Subversion of Identity*, 1990, New York: Routledge

Butler, S, *Conspiracy of Silence: The Trauma of Incest*, 1978, San Francisco, CA: New Glide Publications

Byrne, D, *Social Exclusion*, 1999, Buckingham: Open University Press

Canadian Association of Elizabeth Fry Societies, *Response to the Department of Justice re: Reforming Criminal Code Defences: Self-Defence and Defence of Property*, 1998, Ottawa, ON: CAEFS

Caplan, PJ, 'The role of classroom conduct in the promotion and retention of elementary school children' (1973) 41 Journal of Experimental Education 8

Caplan, PJ, 'Sex, age, behavior, and subject as determinants of report of learning problems' (1977) 10 Journal of Learning Disabilities 314

Caplan, PJ, *The Myth of Women's Masochism*, 1987a, Scarborough, ON: New American Library of Canada

Caplan, PJ, 'The psychiatric association's failure to meet its own standards: the dangers of self-defeating personality disorder as a category' (1987b) 2 Journal of Personality Disorders 178

Caplan, PJ, 'The justice system's endorsement of mental health assessors' sexism and other biases: charter issues and other forms of injustice', in Dickens, B and Ouellette, M (eds), *Health Care, Ethics and Law/Soins de santé, éthique et droit*, 1993, Montreal, QC: Canadian Institute for the Administration of Justice/Institut canadien d'administration de la justice, Les editions Themis, pp 79–87

Caplan, PJ, 'Recovered memories', commissioned by Ms magazine, written in 1994 but not published

Caplan, PJ, *They Say You're Crazy: How the World's Most Powerful Psychiatrists Decide Who's Normal*, 1995, Reading, MA: Addison-Wesley Longman

Caplan, PJ, *The Myth of Women's Masochism*, 2nd edn, 1998, Toronto: University of Toronto Press

Caplan, PJ, *The New Don't Blame Mother: Mending the Mother-Daughter Relationship*, 2nd edn, 2000, New York: Routledge

Caplan, PJ, 'Ambiguity, powerlessness, and the psychologizing of trauma: how backlash affects work with trauma survivors' (2004a) 3(4) Journal of Trauma Practice 1

Caplan, PJ, 'What is it that's being called "Parental Alienation Syndrome"?', in Caplan, PJ and Cosgrove, L (eds), *Bias in Psychiatric Diagnosis*, 2004b, Lanham, MD: Jason Aronson/Rowman & Littlefield, pp 61–67

Caplan, PJ, Awad, G, Wilks, C and White, G, 'Sex differences in a delinquent clinic population' (1980) 20 British Journal of Criminology 311

Caplan, PJ and Caplan, JB, *Thinking Critically About Research on Sex and Gender*, 1999, New York: Addison Wesley Longman

Caplan, PJ and Cosgrove, L (eds), *Bias in Psychiatric Diagnosis*, in press, Livingston, NJ: Jason Aronson

Caplan, PJ and Walton-Allen, N, 'Laypeople's perceptions of spouse abuse', presented to University of Toronto Department of Psychiatry Research Day, 1984 (September)

Caplan, PJ, Watters, J, White, G, Parry, R and Bates, R, 'Toronto multi-agency child abuse research project: the abused and the abuser' (1984) 8 Child Abuse and Neglect: The International Journal 343

Caplan, PJ and Wilson, J, 'Assessing the child custody assessors' (1990) 27 Reports of Family Law, Third Series (October 25) 121

Capponi, P, *Beyond the Crazy House: Changing the Future of Madness*, 2003, Toronto, ON: Penguin Canada

Cardinal, C, 'La police, un intervenant de première ligne pour le réseau de la santé mentale', in Dorvil, H and Mayer, R (eds), *Problèmes sociaux – études de cas et interventions sociales, Tome II*, 2001, Montréal, QC: Presses de l'Université du Québec, pp 447–69

Carlen, P, *Women's Imprisonment: A Study in Social Control*, 1983, London: Routledge

Carlen, P, 'Law, psychiatry and women's imprisonment: a sociological view' (1985) 145 British Journal of Psychiatry 618

Carlen, P, 'Carceral clawback' (2002a) 4 Punishment and Society 115

Carlen, P, 'Controlling measures: the repackaging of common-sense opposition to women's imprisonment in England and Canada' (2002b) 2 Criminal Justice 155

Carlen, P and Worrall, A (eds), *Gender, Crime and Justice*, 1987, Milton Keynes: Open University Press

Carlson, E, Dalenberg, C, Armstrong, J, Daniels, J and Loewenstein, R, 'Multivariate prediction of posttraumatic symptoms in psychiatric patients' (2001) 14 Journal of Traumatic Stress 549

Carmen, EH, 'Masochistic personality disorder DSM-IIIR: critique', unpublished paper, 1985

Carmen, EH, Rieker, PR and Mills, T, 'Victims of violence and psychiatric illness' (1984) 141 American Journal of Psychiatry 378

Cassel, J, *The Secret Plague: Venereal Disease in Canada, 1838–1939*, 1987, Toronto, ON: University of Toronto Press

Castel, R, *La gestion des risques: de l'antipsychiatrie à l'après psychanalyse*, 1981, Paris: Editions de Minuit

Castel, R, *Les métamorphoses de la question sociale. Une chronique du salariat*, 1995, Paris: Fayard

Castel, R, Castel, R and Lovell, A, *The Psychiatric Society*, 1982, New York: Columbia University Press

Castel, R and Harroche, C, *Propriété privée, propriété sociale, propriété de soi. Entretien sur la construction de l'individu moderne*, 2001, Paris: Fayard

Chamberlin, J, 'Women's oppression and psychiatric oppression', in Smith, D and David, S (eds), *Women Look at Psychiatry*, 1975, Vancouver, BC: Press Gang, pp 39–52

Chamberlin, J, *On Our Own: Patient-Controlled Alternatives to the Mental Health System*, 1979, New York: McGraw-Hill

Chamberlin, J, 'The ex-inmates' movement' (1990) 11 Journal of Mind and Behavior 323

Chan, W, 'Legal equality and domestic homicide' (1997) 25 International Journal of the Sociology of Law 203

Chan, W, *Women, Murder and Justice*, 2001, Basingstoke: Palgrave

Chan, W and Mirchandani, K (eds), *Crimes of Colour: Racialization and the Criminal Justice System in Canada*, 2001, Peterborough, ON: Broadview

Chan, W and Rigakos, GA, 'Risk, crime and gender' (2002) 42 British Journal of Criminology 743

Chandler, DB, *Capital Punishment in Canada: A Sociological Study of Repressive Law*, 1976, Toronto, ON: McClelland and Stewart

Chandra, PS and Chaturvedi, SK, 'Cultural variations of premenstrual experience' (1989) 35 International Journal of Social Psychiatry 343

Chesler, P, *Women and Madness*, 1972, New York: Doubleday

Chigwada-Bailey, R, *Black Women's Experiences of Criminal Justice*, 1997, Winchester: Waterside Press

Chunn, DE, 'Regulating the poor in Ontario: from police courts to family courts', in Loo, T and McLean, LR (eds), *Historical Perspectives on Law and Society in Canada*, 1994, Toronto, ON: Copp Clark, pp 184–98

Chunn, DE, 'A little sex can be a dangerous thing: regulating sexuality, venereal disease, and reproduction in British Columbia, 1919–1945', in Boyd, SB (ed), *Challenging the Public/Private Divide: Feminism, Law and Public Policy*, 1997, Toronto, ON: University of Toronto Press, pp 62–86

Chunn, DE and Lacombe, D (eds), *Law as a Gendering Practice*, 2000, Don Mills, ON: Oxford University Press

Chunn, DE and Menzies, R, 'Gender, madness and crime: the reproduction of patriarchal and class relations in a psychiatric court clinic' (1990) 1 The Journal of Human Justice 33

Chunn, DE and Menzies, R, 'Out of mind, out of law: the regulation of "criminally insane" women inside British Columbia's public mental hospitals, 1888–1973' (1998) 10 Canadian Journal of Women and the Law 1–32

Chunn, DE, Adamoski, R and Menzies, R, *Contesting Canadian Citizenship: Historical Readings*, 2002, Peterborough, ON: Broadview

Cohen, N, '661 new crimes – and counting' (2003) New Statesman 18

Cohen, NL and Tsemberis, S, 'Emergency psychiatric intervention on the street' (1991) 52 New Directions for Mental Health Services 3

Cohen, S, *Visions of Social Control: Crime, Punishment and Classification*, 1985, Cambridge: Polity

Colaizzi, J, *Homicidal Insanity, 1800–1985*, 1989, Tuscaloosa, AL: University of Alabama Press

Coleborne, C, 'Making "mad" populations in settler colonies: the work of law and medicine in the creation of the colonial asylum', in Kirkby, D and Coleborne, C (eds), *Law, History and Colonialism: The Reach of Empire*, 2001, Manchester: Manchester University Press, pp 106–22

Coleborne, C and MacKinnon, D (eds), *'Madness' in Australia: Histories, Heritage and the Asylum*, 2003, Brisbane: University of Queensland Press

Coleman, L, *The Reign of Error: Psychiatry, Authority, and Law*, 1984, Boston, MA: Beacon Press

Collier, R, *Masculinity, Law and the Family*, 1995, London: Routledge

Collins, A, *In the Sleep Room: The Story of the CIA Brainwashing Experiments in Canada*, 1988, Toronto, ON: Lester and Orpen Dennys

Comack, E, *Feminist Engagement With the Law: The Legal Recognition of the Battered Woman Syndrome*, 1993, Ottawa, ON: Canadian Research Institute for the Advancement of Women

Comack, E, *Women in Trouble*, 1996, Halifax, NS: Fernwood

Comack, E (ed), *Locating Law: Race/Class/Gender Connections*, 1999, Halifax, NS: Fernwood

Comité de la santé mentale du Québec, *Défis. De la reconfiguration des services de santé mentale. Pour une réponse efficace et efficiente aux besoins des personnes atteintes de troubles mentaux graves* (rapport soumis au ministre de la Santé et des Services sociaux), 1997, Québec: Gouvernement du Québec, Ministère de la Santé et des Services sociaux

Cooper, D, *Psychiatry and Anti-Psychiatry*, 1967, London: Paladin

Cooperstock, R, 'Psychotropic drug use among women' (1976) 115 Canadian Medical Association Journal 760

Cooperstock, R, 'Sex differences in psychotropic drug use' (1978) 12 Social Science and Medicine 176

Cott, NF, *The Bonds of Womanhood: 'Women's Sphere' in New England, 1780–1835*, 1977, New Haven, CT: Yale University Press

Courtois, CA, *Recollections of Sexual Abuse: Treatment Principles and Guidelines*, 1999, New York: Norton

Crean, S, 'Anna Karenina, Scarlett O'Hara, and Gail Bezaire: child custody and family law', in Minas, A (ed), *Gender Basics: Feminist Perspectives on Women and Men*, 2nd edn, 2000, Thomson/Wadsworth, pp 510–14

Crenshaw, K, 'Mapping the margins: identity politics, intersectionality, and violence against women' (1991) 43 Stanford Law Review 1243

Criminal Justice Commission, *Aboriginal Witnesses in Queensland's Criminal Courts*, 1996, Brisbane: Criminal Justice Commission

Crow, I, *The Treatment and Rehabilitation of Offenders*, 2001, London: Sage

Cunneen, C and Kerley, K, 'Indigenous women and criminal justice: some comments on the Australian situation', in Hazlehurst, K (ed), *Perceptions of Justice: Issues in Indigenous and Community Empowerment*, 1995, Aldershot, Sydney: Avebury, pp 71–94

Dain, N, 'Psychiatry and anti-psychiatry in the United States', in Micale, MS and Porter, R (eds), *Discovering the History of Psychiatry*, 1994, Oxford: Oxford University Press

Dallaire, B, McCubbin, M, Morin, P and Cohen, D, 'Civil commitment due to mental illness and dangerousness: the union of law and psychiatry within a treatment-control system', in Busfield, J (ed), *Rethinking the Sociology of Mental Health*, 2001, Oxford: Blackwell, pp 133–52

Dalley, B, '"From demi-mondes to slaveys": a study of the Te Oranga Reformatory for Delinquent Women, 1900–1918', unpublished MA thesis, 1987, Massey University

Daly, K, 'Structure and practice of familial-based justice in a criminal court' (1987) 21 Law and Society Review 267

Daly, K and Chesney-Lind, M, 'Feminism and criminology' (1988) 5 Justice Quarterly 498

Dalziel, R, 'The colonial helpmeet: women's role and the vote in nineteenth-century New Zealand', in Brookes, B, Macdonald, C and Tennant, M (eds), *Women in History*, 1986, Wellington: Bridget Williams Books, pp 55–68

Damousi, J, *Depraved and Disorderly: Female Convicts, Sexuality and Gender in Colonial Australia*, 1997, Cambridge: Cambridge University Press

Dan, AJ and Monagle, L, 'Socio-cultural influences on women's experiences of perimenstrual symptoms', in Gold, JH and Severino, SK (eds), *Premenstrual Dysphoria: Myths and Realities*, 1994, London: American Psychiatric Press, pp 39–52

Davies, MJ, 'The patients' world: British Columbia's mental health facilities, 1910–1935', unpublished MA thesis, 1987, University of Waterloo

de la Cour, L and Reaume, G, 'Patient perspectives in psychiatric case files', in Iacovetta, F and Mitchinson, W (eds), *On the Case: Explorations in Social History*, 1998, Toronto: University of Toronto Press, pp 242–65

Deakin, J and Spencer, J, 'Women behind bars: explanations and implications' (2003) 42 Howard Journal of Criminal Justice 123

Dear, MJ and Wolch, JR, *Landscapes of Despair*, 1987, Princeton, NJ: Princeton University Press

Dell, S, 'Diminished responsibility reconsidered' (1982) Criminal Law Review 809

Dell, S and Gibbens, TCN, 'Remands of women offenders for medical reports' (1971) 11 Medicine, Science and the Law 117

Department of Health/HM Prison Service, *Changing the Outlook: A Strategy for Developing and Modernising Mental Health Services in Prison*, 2001, London: DoH

Department of Health, *Women's Mental Health: Into the Mainstream: Strategic Development of Mental Health Care for Women*, 2002, London: DoH

Devlin, A, *Invisible Women*, 1998, Winchester: Waterside Press

Digby, A, *Madness, Morality and Medicine: A Study of the York Retreat 1796–1914*, 1985, Cambridge: Cambridge University Press

Digman, J, 'Historical antecedents of the five-factor model', in Costa Jr, P and Widiger, T (eds), *Personality Disorders and the Five-Factor Model*, 1994, Washington, DC: American Psychological Association, pp 13–18

Dobash, RP and Dobash, RE, *Violence Against Wives*, 1979, New York: Free Press

Dobash, RP, Dobash, RE and Gutteridge, S, *The Imprisonment of Women*, 1986, Oxford: Basil Blackwell

Doe, J, 'Testimony' (1993) 3 Issues in Child Abuse Accusations 154

Dorvil, H, *De l'Annonciation à Montréal. Histoire de la folie dans la communauté 1962–1987*, 1988, Montréal, QC: Editions Emile-Nelligan

Dorvil, H, 'Reform and reshaping mental health services in the Montreal area' (1997) 43 International Journal of Social Psychiatry 164

Douglas, M, *Risk Acceptability to the Social Sciences*, 1992, London: Routledge and Kegan Paul

Draine, J and Solomon, P, 'Describing and evaluating jail diversion services for persons with serious mental illness' (1999) 50 Psychiatric Services 56

Dubay, D, 'Building alliances' (1985) 7 Madness Network News 3

Dubinsky, K and Iacovetta, F, 'Murder, womanly virtue, and motherhood: the case of Angelina Napolitano, 1911–1922' (1991) 72 Canadian Historical Review 505

Dutton, MA, 'Understanding women's response to domestic violence: a redefinition of Battered Woman Syndrome' (1993) 21 Hofstra Law Review 1191

Dutton, MA, 'Impact of evidence concerning battering and its effects in criminal trials involving battered women', in US Department of Justice and US Department of Health and Human Services, *The Validity and Use of Evidence Concerning Battering and Its Effects in Criminal Trials: Report Responding to Section 40507 of the Violence Against Women Act*, 1996, pt III, pp 1–18, www.ojp.usdoj.gov/ocpa/94Guides/Trials/welcome.html

Dutton, MA, *Expert Testimony in Cases Involving Battered Women: A Resource Monograph*, prepared for the National Association of Women Judges, 1997

Dwyer, E, *Homes for the Mad: Life Inside Two Nineteenth-Century Asylums*, 1987, New Brunswick, NJ: Rutgers University Press

Eaton, M, *Justice For Women? Family, Court and Social Control*, 1986, Milton Keynes: Open University Press

Eaves, D, Ogloff, JRP and Roesch, R (eds), *Mental Disorders and the Criminal Code: Legal Background and Contemporary Perspectives*, 2000, Burnaby, BC: Simon Fraser University, Mental Health, Law and Policy Institute

Edgar, K, 'The criminal justice net widens' (2003) 60 Prison Report 23

Edwards, SSM, *Women on Trial: A Study of the Female Suspect, Defendant, and Offender in the Criminal Law and Criminal Justice Systems*, 1984, Manchester: Manchester University Press

Ehrenreich, B and English, D, *For Her Own Good: 150 Years of the Experts' Advice to Women*, 1979, London: Pluto

Eigen, JP, 'Criminal lunacy in modern early modern England: did gender make a difference?' (1998) 21 International Journal of Law and Psychiatry 409

Elliott, EM, 'The seventh circle of hell: the social responses to murder in Canada', unpublished PhD thesis, 1996, Burnaby, BC: Simon Fraser University

Elphick, J, 'What's wrong with Emma? The feminist debate in colonial Auckland', in Brookes, B, Macdonald, C and Tennant, M (eds), *Women in History*, 1986, Wellington: Bridget Williams Books, pp 69–86

Ernst, W, *Mad Tales from The Raj: The European Insane in British India, 1800–1858*, 1991, London and New York: Routledge

Evans, P, *Verbal Abuse: Survivors Speak Out on Relationship and Recovery*, 1993, Avon, MA: Adams Media

Everett, B, 'Something is happening: the contemporary consumer and psychiatric survivor movement in historical context' (1994) 1(2) Journal of Mind and Behavior 55

Fairclough, N, *Discourse and Social Change*, 1994, Cambridge: Polity

Faith, K, *Unruly Women: The Politics of Confinement and Resistance*, 1993, Vancouver, BC: Press Gang

Faluyi-Smythe, G, 'Prison psychologists: the real deal or just an illusion?' (2003) 40 Inside Time 14

Fee, D (ed), *Psychology and the Postmodern: Mental Illness as Discourse and Experience*, 2000, London: Sage

Feeley, M and Little, DL, 'The vanishing female: the decline of women in the criminal process' (1991) 25 Law and Society Review 719

Feeley, M and Simon, J, 'The new penology: notes on the emerging strategy of corrections and its implications' (1992) 30 Criminology 452

Fegan, EV, 'Ideology after discourse: a re-conceptualisation for feminist analyses of law' (1996) 23 Journal of Law and Society 173

Fegan, EV, 'Subjects of regulation/resistance? Post-modern feminism and women's agency in abortion decision-making' (1999) 7 Feminist Legal Studies 241

Fegan, EV, 'Recovering women: intimate images and legal strategy' (2002) 11 Social and Legal Studies 155

Fegan, EV and Fennell, P, 'Feminist perspectives on mental health law', in Sheldon, S and Thomson, M (eds), Feminist Perspectives on Health Care Law, 1998, London: Cavendish Publishing, pp 73–96

Fegan, EV and Rebouche, R, 'Northern Ireland's abortion law: the morality of silence and the censure of agency' (2003) 11 Feminist Legal Studies 221

Fennell, P, 'Diversion of mentally disordered offenders from custody' (1991) Criminal Law Review 333

Ferguson, G, 'Control of the insane in British Columbia, 1849–78: care, cure, or confinement?', in McLaren, J, Menzies, R and Chunn, DE (eds), Regulating Lives: Historical Essays on the State, Society, the Individual, and the Law, 2002, Vancouver, BC: University of British Columbia Press, pp 63–96

Ferraro, K, 'The words change, but the melody lingers: the persistence of the Battered Woman Syndrome in criminal cases involving battered women' (2003) 9 Violence Against Women 110

Finlayson, A, Making Sense of New Labour, 2003, London: Lawrence and Wishart

Finn, P and Sullivan, M, 'Police handling of the mentally ill: sharing responsibility with the mental health system' (1989) 17 Journal of Criminal Justice 1

Finnane, M, 'Asylums, families and the state' (1985) 20 History Workshop Journal 134

First, MB, Bell, CC, Cuthbert, B et al, 'Personality disorders and relational disorders: a research agenda for addressing crucial gaps in DSM', in Kupfer, D, Michael, B and Regier, D (eds), A Research Agenda for DSM-V, 2002, Washington, DC: American Psychiatric Association, pp 123–99

Fish, V, 'Gender bias in differential diagnosis of "posttraumatic stress disorder", "borderline personality disorder", "dissociative identity disorder", and "schizophrenia"', in Caplan, PJ and Cosgrove, L (eds), Bias in Psychiatric Diagnosis, 2004, Lanham, MD: Jason Aronson/Rowman & Littlefield, pp 213–20

Fleming, PJ, 'Eugenics in New Zealand 1900–1940', unpublished MA thesis, 1981, Massey University

Foner, J, 'A double whammy', in Grobe, J (ed), Beyond Bedlam, 1995, Chicago, IL: Third Side Press, pp 133–47

Forsythe, B and Melling, J (eds), Insanity, Institutions and Society, 1800–1914: A Social History of Madness in Comparative Perspective, 1999, London: Routledge

Foucault, M, Madness and Civilization: A History of Insanity in the Age of Reason, 1965, New York: Pantheon

Foucault, M, Discipline and Punish: The Birth of the Prison, 1977, New York: Pantheon

Foucault, M, 'About the concept of the "dangerous individual" in 19th century legal psychiatry' (1978) 1 International Journal of Law and Psychiatry 1

Foucault, M, Discipline and Punish, 1979a, Harmondsworth: Penguin

Foucault, M, The History of Sexuality, Part 1, 1979b, London: Penguin

Foucault, M, *Birth of the Clinic*, 1989, London: Penguin

Foucault, M, 'Governmentality', in Gordon, C and Miller, P (eds), *The Foucault Effect: Studies in Governmentality*, 1991, Chicago, IL: University of Chicago Press, pp 87–104

Fox, M, 'Feminist perspectives on theories of punishment', in Nicolson, D and Bibbings, L (eds), *Feminist Perspectives on Criminal Law*, 2000, London: Cavendish Publishing, pp 49–70

Fox, M and Murphy, T, 'Irish abortion: seeking refuge in a jurisprudence of doubt and delegation' (1992) 19 Journal of Law and Society 454

Fox, R, *So Far Disordered in Mind: Insanity in California 1870–1930*, 1978, Berkeley, CA: University of California Press

Frank, LR, *The History of Shock Treatment*, 1978, San Francisco, CA: self-published

Fraser, D, 'Still crazy after all these years: a critique of diminished responsibility', in Yeo, SMH (ed), *Partial Excuses to Murder*, 1991, Sydney: The Federation Press, pp 112–24

Fraser, N, *Unruly Practices: Power, Discourse and Gender in Contemporary Social Theory*, 1989, Cambridge: Polity

Freire, P, *Pedagogy of the Oppressed*, 1970, New York: The Seabury Press

Freund, M, 'The politics of naming: constructing prostitutes and regulating women in Vancouver, 1939–45', in McLaren, J, Menzies, R and Chunn, DE (eds), *Regulating Lives: Historical Essays on the State, Society, the Individual, and the Law*, 2002, Vancouver, BC: University of British Columbia Press, pp 231–58

Freyd, P, 'The science of memory: apply with caution' (1996) 10 Traumatic Stress Points 18

Freyd, P and Goldstein, E, *Memory Wars: Recovered vs False Memories*, 1998a, Altadena, CA: Skeptics Society

Freyd, P and Goldstein, E, *Smiling Through Tears*, 1998b, Boca Raton, FL: Upton

Friedberg, J, *Shock Treatment Is Not Good For Your Brain: A Neurologist Challenges the Psychiatric Myth*, 1976, San Francisco, CA: Glide Publications

Friedman, S, Smith, L, Fogel, D, Paradis, C, Viswandathan, R, Ackerman, R and Trappler, B, 'The incidence and influence of early traumatic life events in patients with panic disorder: a comparison with other psychiatric outpatients' (2002) 16 Journal of Anxiety Disorders 259

Friendly Spike Theatre, *The Girls of Grandview*, 2002, Live Performance, Toronto, Tarragon Theatre

Frigon, S (ed), 'Femmes et enfermement au Canada: une décennie de réformes' (2002) 35 Criminologie

Frisman, L, Sturges, GE, Baranosky, MV and Levinson, M, 'Connecticut's Criminal Justice Diversion Program – a comprehensive community forensic mental health model', in Landsberg, G and Smiley, A (eds), *Forensic Mental Health: Working With Offenders with Mental Illness*, 2001, Kingston, NJ: Civic Research Institute

Funk, W, *What Difference Does it Make?*, 1998, Cranbrook: Wild Flower Publishing

Gamberg, H and Thomson, A, *The Illusion of Prison Reform: Corrections in Canada*, 1984, New York: Peter Lang

Gardner, RA, *The Parental Alienation Syndrome: A Guide for Mental Health and Legal Professionals*, 2nd edn, 1998, Cresskill, NJ: Creative Therapeutics

Garfinkel, H, *Studies in Ethnomethodology*, 1967, New York: Prentice Hall

Garland, D, *Punishment and Welfare: A History of Penal Strategies*, 1985, London: Gower

Garland, D, *Punishment and Modern Society*, 1990, Oxford: Oxford University Press

Garland, D, *The Culture of Control*, 2001, Oxford: Oxford University Press

Garton, S, *Medicine and Madness: A Social History of Insanity in New South Wales, 1880–1940*, 1988, Sydney: NSW University Press

Gavigan, SAM, 'Women's crimes: new perspectives and old theories', in Adelberg, E and Currie, C (eds), *Too Few to Count: Canadian Women in Conflict With Law*, 1987, Vancouver, BC: Press Gang

Gavigan, SAM, 'Petit treason in eighteenth century England: women's inequality before the law' (1989–90) 3 Canadian Journal of Women and the Law 335

Gavigan, SAM, 'Feminism, familial ideology and family law: a perilous ménage à trois', in Luxton, M (ed), *Feminism and Families: Critical Policies and Changing Practices*, 1997, Halifax, NS: Fernwood Publishing, pp 98–123

Geller, J and Harris, M, *Women of the Asylum: Voices From Behind the Walls, 1840–1945*, 1994, New York: Anchor Doubleday

Gelsthorpe, L and Morris, A, 'Women and imprisonment: a penal paradox' (2002) 2 Criminal Justice 277

Gerrard, N, 'Damned if you do ...' (2001) *The Observer*, 22 April

Gibbs, B, Butler, A and Beck, J, 'Childhood abuse, depression, and anxiety in adult psychiatric outpatients' (2003) 17 Depression and Anxiety 226

Goff, C, *Corrections in Canada*, 1999, Cincinnati, OH: Anderson

Goffman, E, *Asylums: Essays on the Social Situation of Mental Patients and Other Inmates*, 1961, Garden City, NY: Anchor Books

Goldstein, MS, 'The politics of Thomas Szasz: a sociological view' (1980) 27 Social Problems 570

Goodwin, JM, Cheeves, K and Connell, V, 'Borderline and other severe symptoms in adult survivors of incestuous abuse' (1990) 20 Psychiatric Annals 22

Goodwin, S, 'Sue Goodwin', in Shimrat, I (ed), *Call Me Crazy*, 1997, Vancouver, BC: Press Gang, pp 112–14

Gordon, L, *Heroes of Their Own Lives*, 1988, New York: Viking Penguin

Gorman, K, 'Cognitive behaviourism and the holy grail: the quest for a universal means of managing offender risk' (2001) 48 Probation Journal 3

Gove, WR and Tudor, JF, 'Adult sex roles and mental illness' (1973) 78 American Journal of Sociology 812

Greenhalgh, NM, Wylie, K, Rix, KJB and Tamlyn, D, 'Pilot mental health assessment and diversion scheme for an English metropolitan petty sessional division' (1996) 36 Medicine, Science, and the Law 52

Greenspan, M, *A New Approach to Women and Therapy*, 1983, New York: McGraw-Hill

Greenwood, FM and Boissery, B, *Uncertain Justice: Canadian Women and Capital Punishment, 1754–1953*, 2000, Toronto, ON: Dundurn

Grob, G, *Mental Institutions in America: Social Policy to 1875*, 1973, New York: Free Press

Grobe, J, (ed), *Beyond Bedlam*, 1995, Chicago, IL: Third Side Press

Habermas, J, *The Philosophical Discourse on Modernity: Twelve Lectures*, 1987, Cambridge, MA: Massachusetts Institute of Technology

Hacking, I, 'Making up people', in Heller, T, Sosna, M and Wellbery, D (eds), *Reconstructing Individualism: Autonomy, Individuality and the Self in Western Thought*, 1986, Stanford, CA: Stanford University Press, pp 222–36

Halttunen, K, *Murder Most Foul: The Killer and the American Gothic Imagination*, 1998, Cambridge, MA: Harvard University Press

Hamilton, JA and Gallant, S, 'Problematic aspects of diagnosing premenstrual phase dysphoria: recommendations for psychological research and practice' (1990) 21 Professional Psychology: Research and Practice 60

Hannah-Moffat, K, 'Re-forming the prison – rethinking our ideals', in Hannah-Moffat, K and Shaw, M (eds), *An Ideal Prison? Critical Essays on Women's Imprisonment in Canada*, 2000, Halifax, NS: Fernwood, pp 30–40

Hannah-Moffat, K, *Punishment in Disguise: Penal Governance and Canadian Women's Imprisonment*, 2001, Toronto, ON: University of Toronto Press

Hannah-Moffat, K and Shaw, M (eds), *An Ideal Prison? Critical Essays on Women's Imprisonment in Canada*, 2000, Halifax, NS: Fernwood

Hannah-Moffat, K and Shaw, M, 'Introduction', in Hannah-Moffat, K and Shaw, M (eds), *An Ideal Prison? Critical Essays on Women's Imprisonment in Canada*, 2001, Halifax, NS: Fernwood, pp 11–27

Hannah-Moffat, K and Shaw, M, 'The meaning of "risk" in women's prisons: a critique', in Bloom, B (ed), *Gendered Justice: Addressing Female Offenders*, 2003, Durham, NC: Carolina Academic Press, pp 45–68

Harden, J and Hill, M (eds), *Breaking the Rules: Women in Prison and Feminist Therapy*, 1997, Binghamton, NY: Haworth

Harding, S (ed), *Feminism and Methodology*, 1987, Indianapolis, IN: Indiana University Press

Harding, S, *Whose Science? Whose Knowledge? Thinking From Women's Lives*, 1991, Milton Keynes: Open University Press

Harre, R and Secord, PF, *The Explanation of Social Behaviour*, 1972, Oxford: Basil Blackwell

Harris, R, *Murders and Madness: Medicine, Law, and Society in the Fin de Siècle*, 1989, Oxford: Clarendon

Harris, R, 'Mental disorder and social order: underlying themes in crime management', in Webb, D and Harris, R (eds), *Mentally Disordered Offenders: Managing People Nobody Owns*, 1999, London: Routledge, pp 10–26

Harrison, WF, 'Why I provide abortions' (2002) Summer, British Columbia Pro-Choice Press 15

Hart, L, *Fatal Women: Lesbian Sexuality and the Mark of Aggression*, 1994, London: Routledge

Hartman, MS, *Victorian Murderesses: A True History of Thirteen Respectable French and English Women Accused of Unspeakable Crimes*, 1985, Guernsey: Robson

Harvey, L, Burnham, RW, Kendall, K and Pease, K, 'Gender differences in criminal justice: an international comparison' (1992) 32 British Journal of Criminology 208

Hay, D, Linebaugh, P, Rule, JG, Thompson, EP and Winslow, C, *Albion's Fatal Tree: Crime and Society in Eighteenth-Century England*, 1975, New York: Pantheon

Heidensohn, F, *Women and Crime*, 2nd edn, 1996, Basingstoke: Macmillan

Heidensohn, F, 'Gender and crime', in Maguire, M, Morgan, R and Reiner, R (eds), *The Oxford Handbook of Criminology*, 2002, Oxford: Oxford University Press, pp 491–530

Henning, T, 'Psychological explanations in sentencing women in Tasmania' (1995) 28 Australian and New Zealand Journal of Criminology 298

Henriques, J, Hollway, W, Urwin, C, Venn, C and Walkerdine, V, *Changing the Subject: Psychology, Social Regulation and Subjectivity*, 1984, London: Methuen

Henwood, K and Pigeon, N, 'Beyond the qualitative paradigm: a framework for introducing diversity within qualitative psychology' (1994) 4 Journal of Community and Applied Psychology 225

Her Majesty's Inspectorate of Prisons for England and Wales, *Women in Prison: A Thematic Review by HM Chief Inspector of Prisons*, 1997, London: HMSO

Her Majesty's Chief Inspector of Prisons for England and Wales, *HM Prison Eastwood Park, Report of an Unannounced Follow-Up Inspection, 1–3 October 2001*, 2002a, London: HMSO

Her Majesty's Chief Inspector of Prisons for England and Wales, *Report on a Full Announced Inspection of HM Prison and Young Offenders Institution Styal, 4–8 February 2002*, 2002b, London: HMSO

Her Majesty's Chief Inspector of Prisons for England and Wales, *HM Prison Holloway, Report on a Full Announced Inspection, 8–12 July 2002*, 2002c, London: HMSO

Her Majesty's Inspectorate of Prisons for England and Wales, *Annual Report of HM Chief Inspector of Prisons for England and Wales*, 2002, London: HMSO

Her Majesty's Prison Service, *HM Prison Service Annual Report and Accounts, April 2001–March 2002*, 2002, London: HMSO

Herman, JL, 'Complex PTSD: a syndrome in survivors of prolonged and repeated trauma' (1992a) 5 Journal of Traumatic Stress 377

Herman, JL, *Trauma and Recovery: The Aftermath of Violence – From Domestic Abuse to Political Terror*, 1992b, New York: Basic Books

Herman, JL, Perry, JC and van der Kolk, BA, 'Childhood trauma in borderline personality disorder' (1989) 146 American Journal of Psychiatry 460

Hiday, VA, 'Civil commitment: a review of empirical research' (1988) 6 Behavioral Sciences and the Law 15

Hill, A, *Speaking Truth to Power*, 1998, New York: Doubleday

Hillyard, P, Sim, J, Tombs, S and Whyte, D, '"Leaving a stain upon the silence": contemporary criminology and the politics of dissent' (2004) 44 British Journal of Criminology 1

Hoff, RA, Baranosky, MV, Buchanan, J, Zonana, H and Rosenheck, RA, 'The effects of a jail diversion program on incarceration: a retrospective cohort study' (1999) 27 Journal of the American Academy of Psychiatry and the Law 377

Hollway, W, *Subjectivity and Method in Psychology: Gender, Meaning and* Science, 1989, London: Sage

Holstein, JA, *Court-Ordered Insanity: Interpretive Practice and Involuntary Commitment*, 1993, New York: Aldine de Gruyter

Home Office, *The Government's Strategy for Women Offenders*, 2000, London: HMSO

Home Office, *Statistics for Women and the Criminal Justice System*, 2002, London: HMSO

Home Office, *Prison Statistics England and Wales 2001*, Cm 5743, 2003, London: HMSO

Horlick-Jones, T, 'The language and technologies of risk', in Gray, N, Laing, J and Noaks, L (eds), *Criminal Justice, Mental Health and the Politics of Risk*, 2002, London: Cavendish Publishing, pp 149–68

Horney, K, 'Die praemenstruellen Verstimmungen' (1931) 5 Zeitschrift fuer Psychoanalytische Paedagogik 1, reprinted in Horney, K, *Feminine Psychology*, 1967, London: Norton, pp 99–106

Horwitz, AV, *Creating Mental Illness*, 2002, Chicago, IL: University of Chicago Press

Houston, RA, 'Madness and gender in the long eighteenth century' (2002) 27 Social History 309

Hudson, B, *Understanding Justice*, 1996, Buckingham: Open University Press

Hudson, B, 'Punishing the poor: dilemmas of justice and difference', in Heffernan, W and Kleinig, J (eds), *From Social Justice to Criminal Justice: Poverty and the Administration of Criminal Law*, 2000, New York: Oxford University Press, pp 189–216

Hudson, B, 'Gender issues in penal policy and penal theory', in Carlen, P (ed), *Women and Punishment: The Struggle for Justice*, 2002, Cullompton: Willan Publishing, pp 21–46

Hudson, D, 'You can't commit violence against an object: women, psychiatry and psychosurgery', in Hanmer, J and Maynard, M (eds), *Women, Violence and Social Control*, 1987, Atlantic Highlands, NJ: Humanities Press International, pp 110–21

Hughes, J, 'The madness of separate spheres: insanity and masculinity in Victorian Alabama', in Carnes, M and Griffen, C (eds), *Meanings for Manhood: Constructions of Masculinity in Victorian America*, 1990, Chicago, IL: University of Chicago Press, pp 53–66

Hunter, MS, Ussher, J, Browne, S, Cariss, M, Jelly, R and Katz, M, 'A randomised comparison of psychological (cognitive behaviour therapy), medical (fluoxetine) and combined treatment for women with premenstrual dysphoric disorder' (2002) 23 Journal of Psychosomatic Obstetrics and Gynaecology 193

Hustak, A, *They Were Hanged*, 1987, Toronto, ON: Lorimer

Ignatieff, M, 'Total institutions and working classes: a review essay' (1983) 15 History Workshop Journal 167

Ingleby, D (ed), *Critical Psychiatry: The Politics of Mental Health*, 1980, New York: Pantheon

Ingleby, D, 'Mental health and social order', in Cohen, S and Scull, A (eds), *Social Control and the State*, 1983, New York: Macmillan, pp 141–88

Ingratta, B and Patriasz, L (Producer), *Still Sane*, 1984, Video, Vancouver, BC: Women in Focus

Inquest, *Response to the Ministerial Statement on Styal Prison and the Ombudsman Inquiry*, 2004, London: Inquest

Jaffe, PG, Wolfe, DA and Wilson, SK, *Children of Battered Women*, 1990, Newbury Park, CA: Sage

James, DV and Hamilton, LW, 'The Clerkenwell scheme: assessing efficacy and cost of a psychiatric liaison service to a magistrates' court' (1991) 303 British Medical Journal 282

James, DV and Hamilton, LW, 'Setting up psychiatric liaison schemes to magistrates' courts: problems and practicalities' (1992) 32 Medicine, Science, and the Law 167

Jones, A, *Women Who Kill*, 1996, Boston, MA: Beacon Press

Jones, J, *Medea's Daughters: Forming and Performing the Woman Who Kills*, 2003, Columbus, OH: Ohio State University Press

Jordanova, LJ, 'Mental illness, mental health: changing norms and expectations', in The Cambridge Women's Studies Group (ed), *Women in Society: Interdisciplinary Essays*, 1981, London: Virago, pp 95–114

Joseph, PLA and Potter, M, 'Diversion from custody. I: Psychiatric assessment at the magistrates' court' (1993a) 162 British Journal of Psychiatry 325

Joseph, PLA and Potter, M, 'Diversion from custody. II: Effect on hospital and prison resources' (1993b) 162 British Journal of Psychiatry 330

Kaplan, M, 'A woman's view of DSM-III' (1983) 38 American Psychologist 786

Karls, J and Wandrei, K, 'PIE: a new language for social work' (1992) 37 Social Work 80

Karls, J and Wandrei, K, 'PIE: a system for describing and classifying problems of social functioning', in Karls, J and Wandrei, K (eds), *Person-in-Environment System: The PIE Classification System for Social Functioning Problems*, 1994a, Washington, DC: NASW Press, pp 3–21

Karls, J and Wandrei, K, *PIE Manual: Person-in-Environment System*, 1994b, Washington, DC: NASW Press

Kaslow, F (ed), *Handbook of Relational Diagnosis and Dysfunctional Family Patterns*, 1996, New York: John Wiley and Sons

Kaysen, S, *Girl Interrupted*, 1993, New York: Turtle Bay Books

Keat, R, 'Positivism and statistics in social science', in Irvine, J, Miles, I and Evans, J (eds), *Demystifying Social Statistics*, 1979, London: Routledge, pp 75–86

Keenan, C, 'The same old story: examining women's involvement in the initial stages of the criminal justice system', in Nicolson, D and Bibbings, L (eds), *Feminist Perspectives on Criminal Law*, 2000, London: Cavendish Publishing, pp 29–48

Kelleher, MD and Kelleher, CL, *Murder Most Rare: The Female Serial Killer*, 1998, Westport, CT: Praeger

Keller, EF, *Reflections on Gender and Science*, 1985, London: Yale University Press

Keller, R, 'Madness and colonisation: psychiatry in the British and French Empires, 1800–1962' (2001) 35 Journal of Social History 295

Kelm, M-E, '"The only place likely to do her any good": the admission of women to British Columbia's Provincial Hospital for the Insane' (1992) 66 BC Studies 66

Kelm, M-E, 'Women, families and the Provincial Hospital for the Insane, British Columbia, 1905–1915' (1994) 19 Journal of Family History 177

Kendall, K, 'The politics of premenstrual syndrome: implications for feminist justice' (1991) 2 The Journal of Human Justice 77

Kendall, K, 'Mental illness – tales of madness: from the asylum to Oprah', in Schissel, B and Mahood, L (eds), *Social Control in Canada: Issues in the Social Construction of Deviance*, 1996, Toronto, ON: Oxford University Press, pp 111–19

Kendall, K, 'Beyond Grace: criminal lunatic women in Victorian Canada' (1999a) 19 Canadian Woman Studies 110

Kendall, K, 'Criminal lunatic women in 19th century Canada' (1999b) 11 Forum on Corrections Research 46

Kendall, K, 'Psy-ence fiction: inventing the mentally-disordered female prisoner', in Hannah-Moffat, K and Shaw, M (eds), *An Ideal Prison? Critical Essays on Women's Imprisonment in Canada*, 2000, Halifax, NS: Fernwood, pp 82–93

Kendall, K, 'Time to think again about cognitive behavioural programmes', in Carlen, P (ed), *Women and Punishment*, 2002, Cullompton: Willan Publishing, pp 182–98

Kendall, R, 'Five criteria for an improved taxonomy of mental disorders', in Helzer, J and Hudziak, J (eds), *Defining Psychopathology in the 21st Century: DSM-V and Beyond*, 2002, Washington, DC: American Psychiatric Association, pp 3–17

Kennedy, D, *On a Killing Day*, 1992, Chicago, IL: Bonus Books

Kennedy, H, *Eve Was Framed: Women and British Justice*, 1993, London: Vintage

Kenney-Herbert, J, 'The health care of women prisoners in England and Wales: a literature review' (1999) 38 The Howard Journal 54

Kerwin, S, 'The Janet Smith Bill of 1924 and the language of race and nation in British Columbia' (1999) 121 BC Studies 83

Kessler, RC and Macleod, J, 'Social support and mental health in community samples', in Cohen, S and Syme, L (eds), *Social Support and Health*, 1985, New York: Academic Press, pp 620–31

Kesteven, S, 'Women who challenge' (2002) Summer, Safer Society 24

Kim, N and Ahn, W, 'Clinical psychologists' theory-based representations of mental disorders predict their diagnostic reasoning and memory' (2002) 131 Journal of Experimental Psychology: General 451

Kimball, M, 'Women, sex role stereotypes, and mental health: Catch 22', in Smith, D and David, S (eds), *Women Look at Psychiatry*, 1975, Vancouver, BC: Press Gang, pp 121–42

King, D, 'Religious leaders stand up in support of reproductive freedom' (2003) Chicago Newswire, 12 April

King, E, 'How the psychiatric profession views women', in Smith, D and David, S (eds), *Women Look at Psychiatry*, 1975, Vancouver, BC: Press Gang, pp 21–37

Kirk, SA and Kutchins, H, *The Selling of DSM: The Rhetoric of Science in Psychiatry*, 1992, New York: Aldine de Gruyter

Kirk, SA and Kutchins, H, 'How scientific is the DSM-IV?', paper presented at the American Psychological Association Convention, 1995, New York

Knelman, J, *Twisting in the Wind: The Murderess and the English Press*, 1998, Toronto, ON: University of Toronto Press

Koegel, P, 'Through a different lens: an anthropological perspective on the homeless mentally ill' (1992) 16 Culture, Medicine and Psychiatry 1

Koeske, R, 'Sociocultural factors in the premenstrual syndrome: review, critiques and future directions', paper presented at the Premenstrual Syndrome Workshop, 1983, Rockville, MD: NIMH, 14–15 April

Kramar, KJ, 'Unwilling mothers and unwanted babies: "infanticide" and medico-legal responsibility in 20th century Canadian legal discourse', 2000, PhD dissertation, University of Toronto

Kramer, M, *Psychiatric Services and the Changing Institutional Scene 1950–1975*, 1977, Washington, DC: National Institute of Mental Health

Kramer, R and Mitchell, T, *Walk Toward the Gallows: The Tragedy of Hilda Blake, Hanged 1899*, 2002, Don Mills, ON: Oxford University Press

Kuhn, T, *The Structure of Scientific Revolutions*, 3rd edn, 1996, Chicago, IL: University of Chicago Press

Kupers, T, *Prison Madness: The Mental Health Crisis Behind Bars and What We Must Do About It*, 1999, San Francisco, CA: Jossey-Bass

Kupfer, D, First, M and Regier, D (eds), *A Research Agenda for DSM-V*, 2002, Washington, DC: American Psychiatric Association

Kutchins, H and Kirk, SA, *Making Us Crazy: DSM: The Psychiatric Bible and the Creation of Mental Disorders*, 1997, New York: Free Press

Laberge, D, Landreville, P and Morin, D, 'The criminalization of mental illness: a complex process of interpretation', in Beaman, LG (ed), *New Perspectives on Deviance: The Construction of Deviance in Everyday Life*, 2000a, Scarborough, ON: Prentice Hall Allyn and Bacon Canada, pp 85–108

Laberge, D, Landreville, P and Morin, D, 'Pratiques de déjudiciarisation de la maladie mentale: le modèle de l'urgence psychosociale-justice' (2000b) 33 Criminologie 81

Laberge, D and Morin, D, *'Les clientèles psychiatrie-justice': problèmes de prise en charge et d'intervention*, 1992, Montréal, QC: Les cahiers du GRAPPP

Laberge, D and Morin, D, 'The overuse of criminal justice dispositions: failure of diversionary policies in the management of mental health problems' (1995) 18 International Journal of Law and Psychiatry 389

Labour Party, *Local Policy Forum 1998, Crime and Justice Consultation Paper*, 1998, London: The Labour Party

Labrum, B, '"For the better discharge of our duties": women's rights in Wanganui 1893–1903' (1990) 6 Women's Studies Journal 136

Labrum, B, 'Looking beyond the asylum: gender and the process of committal in Auckland, 1870–1910' (1992) 26 New Zealand Journal of History 125

Labrum, B, *Women's History: A Short Guide to Researching and Writing Women's History in New Zealand*, 1993, Wellington: NZ Historical Branch

Labrum, B and Dalley, B, *Fragments: New Zealand Social and Cultural History*, 2000, Auckland: Auckland UP

Lacey, N, *Unspeakable Subjects: Feminist Essays in Legal and Social Theory*, 1998, Oxford: Hart Publishing

Laing, RD, *The Divided Self: An Existential Study in Sanity and Madness*, 1969, London: Tavistock

Laing, RD, *Wisdom, Madness, and Folly: The Making of a Psychiatrist*, 1985, New York: McGraw-Hill

Lamberti, S, 'Prevention of jail and hospital recidivism among persons with severe mental illness' (1999) 50 Psychiatric Services 1477

Landreville, P, Morin, D and Laberge, D, 'Déjudiciarisation en santé mentale à Montréal' (2003) 1–2 Politiques sociales 94

Landrine, H, *The Politics of Madness*, 1992, New York: Peter Lang

Lapon, L, *Mass Murderers in White Coats*, 1986, Springfield, IL: Psychiatric Genocide Research Institute

Laqueur, T, *Making Sex: Body and Gender From the Greeks to Freud*, 1990, Cambridge, Mass: Harvard University Press

Laster, K, 'Infanticide: a litmus test for feminist criminological theory' (1989) 22 Australian and New Zealand Journal of Criminology 151

Leader-Elliott, I, 'Battered but not beaten: women who kill in self-defence' (1993) 15 Sydney Law Review 403

Leary, T, *Interpersonal Diagnosis of Personality: A Functional Theory and Methodology for Personality Evaluation*, 1957, New York: Ronald Press

Lee, E, 'The context for the development of "post-abortion syndrome"', presented at The Psychological Sequelae of Abortion – Myths and Facts Symposium, 2001, Berne, Switzerland

Lee, E, 'Tough life choices' (2002) *The Guardian*, 14 June, 'Comment and Analysis'

Leps, MC, *Apprehending the Criminal: The Production of Deviance in Nineteenth-Century Discourse*, 1992, Durham, NC: Duke University Press

Lerman, H, *Pigeonholing Women's Misery: A History and Critical Analysis of the Psychodiagnosis of Women in the Twentieth Century*, 1996, New York: Basic Books

Leyton, E, *Men of Blood: Murder in Everyday Life*, 1996, Toronto, ON: McClelland and Stewart

Liebling, H, Chipchase, H and Velangi, R, 'An evaluation of nurse training and support needs: Working with women patients who harm themselves in a special hospital', in Stephenson, GM and Clark, NK (eds), *Procedures in Criminal Justice: Contemporary Psychological Issues*, 1997, Leicester: British Psychological Society

Lindsay, W, Taylor, JL and Sturmey, P (eds), *Offenders with Developmental Disabilities*, 2004, London: John Wiley & Sons

Littlewood, R and Lipsedge, M, *Aliens and Alienists: Ethnic Minorities and Psychiatry*, 1982, Harmondsworth: Penguin

Lloyd, A, *Doubly Deviant, Doubly Damned: Society's Treatment of Violent Women*, 1995, Harmondsworth: Penguin

Loring, M and Powell, B, 'Gender, race and DSM-III: a study of the objectivity of psychiatric diagnostic behavior' (1988) 29 Journal of Health and Social Behavior 1

Luke, P, 'Suicide in Auckland 1848–1939', unpublished MA thesis, 1982, University of Auckland

Macdonald, C, 'Crime and punishment in New Zealand 1840–1913: a gendered history' (1989) 23 The New Journal of History 5

Macdonald, C, *A Woman of Good Character: Single Woman as Immigrant Settlers in Nineteenth Century New Zealand*, 1990, Wellington: Bridget Williams Books

Macdonald, C, 'Too many men and too few women: gender's "fatal impact" in nineteenth century colonies', in Daley, C and Montgomerie, D (eds), *The Gendered Kiwi*, 1999, Auckland: Auckland University Press, pp 17–36

MacDonald, I and O'Keefe, B, *Canadian Holy War: A Story of Clans, Tongs, Murder, and Bigotry*, 2000, Surrey, BC: Heritage House

Mack, K and Roach Anleu, S, 'Balancing principle and pragmatism: guilty pleas' (1995) 4 Journal of Judicial Administration 233

MacKay, RD, 'Insanity and unfitness to stand trial in Canada and England: a comparative study of recent developments' (1995) 6 Journal of Forensic Psychiatry 121

MacKay, RD, 'The abnormality of mind factor in diminished responsibility' (1999) Criminal Law Review 117

MacMillan, HL, Fleming, JE, Streiner, DL, Lin, E, Boyle, MH, Jamieson, E, Duku, EK, Walsh, CA, Wong, Y-Y and Beardslee, WR, 'Childhood abuse and lifetime psychopathology in a community sample' (2001) 158 American Journal of Psychiatry 1878

Maidment, MR, 'Towards a "woman centred" approach to community-based corrections: a gendered analysis of electronic monitoring (EM) in Eastern Canada' (2002) 13 Women and Criminal Justice 47

Mair, G (ed), *What Matters in Probation*, 2004, Cullompton: Willan Publishing

Margulies, P, 'Battered bargaining: domestic violence and plea negotiation in the criminal justice system' (2001) 11 Southern California Review of Law and Women's Studies 153

Marquis, G, *Policing Canada's Century: A History of the Canadian Association of Chiefs of Police*, 1993, Toronto, ON: University of Toronto Press

Martin, DJ, Abramson, LY and Alloy, LB, 'Illusion of control for self and others in depressed and non-depressed college students' (1984) 46 Journal of Personality and Social Psychology 125

Martinson, D, MacCrimmon, M, Grant, I and Boyle, C, 'A forum on *Lavallee v R*: women and self defence' (1991) 25 University of British Columbia Law Review 23

Mason, T and Mercer, D, *A Sociology of the Mentally Disordered Offender*, 1999, Harlow: Pearson

Masson, JM, *The Assault on Truth: Freud's Suppression of the Seduction Theory*, 1984, New York: Farrar, Straus and Giroux

Mathiesen, T, 'The viewer society: Michel Foucault's "Panopticon" revisited' (1997) 1 Theoretical Criminology 215

Matthews, J, *Good and Mad Women: The Historical Construction of Femininity in Twentieth Century Australia*, 1984, Sydney: George Allen and Unwin

Mawani, R, 'Regulating the "respectable" classes: venereal disease, gender, and public health initiatives in Canada, 1914–35', in McLaren, J, Menzies, R and Chunn, DE (eds), *Regulating Lives: Historical Essays on the State, Society, the Individual, and the Law*, 2002, Vancouver, BC: University of British Columbia Press, pp 170–95

McCallum, D, *Personality and Dangerousness: Genealogies of Antisocial Personality Disorder*, 2001, Cambridge: Cambridge University Press

McCrae, R and John, O, 'An introduction to the Five-Factors model and its applications' (1992) 60 Journal of Personality 175

McFadyean, M and Renn, R, *Thatcher's Blues*, 1984, London: The Hogarth Press

McGowen, R, 'The well-ordered prison: England, 1780–1865', in Morris, N and Rothman, D (eds), *The Oxford History of Prison: The Practice of Punishment in Western Society*, 1995, Oxford: Oxford University Press, pp 71–99

McLaren, A, 'Illegal abortions: women, doctors, and abortion, 1886–1939' (1993) 26 Journal of Social History 797

McLaren, A and McLaren, AT, *The Bedroom and the State: The Changing Practices and Politics of Contraception and Abortion in Canada, 1880–1997*, 2nd edn, 1997, Toronto, ON: Oxford University Press

McLaren, J, Menzies, R and Chunn, DE (eds), *Regulating Lives: Historical Essays on the State, Society, the Individual, and the Law*, 2002, Vancouver, BC: University of British Columbia Press

McLaren, JPS, 'White slavers: The reform of Canada's prostitution laws and patterns of enforcement, 1900–1920' (1987) 8 Criminal Justice History 53

McLaughlin, E and Muncie, J, 'The silent revolution: market based criminal justice in England' (1993) 9 Socio-Legal Bulletin 4

McNamee, S and Gergen, K (eds), *Therapy as Social Construction*, 1992, London: Sage

McWinney, S, 'Petite treasons: crimes against the matriarchy', in Scholder, A (ed), *Critical Condition: Women on the Edge of Violence*, 1993, San Francisco, CA: City Lights Books, pp 48–53

Mechanic, D, 'Mental health and mental illness: definitions and perspectives', in Horwitz, AV and Scheid, TL (eds), *A Handbook for the Study of Mental Health: Social Contexts, Theories, and Systems*, 1999, Cambridge: Cambridge University Press, pp 12–28

Melling, J and Forsythe, B (eds), *Insanity, Institutions and Society, 1800–1914*, 1999, London: Routledge

Memmott, P, *Violence in Indigenous Communities*, 2001, Barton, ACT: Crime Prevention Branch, Commonwealth Attorney General's Department

Menkes, DB, Taghavi, E, Mason, PA and Howard, RC, 'Fluoxetine's spectrum of action in premenstrual syndrome' (1993) 8 International Clinical Psychopharmacology 92

Menzies, R, 'Psychiatry, dangerousness and legal control', in Boyd, N (ed), *The Social Dimensions of Law*, 1986, Scarborough, ON: Prentice Hall, pp 182–211

Menzies, R, 'Psychiatrists in blue: police apprehension of mental disorder and dangerousness' (1987) 25 Criminology: An Interdisciplinary Journal 429

Menzies, R, *Survival of the Sanest: Order and Disorder in a Pre-Trial Psychiatric Clinic*, 1989, Toronto, ON: University of Toronto Press

Menzies, R, 'Contesting criminal lunacy: narratives of law and madness in west coast Canada, 1874–1950' (2001) 7 History of Psychiatry 123

Menzies, R, 'Historical profiles of criminal insanity' (2002) 25 International Journal of Law and Psychiatry 379

Menzies, R and Chunn, DE, 'The gender politics of criminal insanity: "Order-in-Council" women in British Columbia, 1888–1950' (1999) 31 Histoire sociale/Social History 241

Menzies, R, Chunn, DE and Webster, CD, 'Female follies: the forensic psychiatric assessment of women defendants' (1992) 15 International Journal of Law and Psychiatry 179

Miller, P and Rose, N (eds), *The Power of Psychiatry*, 1986, Cambridge: Polity

Millett, K, *The Loony-Bin Trip*, 1990, New York: Simon & Schuster

Mills, A, 'Mental health in-reach – the way forward for prison?' (2002) 49 Probation Journal 107

Mills, JH, *Madness, Cannabis and Colonialism: The 'Native-Only' Lunatic Asylums of British? India, 1857–1900*, 2000, Basingstoke: Palgrave

Ministère de la Santé et des Services sociaux (MSSS) and Ministère de la Sécurité publique (MSP), *Les services de santé et les services sociaux pour la personne contrevenante*, 1990, Québec: Gouvernement du Québec

Ministerial Group on the Family, *Supporting Families*, 1998, London: HMSO

Mitchinson, W, 'Gender and insanity as characteristics of the insane: a nineteenth-century case' (1987) 4 Canadian Bulletin of Medical History 99

Mitchinson, W, *The Nature of Their Bodies: Women and Their Doctors in Victorian Canada*, 1991, Toronto, ON: University of Toronto Press

Moran, JE, *Committed to the State Asylum: Insanity and Society in Nineteenth-Century Quebec and Ontario*, 2000, Montréal, QC and Kingston, ON: McGill-Queen's University Press

Moran, R, *Knowing Right From Wrong: The Insanity Defense of Daniel McNaughtan*, 1981, New York: Free Press

Morris, A and Gelsthorpe, L (eds), *Women and Crime: Papers Presented to the Cropwood Round-Table Conference*, 1981, Cambridge: University of Cambridge, Institute of Criminology

Morrissey, B, *When Women Kill: Questions of Agency and Subjectivity*, 2003, London: Routledge

Mort, F, *Dangerous Sexualities: Medico-Moral Politics in England Since 1830*, 2nd edn, 1987, London: Routledge

Mosoff, J, 'Motherhood, madness and law' (1995) 45 University of Toronto Law Journal 107

Mosoff, J, '"A jury dressed in medical white and judicial black": mothers with mental health histories in child welfare and custody', in Boyd, SB (ed), *Challenging the Public/Private Divide: Feminism, Law and Public Policy*, 1997, Toronto, ON: University of Toronto Press, pp 227–52

Mouzos, J, 'Homicide in Australia 1999–2000' (2001a) 187 Trends and Issues, Australian Institute of Criminology

Mouzos, J, 'Indigenous and non-indigenous homicides in Australia: a comparative analysis' (2001b) 210 Trends and Issues, Australian Institute of Criminology

Mullen, P, 'Jealousy: the pathology of passion' (1991) 158 British Journal of Psychiatry 593

Myers, A and Wight, S (eds), *No Angels: Women Who Commit Violence*, 1996, London: Pandora

Myers, T, 'Qui t'a debauchée?: female adolescent sexuality and the Juvenile Delinquent's Court in early twentieth-century Montreal', in Chambers, L and Montigny, E (eds), *Family Matters: Papers in Post-Confederation Canadian Family History*, 1998, Toronto, ON: Canadian Scholars Press

Naar-King, S, Silvern, V, Ryan, V and Sebring, D, 'Type and severity of abuse as predictors of psychiatric symptoms in adolescence' (2002) 17 Journal of Family Violence 133

Naffine, N, *Law and the Sexes: Explorations in Feminist Jurisprudence*, 1990, Sydney: Allen and Unwin

Navarro, V, *Medicine Under Capitalism*, 1976, New York: Prodist

Neave, MA, 'The gender of judging' (1995) 2 Psychiatry, Psychology and Law, ANZAPPL in association with Swinburne University of Technology 3

Ney, P, 'Abortion wounds: the deeply damaging impact of abortion on women and the family', in Wagner, T (ed), *Back to the Drawing Board: The Future of the Pro-Life Movement*, 2003, South Bend, IN: St Augustine's Press

Nicolson, D, 'Telling tales: gender discrimination, gender construction and battered women who kill' (1995) 3 Feminist Legal Studies 185

Nicolson, D, 'What the law giveth it also taketh away', in Nicolson, D and Bibbings, L (eds), *Feminist Perspectives on Criminal Law*, 2000, London: Cavendish Publishing, pp 159–82

Nicolson, P, 'Developing a feminist approach to depression following childbirth', in Wilkinson, S (ed), *Feminist Social Psychology*, 1986, Milton Keynes: Open University Press, pp 53–67

Norrie, AW, *Crime, Reason and History: A Critical Introduction to Criminal Law*, 2nd edn, 2001 [1993], London: Butterworths

North American Nursing Diagnosis Association, *NANDA Nursing Diagnoses: Definitions and Classifications 1995–1996*, 1994, Philadelphia, PA: Author

NSWLRC, *Sentencing: Aboriginal Offenders*, Report 96, 2000, Sydney: NSWLRC

Nunnally, J, 'Classification in psychology: purposes and methods', in Theodore B *et al* (eds), *Report of the Ad Hoc Task Force on Behavioral Classification. I Classification. II The State of the Art in Application*, 1975, Washington, DC: American Psychological Association, pp 15–30

O'Brien, M, Mortimer, L, Singleton, N and Meltzer, H, *Psychiatric Morbidity Among Women Prisoners in England and Wales*, 2001, London: Office for National Statistics

O'Donovan, K, 'Law's knowledge: the judge, the expert, the battered woman and her syndrome' (1993) 20 Journal of Law and Society 427

O'Marra, JC, 'Hadfield to Swain: the Criminal Code amendments dealing with the mentally disordered accused' (1994) 36 The Criminal Law Quarterly 49

Ogata, SN, Silk, KR, Goodrich, S, Lohr, NE, Westen, D and Hill, EM, 'Childhood sexual and physical abuse in adult patients with borderline personality disorder' (1990) 147 American Journal of Psychiatry 1008

Ogloff, JRP and Whittemore, KE, 'Fitness to stand trial and criminal responsibility in Canada', in Schuller, RA and Ogloff, JRP (eds), *Introduction to Psychology and Law: Canadian Perspectives*, 2001, Toronto, ON: University of Toronto Press, pp 3–28

Olio, K, 'The truth about "false memory syndrome"', in Caplan, PJ and Cosgrove, L (eds), *Bias in Psychiatric Diagnosis*, 2004, Lanham, MD: Jason Aronson/Rowman & Littlefield, pp 163–70

Olssen, E, 'Truby King and the Plunket Society: an analysis of a prescriptive ideology' (1981) 15 The New Zealand Journal of History 3

Olssen, E and Levesque, A, 'Towards a history of the New Zealand family', in Koopman-Boyden, P (ed), *Families in New Zealand Society*, 1978, Wellington: Methuen, pp 1–26

Ontario Coalition to Stop Electroshock, *The Case Against Electroshock*, 1984, Toronto, ON: Ontario Coalition to Stop Electroshock

Orme, J, *Gender and Community Care*, 2001, Basingstoke: Palgrave

Otero, M, 'Les stratégies d'intervention psychothérapeutique et psychosociale au Québec. La régulation des conduites' (2000) 32 Sociologie et Sociétés 213

Otero, M, *Les règles de l'individualité contemporaine: Santé mentale et société*, 2003, Sainte-Foy: Les Presses de l'Université Laval

Oudshoorn, N, 'On measuring sex hormones: the role of biological assays in sexualizing chemical substances' (1990) 64 Bulletin of History of Medicine 243

Owen, T and Sim, J, 'Doctors, discipline and prison medicine: the case of George Wilkinson', in Scraton, P and Gordon, P (eds), *Causes for Concern*, 1984, Harmondsworth: Penguin, pp 228–55

Parker, I, *Discourse Dynamics: Critical Analysis for Social and Individual Psychology*, 1992, London: Sage

Parker, I, Georgaca, E, Harper, D, McLaughllin, T and Stowell-Smith, M, *Deconstructing Psychopathology*, 1995, London: Sage

Parlee, M, 'The science and politics of PMS research', presented at the annual research conference of the Association for Women in Psychology, 1989, Newport, RI

Parlee, M, 'The social construction of PMS: a case study of scientific discourse as cultural contestation', presented to the conference The Good Body: Asceticism in Contemporary Culture, Institute for the Medical Humanities, 1991, University of Texas, Galveston, 12–13 April

Parrish, J, 'Trend analysis: expert testimony on battering and its effects in criminal cases', in US Department of Justice and US Department of Health and Human Services, *The Validity and Use of Evidence Concerning Battering and Its Effects in Criminal Trials: Report Responding to Section 40507 of the Violence Against Women Act*, 1996, Pt II, pp 31–75, www.ojp.usdoj.gov/ocpa/94Guides/Trials/welcome.html

Patel, N and Fatimilehin, I, 'Racism and mental health', in Newness, C, Holmes, G and Dunn, C (eds), *This is Madness*, 1999, Ross-on-Wye: PCCS Books, pp 51–73

Pavkov, T, Lewis, D and Lyons, J, 'Psychiatric diagnoses and racial bias: an empirical investigation' (1989) 20 Professional Psychology: Research and Practice 364

Payer, L, *Medicine and Culture*, 1988, New York: Henry Holt and Company

Pearson, G, *The Deviant Imagination: Psychiatry, Social Work and Social Change*, 1975, London: Macmillan

Pearson, P, *When She Was Bad*, 1998, London: Virago

Penfold, PS, *Sexual Abuse by Health Professionals: A Personal Search for Meaning and Healing*, 1998, Toronto, ON: University of Toronto Press

Penfold, PS and Walker, G, *Women and the Psychiatric Paradox*, 1984, Milton Keynes: Open University Press

Petrunik, M, 'The hare and the tortoise: dangerousness and sex offender policy in the United States and Canada' (2003) 45 Canadian Journal of Criminology and Criminal Justice 43

Pfohl, S, *Predicting Dangerousness: The Social Construction of Psychiatric Reality*, 1978, Lexington, MA: Lexington Books

Phillips, J, *A Man's Country? The Image of the Pakeha Male – A History*, 1987, Auckland: Penguin

Phillips, R, *Divorce in New Zealand: A Social History*, 1981, Auckland: Oxford University Press

Phoenix Rising, 'Lesbian and gay supplement' (1990) 8 Phoenix Rising 1

Pilgrim, D and Rogers, A, 'Mental health, critical realism and lay knowledge', in Ussher, JM (ed), *Body Talk: The Material and Discursive Regulation of Sexuality, Madness and Reproduction*, 1997, London: Routledge, pp 67–82

Pool, D, *The Maori Population of New Zealand 1769–1971*, 1977, Auckland: Auckland University Press

Porter, R, *Madness: A Brief History*, 2002, Oxford: Oxford University Press

Porter, R and Wright, D (eds), *The Confinement of the Insane: International Perspectives, 1800–1965*, 2003, Cambridge: Cambridge University Press

Potter, J and Wetherell, M, *Discourse and Social Psychology*, 1986, London: Sage

Prestwich, P, 'Family strategies and medical power: "voluntary" committal in a Parisian asylum, 1876–1914' (1994) 27 Journal of Social History 803

Prior, P, 'Mad, not bad: crime, mental disorder and gender in nineteenth-century Ireland' (1997) 8 History of Psychiatry 501

Prior, P, *Gender and Mental Health*, 1999, Basingstoke: Macmillan

Prison Reform Trust, *Inside Prisons*, Prison Report, 2003, London: Prison Reform Trust, p 4

Procek, E, 'Psychiatry and the social control of women', in Morris, A and Gelsthorpe, L (eds), *Women and Crime*, 1980, Cambridge: Institute of Criminology, pp 19–32

Quen, JM, 'Anglo-American criminal insanity: an historical perspective' (1974) 4 Journal of the History of the Behavioral Sciences 313

Rafter, NH, *Partial Justice: Women, Prisons and Social Control*, 1990, New Brunswick, NJ: Transaction Books

Rafter, NH, 'Psychopathy and the evolution of criminological knowledge' (1997) 1 Theoretical Criminology 235

Raitt, FE and Zeedyk, MS, *The Implicit Relation of Psychology and Law: Women and Syndrome Evidence*, 2000, London: Routledge

Rapaport, E, 'Staying alive: equal protection, re-election, and the execution of women' (2000) 4 Buffalo Criminal Law Review 967

Ratushny, J, *Self Defence Review: Final Report*, Minister of Justice Canada and Solicitor General Canada (11 July 1997), www.justice.gc.ca/en/dept/pub/sdr/rtush.html

Raymond, V *et al*, 'Mental health and violence against women' (1985) 5 Phoenix Rising 6

Reardon, DC, 'How to become a "stealth healer"' (1998) www.afterabortion.org

Reardon, DC, 'A list of major psychological sequelae of abortion' (2000), www.lifeissues.net

Reaume, G, *Remembrance of Patients Past: Patient Life at the Toronto Hospital for the Insane, 1870–1940*, 2000, Don Mills, ON: Oxford University Press

Reaume, G, 'Archives, activists, and history' (2002) Sigerist Circle Newsletter 6

Reznek, L, *Evil or Ill? Justifying the Insanity Defence*, 1997, London: Routledge

Rice, C, 'Should we blame the lawyers?', in Wagner, T (ed), *Back to the Drawing Board: The Future of the Pro-Life Movement*, 2003, South Bend, IN: St Augustine's Press

Richards, D, 'Self-defense and relations of domination: moral and legal perspectives on battered women who kill: introduction' (1996) 57 University of Pittsburgh Law Review 461

Ripa, Y, *Women and Madness: The Incarceration of Women in Nineteenth-Century France*, 1990, Minneapolis, MN: University of Minnesota Press

Roach Pierson, R, 'They're Still Women After All': The Second World War and Canadian Womanhood, 1990, Toronto, ON: McClelland and Stewart

Roberts, Y, 'Mad as a desperate woman' (2003) The Observer, 18 May, p 29

Robertson, GB, Mental Disabililty and the Law in Canada, 1987, Toronto, ON: Carswell

Robinson, J, 'Of diverse persons, men, women and whores: women and crime in nineteenth century Canterbury', unpublished MA thesis, 1983, University of Canterbury

Roelofs, K, Keijsers, GPJ, Hoogduin, KAL, Näring, GWB and Moene, FC, 'Childhood abuse in patients with conversion disorder' (2002) 159 American Journal of Psychiatry 1908

Rose, N, 'Calculable minds and manageable individuals' (1988) 1 History of the Human Sciences 179

Rose, N, Inventing Ourselves: Psychology, Power and Personhood, 1996, Cambridge: Cambridge University Press

Rose, N, Governing the Soul: The Shaping of the Private Self, 2nd edn, 1999a, London: Free Association Books

Rose, N, Powers of Freedom: Reframing Political Thought, 1999b, Cambridge: Cambridge University Press

Rosenthal, R, 'Dilemmas of local movements', in Baumohl, J (ed), Homelessness in America, 1996, Phoenix, AZ: Onyx Press, pp 200–12

Rosewater, L, 'A critical analysis of the proposed self-defeating personality disorder' (1987) 1 Journal of Personality Disorders 190

Ross, S, 'Battered wife syndrome and the role of lawyers' (1998) 72 Law Institute Journal 39

Roth, M, 'The New Zealand family: cornerstone of colonisation', unpublished MA thesis, 1980, University of Auckland

Roth, R and Lerner, J, 'Sex-based discrimination in the mental institutionalization of women', in Weisberg, D (ed), Women and the Law, Vol I, 1982, Cambridge, MA: Schenkman

Rothman, D, The Discovery of the Asylum: Social Order and Disorder in the New Republic, 1971, Boston, MA: Little Brown

Rounsaville, BJ, Alarcon, RD, Andrews, G, Jackson, JS, Kendell, RE and Kendler, K, 'Basic nomenclature issues for DSM-V', in Kupfer, D, First, M and Regier, D (eds), A Research Agenda for DSM-V, 2002, Washington, DC: American Psychiatric Association

Roy, A, 'Childhood trauma and neuroticism as an adult: possible implications for the development of the common psychiatric disorders and suicidal behavior' (2002) 32 Psychological Medicine 1471

Rue, V, 'Post-abortion syndrome: a variant of post-traumatic stress disorder', in Doherty, P (ed), Post-abortion Syndrome – Its Wider Ramifications, 1995, Dublin: Four Courts Press

Rush, F, The Best Kept Secret: Sexual Abuse of Children, 1980, New York: Prentice Hall

Russell, D, Women, Madness and Medicine, 1995, Cambridge: Polity

Russell, D, Scenes from Bedlam: A History of Caring for the Mentally Disordered at Bethlem Royal Hospital and the Maudsley, 1997, London: Baillière Tindall

Russell, S, Damsel of Death: The Inside Story of the World's First Female Serial Killer, 1992, London: True Crime

Russo, NF and Zierk, K, 'Abortion, childbearing, and women's well-being' (1992) 23 Professional Psychology: Research and Practice 269

Salter, S, 'Taking the politics out of abortion counseling' (2002) *The San Francisco Chronicle*, 3 November

Sangster, J, *Girl Trouble: Female Delinquency in English Canada*, 2002, Toronto, ON: Between the Lines

Sansone, R, Gaither, G and Songer, D, 'The relationships among childhood abuse, borderline personality and self-harm behavior in psychiatric inpatients' (2002) 17 Violence and Victims 49

Sartori, G, 'Geseila Sartori', in Shimrat, I (ed), *Call Me Crazy*, 1997, Vancouver, BC: Press Gang, pp 124–38

Sayer, A, *Realism and Social Science*, 2000, Sage: London

Scheff, TJ, *Being Mentally Ill: A Sociological Theory*, 1966, Chicago, IL: Aldine

Scheff, TJ (ed), *Labelling Madness*, 1975, Englewood Cliffs, NJ: Prentice Hall

Scheper-Hughes, N and Lovell, AM, *Psychiatry Inside Out: Selected Writings of Franco Basaglia (European Perspectives)*, 1987, New York: Columbia University Press

Schnapp, W, Nguyen, T and Johnson, J, 'Services for offenders with mental impairments: a Texas model' (1996) 23 Administration and Policy in Mental Health 361

Schneider, EM, 'Describing and changing women's self-defence work: the problem of expert testimony' (1986) 9 Women's Rights Law Reporter 195

Schneider, EM, 'Particularity and generality: challenges of feminist theory and practice in work on woman abuse' (1992) 67 New York University Law Review 520

Schneider, EM, 'Self-defense and relations of domination: moral and legal perspectives on battered women who kill: Resistance to equality' (1996) 57 University of Pittsburgh Law Review 477

Schneider, EM, *Battered Women and Feminist Lawmaking*, 2000, New Haven, CT: Yale University Press

Schrag, P, *Mind Control*, 1978, New York: Pantheon

Schultz, J and Videbeck, S, *Manual of Psychiatric Nursing Care Plans*, 4th edn, 1994, Philadelphia, PA: JB Lippincott

Scott, JW, 'Experience', in Butler, J and Scott, JW (eds), *Feminists Theorise the Political*, 1992, New York: Routledge

Scott, S, 'The training needs of staff working with women in secure settings', presented at the Women in Secure Environments Conference, 2000, Nottingham

Scott, S and Parry-Crooke, G, 'Gender training needs of staff working in secure services' (2001) 7 Mental Health Review 18

Scull, A, *Museums of Madness: The Social Organisation of Insanity in Nineteenth Century England*, 1979, London: Allen Lane

Scull, A (ed), *Madhouses, Mad-doctors and Madmen: The Social History of Psychiatry in the Victorian Era*, 1981, Philadelphia, PA: University of Pennsylvania Press

Second Opinion Society, 'News' (1994) Summer, Second Opinion 26

Sedgwick, P, *Psychopolitics: Laing, Foucault, Goffman, Szasz, and the Future of Mass Psychiatry*, 1982, New York: Harper and Row

Seifman, R and Frieberg A, 'Plea bargaining in Victoria: the role of counsel' (2001) 25 Criminal Law Journal 64

Shaffer, M, 'The battered woman syndrome revisited: some complicating thoughts five years after *R v Lavallee*' (1997) 47 University of Toronto Law Journal 1

Sheehy E, 'Review of the self defence review' (2000) 12 Canadian Journal of Women and the Law 197

Sheehy, E, 'Battered women and mandatory minimum sentences' (2001) 39 Osgoode Hall Law Journal 529

Sheehy, E, Stubbs, J and Tolmie, J, 'Defending battered women on trial: the battered woman syndrome and its limitations' (1992) 16 Criminal Law Journal 369

Sheldon, S, 'Who is the mother to make the judgement? Constructions of "woman" in the Abortion Act' (1993) 1 Feminist Legal Studies 3

Shimrat, I, *Call Me Crazy: Stories from the Mad Movement*, 1997, Vancouver, BC: Press Gang

Shipley, SL and Arrigo, BA, *The Female Homicide Offender: Serial Murder and the Case of Aileen Wuornos*, 2004, Upper Saddle River, NJ: Prentice Hall

Shotter, K and Gergen, KJ (eds), *Texts of Identity*, 1989, London: Sage

Showalter, E, *The Female Malady: Women, Madness, and English Culture, 1803–1980*, 1987, Harmondsworth: Penguin

Sicot, F, *Maladie mentale et pauvreté*, 2001, Paris: L'Harmattan

Sim, J, *Medical Power in Prisons: The Prison Medical Service in England 1774–1989*, 1990, Milton Keynes: Open University Press

Sim, J, '"One thousand days of degradation": New Labour and old compromises at the turn of the century' (2000) 27 Social Justice 168

Sim, J, 'The future of prison health care: a critical analysis' (2002) 22 Critical Social Policy 300

Sim, J and Fitzgerald, M, *British Prisons*, 1982, Oxford: Blackwell

Sim, J, Ruggiero, V and Ryan, M (eds), *Western European Penal Systems*, 1995, London: Sage

Sim, J, Scraton, P and Skidmore, P, *Prisons Under Protest*, 1991, Milton Keynes: Open University Press

Simon, RJ, *Women and Crime*, 1975, Lexington, MA: Lexington Books

Sjostrom, S, *Party or Patient: Discursive Practices Relating to Coercion in Psychiatric and Legal Settings*, 1997, Umea, Sweden: Borea Bokforlag

Skrapec, C, 'The female serial killer: an evolving criminality', in Birch, H (ed), *Moving Targets: Women, Murder and Representation*, 1994, Berkeley, CA: University of California Press, pp 241–68

Smart, C, *Women, Crime and Criminology: A Feminist Critique*, 1976, London: Routledge and Kegan Paul

Smart, C, *Feminism and the Power of Law*, 1989, London: Routledge

Smart, C, 'The woman of legal discourse' (1992) 5 Social and Legal Studies 29

Smith, C, *The Imprisoned Body: Women, Health and Imprisonment*, 1996, unpublished PhD thesis, University of Wales, Bangor

Smith, D, 'The statistics on mental illness (what they will not tell us about women and why)', in Smith, D and David, S (eds), *Women Look at Psychiatry*, 1975, Vancouver, BC: Press Gang, pp 73–119

Smith, D, *The Conceptual Practices of Power*, 1990, Toronto, ON: University of Toronto Press

Smith, D and David, S (eds), *Women Look at Psychiatry*, 1975, Vancouver: Press Gang

Smith, R, *Trial by Medicine: Insanity and Responsibility in Victorian Trials*, 1981, Edinburgh: Edinburgh University Press

Smith Rosenberg, C, *Disorderly Conduct: Visions of Gender in Victorian America*, 1986, New York: AA Knopf

Soloff, P, Lynch, K and Kelly, T, 'Childhood abuse as a risk factor for suicidal behavior in borderline personality disorder' (2002) 16 Journal of Personality Disorders 201

Sommers, EK, *Voices from Within: Women Who Have Broken the Law*, 1995, Toronto, ON: University of Toronto Press

Sowa, CJ and Lustman, PJ, 'Gender differences in rating stressful events, depression, and depressive cognition' (1984) 40 Journal of Clinical Psychology 1334

Spierenburg, P, 'The body and the state: early modern Europe', in Morris, N and Rothman, D (eds), *The Oxford History of Prison: The Practice of Punishment in Western Society*, 1995, Oxford: Oxford University Press, pp 44–70

Stafford, P, *Defining Gender Issues ... Redefining Women's Services*, 1999, London: WISH

Stainton-Rogers, W, *Explaining Health and Illness*, 1996, Hemel Hempstead: Harvester Wheatsheaf

Stanton, M, 'U-Turn on memory lane' (1997) Columbia Journalism Review 44

Stark, E, 'Re-presenting woman battering: from battered woman syndrome to coercive control' (1995) 58 Albany Law Review 973

Steadman, HJ, Cocozza, JJ and Veysey, BM, 'Comparing outcomes for diverted and nondiverted jail detainees with mental illnesses' (1999) 23 Law and Human Behavior 615

Steadman, HJ and Morrissey, JP, 'The impact of deinstitutionalization on the criminal justice system: implications for understanding changing modes of social control', in Lowman, J, Menzies, RJ and Palys, TS (eds), *Transcarceration: Essays in the Sociology of Social Control*, 1987, Cambridge: Gower, pp 226–48

Stefan, S, 'Impact of the law on women with diagnoses of borderline personality disorder related to childhood sexual abuse', in Levin, BL, Blanch, AK and Jennings, A (eds), *Women's Mental Health Services: A Public Health Perspective*, 1998, Thousand Oaks, CA: Sage, pp 240–78

Stephen, J, 'The "incorrigible", the "bad", and the "immoral": Toronto's "factory girls" and the work of the Toronto Psychiatric Clinic', in Knafla, LA and Binnie, S (eds), *Law, Society and the State: Essays in Modern Legal History*, 1995, Toronto, ON: University of Toronto Press, pp 405–39

Stewart, C, 'Responding to the needs of women in prison' (2000) 132 Prison Service Journal 41

Stonier-Newman, L, *Policing a Pioneer Province: The BC Provincial Police, 1858–1950*, 1991, Madeira Park, BC: Harbour Publishing

Stoppard, J, *Women's Depression: A Social Constructionist Account*, 1999, London: Routledge

Stoppard, J, *Understanding Depression*, 2000, London: Routledge

Strange, C, *Toronto's Girl Problem: The Perils and Pleasures of the City, 1880–1930*, 1995, Toronto, ON: University of Toronto Press

Strange, C, 'The lottery of death: capital punishment, 1867–1976' (1996) 23 Manitoba Law Journal 594

Stubbs, J, *Women, Male Violence and the Law*, 1994, Sydney: Institute of Criminology

Stubbs, J and Cunneen, C, *Gender, Race and International Relations*, 1997, Sydney: Institute of Criminology

Stubbs, J, Kaye, M and Tolmie, J, *Negotiating Child Residence and Contact Arrangements Against a Background of Domestic Violence*, 2003, Griffith University Law and Social Policy Research Unit

Stubbs, J and Tolmie, J, 'Race, gender, and the battered woman syndrome: an Australian case study' (1995) 8 Canadian Journal of Women and the Law 122

Stubbs, J and Tolmie, J, 'Falling short of the challenge? A comparative assessment of the Australian use of expert expertise on the battered woman syndrome' (1999) 23 Melbourne University Law Review 709

Sudbury, J, 'Celling black bodies: black women in the global prison industrial complex' (2002) 70 Feminist Review 57

Surrey, J, Swett, C, Michaels, A and Levin, S, 'Reported history of physical and sexual abuse and severity of symptomatology in women psychiatric outpatients' (1990) 60 American Journal of Orthopsychiatry 412

Suyemoto, KL, 'Constructing identities: a feminist culturally contextualized alternate to "personality"', in Ballou, M and Brown, L (eds), *Rethinking Mental Health and Disorder: Feminist Perspectives*, 2002, New York: Guilford, pp 71–98

Swainger, J, 'A distant edge of authority: capital punishment and the prerogative of mercy in British Columbia, 1872–1880', in Foster, H and McLaren, M (eds), *Essays in the History of Canadian Law. Vol VI: British Columbia and the Yukon*, 1995, Toronto, ON: Osgoode Society and University of Toronto Press, pp 204–41

Szasz, TS, *The Myth of Mental Illness: Foundations of a Theory of Personal Conduct*, 1961, New York: Hoeber-Harper

Szasz, TS, *Law, Liberty, and Psychiatry: An Inquiry into the Social Uses of Mental Health Practices*, 1963, New York: Macmillan

Tennant, M, 'Magdalens and moral imbeciles: women's homes in nineteenth century New Zealand' (1986) 9 Women's Studies International Forum 491

Teplin, LA, 'Policy discretion and mentally ill persons', in Landsberg, G and Smiley, A (eds), *Forensic Mental Health: Working With Offenders With Mental Illness*, 2001, Kingston, NJ: Civic Research Institute

Theriot, NM, 'Women's voices in nineteenth-century medical discourse: a step toward deconstructing science' (1993) 19 Signs: Journal of Women in Culture and Society 1

Thompson, JB, *Studies in the Theory of Ideology*, 1984, Cambridge: Polity

Tiefer, L, 'In pursuit of the perfect penis: the medicalization of male sexuality' (1986) 29 American Behavioural Scientist 579

Tilt, Sir R, *Report of the Review of Security at the High Security Hospitals*, 2000, www.doh.gov.uk

Tobin, P, 'Clinical recommendations for sole custody in child custody disputes: an analysis of sex-related factors in the decision-making and assessment process', 1989, unpublished doctoral dissertation, Toronto, ON: Ontario Institute for Studies in Education

Tomes, N, 'Historical perspectives on women and mental illness', in Apple, R (ed), *Women, Health, and Medicine in America*, 1990, New York and London: Garland Publishing, pp 143–71

Turner, BS, *The Body and Society*, 1984, Oxford: Blackwell

Ulysse, P-J and Lesemann, F, *Citoyenneté et pauvreté. Politiques, pratiques et stratégies d'insertion en emploi et de lutte contre la pauvreté*, 2004, Montréal, QC: Presses de l'Université du Québec

US Department of Justice and US Department of Health and Human Services, *The Validity and Use of Evidence Concerning Battering and Its Effects in Criminal Trials: Report Responding to Section 40507 of the Violence Against Women Act*, 1996, www.ojp.usdoj.gov/ocpa/94Guides/Trials/welcome.html

Ussher, JM, *The Psychology of the Female Body*, 1989, London: Routledge

Ussher, JM, *Women's Madness: Misogyny or Mental Illness?*, 1991, Amherst, MA: University of Massachusetts Press

Ussher, JM, 'Research and theory related to female reproduction: implications for clinical psychology' (1992) 31 British Journal of Clinical Psychology 129

Ussher, JM, 'Premenstrual syndrome: reconciling disciplinary divides through the adoption of a material-discursive epistemological standpoint' (1996) 7 Annual Review of Sex Research 218

Ussher, JM, *Body Talk: The Material and Discursive Regulation of Sexuality, Madness and Reproduction*, 1997a, London: Routledge

Ussher, JM, *Fantasies of Femininity: Reframing the Boundaries of Sex*, 1997b, London: Penguin

Ussher, JM, 'Living with drink from a feminist perspective: a material-discursive-intra psychic standpoint', in Velleman, R, Copello, A and Maslin, J (eds), *Living With Drink*, 1997c, London: Longman, pp 150–61

Ussher, JM, 'Feminist approaches to qualitative health research', in Murray, M (ed), *Qualitative Health Psychology*, 1999a, London: Sage, pp 98–114

Ussher, JM, 'Premenstrual syndrome: reconciling disciplinary divides through the adoption of a material-discursive-intrapsychic approach', in Kolk, A, Bekker M and Van Vliet, K (eds), *Advances in Women and Health Research*, 1999b, Tilburg: Tilberg University Press, pp 47–64

Ussher, JM, 'Women's madness: a material-discursive-intra psychic approach', in Fee, D (ed), *Psychology and the Postmodern: Mental Illness as Discourse and Experience*, 2000, London: Sage, pp 207–30

Ussher, JM, 'Processes of appraisal and coping in the development and maintenance of Premenstrual Dysphoric Disorder' (2002) 12 Journal of Community and Applied Social Psychology 1

Ussher, JM, 'The ongoing silencing of women in families: an analysis and rethinking of premenstrual syndrome and therapy' (2003a) 25 Journal of Family Therapy 387

Ussher, JM, 'The role of premenstrual dysphoric disorder in the subjectification of women' (2003b) 24 Journal of Medical Humanities 131

Ussher, JM, 'Postnatal depression: a critical feminist perspective', in Stewart, M (ed), *Pregnancy, Birth and Maternity Care – A Feminist Perspective*, 2004, London: Butterworths

Ussher, JM, *Managing the Monstrous Feminine: Regulating the Reproductive Body*, 2005, London: Routledge

Ussher, JM and Nicolson, J (eds), *Gender Issues in Clinical Psychology*, 1992, London: Routledge

Ussher, JM and Wilding, JM, 'Interactions between stress and performance during the menstrual cycle in relation to the premenstrual syndrome' (1992) 10 Journal of Reproductive and Infant Psychology 83

Valenstein, E, *Great and Desperate Cures: The Rise and Decline of Psychosurgery and Other Radical Treatments for Mental Illness*, 1986, New York: Basic

Van Houdenhove, B, Neerinckx, E, Lysens, R, Vertommen, H, Van Houdenhove, L, Onghena, P, Westhovens, R and D'Hooghe, MB, 'Victimization in chronic fatigue syndrome and fibromyalgia in tertiary care: a controlled study on prevalence and characteristics' (2001) 42 Psychosomatics: Journal of Consultation Liaison Psychiatry 21

Vatz, RE and Weinberg, LS (eds), *Thomas Szasz: Primary Values and Major Contentions*, 1983, Buffalo, NY: Prometheus

Verdun-Jones, SN, 'The evolution of the defences of insanity and automatism in Canada from 1843–1979: a saga of judicial reluctance to sever the umbilical cord to the mother country?' (1980) 14 University of British Columbia Law Review 1

Vice, J, *From Patients to Persons: The Psychiatric Critiques of Thomas Szasz, Peter Sedgwick, and RD Laing*, 1992, New York: Lang

Wahl, OF, *Media Madness: Public Images of Mental Illness*, 1995, New Brunswick, NJ: Rutgers University Press

Wainwright, S and Forbes, A, 'Philosophical problems with social research on health inequalities' (2000) 8 Health Care Analysis 259

Wakefield, J and Spitzer, R, 'Why requiring clinical significance does not solve epidemiology's and DSM's validity problem: response to Regier and Narrows', in Helzer, J and Hudziak, J (eds), *Defining Psychopathology in the 21st Century: DSM-V and Beyond*, 2003, Washington, DC: American Psychiatric Association, pp 31–40

Walker, A, 'Theory and methodology in premenstrual syndrome research' (1995) 41 Social Science and Medicine 793

Walker, A, *The Menstrual Cycle*, 1997, London: Routledge

Walker, J, *Couching Resistance: Women, Film and Psychoanalytic Psychiatry*, 1993, Minneapolis, MN: University of Minnesota Press

Walker, L, *The Battered Woman*, 1979, New York: Harper and Row

Walker, L, 'Statement on proposed diagnosis of masochistic personality disorder', presented to the American Psychiatric Association's Work Group to Revise DSM-III, 1985, Washington, DC

Walker, L, 'Diagnosis and politics: abuse disorders', paper presented at the Convention of the American Psychological Association, 1986, Washington, DC

Walker, N, *Crime and Insanity in England, Vol 1*, 1968, Edinburgh: Edinburgh University Press

Walklate, S, *Gender and Crime: An Introduction*, 1995, London: Prentice Hall/Harvester Wheatsheaf

Walton, JK, 'Casting out and bringing back in Victorian England: Pauper lunatics, 1840–70', in Bynum, W, Porter, R and Shepherd, M (eds), *The Anatomy of Madness: Essays in the History of Psychiatry 2: Institutions and Society*, 1985, London: Routledge, pp 132–46

Ward, T, 'Law's truth, lay truth and the authority of science: expert witnesses and criminal insanity in England, ca 1840–1940' (1997) 6 Social and Legal Studies 343

Ward, T, 'The sad subject of infanticide: law, medicine and child murder, 1860–1938' (1999) 8 Social and Legal Studies 163

Warner, K, 'Sentencing the violent spouse' (1996) 3 Psychiatry, Psychology and Law 107

Warren, CAB, *The Court of Last Resort: Mental Illness and the Law*, 1982, Chicago, IL: University of Chicago Press

Warren, CAB, *Madwives: Schizophrenic Women in the 1950s*, 1987, New Brunswick: Rutgers University Press

Wassom, BD, 'Exception that swallowed the rule? *Women's Medical Professional Corporation v Voinovich* and the mental health exception to post-viability abortion bans' (1999) 49 Case Western Reserve Law Review 799

Watson, MA, Segal, SP and Newhill, CE, 'Police referral to psychiatric emergency services and its effect on disposition decisions' (1993) 44 Hospital and Community Psychiatry 1085

Watson, NR, Studd, JW, Savvas, M and Garnett, T, 'Treatments of severe premenstrual syndrome with oestradiol patches and cyclical oral norethisterone' (1989) 297 British Medical Journal 900

Watters, J, Caplan, PJ, White, G, Bates, R and Parry, R, *Toronto Multi-agency Child Abuse Research Project Report*, 1986, Toronto, ON: Hospital for Sick Children Foundation

Way, BB, Evan, ME and Banks, SM, 'An analysis of police referrals of 10 psychiatric emergency rooms' (1993) 21 Bulletin of the American Academy of Psychiatry and the Law 389

Weaver, TL and Clum, GA, 'Early family environments and traumatic experiences associated with borderline personality disorder' (1993) 61 Journal of Consulting and Clinical Psychology 1068

Webster, D, 'Somotoform and pain disorders', in Ballou, M and Brown, L (eds), *Mental Health and Disorder: Feminist Perspectives*, 2002, New York: Guilford, pp 145–73

Weitz, D *et al*, 'Testimony on electroshock movement' (1984) 4 Phoenix Rising 16A

Welter, B, 'The cult of true woman, 1820–1860' (1966) 18 American Quarterly 18

Wenegrat, B, *Illness and Power: Women's Mental Disorders and the Battle Between the Sexes*, 1995, New York: New York University Press

White-Mair, K, 'Experts and ordinary men: locating *R v Lavallee*, battered woman syndrome, and the "new" psychiatric expertise on women within Canadian history' (2000) 13 Canadian Journal of Law and Society 406

White-Mair, K, 'Negotiating responsibility: representations of criminality and mind-state in Canadian law, medicine and society, 1920–1950' (2001) PhD dissertation, University of Toronto

Widiger, T and Costa, PT, 'Personality and personality disorders' (1994) 103 Journal of Abnormal Psychology 5

Widiger, T and Trull, T, 'Personality and psychopathology: an application of the Five-Factor Model' (1992) 60 Journal of Personality 363

Wilkinson, S and Kitzinger, C (eds), *Feminism and Discourse: Psychological Perspectives*, 1995, London: Sage

Williams, J, *The Law of Mental Health*, 1990, London: Fourmat

Williams, J, 'Social inequalities and mental health', in Newnes, C, Holmes, G and Dunn, C (eds), *This is Madness*, 1999, Ross-on-Wye: PCCS Books, pp 29–50

Williams, J and Scott, S, 'Framework feature: service responses to women with mental health needs' (2001) 7 Mental Health Review 6

Williams, J, Scott, S and Waterhouse, S, 'Mental health services for "difficult women": reflections on some recent developments' (2001) 68 Feminist Review 89

Williams, S, 'Beyond meaning, discourse and the empirical world: critical realist reflections on health' (2003) 1 Social Theory and Health 42

Willie, CV, Perri Reiker, P, Kramer, BM and Brown, BS (eds), *Mental Health, Racism, and Sexism*, 1995, Pittsburgh, KS: University of Pittsburgh Press

WISH (Women in Secure Hospitals), *Annual Report 2000–2001: Time for Change*, 2002, London: WISH

Wolff, N, 'Interactions between mental health and law enforcement systems: problems and prospects for cooperation' (1998) 23 Journal of Health Politics, Policy and Law 133

World Health Organisation, 2003, www5.who.int/mental_health/en

Worrall, A, *Offending Women: Female Lawbreakers and the Criminal Justice System*, 1990, London: Routledge

Wright, D, 'Discussion point. Getting out of the asylum: understanding the confinement of the insane in the nineteenth century' (1997) 10 Social History of Medicine 137

Wright, M-E, 'Unnatural mothers: infanticide in Halifax, 1850–1875' (1987) 7 Nova Scotia Historical Review 13

Yardley, L, 'Reconciling discursive and materialist perspectives on health and illness: a reconstruction of the bio-psychosocial approach' (1996) 6 Theory and Psychology 485

Yardley, L (ed), *Material Discourses of Health and Illness*, 1997, London: Routledge

Zanarini, MC, Gunderson, JG, Marino, MF, Schwartz, EO and Frankenburg, FR, 'Childhood experiences of borderline patients' (1989) 30 Comprehensive Psychiatry 18

Zedner, L, *Women, Crime and Custody in Victorian England*, 1991, Oxford: Clarendon

Zedner, L, 'Wayward sisters: the prison for women', in Morris, N and Rothman, D (eds), *The Oxford History of Prison: The Practice of Punishment in Western Society*, 1995, Oxford: Oxford University Press, pp 295–324

Zimmerman, M, 'Why are we rushing to publish the DSM-IV?' (1988) 45 Archives of General Psychiatry 1137

Zylberberg, P, Personal Communication, 1993

Legal cases

Australia

R v Burke [2000] NSWSC 356

R v Churchill [2000] WASCA 230 (28 August 2000)

R v Chhay (1994) 72 A Crim R 1

R v Denney [2000] VSC 323

R v Fernando (1992) 76 A Crim R 58

R v Gutsche (2002) unreported, 30 May (Supreme Court of the Northern Territory, SCC 20112237)

R v Kennedy [2000] NSWSC 109 (1 March 2000)

R v Kirkwood [2000] NSWSC 184 (3 March 2000)

R v MacKenzie [2000] QCA 324 (11 August 2000)

R v Melrose [2001] NSWSC 847 (31 August 2001)

R v Thomson (2000) 115 A Crim R 104

Canada

Bezaire v Bezaire (1980) 20 RFL (2d) 358 (Ont CA)

R v Chaulk [1990] 3 SCR 1303, *R v Swain* [1991] 1 SCR 933

R v Lavallee [1990] 1 SCR 852; 55 CCC (3rd) 97

R v Malott [1998] 1 SCR 123, 140–41; 155 DLR (4th) 513, 526–27

Sherrett v Sherrett (1987) 6 RFL (3d) 172 (Ont CA)

Winko v British Columbia (Forensic Psychiatric Institute) [1999] 2 SCR 625

Ireland

Attorney General v X and Others [1992] 1 IR 1

New Zealand

R v Oakes [1995] 2 NZLR 673

The Queen v Zhou (1993) unreported, 4 October (High Court, Auckland)

United Kingdom

R v Byrne [1960] 3 All ER 1

R v O'Connell [1997] Crim LR 683

R v Gomez (1964) Cr App R 310 (CCA)

R v Sanderson (1994) 98 Cr App R 325

The Family Planning Association of Northern Ireland (fpaNI) v The Department of Health, Social Services and Public Safety (DHSSPS) (Northern Ireland) (2003) NILQ 48

USA

Loving v Virginia 388 US 1 (1967)

Palmore v Sidoti 466 US 429 (1984)

Roe v Wade 410 US 164 (1973)

State of Washington v Wanrow 88 Wash 2d 221; 559 P 2d 548 (1977)

Index